Failed States and Institutional Decay

Understanding Instability and Poverty in the Developing World

NATASHA M. EZROW AND ERICA FRANTZ

BLOOMSBURY

NEW YORK • LONDON • NEW DELHI • SYDNEY

Bloomsbury Academic

An imprint of Bloomsbury Publishing Plc

1385 Broadway	50 Bedford Square
New York	London
NY 10018	WC1B 3DP
USA	UK

www.bloomsbury.com

First published 2013

Library of Congress Cataloging-in-Publication Data
Ezrow, Natasha M.
Failed states and institutional decay : understanding instability and poverty in the developing world / Natasha M. Ezrow and Erica Frantz.
pages cm
Includes bibliographical references and index.
ISBN 978-1-4411-5051-6 (pbk.) – ISBN 978-1-4411-1102-9 (hardcover) 1. Failed states–Developing countries. 2. Political stability–Developing countries. 3. National security–United States. 4. Poverty–Developing countries. I. Frantz, Erica. II. Title.
JC328.7.E97 2013
320.9172′4–dc23
2013006003

ISBN: HB: 978-1-4411-1102-9
PB: 978-1-4411-5051-6
epub: 978-1-4411-1342-9
ePDF: 978-1-4411-7829-9

Typeset by Newgen Imaging Systems Pvt Ltd, Chennai, India
Printed and bound in the United States of America

CONTENTS

Introduction

Since the end of the Cold War, one of the most pressing concerns in the policy and development communities is the problem posed by "failed states." There is near consensus in these circles that state failure is "a challenge to both development and security."[1] Policy makers are concerned with failed states primarily because of their security implications, which they argue transcend regional boundaries and affect the global community at large. Development agencies share these concerns, but emphasize the obstacles that state failure poses for development. As then–secretary general of the UN Kofi Annan warned in 2005, "if states are fragile, the peoples of the world will not enjoy the security, development, and justice that are their right."[2] Members of the academic world have also contributed to the buzz surrounding failed states, publishing a wide array of articles dedicated to the causes and consequences of state failure. The overall message to emerge from these discussions is that state failure is intimately tied to political disorder and poor economic performance and all of their pernicious consequences.

The result of this line of inquiry has been a concerted effort among policy makers and the development community to tackle state failure by implementing comprehensive state-building efforts.[3] Yet, in the last decade or so, particularly given the difficulties state-building efforts encountered in Afghanistan and Iraq, some have began to reexamine the concept of failed states with a critical eye.[4] Indeed, a rising tide of researchers have questioned the utility of branding states as "failed" (or "failing") and engaging in scholarly inquiry into the concept of state failure.[5] These critics

---

[1]Boege et al. (2009: 15).
[2]Annan (2005: 6).
[3]Rice (2003).
[4]Coyne (2006); Bilgin and Morton (2002). Criticism of the concept of "state failure" emerged for a number of other reasons, as well, which we discuss in greater detail later in this chapter and in Chapter Two.
[5]Throughout this book, we use the term "researchers" to refer to both academics and individuals in the policy and development communities engaging in research on this subject.

of the failed states literature argue that state failure is an immeasurable and amorphous concept, plagued by ambiguity, and molded to address the concerns of the particular researcher interested in it. They argue that the problems are so dire that they muddle any attempts to develop strategies to "re-build" states.

Despite the controversies surrounding the concept of state failure, the reality remains that the types of countries this literature addresses face very serious challenges in terms of their political stability and economic performance. For those interested in better understanding and improving the conditions of the developing world and /or mitigating threats to international security, these countries lie at the epicenter of inquiry.

Somalia, for example, is consistently featured in the literature as the epitome of a failed state. The country has operated without a central government since 1991. One of the poorest countries in the world, Somalia lags behind the world and its peers in its economic performance. Life expectancy is low, infant mortality rates are high, and humanitarian crises, such as famine, are recurring. For these reasons, Somalia is a key target of development and humanitarian programs. To make matters worse, Somalia is politically unstable. It is a battleground for warlords and a base for international piracy. Most observers agree that the country's political instability is a threat to global security. Regardless of whether Somalia is or is not a failed state, it is indisputably a country that is high on the international agenda.

The economic and security struggles endemic to the countries the failed states literature highlights undoubtedly demand our attention. Yet, given the serious criticism of the failed states literature, the concept of "state failure" appears to have yielded little analytical leverage in our understanding of these countries and their challenges. While it is of top concern to better understand the dynamics underlying the most troubled countries of the developing world, focusing on state failure is perhaps not the most effective means for doing so.

In this book, we promote an institutional approach instead. A large body of research in the political science and economics literatures has shown that *state institutions* are critical to both political stability and economic performance (and vice versa). State institutions structure political dynamics and policy choices, just as these institutions are molded and shaped by actors responding to political conditions and realities. Narrowing the focus from the strength of *the state* to the strength of *state institutions* extracts the underlying essence of the state failure literature, while restricting its scope to a concept that is less general and therefore less analytically and empirically slippery.

We note here that the causal arrow between state institutions and both political stability and economic performance can go both ways. In our individual chapters, we are careful to differentiate between arguments and findings that address one relationship versus the other and leave it to researchers to disentangle any methodological issues of endogeneity. Centering the discussion on whether state institutions are weak or strong, as opposed to whether the state is failing or not (i.e. state failure), improves the clarity with which we comprehend and assess the politics of the developing world. This, in turn, makes it easier for researchers to identify causal relationships, while also providing more precise advice for policy makers and others concerned with combating political instability and poor economic performance in the countries experiencing them.

The goal of this book is to provide readers with an in-depth understanding of: (1) the concept of state failure and its analytical limitations, and (2) the complex interrelationship between state institutions, on the one hand, and political stability and economic performance, on the other. To do so, we summarize and synthesize a large body of research across multiple disciplines in a manner that is clear and easily accessible. Throughout, we integrate in-depth examples across key regions of the developing world to provide context to the theoretical discussion. For these reasons, this book should be of interest to students, researchers, and members of the policy and development communities looking to broaden their understanding of some of the key challenges of the developing world.

We should note that our emphasis on the developing world is intentional. This part of the world hosts the world's most politically unstable and poorest performing countries—those most commonly featured in the failed states literature. For example, none of the countries in the top ten of the oft-cited Fund for Peace's 2012 Failed States Index are in Western Europe.[6] Instead, they lie in the world's developing regions, as classified by their GDP per capita (a standard proxy for a country's level of development). The GDP per capita levels of the top two countries on the Index, Somalia and the Democratic Republic of Congo (DRC), for example, are among the lowest in the world.[7] While it is true that "the weakest states are not necessarily the poorest,"[8] the fact remains that concerns about state failure are rarely (if ever) directed toward states in the developed world.

In this introductory chapter, we first offer some historical background on the concept of state failure and then discuss the central theme of the

---

[6]See "2012 Failed State Index," The Fund for Peace, www.fundforpeace.org/global/?q=fsi (accessed August 10, 2012). There are a variety of ways of measuring state failure, as we discuss in-depth in this book. We choose the Fund for Peace's index for this example because it is one of the most well known. The countries in the top ten are (in order): Somalia, the Democratic Republic of Congo (DRC), Sudan, Chad, Zimbabwe, Afghanistan, Haiti, Yemen, Iraq, and the Central African Republic.
[7]Both countries have GDP per capita that ranks in the bottom five in the world, according the CIA World Factbook's assessment. The data were estimated in 2010 for Somalia and 2011 for the DRC.
[8]Patrick (2006a: 31).

book at greater length. We close by detailing how the book is organized and providing chapter summaries.

History of the failed states concept

"State failure" is still a relatively new and contested concept in international legal discourse, one that first came to the fore after the end of the Cold War.[9] As early as 1990, Robert Jackson identified a set of countries, primarily located in Sub-Saharan Africa, which had never achieved institutions of statehood. He dubbed these countries, "quasi states." Members of the policy community picked up on this idea, observing that a relationship appeared to exist between states that lacked the internal features of the developed world and zones of political instability and poor economic performance, including then–US secretary of state Madeline Albright and key officials within the United Nations (UN).[10] Because many developed nations, particularly the United States, viewed prolonged political and economic crises in pockets around the world as a security concern, they placed increasing emphasis on the types of countries that harbored it, which they termed failed states. These countries shared in common an inability to meet the basic needs of their citizens. The concept of the failed state, then, was formulated to help identify those states that were unable to provide for their own citizens and were, therefore, a threat to security.[11] Before long, a number of academics, journalists, and members of the wider policy and development communities had taken an interest in failed states and the term had entered the lexicon.

It is important to note a few things here. The first is that at this time much of the focus was on failed states in Sub-Saharan Africa (hereafter Africa); observers viewed state failure to be a problem primarily confined to this region. William Zartman's seminal 1995 edited volume, *Collapsed States,* for example, which discusses the processes and causes of state collapse, is dedicated exclusively to cases in Africa.[12] The scope of the literature eventually expanded beyond Africa, but this took some time. The second is that early work on state failure primarily emphasized the most extreme cases of state collapse. This also gradually changed over time, as scholars and researchers eventually focused more on cases of state weakening, the incapacity of states to govern effectively, and gradations of state failure. Last, though the development community also became concerned with state failure (due to its associations with underdevelopment), the initial

---

[9]Gros (1996).
[10]Ibid., 455; François and Sud (2006: 142).
[11]Dorff (2005).
[12]Zartman (1995).

driving force behind the explosion of the failed states literature was the policy community, which saw state failure as a security threat, a subject to which we now turn.

Observers tied state failure to threatened security for a number of reasons. Most importantly, failed states lacked the capacity to monitor or constrain activities within their borders. This made these countries vulnerable to the growth of non-state actors, particularly terrorists and organized crime groups, who could operate freely within their borders and use their territories as launching pads for their activities.[13] It also made them vulnerable to the proliferation of weapons of mass destruction, international piracy, smuggling, as well as disease and other humanitarian crises.[14]

To make matters worse, observers saw state failure as contagious.[15] A consensus position during the 1990s quickly emerged, particularly among policy makers, that the spread of failed states was one of the world's most pressing security threats. Robert Kaplan, for example, argued in a 1994 article in the *Atlantic Monthly* titled "The Coming Anarchy" that the threat failed states posed to international security and stability was grave.[16] That same year, Brian Atwood of the US Agency for International Development (US AID) stated that "disintegrating societies and failed states with their civil conflicts and destabilizing refugee flows have emerged as the greatest menace to global stability."[17] Similarly, in 1993, Gerald Helman and Steven Ratner published a *Foreign Policy* article called "Saving Failed States."[18] In it, they argued that the security risk posed by failed states was such that UN conservatorship was needed in many.[19] These views were soon echoed by a number of others in the policy, development, and academic communities, and, for a brief period, there was an effort to establish an international policy on the right to intervene when states are not fulfilling their responsibilities.[20]

Concerns with the security repercussions of failed states were such that in 1994, the CIA began funding a massive research project, called the "State Failure Task Force" (referred to as the "Political Instability Task Force" since 2003), whose goal was to identify the causes of state failure.[21] The logic behind the establishment of the task force was that developing a

---

[13]Rotberg (2003).
[14]Patrick (2006a); Dunlap (2004).
[15]François and Sud (2006: 144).
[16]Kaplan (1994).
[17]Bilgin and Morton (2004: 170).
[18]Helman and Ratner (1992–3).
[19]They did not call for a conservatorship in all failed states given that "the U.N.'s responsibility for international peace and security is not, however, a sufficient basis for its action to resurrect all failed or failing states" (see ibid.).
[20]Dorff (2005).
[21]The goal of this project changed in 2003 to understanding the causes of political instability, a subtle, yet important, change that we explore in greater detail in the following chapter.

better understanding of the specific predictors of failed states would help policy makers develop long-term policies to reduce the likelihood of their onset, just as generating predictions of state failure would enable them to move quickly to prevent it.

The terrorist attacks on September 11, 2001, amplified all of these concerns, most notably within the United States. Suddenly addressing the problem of failed states became extremely urgent, and the topic rose to prominence in US foreign policy discourse.[22] The 2002 US National Security Strategy, for example, stated that "America is now threatened less by conquering states than we are by failing ones."[23] In response, the United States enacted new policies to prevent state failure, which emphasized prevention, and the early diagnosis basic message was that weak states posed a danger to US national security because of their vulnerability to the proliferation of terrorist networks and drug cartels.[24]

US concerns with failed states were soon shared by governments and organizations. Then–prime minister of the United Kingdom Tony Blair, for example, stated in 2007 that failed states were breeding grounds for terrorism.[25] In turn, international organizations, financial institutions, and development agencies began placing greater emphasis on good governance in their programs.[26] As evidence of this, the Organization for Economic Cooperation and Development (OECD), the World Bank, and the UN have each developed policies (at one time or another) aimed at preventing state failure and the dangerous spill-over effects of state weakness. As then–secretary general of the UN Kofi Annan warned in 2005, "ignoring failed states creates problems that sometimes come back to bite us."[27]

Narrowing the focus

Some 20 years later, the concept of state failure continues to be at the top of the foreign policy agendas of many policy makers and a major subject of interest for researchers, journalists, and members of the larger policy and development communities. The central reason for this is that state failure is associated with political instability and poor economic performance, which can manifest in a number of ways, including civil war, coup d'états, the proliferation of terrorist and criminal networks, and persistent underdevelopment.

---

[22]Patrick (2006a: 27).
[23]See Rice (2003).
[24]Bilgin and Morton (2004: 171). Patrick (2006a).
[25]Blair (2007).
[26]Buira (2003).
[27]"Press Release SG/SM/9772," United Nations, March 21, 2005, www.un.org/News/Press/docs/2005/sgsm9772.doc.htm (accessed March 7, 2012).

The discussion that surrounds failed states has improved international awareness of some of the major contemporary issues and challenges that developing countries face. Yet, the concept of state failure has proven to be limited in its utility, prompting a growing number of researchers to sharply criticize the failed states literature. Their primary contention is that the concept lacks definitional specificity, so much so that it provides us with little analytical leverage. This lack of specificity raises major theoretical, normative, empirical, and practical concerns, which we discuss in great detail in the following chapter.

One reflection of the generality of the concept is the heterogeneity of the set of countries that has been designated as "failed" or "failing" by one organization or another. This set includes countries as diverse as Colombia, Afghanistan, Haiti, and Iraq. Often times, the only characteristic that countries branded as failed or failing share in common is their location in the developing world. Because the concept of state failure is so broadly defined, its application often adds little to our understanding of the key challenges in the developing world.

This begs the question, should the concept of state failure be abandoned entirely? In this book, we assess that the underlying relationship that is truly at the heart of much of our interest in state failure is the tie between *state institutions* and *economic performance and political stability*. On the one hand, understanding these interrelationships remains of paramount importance. Yet on the other hand, our ability to do so is severely limited by the emphasis on the overly general concept of state failure. Because of this, in this book we advocate an *institutional approach* instead. Weak or absent state institutions capture many of the underlying components alluded to by the concept of state failure but are more specific and easier to define and measure. Narrowing our focus from the state to state institutions will improve our understanding of how domestic political environments affect political stability and economic performance (and vice versa), in turn providing us with new insights about some of the key contemporary challenges of the developing world.

For clarity, in this book we disaggregate state institutions into four categories: political institutions, security institutions, administrative institutions, and judicial institutions. We do so because states may have strong institutions in one domain, but weak ones in others. Identifying which types of state institutions matter for political stability and economic performance and in what ways is desirable because it provides us with greater analytical clarity, paving the way for more precise policy guidance. We highlight these four types of institutions because they encapsulate the major institutions of the state. Throughout the book, we synthesize, where possible, the major arguments and findings in the literature regarding which of them bear on political stability and economic performance (and vice versa) and which do not.

Organization of the book

This book is roughly divided into three parts. The first portion of the book gives readers a general background on the failed states literature and its controversies, as well as a summary of the literature on state institutions. We next direct the discussion to the issue of understanding what causes institutions to be weak and the challenges that developing states face. The second portion of the book provides an in-depth discussion of the four types of institutions, offering an assessment of how these institutions can be categorized and evaluated. Here the book briefly discusses the major arguments and findings in the failed states literature with respect to coups, organized crime, civil war, terrorism, and poor economic performance (some of the major themes of this literature), before examining what the institutionalist literature tells us about them. For contextual clarity, we supplement each of these discussions with detailed examples from the developing world, providing a landscape of the comparative institutional strength of these regions. We conclude by pointing out what warning signs exist for predicting when states are starting to falter and what solutions have been set forth by the literature. Here we summarize existing research in the area of state building, examine the particular ways in which state institutions can be strengthened to foster political stability and economic growth, and point out the critical questions to be answered in this regard.

In what follows, we provide brief summaries of the book's individual chapters.

Part one: Definitions, controversies, and challenges

Chapter One examines the concept of the failed state, briefly explaining how it has been defined, measured, categorized, and evaluated by scholars, policy makers, and assessment organizations, and why the topic has been awash with controversy. One of the first criticisms of the term failed state is that it has been associated with Western biases about what constitutes the state. Along these lines, it has been argued that some states in the developing world were granted sovereignty automatically before they had achieved statehood. The concept itself has come under fire for being difficult to define and not a useful tool in diagnosing instability in the developing world. Instead, it has been argued that the concept has been conceived in order to justify interventionist foreign policies. Scholars and policy makers have also conflated the causes and effects of state failure, coming up with a concept that is neither helpful in preventing nor in solving the problems that developing nations face. In spite of these controversies, the chapter will explain why it is important to study the state and how the state relates to development and stability.

Chapter Two builds on the explanations from the first chapter and provides a theoretical overview of the approaches to studying institutions and why this area of study is so important. Institutions are clearly defined, and an overview of how institutions can be measured, evaluated, and categorized is set forth. We emphasize the important of disaggregating the "state" into different types of formal institutions in order to better understand the effects of the state. This chapter spells out what these different types of formal institutions are and why it's important to understand how they function.

As preceding chapters highlighted, the state failure literature is primarily concerned with understanding the relationship between the state on the one hand, and instability (coups, crime, conflict, and terrorism) and economic decline (since corruption is linked with economic performance, corruption is also examined) on the other. This book explores whether or not studying institutions can help us understand more about why coups, conflict, crime, terrorism, and economic decline occur.

Chapter Three provides an overview of the challenges to institution building, identifying the macro-historical and situational micro-level causes of institutional weakness in the developing world. We first explain the legacies of the Westphalian system, illustrating how the process of state building and definitions of sovereignty for Western states have varied from non-Western states. We then outline the effects of colonialism, the Cold War, neoliberal economic policies, and globalization on the development of institutions in the developing world. In addition to these historical and international factors, the chapter examines internal factors that have made state building more challenging for some countries in the developing world, focusing specifically on the environment, resources, and demographic challenges.

Part two: Institutions in the developing world

This book highlights the importance of getting the state back into the discussion of understanding the causes of instability and poverty. The state, however, is often too vague a term. We argue that it's important to disaggregate the institutions of the state into administrative, political, security, and judicial functions in order to illuminate how institutions can foster stability or chaos, economic growth or decline. We provide an overview of studies that examine the link between specific types of institutions and coups, conflict, terrorism and organized crime, and economic performance.

Though no cross-national data exists examining the quality of institutions on all of these dimensions, we offer many examples from the developing world to illustrate how institutions perform. Our analysis includes but is not restricted to countries in Latin America, Africa, Asia (including

South Asia, East Asia, and Southeast Asia), the Middle East, and the former Soviet Union (referred to as the post-Soviet states). Where possible, for area specialists, we provide generalized comments about regional institutional developments, while also giving more detailed examples of specific cases. To demonstrate the link between institutions and outcomes, the case studies and examples illustrate that countries with high functioning institutions are also generally more stable and perform better economically.

Chapter Four discusses the role of administrative institutions in the functioning of the state. After briefly defining what is meant by administrative institutions and what their functions entail, we delineate the defining features of high-quality (versus low-quality) administrative institutions and offer numerous examples comparing and contrasting administrative institutions to illustrate these points. We next provide information about how administrative institutions are measured by different assessment organizations. We then examine how variations in the quality of administrative institutions affect key outcomes of interest—in this case economic performance, corruption, conflict, terrorism, and organized crime. Finally we offer suggestions on how to move forward and what future research should focus on.

Chapter Five discusses the role that judicial institutions play in the functioning of the state. After a brief definition, we examine the defining features of high-quality (versus low-quality) judicial institutions and provide detailed examples throughout the developing world to highlight our main points. We then discuss the relationship between judicial institutions and the rule of law and enforcement of property rights. After providing information about how judicial institutions are measured by different assessment organizations, we then evaluate how judicial institutional quality affects other outcomes—in this case economic performance and crime. The chapter concludes by offering suggestions on how to move forward and what gaps exist in the literature.

Chapter Six examines the purpose of security institutions in the functioning of the state. We discuss what high-quality and low-quality security institutions look like in practice and outline the key features that differentiate them, offering numerous examples to illustrate these points. We then offer information about how the quality of security institutions is primarily captured by various assessment organizations, specifically with respect to the military. We then turn to a discussion of how the quality of security institutions impact key outcomes of interest, namely coups, conflict, terrorism, and crime. Finally we offer suggestions on how to move forward in this area of study and what future studies should tackle.

Chapter Seven is in a slightly different format than the prior three. Though we define political institutions and their functions, we do not categorize political institutions as high quality or low quality. Unlike other institutions of the state, there is no unique set of political institutions that uniformly leads to positive state performance. That being said, this does not mean that political institutionalization does not matter. Rather, the effects of political institutions vary depending on the outcome of interest. We examine political parties, legislatures, and elections (and electoral laws in democracies) specifically and provide detailed criteria for how to measure how well institutionalized these institutions are. We then explore what ways these institutions are important in democracies and non-democracies. The chapter also examines the key findings on the effects of political institutions, both in democracies and non-democracies, specifically looking at economic performance, coups, conflict, and terrorism. We then highlight some of the methodological issues of measuring political institutions and the shortcomings of past research in this area. To conclude we offer suggestions on how to move forward.

Part three: Warning signs and solutions

Chapter Eight highlights the effects of corruption, one of the most important warnings signs of institutional decay. The chapter delineates the different types of corruption, offers explanations for the causes, and elucidates the impact that different types of corruption can have on state performance. By providing an overview of different types of corruption, this chapter sheds light on why institutions stop performing and why corruption is such a negative omen for the state's future. Throughout we offer in-depth examples of how corruption manifests in developing countries and demonstrate its harmful effects. Through case studies we demonstrate that strengthening institutions can reap valuable rewards in reducing corruption.

Chapter Nine outlines the literature on state building and explores the controversies in state building, foreign aid, and foreign intervention. It provides an overview of what state building is and offers examples that illustrate the challenges involved in reconstructing new institutions in the developing world, particularly in post-conflict situations. The chapter highlights the importance of *conceptual clarity* in defining with greater precision the variables and outcomes of state building, *empirical grounding* to guide behavior based on what has proven to work in the past, and *realistic expectations* on the part of the international community to better understand the massive undertaking that state building entails. The chapter concludes that in spite all of the challenges posed by state building, the goal of strengthening state institutions in the developing world is a necessary one, and therefore acting early to help states that are interested in reforming their institutions is important.

Concluding remarks

One might question, given its limitations, why discuss state failure at all in this book? The primary reason for doing so is due to the dominance of this concept in discussions of the politics of the developing world, particularly in the policy and development communities. Innumerable news articles, journal articles, and policy briefs reference failed states (or some variant of them). To be able to participate in and contribute to these discussions, it is essential to have a solid understanding of what state failure means, what the shortcomings are of this concept, and how analyses can be improved by emphasizing state institutions instead.

This book provides readers with the tools to accomplish these tasks, exploring what the concept of state failure refers to and what its limitations are, before turning to an in-depth discussion of how state institutions interrelate with political stability and economic performance. In doing so, the book synthesizes two very abundant and complex literatures (*the state failure and institutionalist literatures*) in a manner that is clear and accessible. Where possible, we identify for readers the central insights and underlying relationships of interest in the failed states literature and offer suggestions for how they can be better understood by narrowing the focus from the state to state institutions. We also point out in these discussions the key unanswered questions that remain. We emphasize throughout that state institutions are a critical component of political stability and economic performance, showing readers how and in what ways, thereby deepening their understanding of the politics of the developing world.

PART ONE

Definitions, controversies, and challenges

CHAPTER ONE

What is state failure?

Before we can generate an understanding of whether the concept of a failed state is useful for analysis and policy formulation, it is first necessary to define what is meant by state failure. The concepts failed states and state failure are interrelated. *Failed states* are simply states that have undergone *state failure*, just as *state failure* is the process of becoming a *failed state*. Not all states that experience state failure, however, eventually become failed states. In fact, rarely do those in the literature consider states to be truly "failed" in practice. Typically only a handful of countries (like Somalia) are considered as such in any given year.[1] A much larger number of countries, however, are *at risk* of becoming failed states.

These states are referred to in a variety of ways in the literature, such as weak states, failing states, disrupted states, distressed states, or fragile states. Some, particularly within the donor literature, prefer to use the term "fragile" instead of "failing" due to the negative connotations associated with failure.[2] The UK Department for International Development (DFID), the World Bank, and the US Agency for International Development (USAID), for example, all use the term fragile. Others avoid using the term failing because it implies that the state is on the verge of being nonexistent, as opposed to simply incapable of governing.[3] Regardless of the particular term used, the underlying concept being referenced is generally the same. For consistency, throughout this book, we use the terms failing or weak.

What both failed states and failing states share in common is that they have undergone or are experiencing *state failure*. For this reason, we concentrate on defining state failure in this chapter. We begin by providing an

---

[1]Only two states (Somalia and the DRC), for example, received the Fund for Peace's "Alert" categorization on its 2012 Failed States Index.
[2]Hameiri (2007: 126).
[3]Sørensen (1999a).

in-depth overview of what state failure is as a concept and how it is measured, before turning to the criticism that surrounds it.

Definitions

What do we mean when we refer to state failure? Defining state failure is not a straightforward endeavor, and measuring it even less so. To grasp what state failure is, we must first understand the concept of "the state" more generally, as well as what constitutes a strong versus a weak state.

The modern state

The modern state emerged in the sixteenth and seventeenth centuries, with the Peace of Westphalia codifying external sovereignty between states.[4] The process of forming the modern state was long and complex, often interrupted due to the frequency of war. During this period of modern state formation in Europe, unsuccessful states were absorbed by more powerful states, and even these states lacked full control over their territory.[5] Therefore, providing security for citizens was of critical importance. States consolidated their power by offering minimal levels of security for citizens in return for extraction, which was needed to provide funding for wars and national security efforts.[6] As the state established institutions for extraction, other institutions of the state developed as well. Representative institutions, for example, were slowly built over time to compensate citizens for the state's need to extract.[7]

Some scholars have argued that the emergence of capitalism was also important for modern state formation.[8] Anthony Giddens writes that the wheels of capitalism generated the need for a stable political and legal framework that can protect property rights, enforce contracts, and maintain the rule of law, all critical to economic growth and development. In other words, the demands of a capitalistic economy paved the way for the emergence of the modern state. By providing citizens with welfare at the same time, the state essentially bound citizens to its existence.[9]

This relationship between a state and its citizens is an important one, as a number of political philosophers have pointed out. Thomas Hobbes, Jean-Jaques Rousseau, and John Locke, for example, all argue that the role

---

[4]Milliken and Krause (2002: 755).
[5]Ibid., 758.
[6]Tilly (1990).
[7]Milliken and Krause (2002: 756).
[8]Giddens (1987).
[9]Milliken and Krause (2002: 760).

of the state is to provide a binding social contract with its citizens. A state's authority rests on the willingness of citizens to acknowledge the rules it has established. This does not necessarily mean that states must be democratic, but rather that they must meet the expectations of at least some segments of society. Today, the emphasis on the contract between states and citizens continues. The OECD asserts, for example, that the ability of the state to fulfill the needs of the population for basic services lies at the heart of the state–citizen relationship.

The philosopher Max Weber also explored the concept of the state. According to Weber, the state is a "human community that (successfully) claims the monopoly of the legitimate use of force within a given territory."[10] In the Weberian view, what differentiates a state from anarchy is the legitimization of violence. In a state, the right to use physical force is given to institutions and individuals only so long as the state permits it.

The Montevideo Convention of the Rights and Duties of States, a treaty signed in 1933, was a product of these philosophical discussions on the definition of statehood. To this day, the convention sets the international legal boundaries for what constitutes statehood, the criteria for which include a defined territory, a permanent population, an effective government, and the capacity to enter into formal relations with other states.[11]

Strong states versus weak states

Understanding what constitutes statehood paves the way for discussing what it means to be a strong state versus a weak state, the latter of which is a precursor to a failed state. Strong states are states that are stable, with the bond between states and citizens firmly intact. Weak states, by contrast, are unstable, with the state barely able to fulfill its end of the bargain in its relationship with citizens. As noted political scientist Joel Migdal writes, "state strength is weighed in terms of a state's capacity to penetrate society, regulate relationships, extract resources and appropriate or use resources in determined ways. Weakness is a syndrome characterized by corruption, the collapse of a state's coercive power, the rise of strongmen and the segmentation of the political community."[12]

It is important to note that, in theory, the strength of the state is not synonymous with regime type. Whether a state is democratic or autocratic is not necessarily a predictor of whether it is weak or strong (a discussion that we return to in far greater depth in Chapter Seven). Autocracies like the Chinese Communist dictatorship (in power since 1949) basically meet all of the criteria of state strength Migdal identifies, for example, as does

---

[10]Weber (1972).
[11]Chesterman et al. (2005: 15).
[12]Migdal (1988: 4).

Chile's democracy. At the same time, autocracies like the current regime in Chad (in power since 1990) meet many of the criteria of state weakness Migdal mentions, as does Pakistan's current democracy. According to Robert Bates, lack of control over the means of coercion is what distinguishes a weak state from an autocracy.[13] In weak states, political competition primarily occurs among armed groups, whereas in a strong state it occurs among political parties.

Scholars are not in full agreement, however, of what constitutes a strong versus a weak state (a tension that helps to explain the divisions in the literature on the definition of a failed state that we address shortly). For example, Robert Rotberg argues that there is a hierarchy of functions strong states provide, which include: security; institutions to regulate and adjudicate conflicts and enforce the rule of law, property rights, and contracts; political participation; and social service delivery, provision of infrastructure, and regulation of the economy.[14] Ashraf Ghani et al. identify a number of these same functions as important as well, but expand the list to include additional functions, such as effective public borrowing.[15]

Though there is substantial overlap in the attributes of strong states that scholars have put forth, there is by no means a clear-cut, universal list. Scholars do agree, however, that weak states are often precursors to failed states, a subject to which we now turn.

State failure

Most researchers view state failure as a matter of degree, because multiple gradations of state weakness are possible. Some consider state failure to reflect a continuum, where the gradations blend into one other, whereas others place the gradations of state failure into concrete categories. In their edited volume on state failure, for example, Simon Chesterman and co-authors treat state failure as "as continuum of circumstances that afflict states with weak institutions—ranging from states in which basic public services are neglected to the total collapse of governance."[16] Paul Collier, by contrast, puts countries undergoing state failure into categories, according to whether they are failing, falling behind, or falling apart.[17] Though the extents to which researchers distinguish between the degrees of state failure differ, the consensus position is that there are multiple levels of state failure.

---

[13]Bates (2008b).
[14]Rotberg (2003).
[15]Ghani et al. (2009).
[16]Von Einsiedel, (2005: 13–35); see also Bøås and Jennings (2005: 385–95).
[17]Collier (2007).

But what exactly is state failure? In general, most definitions of state failure are based on the idea that the state is in some way failing to fulfill the expectations of its citizens. As Jean-German Gros writes, the state fails when "public authorities are either unable or unwilling to carry out their end of what Hobbes long ago called the *social contract*, but which now includes more than maintaining the peace among society's many factions and interests."[18] This position is echoed by Martin Doornbos as well.[19] State failure, in other words, is the result of the state's inability to meet the needs of its citizens—a critical component of the state–citizen relationship. Simply put, state failure occurs when "the basic functions of the state are no longer performed."[20]

Though most definitions of state failure center on this basic theme, there are nuanced differences among them. Some scholars place greater emphasis on one function of the state than on another, for example, or highlight some functions, but ignore others. We list a handful of definitions of state failure from within both the policy community and academia below:

- The Crisis States Research Center: State failure is "a condition of state collapse, whereby the state can no longer perform its basic security and development functions and has no effective control over its territory and borders."[21]

- The Fund for Peace: "A state is failing when its government is losing physical control of its territory or lacks a monopoly on the legitimate use of force."[22]

- Robert Rotberg: State failure occurs when a polity "is no longer able or willing to perform the fundamental tasks of a nation-state in the model world."[23]

- State failure is "marked by the collapse of the central government authority to impose order, resulting in the loss of physical control of territory and the monopoly over the legitimate use of force."[24]

In general, definitions of state failure emphasize one or more of the following (often interrelated) dimensions as important functions of the state:

- Monopoly over violence

- Administrative services and infrastructure

---

[18]Gros (1996: 456).
[19]Doornbos (2006).
[20]Zartman (1995: 5).
[21]Crisis States Workshop, London, March 2006, 1.
[22]Fund for Peace (2006).
[23]Rotberg (2003: 7).
[24]Stewart and Brown (2010: 1).

- Social services
- Judicial services
- Economic performance

The first dimension is by far the most frequently highlighted in the literature, and for this reason we discuss it in greater detail than the latter four dimensions.[25] Common to all of these dimensions is the state's breaching of its "contract" with citizens. Because the state no longer offers valuable goods to citizens, the state starts to lose their support.[26] In such an environment, the state's legitimacy in the eyes of the citizenry deteriorates, which in turn intensifies the state's weakness and inability to maintain control over society.[27]

Monopoly over violence

The first dimension scholars point to as critical to state failure is loss of control over the use of force. Emphasis on this feature builds on the early scholarship on statehood discussed earlier, particularly Weber, who argued that the monopoly over violence is a key component of the modern state. As Bates directly puts it, the key feature of state failure "is the inability of governments to secure a monopoly of violence."[28]

States that lack the capacity to control the use of force within their borders implicitly are incapable of providing security for their citizens, one of the key components of the state–citizen relationship. According to William Zartman, for example, state failure occurs when few or no state institutions can ensure the population's security.[29] This view is supported by Rotberg, who argues that when states lack the capacity to provide security for citizens, the delivery of "a range of other desirable political goods" becomes impossible.[30]

When the state loses its monopoly over violence, its sovereignty is also under threat because the state can no longer maintain security within its borders.[31] In some cases, this results in the state losing international recognition.[32]

---

[25]See, for example, Ignatieff (2002) and Stewart and Brown (2010).
[26]Rotberg (2003: 1); some scholars, such as Hawkins and Semerad (2001), view lack of legitimate governance itself as a key component of state failure.
[27]Stewart and Brown (2010).
[28]Bates (2005: 6).
[29]Zartman (1995).
[30]Rotberg (2003: 3).
[31]Ibid.
[32]Bøås and Jennings (2005).

Lack of control over the use of force creates a situation amenable to outbreaks of violence. For Rotberg, failed states are nearly always violent battlegrounds. He writes: "In most failed states, government troops battle armed revolts led by one or more warring factions."[33] Violence against the government breaks out because the state is powerless at forcefully eliminating threats to its rule. Non-state actors like ethnic militias, secessionist groups, warlords, guerrilla groups, and other militias may hold power over parts of the territory, given that the state is unable to disarm and disband them. There may even be zones that have a "state within a state" operating, with independent policy forces, judiciaries, and economies.[34] At the same time, criminal violence may erupt because the state cannot control the sale and distribution of firearms nor protect its people from unauthorized violence.[35] In other words, violent instability is a symptom of the loss of control over the use of coercion.[36]

Though all states are subject to episodes of violence (even intense ones), these periods of violence are prolonged when a state has failed.[37] In failed states, violence is persistent because the state is incapable of enforcing order.

Many scholars are quick to point out that state failure is not synonymous with violence, however. This is because violence can occur even in strong states. According to Bates, loss of the monopoly over violence is what distinguishes state failure from episodes of political instability, like revolutions and civil wars.[38] Though during a revolution, a state may briefly lose control, revolutions lead to a "new order, whereas state failure yields disorder."[39] At the same time, though civil wars can erupt in failed states, strong states can also become involved in civil wars.

Administrative services and infrastructure

A second dimension of state failure is the state's inability to handle its administrative duties and develop its infrastructure. Strong states provide several administrative services for citizens, many of which are important for the state's ability to extract resources and function. When states cease to offer these services (regardless of whether they lack the will or ability to do so), this creates an environment in which taxes are not collected, laws are not implemented, state employees are not paid, and even mail is

---

[33]Rotberg (2003: 5).
[34]Bøås and Jennings (2005).
[35]Boutwell and Klare (1999: 9–28).
[36]Bates (2005: 6).
[37]Rotberg (2003).
[38]Bates (2008a: 1–12).
[39]Ibid., 1.

not delivered.[40] The use of bribes dominates the functioning of whatever administrative bureaucracy exists.

The neglect or absence of infrastructure also signifies state failure. Roads, ports, harbors, and railways, if they exist, are not maintained. Telephone lines do not function, water supplies are scarce, and electricity provision is sporadic or nonexistent.[41] As Rotberg writes: "Metaphorically, the more potholes . . . the more a state will exemplify failure."[42] The state's abandonment of infrastructure, in turn, makes it impossible for many economic and commercial activities to function.

Social services

A third dimension of state failure is the state's inability to provide basic social services for its people (or opposition to doing so).[43] This means that the state fails to ensure that its citizens receive a minimal standard of living and that there is no safety net.[44] Schools and hospitals are neglected, causing low literacy rates and high infant mortality rates.[45]

Because the state has virtually abandoned its citizens, there are high-income disparities and no middle class. The absence of a middle class, in turn, polarizes the citizenry and can trigger violent confrontations.[46] It is important that the state help people cultivate a sense of belonging.[47] Yet in such a scenario, the citizenry lacks cohesion and a common identity.

Judicial services

A fourth dimension of state failure is the absence of adequate judicial services. For a state to function, it is important that it provides some judicial services, including independent and effective courts and the rule of law. Without working judicial services, corruption becomes rampant.[48] This corruption can take the form of kickbacks, wasteful construction projects that enable rent-seeking, extortion, currency speculation, and using state resources to fund extravagant, personal purchases.

The lack of judicial services enables leaders (and citizens) to behave as they please, irrespective of the law. This leaves citizens with few resources to adjudicate disputes and the government incapable of regulating the

---

[40]Bøås and Jennings (2005).
[41]Rotberg (2003).
[42]Rotberg (2002: 88).
[43]UK DFID (2005).
[44]Patrick (2006b: 1–31).
[45]Rotberg (2003).
[46]Lipset (1959: 69–105).
[47]Bøås and Jennings (2005).
[48]Rotberg (2003).

norms of society.[49] The consequences of inadequate judicial services can include the escalation of violence (because citizens have few other means for resolving disputes beyond using force) and the disruption of economic activities (because citizens and international investors are hesitant to invest in corrupt economies where contracts are not enforced).

Economic performance

A fifth dimension of state failure is poor economic performance. A state is failing when it is a "low-income country in which economic policies, institutions, and governance are so poor that growth is highly unlikely. The state is failing its citizens because even if there is peace they are stuck in poverty."[50] In failing states, the Gross Domestic Product (GDP) falls continuously from one year to the next, leading to negative growth rates.[51]

States that experience a persistent decline in the size of their economies (particularly when they are less developed to begin with) have proven incapable of prioritizing the health of the economy. This robs citizens of opportunities to contribute to a productive economy and better their social standing in legitimate ways. It also usually means that those who are poor will become even more impoverished.

The five dimensions of state failure that we discuss here touch on the key components of state failure that have been raised in the literature. Though there is little consensus on the definition of what constitutes state failure, this discussion should provide a picture of the types of environments that researchers, journalists, and policy makers are referring to when they mention failed states.

Typologies of failed states

A few scholars have created typologies of those states that lie at the end of the failed state continuum (i.e. weak and failed states). (For ease of discussion, throughout this section we use the term failed states to refer to these states, as opposed to weak and failed states.) The motivation for identifying different types of failed states is the idea that these states are not one and the same and that differences among them have implications for the kinds of policies external actors should pursue to engage them.[52] Here we discuss

---

[49]Rotberg (2002).
[50]Lisa Chauvet and Paul Collier, "What Are the Preconditions for Turnarounds in Failing States?" Center for the Study of African Economies, University of Oxford (January 2007): 1–19.
[51]Patrick (2006a); Rotberg (2003, 2004).
[52]Patrick (2006a: 30).

two typologies of failed states: one which disaggregates them based on two dimensions, the other which disaggregates them based on type.

Dimensions that differentiate failed states

The first typology we discuss, highlighted by Stewart Patrick, differentiates failed states according to how they fare along two dimensions: capacity and will.[53] Capacity is important because it captures the extent to which the government has the means to provide citizens with the basic goods associated with statehood. In Patrick's view, these goods are physical security, legitimate political institutions, economic management, and social welfare. States that lack capacity are unable to do basic things, such as protect the country's borders and ensure public order, maintain government institutions that are effective and legitimate, implement economic policies conducive to the growth of the economy, or provide citizens with basic social services. According to Patrick, "failed states" can lack capacity in one or more of these areas. Will, however, is also important. If the government is corrupt or incompetent, all the assistance in the world will not improve the state's performance.

This creates four categories of failed states: states that are both capable and committed (i.e. Senegal and Honduras), states that are incapable but committed (i.e. Mozambique and East Timor), states that are capable but lacking in will (i.e. Burma and Zimbabwe), and states that are both incapable and lacking in will (i.e. Haiti and Sudan).[54] Patrick argues that these categorizations help to explain differences across failed states in a number of areas. As Patrick sees it, failed states that have inadequate will (but are capable) are more prone to terrorism and the proliferation of weapons of mass destruction (WMDs), for example, while failed states that have weak capacity (but are willing) are particularly vulnerable to outbreaks of disease and the spread of small arms.[55]

Categories that differentiate failed states

The second typology we turn to was developed by Jean-Germain Gros.[56] It groups failed states according to their type, specifically whether they are anarchic, phantom, anemic, captured, or aborted.

Anarchic states have no central government. Instead armed groups battle one another for control under orders from warlords. Many of the armed confrontations in anarchic states have no objectives; conflicts may be triggered by boredom more frequently than political injustices. Classic

---

[53]Ibid.
[54]Ibid., 30.
[55]Ibid., 46.
[56]Gros (1996).

examples of anarchic states are Somalia (since 1991) and Liberia during its civil war from 1989 to 1996.

Mirage states (also referred to as phantom states) have a greater semblance of authority than anarchic states. The only state institutions that exist, however, function solely to ensure the security of the leader, his cronies, and his family members. The state provides virtually no services to citizens. An example of a mirage state is Zaire (today's Democratic Republic of Congo) under Joseph Mobutu (1965–97). During this time, the security apparatus revolved around the protection of Mobutu, the currency was not used, and the military rampaged communities and commercial districts, rather than protect the citizens.[57]

Anemic states are states that lack the ability to assert control. They are incredibly weak because counterinsurgency groups are seeking to supplant their authority and/or because overpopulation due to modernity has proven too demanding for them to withstand. In anemic states, the state was already weak to begin with, but new pressures or catastrophic events make them even more emaciated. The state may provide a few services, but they are offered infrequently. Haiti is an example of an anemic state.[58] According to Gros, anemic states are not beyond the hope of reconstruction.

Captured states have a strong centralized authority, but have been "captured" by insecure elites as a means of challenging (and in some cases destroying) their elite rivals. To accomplish this they often implement discriminatory and exclusive policies, which can incite conflict. The classic example of a captured state is Rwanda in the years leading up to its 1994 genocide. During this time, members of the ruling elite, who were Hutus, initiated policies intended to marginalize the Tutsis. The state was organizationally strong, as manifest by the government's ability to kill around one million people in a three-month period during the genocide.

Aborted states are unlike the others in that they experienced failure before the state even formed. In these scenarios, the consolidation of the state never took place. This can occur because the shift to independence occurred too quickly or because neighbors took advantage of the state's weakness, as was the case in Bosnia.

These typologies of failed states illustrate that there are nuanced differences among them, including the extent to which the state exerts control over society and in elite behavior.

Measurements

Measuring state failure is important because otherwise it is impossible for scholars to test (either qualitatively or quantitatively) the causes or

---

[57]Ibid., 458.
[58]Ibid., 459.

consequences of the concept. It is also valuable for identifying the set of countries that are troubled.

Just as there are a variety of ways in which researchers define and categorize state failure, however, there are also a variety of ways in which they measure it. A plethora of organizations and researchers have (either directly or indirectly) derived unique measures of state failure. For instance, in Susan E. Rice and Stewart Patrick's summary of the major efforts to quantify state weakness, they identify a dozen![59] And a bevy of additional measures exist beyond these twelve.

A reflection of this is the literature's divergent estimates of the number of weak and failing states in the world. In 2006, the Commission on Weak States and US National Security put this number at between 50 and 60; the UK Department for International Development put it at 46, and the World Bank put it at 30.[60] As Patrick writes, "these divergent estimates reflect differences in the criteria used to define state weakness, the indicators used to gauge it, and the relative weighting of various aspects of governance."[61]

We should note that most measures of state failure include a mixture of indicators that capture political outcomes (e.g. civil war, economic growth, riots) and characteristics of the state (e.g. political freedoms, judicial bodies, civil rights). No measure, to our knowledge, solely looks at characteristics of the state; political outcomes are incorporated in all of them.[62] This makes it difficult to assess how state failure impacts political outcomes, however, because these same outcomes are included in the measure of state failure. We discuss this empirical issue in greater detail later in this chapter and merely draw attention to it briefly here.

To provide a portrait of the types of measures that have been used by researchers, we review a handful of them below. We focus on the measures released by major organizations, but note that a number of researchers have developed their own measures as well.[63]

The State Failure Task Force

The State Failure Task Force, funded by the CIA's Directorate of Intelligence, was an organization started in 1994 tasked with identifying the conditions that contribute to state failure.[64] This group focused solely on the causes of state failure (not the consequences), the idea being that doing so would help policy makers tailor policies aimed at preventing it. The group's 2003

---

[59]Rice and Patrick (2008: 1–47).
[60]Patrick (2006a: 29).
[61]Ibid.
[62]Though Iqbal and Starr (2008) argue that the Polity IV Project's measure of interregnum (which we discuss in what follows) avoids this pitfall, Easterly and Freschi (2010) point out that this measure really just captures incidences of internal war.
[63]See, for example, Goldstone (2003); Ghani et al. (2009); Rotberg (2003); Rice and Stewart (2008).
[64]See Gurr et al. (2003).

report on state failure is considered to be one of the most extensive ever carried out. In it, the group define state failure as "serious political instability," encapsulated by four types of events: revolutionary wars, ethnic war identifiers, adverse regime changes (movements from democracy to autocracy), and genocides and politicides.[65] Though the State Failure Task Force did not construct a single index of state failure, countries experiencing any of these four events were considered to be at risk of collapse. As the definition makes clear, state failure here is measured entirely by outcomes (as opposed to characteristics of the state).

Some of the central findings of the report are that states bordering major civil conflicts are more at risk of state failure, as are states with low levels of material well being (as captured by their infant mortality rates), low levels of trade openness, and high population densities.

It is important to note that the group has since become the Political Instability Task Force and it has changed its focus from state failure to political instability, which it measures using the same four events mentioned earlier.[66] We touch on the significance of this change in Chapter Two.

The Fund for Peace

The Fund for Peace is a nongovernmental organization dedicated to preventing violent conflict and promoting sustainable security.[67] It compiles the Failed States Index, which is published annually by *Foreign Policy* magazine and is one of the more widely used measures of state failure in the literature. The index ranks 177 countries based on their susceptibility to state failure. According to the Fund for Peace, a state that is failing has the following characteristics: "the loss of physical control of its territory or a monopoly on the legitimate use of force . . . the erosion of legitimate authority to make collective decisions, an inability to provide reasonable public services, and the inability to interact with other states as a full member of the international community."[68]

To capture this conceptualization of state failure, the index consists of the following 12 indicators:

1   Mounting demographic pressures

2   Massive movement of refugees or internally displaced persons

---

[65]Ibid., 1.
[66]See Robert Bates Goldstone, Ted Robert Gurr, Michael Lustik, Monty G. Marshall, Jay Ulfelder, and Mark Woodward, "A Global Model of Political Instability," The Political Instability Task Force, 2005, paper presented at the Annual Meeting of the American Political Science Association in Washington, DC, September 3, 2005.
[67]See "About the Fund for Peace," The Fund for Peace, www.fundforpeace.org/global/?q=aboutus (accessed August 13, 2012).
[68]See "The Failed States Index: Frequently Asked Questions," The Fund for Peace, www.fundforpeace.org/global?q=fsi-faq#5 (accessed August 13, 2012).

3   Legacy of vengeance-seeking group grievance or group paranoia

4   Chronic and sustained human flight

5   Uneven economic development along group lines

6   Sharp and/or severe economic decline

7   Criminalization and/or delegitimization of the state

8   Progressive deterioration of public services

9   Suspension of arbitrary application of the rule of law and widespread human rights abuse

10 Security apparatus operates as a "state within a state"

11 Rise of factionalized elites

12 Intervention of other states or external political actors

Each of these 12 indicators is then split into an average of 14 sub-indicators, which are weighted using a special algorithm to produce a ranking for each country. The first indicator, "mounting demographic pressures," for example, is measured by 21 sub-indicators, including the HIV AIDS growth rate, population growth, and infant mortality.[69] This means that over 100 sub-indicators underlie each country's ranking in the Failed States Index. The index ranges in value from 1 to 10, with 1 representing the most stable countries and 10 representing those most at risk of state collapse. The Failed States Index includes sub-indicators that capture both characteristics of the state (e.g. existence of a legal system) and political outcomes (e.g. attacks by armed insurgents).

The World Bank

The World Bank is an international institution that offers financial and technical assistance to countries in the developing world. It runs the Worldwide Governance Indicators (WGI) Project, produced by Daniel Kaufmann, Aart Kraay, and Massimo Mastruzzi. According to the World Bank, governance refers to:

the traditions and institutions by which authority in a country is exercised. This includes (a) the process by which governments are selected, monitored and replaced; (b) the capacity of the government to effectively formulate and implement sound policies; and (c) the respect of

---

[69]For more on the sub-indicators, see "Conflict Assessment Indicators," The Fund for Peace, www.fundforpeace.org/global/library/cr-10–97-ca-conflictassessmentindicators-1105c.pdf (accessed August 13, 2012).

citizens and the state for the institutions that govern economic and social interactions among them.[70]

The project is based on the idea that good governance is a critical component of development. It argues that, through multiple mechanisms, capable public sector institutions, the protection of property rights, and the protection of civil liberties will lead to sustained economic development and the reduction of poverty.[71] Through the project, the World Bank produces the Governance Matters data set, which aggregates a number of indicators of governance for over 200 countries and groups them into six dimensions. (Note that the project does not compile for researchers an index that combines these dimensions.) The dimensions are:

1 Voice and accountability
2 Political stability and absence of violence/terrorism
3 Government effectiveness
4 Regulatory quality
5 Rule of law
6 Control of corruption

To measure each of these dimensions, the World Bank uses primarily survey data, meaning that scores are mainly based on the perceptions of respondents. Those surveyed include employees at domestic firms and country analysts at major multilateral development agencies. Some of the dimensions are intended to capture characteristics of the state (e.g. regulatory quality), while others are intended to capture political outcomes (e.g. political stability and absence of violence/terrorism).

Though not synonymous with state failure, governance failure is a closely correlated concept. As such, the Governance Matters data are often used as proxies for state failure.[72]

We note that in addition to measuring governance, the World Bank also runs the Fragile and Conflict-Affected Countries Group (formerly the Low-Income Countries Under Stress Initiative or LICUS). This group designates countries as fragile or not (World Bank, 2002).[73] Within the

---

[70]Daniel Kaufmann, Aart Kraay, and Massimo Mastruzzi, "The Worldwide Governance Indicators: Methodology and Analytical Issues," The World Bank Development Research Group Macroeconomics and Growth Team, *Policy Research Working* Paper 5430 (September 2010): 4.
[71]See "Governance Matters 2010: Worldwide Governance Indicators Highlight Governance Successes, Reversals, and Failures," Brookings Institution, September 24, 2010, www.brookings.edu/research/opinions/2010/09/24-wgi-kaufmann (accessed August 13, 2012).
[72]Williams (2007: 24).
[73]Iqbal and Starr (2008: 315–31).

category of fragile, countries are further divided according to whether their fragility is severe, core, or marginal. Fragile countries are characterized by "a debilitating combination of weak governance, policies and institutions" (World Bank, 2002). They are identified by their ranking on the World Bank's Country Policies and Institutional Performance Assessment (CPIA), the indicators of which are not publicly disclosed.

Polity IV Project

Another measure of state failure used in the literature comes from the Polity IV Project, a research effort geared toward coding characteristics of states in the world. The project's data set places countries along an autocratic-democratic continuum (based on a number of components).[74] When there is a complete collapse of authority, countries receive a code of "-77," which is referred to as a period of "interregnum." According to the Polity project: "Interregnal periods are equated with a collapse, or failure, of central state authority, whether or not that failure is followed by a radical transformation, or revolution, in the mode of governance."[75] The interregnum coding is intended to capture countries that have lost central political authority. Scholars using the data consider states "failed" when they have received this coding. In practice, the interregnum coding primarily captures countries that are experiencing internal war, a political outcome.[76]

US Agency for International Development

USAID is a governmental organization that offers economic, development, and humanitarian assistance to countries around the world in line with US foreign policy goals. In 2006, the organization released a report, "Measuring State Fragility," which identified 33 indicators of state effectiveness and legitimacy that could be used to rank countries.[77] According to USAID, the key factor that differentiates fragile states and more capable ones is the relationship between the government and the governed.[78] In fragile states, the relationship is poor and "the government acts in ways that create conditions (or outcomes) that are broadly seen as ineffective, illegitimate, or both."[79] This, in turn, makes citizens less willing to engage with the government in constructive ways.

---

[74] See, for example, ibid.
[75] See Marshall and Jaggers (2002: 17–18).
[76] Easterly and Freschi (2010).
[77] Rice and Patrick (2008).
[78] US AID (2005: 1).
[79] Ibid.

USAID grouped the indicators into four categories of governance: economic, political, security, and social. Example indicators include the number of state coups in a given year, the extent of citizen participation, and asylum requests. This sampling of indicators illustrates that the indicators capture both characteristics of the state and political outcomes. The program, however, was suspended in 2006. The organization did not release a list of comparative rankings of state fragility, but did provide recommendations for researchers for how to use the indicators to construct composite indices.

The measures of state failure that we discuss here are by no means exhaustive, as mentioned earlier. They should provide readers, however, with a good idea of the types of indicators that organizations and researchers consider when deriving a measure of state failure. We now turn to discussing some of the problems associated with existing measures of state failure, and with the concept of state failure itself.

Criticism

Despite the proliferation of research devoted to state failure and the significant financial and physical resources that governments and developmental agencies have allotted to combat it, the utility of the concept of state failure is increasingly questioned by researchers, primarily within academia.[80] As Tobias Hagmann and Markus V. Hoehne write: "The state failure debate is confronted by . . . shortcomings of considerable proportions."[81] A growing chorus of critics asserts that state failure is *too broad* a concept, so much so that it offers us little analytical leverage in our efforts to better understand the challenges of the developing world.

We examine the central problems with the failed states literature in detail in this section. We note that the key theme that underlies these criticisms is an emphasis on the concept's lack of specificity. For clarity, we group these problems into four interrelated categories: theoretical concerns, empirical concerns, normative concerns, and practical concerns.[82]

---

[80]The term "state failure" is itself controversial, as alluded to earlier. There are many debates over semantics, i.e. the precise term that should be used to refer to the underlying concept of "state failure." We do not discuss the positives and negatives of the particular *terms* used to capture this concept here, and instead focus on the *utility of the concept itself.*
[81]Hagmann and Hoehne (2009: 44).
[82]These groupings are fairly similar to Hagmann and Hoehne's identification of the "empirical, analytical, normative and practical shortcomings" of the state failure literature (see ibid.).

Theoretical concerns

Theoretical concerns over the concept of state failure center on the fact that there is substantial variation across the literature regarding what state failure is. As William Easterly and Laura Freschi point out: "'State failure' has no coherent definition."[83] Though most researchers agree that state failure deals with a state's loss of control over the use of force, what this means in practice varies greatly from one researcher to the next. To make matters more confusing, some researchers include additional features of the state— such as a state's inability to perform development functions—to their definitions of state failure.

The lack of consensus regarding the meaning of state failure creates substantial ambiguity regarding what the concept of state failure actually refers to in practice. This is troublesome because it generates confusion over state failure's causes and consequences, a central focus of most research on the subject, in turn muddling the solutions identified to ameliorate state failure. As Shahar Hameiri writes: "I do not suggest that there are no serious problems associated with the disintegration of the state apparatus in some states; rather there is a need for a more sophisticated theorization of state dynamics than advanced in the failed states literature."[84]

Ambiguity surrounding the concept of state failure leads to significant variation across researchers in the set of countries classified as failed or failing. Identifying these countries is crucial not only for research investigating the causes and consequences of state failure, but also for governments and organizations seeking to assist failing states. Yet because researchers and organizations have different definitions of state failure, they also have different ways of measuring it. As Zaryab Iqbal and Harvey Starr write, "although addressing important issues, [definitions of state failure] fail to provide us with a definitive and measurable conceptualization of state failure."[85]

Most measures emphasize some combination of political instability, poor economic performance, and weak state institutions (depending on the particularly definition used). The extent to which they consider each factor, however, varies considerably. Morten Bøås and Kathleen Jennings point to this, critiquing the variety of circumstances to which the failed state label is or is not applied. They write: "Many states experience at least some of the security, humanitarian, and governance crises commonly associated with failed states, but it is only to some that the label is attached."[86] These classification differences are so significant, that the set of countries identified

---

[83]Easterly and Freschi (2010).
[84]Hameiri (2007: 123).
[85]Iqbal and Starr (2008: 318).
[86]Bøås and Jennings (2007: 476).

by one researcher as "failing" can vary markedly from the set of countries identified by another.

Definitions that elicit measurements that weigh political violence heavily, for example, will be likely to classify Colombia as a failing state, due to the government's history of armed conflict with guerrilla groups. A country like Haiti, however, is unlikely to be classified as failing, given that it has not endured sustained political violence. Definitions that elicit measurements that weigh economic underperformance heavily, by contrast, will be likely to classify Haiti as a failing state, given its poor record of economic growth, but not Colombia, because its economy has been performing well. In 2006, Colombia in spite of a strong economic record was categorized as failing (ranked by Foreign Policy as high as #14) and deemed in worse condition than Zimbabwe.

Because the concept is ambiguous, it can be (and has been) applied to a wide range of countries that have very different political realities, based on different interpretations of state failure. Ambiguity in the meaning of state failure leads to a situation where a heterogeneous set of countries are classified as failing from one study to the next. Charles Call points out, for example, that "the term 'failing state' . . . has grown to encompass states as diverse as Colombia, East Timor, Indonesia, North Korea, Ivory Coast, Haiti, Iraq, and the Sudan."[87] He goes on to say: "The most serious problem with the concept of failed states is the problem of definition, and more specifically of super-aggregation of very diverse sorts of states and their problems."[88] With such a dissimilar group of countries lumped together, the exercise of categorization loses meaning. The end result is that "crucial differences in state formation and recession" are "smoothed over and obscured," only to "inform and perpetuate misguided policy responses."[89]

While it is true that theoretical disagreements among researchers over definitions of concepts are common in many fields, here they create so much ambiguity that there are significant differences in how the concept is measured and applied to classify countries.[90] For researchers, these classification differences bring about dissimilar results in their analyses of what causes state failure and what its effects are. Perhaps more troubling, for policy makers and members of the development community, these differences create

---

[87]Call (2008: 1492).
[88]Ibid., 1494.
[89]Bøås and Jennings (2007: 476).
[90]For example, in political science, there is dissention over how to define the concept of "democracy." Despite these disputes, however, democracies are measured in fairly similar ways, such that there is usually significant overlap in the set of countries considered to be democratic. This occurs because nearly all definitions of democracy (to our knowledge) at a minimum included the maintenance of free and fair elections, giving the concept some clarity and continuity.

confusion regarding which states should be the targets of their efforts and which should not. According to Charles Call:

> The failed state concept has led the Western policy community to apply a blunt instrument . . . to strong states with limited areas out of control (Colombia) as much as to weak and legitimate states with low capacity but high legitimacy (East Timor) or to predatory states deliberately looting the state for personal or corrupt ends (Liberia).[91]

A wide range of countries end up targeted by similar policy efforts, even though they share very little in common.

Normative concerns

Researchers also express normative concerns with the concept of state failure, arguing that it is easily molded to suit political agendas. Because there is a lack of consensus regarding what state failure means, the concept can be shaped according to the motivations of the researcher or organization. Policy groups, in particular, are criticized on this front.

Bøås and Jennings summarize the nature of this criticism well:

> The use of the failed state label is inherently political, and based primarily on Western perceptions of Western security and interests. In order to bring meaning to the failed state concept, one must first ask: For whom is the state failing, and how? . . . We maintain that states called "failed" are primarily those in which [the] recession and informalization of the state is perceived to be a threat to Western interests . . . Crucially, labeling states as failed (or not) operates as a means of delineating the range of acceptable policy responses to those states.[92]

They are not the only researchers, however, to criticize the concept of state failure for being easily manipulated for political motives. These sentiments are also shared by Pinar Bilgin and Adam David Morton, who write: "Labeling certain states as 'failed' states serves to facilitate different kinds of policies that are simplistically aimed at two different groups of states: 'friends' and 'foes.'"[93] According to Susan Woodward, the politicization of the concept of state failure is overt. She writes that one policy analysis "even admitted the terms 'failing states' and 'failed states' were used 'for convenience.'"[94] She argues that the term is only prominent internationally

---

[91]Call (2008: 1496).
[92]Bøås and Jennings (2007: 476).
[93]Bilgin and Morton (2002: 66).
[94]Woodward (2004: 4).

due to the US war on terror, prompting some countries, such as France, Germany, and China, to refuse to reference the term at all.[95]

In summary, many researchers criticize the state failure literature because they believe the concept of state failure is too easily politicized. Because the concept is so broad to begin with, it can be molded and shaped to suit the needs of the individual researcher or organization.

Empirical concerns

Empirical concerns with the state failure literature have to do with the way that measures of state failure are used in empirical analyses (regardless of whether they are qualitative or quantitative). As mentioned earlier, measures of state failure are required for inquiry into the causes and effects of this concept. They enable researchers to classify countries according to whether they are failed or failing (or whichever classification of state failure is used). With these classifications, researchers can then investigate the effects of state failure on particular outcomes (or, if desired, the reverse—the effects of particular factors on the risk of state failure). Existing measures of state failure, however, generally include the very outcomes that are of interest, making it impossible for researchers to understand the nature of the relationship between state failure and these outcomes. As noted in the measurement section above, no measure of state failure, to our knowledge, solely includes state characteristics; outcomes are always included as well.

A number of researchers have identified this problem. Iqbal and Starr, for example, point out:

> Most existing measures or indices of state failure incorporate a number of factors that may, in fact, be determinants of state collapse—such as civil strife and poverty. This causes endogeneity issues that make it a challenge to study state failure as a dependent variable.[96]

Woodward puts the empirical problem bluntly, arguing:

> The measures are abysmal, the studies are tautological (the exact same empirical measures are used for both cause and outcome), and there is no real effort at causal analysis, identifying the causal links between state fragility and these outcomes of concern.[97]

This problem occurs primarily because most definitions of state failure do not lend themselves to direct measurement; researchers must instead use

---

[95]Ibid., 5.
[96]Iqbal and Starr (2008: 317).
[97]Woodward (2004: 5).

indicators of state failure to capture the concept, which are usually outcomes.[98] An example helps illustrate this. Suppose the definition of state
failure used is that a state has lost its monopoly over violence. This definition of state failure is difficult (if not impossible) to measure. One indication that a state has lost control over the monopoly of force, however, is
that it is experiencing civil war. Civil war, then, is an indicator of state
failure in this scenario and would be included in the measure of state failure. This, in itself, is not problematic. The problem arises when researchers use this measure of state failure (which includes whether a country is
experiencing civil war) to examine the relationship between state failure
and civil war. Because the measure of state failure is endogenous to civil
war *by construction*, any efforts to assess the causality of this relationship
are rendered futile.[99]

The Fund for Peace's Failed States Index, for example, includes around
100 sub-indicators to capture state failure, many of which measure conflict,
such as the number of attacks by armed insurgents. The organization's categorization of a failed state, then, is determined, at least partially, according to whether the state is experiencing conflict. As Bøås and Jennings
argue, indices such as these "conflate failed states with conflict, despite
the fact that countries with relatively robust institutions also experience
conflict."[100] The conflation of state failure with key outcomes of interest,
like conflict, makes it impossible to determine which causes which.[101]

Unfortunately, this empirical problem occurs quite frequently in the
state failure literature. Researchers examine the effects of state failure using
measures of state failure that consist of these very effects. We can only
examine the effects of state failure on outcomes that are not defining features or indicators of state failure, however. The same is true when we look
at the causal factors of state failure. This leads us to the practical concerns
with the concept of state failure.

Practical concerns

Practical concerns with the concept of state failure deal directly with the
broadness of existing measures that are used to capture it.[102] Most measures of state failure include a wide array of indicators (see the section on

---

[98]It can also occur because the definition of state failure used itself includes the outcome of
interest.
[99]See Geddes (2003) and King et al. (1994) research design book for more on the basics
of research design. Though endogeneity issues are by no means impossible to overcome
methodologically, here the variables are endogenous by construction.
[100]Bøås and Jennings (2007: 478); see, also Von Einsiedal (2005); Ignatieff (2002); Morten
and Jennings (2007).
[101]See, also, Woodward (2004: 4), who argues that state failure is often equated with "threats."
[102]This occurs even if the definition that is used is not broad.

measurement above), covering a mixture of political instability, poor economic performance, and weak state institutions. As a result, they are very general, incorporating a lot of distinct experiences and features of a state.

This has two negative consequences. The first is that it reduces the number of outcomes that can be investigated because so many are already included in the measure. Woodward, for example, refers to existing measures of state failure as "overly aggregated."[103] This is fine if the goal is simply classifying whether states are failed or failing, but it is troublesome if we are interested in how states get this way or what the consequences of being this way are (for the reasons examined in the discussion on empirical concerns). Yet these are the very reasons why the concept of state failure was introduced in the first place! The broadness of existing measures of state failure restricts the set of causes and consequences that we can examine.

The second negative consequence is that the use of broad measures of state failure makes it more difficult to pinpoint exactly what policy suggestions should be offered to combat it. For example, if a study finds that state failure increases the likelihood that citizens will contract HIV/AIDS, it becomes important to try to prevent state failure or lessen it (to reduce the spread of the disease). Yet, because measures of state failure include an amalgam of indicators, it is impossible to know exactly what should be targeted. As Hagmann and Hoehne write, "the state failure debate gloss[es] over important differences between existing states rather than accounting for these differences."[104]

A common theme throughout these four categories of criticism is the lack of specificity in discussions of the concept of failed states. A more precise and universally accepted definition of state failure would alleviate many of the central problems identified in the literature. Greater conceptual specificity would: (1) provide greater clarity, reducing the variety of definitions proposed, (2) limit the ability of researchers and organizations to shape the concept for political purposes, and (3) reduce the likelihood that such a wide range of indicators would be included in measures of state failure (in turn reducing the likelihood of empirical problems of endogeneity).

The need for greater specificity, however, calls into question the utility of the concept of state failure itself. If by state failure, we really mean political instability or poor economic performance or weak state institutions, why not examine these particular concepts instead? What is the purpose of emphasizing the concept of state failure, when it lacks the specificity needed to carry out empirical research and provide policy guidance?

---

[103]Woodward (2004: 2, 5).
[104]Hagmann and Hoehne (2009: 45).

Indeed, researchers (primarily within academia) are increasingly advocating abandoning the use of the concept entirely. We include a sampling of their statements here:

● Hameiri argues that "the label 'failed state' is itself problematic," so much so that it "stifle[s] efforts . . . that might explain these very states."[105]

● Bøås and Jennings echo this point, stating: "The way in which the failed state concept has been understood and operationalized, especially since 2001, is problematic. From an analytical standpoint, the concept's usefulness to effective policy formulation is in fact sharply limited."[106]

● Charles Call writes: "The 'failed states' concept—and related terms like 'failing,' 'fragile,' 'stressed,' and 'troubled' states—has become more of a liability than an asset . . . [It] is largely useless and should be abandoned."[107]

● Hagmann and Hoehne assert that the "failed states debate has failed to provide appropriate analytical tools."[108]

● Economists William Easterly and Laura Freschi, in their editorial "Top 5 reasons why 'failed state' is a failed concept," point out that "the only possible meaningful definition adds nothing new to our understanding of state behavior, and is not measurable." Because of this, "while there has been research on state failure, it failed to generate any quality academic publications in economics."[109]

Though the concept of failed states offers a convenient way for researchers and organizations to refer to states in the developing world that face serious challenges, the emerging concern is that it has provided us with little analytical leverage about these challenges and, in many ways, only created greater confusion in the policy, development, and academic communities about the political problems of the developing world.

Moving beyond state failure

To understand where to go from here, it is important to take a step back and identify exactly why the concept of state failure emerged to begin

---

[105]Hameiri (2009: 123).
[106]Bøås and Jennings (2007: 476).
[107]Call (2008: 1491–2).
[108]Hagmann and Hoehne (2009: 43).
[109]Easterly and Freschi (2010).

with. Policy makers and members of the development community first turned their focus to failed states because of their potential implications for *political stability* and *economic performance*. From the perspective of policy makers, political stability and economic performance were of interest because they could potentially lessen threats to international security. From the perspective of the development community, they were of interest because they could potentially foster a country's development and lessen citizen suffering.[110] To better understand both, the failed states literature emphasized the domestic political environment, specifically the state itself.

It becomes clear, then, that the key contribution of the failed states literature is its *association of the weakness of the state with political instability and poor economic performance*.

State weakness, however, is a vague and broad concept, just as state failure is its close cousin. It is here where the failed states literature loses its coherence and the problems discussed above arise. Lack of specificity engenders confusion and limits the analytical leverage derived from studying state failure. Hameiri writes in his critique of the failed states literature, for example: "The problem with this literature, hence, is not that it has 'invented' problems that do not exist, but with the frameworks within which these problems are interpreted and evaluated and the blueprints for intervention and action these sorts of analyses invite."[111]

This begs the question, how can we move forward and examine the features of the state, without running into the same problems as the failed states literature? One way to do so is to narrow the scope from the *strength of the state* to the *strength of state institutions*. The closeness of these concepts is reflected in the frequent reference in the failed states literature to the importance of state institutions. Rotberg mentions this here:

Failed states contain weak or flawed institutions—that is, only the executive institution functions. If legislatures exist at all, they are rubber-stamp machines. Democratic debate is noticeably absent. The judiciary is derivative of the executive rather than being independent, and citizens know that they cannot rely on the court system for significant redress or remedy, especially against the state. The bureaucracy has long ago lost its sense of professional responsibility and exists solely to carry out the orders of the executive and, in petty ways, to oppress citizens. The military is possibly the only institution with any remaining integrity, but the armed forces of failed states are often highly politicized, without the esprit that they once exhibited.[112]

---

[110]We do not argue that these relationships indeed exist between political stability and economic performance, on the one hand, and international security and development, on the other, but just point out the original motivations underlying inquiries into state failure.
[111]Hameiri (2009: 123).
[112]Rotberg (2002: 87).

Though the failed states literature identifies the strength of state institutions as important to understanding political instability and poor economic performance (and vice versa), the focus is not overtly on this concept. Indeed, state failure and "institutional weakness" are very similar ideas. The major difference is that state institutions are a subset of the state itself, giving this line of inquiry greater specificity. We should note that like most analytical concepts, the concept of institutional weakness also lacks definitional unanimity. It is less nebulous and general, however, than the concept of state failure, and therefore does not suffer from the same drawbacks.

Given the limitations of the concept of state failure to improving our understanding of the politics of the developing world, and yet the tight association of features of the state with political stability and economic performance, it appears clear that the way to move forward is to narrow the focus of analytical inquiry to state institutions.

The key question explored in the bulk of this book, then, is how do state institutions affect political stability and economic performance (and vice versa)? Thus, first it is important to explain what is meant by political instability and economic performance.

Political instability most often refers to coup d'états, civil conflict, and terrorism, with some studies also investigating organized crime. We provide a brief definition of these variables.

A *coup* consists of the rapid "infiltration of a small but critical segment of the state apparatus, which is then used to displace the government from its control of the remainder."[113] Coups are often an expression of protest against a government that is not functioning. (see Boxes 1.1 and 1.2) According to Samuel Huntington, coups are a clear sign of *political decay*, in that the mechanisms for institutionalized turnover in power are overlooked in favor of quickly using force or the threat of force.[114]

BOX 1.1 Political decay

Political decay is the precursor to the idea of state failure. Samuel Huntington defined political decay as states plagued by high levels of corruption, authoritarianism, domestic violence, political disintegration, and institutional decline.[115] In particular, coups and military interventions are an indicator of low levels of institutionalization. These types of interventions are signs that the political institutions, in particular, lack autonomy and

(*Continued*)

---

[113]Luttwak (1968: 26–7). It is assumed that coups are executed by the military
[114]Huntington (1968).
[115]Ibid., 393.

BOX 1.1 *Continued*

coherence.[116] Another indicator of political decay is the rise of charismatic leaders. This type of leadership deliberately weakens other institutions such as party organizations.[117] The reason is that leaders "cannot create institutions without relinquishing personal power."[118] Huntington claims that "the simplest political system is that which depends on one individual. It is also, of course, the least stable."[119]

BOX 1.2 Coup trap

Countries such as Thailand that have experienced many coups in the past are also more likely to experience coups in the future. The *coup trap* is the probability that a country will experience a coup will increase if the country has had a past experience of a coup. There are several reasons for this. First, a political culture develops where military coups are the norm.[120] Where there has been no precedent of military intervention, coup plotters are less likely to opt to stage a coup to achieve their objectives. Second, once this boundary has been crossed by the military a coup becomes a much easier method to solve disputes and to implement a changeover in power. In Africa, which has experienced so many coups, previous coups have increased the probability of more coups, often taking place not long after a previous coup. A number of countries in Africa "experienced a succession of coups and attempted coups following an initial event."[121]

Civil war is defined as a "a violent conflict within a country fought by organized groups that aim to take power at the center or in a region, or to change government policies."[122] Scholars are not in agreement in terms of the death toll, but the general consensus is that an active conflict will have at least 1,000 casualties per year. The International Crisis Group claims that civil wars cost the country in conflict and its neighbors an average of $55 billion dollars. Civil wars also tend to be long in duration, by some

---

[116]Ibid., 408.
[117]Ibid., 423.
[118]Ibid.
[119]Ibid., 400.
[120]Londregan and Poole (1990: 175).
[121]Wang (1998: 663).
[122]James D. Fearon, "Iraq's Civil War" *Foreign Affairs* 86, no. 2 (March/April 2007): 3.

estimates averaging almost 16 years.[123] Therefore, better understanding the causes of civil conflict is important since they are so long and costly.

Terrorism is defined as "premeditated, politically motivated violence perpetrated against non-combatant targets by sub-national groups or clandestine agents, usually intended to influence an audience."[124] The type of violence is unconventional and considered outside of the context of legitimate warfare activities. It is therefore distinct from insurgency, civil war, mass murder, or any purely criminal act.[125]

Organized crime constitutes economic activity of groups that have a permanent structure that aim to maximize profits by exploiting opportunities to violate state rules and regulations.[126] It is distinguished from political insurgencies and terrorist networks due to the fact that the motivations of organized criminal groups are purely economic. According to the World Bank, organized crime represents 2.5–4.5 percent of global GDP and somewhere between 14–27 percent of global trade. Because of this, organized crime has become a growing area of research in the "failed state" literature.

In addition to the focus on political instability, economic performance is also commonly examined. Economic performance most often refers to economic growth rates, but studies may also look at poverty rates (such as those living under $2 a day), inequality rates, levels of foreign direct investment, infant mortality rates, literacy rates, rates of calorie consumption, unemployment rates, inflation, and GDP/capita figures.

To lead off this discussion, we examine what researchers mean by state institutions and how they assess their strength or weakness in the following chapter. Relating the state to these challenges (problems) is the essence of what the "failed state" literature aims to understand.

---

[123]James D. Fearon, "Why Do Some Civil Wars Last So Much Longer Than Others?" *Journal of Peace Research* 41, no. 3 (2004): 275.

[124]Larry J. Siegel, *Criminology* (Andover, UK: Cenage Learning Publications, 2008), 328.

[125]Dominic Lisanti, "Do Failed States Really Breed Terrorists?: An Examination of Terrorism in Sub-Saharan Africa-Comparing Statistical Approaches with a Fuzzy Set Qualitative Comparative Analysis," Paper Prepared for the CAPERS Workshop at NYU, May 14th, 2010, 1–26.

[126]Alfred Pfaller and Marika Lerch, *Challenges of Globalization: New Trends in International Politics and Society* (New Brunswick, NJ: Transaction Publishers, 2005), 54.

CHAPTER TWO

What are state institutions?

Having discussed in detail the analytical limitations of the concept of state failure, we now narrow the focus of the discussion to state institutions, specifically. We advocate that doing so provides researchers with greater leverage and reduces the confusion and controversy that has shrouded the failed states literature.

In this chapter, we first review the major theoretical approaches to the study of institutions, discuss why institutions are an important subject of inquiry, and define what we mean by institutions (and state institutions specifically). We close by briefly discussing the four major types of state institutions that we highlight in this book: political institutions, administrative institutions, judicial institutions, and security institutions.

Theoretical approaches to institutions

The literature on political institutions is both vast and robust.[1] As R. A. W. Rhodes, Sarah A. Binder, and Bert A. Rockman write: "The study of political institutions is central to the identity of the discipline of political science."[2] As a result, there are a wide variety of theoretical approaches used in this line of inquiry. We offer some brief background on three of the major approaches here, relying on the review of this literature provided by Rhodes, Binder, and Rockman (2006).

---

[1]See Rhodes et al. (2006) for a review of this literature.
[2]Ibid., xii.

Historical institutionalism

The first theoretical approach is the historical institutionalist approach. Historical institutionalists view institutions as continuities.[3] In this approach, institutions are a product of history and are very resistant to change. They reflect the accumulation of events; once in place, they are quite sticky. As Rhodes, Binder, and Rockman put it, here "[i]nstitutions are like dried cement. Cement can be uprooted when it has dried, but the effort to do so is substantial. It is easier to alter the substance before it hardens."[4] Historical institutionalists compare why certain paths were followed, but not others, examining the particular conditions at the root of the emergence of different institutions.

Sociological institutionalism

The second approach is referred to as sociological institutionalism. Sociological institutionalists conceptualize institutions as "norms and culture."[5] They are "independent entities that over time shape a polity by influencing actors' preferences, perceptions, and identities."[6] In this approach, institutions are exogenous, meaning that they are the product of the history and norms of society as opposed to the strategic maneuvering of political actors. Individuals do not act out of their own self-interest; instead, they act in accordance with their sense of duty, which is molded by existing rules and patterns of behavior.

Rational-Choice Institutionalism

The third approach we discuss is rational-choice institutionalism. This approach views institutions as systems of rules and incentives.[7] Here, institutions are endogenous, created to advantage some political actors over others. As Rhodes, Binder, and Rockman write, "institutions in this sense provide arenas for conflict, and efforts to alter them stimulate conflict inasmuch as they change the rules of the game in such a way as to alter the allocation of advantages and disadvantages."[8] According to rational-choice institutionalists, institutions are the result of the struggle for power between those who hold power and those who want it.

---

[3]Ibid., xv.
[4]Ibid.
[5]Ibid.
[6]Ibid., xvi.
[7]Ibid., xiii.
[8]Ibid., xiv.

All of these approaches have merit; the most useful approach in many ways depends on the particular subject of inquiry. In this book, we are concerned with both the consequences of state institutions—looking at how state institutional frameworks affect political outcomes—and the causes of political institutions—looking at how political circumstances shape individual incentives and strategic behavior. Because of this emphasis on both formal institutions (which we define below) and their endogeneity, the definitions and discussions that follow primarily use the rational-choice institutionalist approach.

The importance of institutions

Researchers have for some time argued that institutions are an important feature of the state, one that is at the root of many differences across states in their political outcomes. In some states, institutions are all but nonexistent; while in others they are abundant and pervade society. As Samuel Huntington wrote in 1991, "the most important political distinction among countries concerns not their form of government but their degree of government."[9] Differences in the institutional landscapes of states help to explain differences in their political behavior. This is particularly true for researchers in the field of development studies. Institutions play a critical role "in furthering peace, development, and prosperity."[10]

We should note that the institutionalist literature does not universally claim that institutions are "good" or "bad." Though in general "good" institutions produce "good and prosperous societies" and "bad" institutions produce "bad behavior and poor societies," this is highly contextual.[11] For example, "good" institutions can be associated with stable, firmly entrenched democracies, as well as stable, firmly entrenched dictatorships.[12] Whether institutions elicit positive or negative outcomes for states depends on both the type of institution in question and the context in which it is examined (a subject we discuss in greater detail at the end of this chapter). Rather, what this literature shares in common is its emphasis on the importance of looking to institutions to account for variations in patterns of behavior.

---

[9]Huntington (1991: 28).
[10]Hagmann and Hoehne (2009: 43).
[11]Goldstone (2008: 287).
[12]Rodrik writes, for example, "The central dilemma . . . is that a political entity that is strong enough to establish property rights and enforce contracts, is also strong enough, by definition, to violate these same rules for its own purpose" (2005: 972).

Defining institutions

What are institutions? One of the most widely cited definition of institutions comes from Douglass North, who writes: "Institutions are the rules of the game in a society or, more formally, are the humanly devised constraints that shape human interaction."[13] This emphasis on "rules" is common to most definitions of institutions. We list a sampling of them here:

- William Riker refers to institutions as, "rules about behavior, especially about making decisions."[14]

- Charles Plott states that institutions are "rules for individual expression, information transmittal, and social choice.[15]

- According to Geoffrey Hodgson, institutions are "established and embedded social rules that structure social interactions."[16]

- Guillermo O'Donnell writes that "institutions are regularized patterns of interaction that are known, practiced, and regularly accepted (if not necessarily normatively approved) by social agents who expect to continue interacting under the rules and norms formally or informally embodied in these patterns.[17]

As these definitions indicate, institutions are rules that are created by humans to govern their behavior. The existence of institutions provides boundaries for human activities and shapes their interactions. As North writes, they "structure incentives in human exchange, whether political, social, or economic . . . [Institutions] define and limit the set of choices of individuals."[18]

Because institutions provide structure to human behavior, they can be molded and shaped in ways to achieve certain outcomes. Humans have an incentive to create institutions that will elicit outcomes that suit their individual interests or the common interests of society. In other words, institutions are not exogenous creations; they are the products of the very societies that they in turn shape.[19]

---

[13]North (1990: 3). We remind readers that we are relying on the rational-choice institutionalist approach in this book.
[14]Riker (1982: 435).
[15]Plott (1979: 156).
[16]Hodgson (2006: 2).
[17]O'Donnell (1994: 57).
[18]North (1990: 3–4).
[19]Because the relationship between institutions and behavior runs in both directions, throughout the book we examine both the causes of particular institutional configurations and their consequences. We leave it to researchers to sort out the endogeneity of these relationships.

We should note that the term "institution" is often used synonymously with the term "organization." They are slightly different concepts, however. Organizations are *types* of institutions. As North writes: "If institutions are the rules of the game, organizations and their entrepreneurs are the players. Organizations are made up of individual rules bound together by some common purpose to achieve certain objectives."[20] Organizations include things like political parties, trade unions, schools, and so forth. In this book, we discuss the broader concept of institutions. Some of the institutions that we discuss are organizations, like state ministries, but others are not, like elections.[21]

Defining state institutions

Institutions can be either formal or informal. Formal institutions are in many ways more conceptually straightforward. Formal institutions are legal rules that are enforced through third parties.[22] Examples include constitutions, bureaucracies, and political parties.[23] Informal institutions are more ambiguous. They refer to norms of behavior, such as moral codes, social conventions, and self-enforcing agreements.[24]

In this book, we concentrate on formal institutions. We do so because formal institutions have received greater attention in the institutionalist literature, largely because they are easier to identify and measure. In his summary of the evolution of the field of development studies, for example, Adrian Leftwich writes that the focus has been primarily on formal institutions.[25] Though most researchers concur that informal institutions are also important subjects of inquiry and help to explain key differences in political behavior and outcomes, the reality is that they are more difficult to study in methodologically rigorous fashion.

Within the category of formal institutions, we focus solely on the institutions of the state.[26] By this we mean, quite simply, institutions that are government created and/or supported. Institutions do not necessarily have to be government run to be state institutions; they simply have to be part of the state's constitutional or legal framework. For example, we consider a political party that is legal, but not affiliated with the government, to be a

---

[20]North (1994: 361).
[21]See Hodgson (2006) for a discussion of how North conceptualizes and distinguishes between institutions and organizations.
[22]Rodrik (2008: 51).
[23]North (1994: 360).
[24]Ibid.; Rodrik (2008).
[25]Leftwich (2006: 2).
[26]We exclude from the analysis other forms of formal institutions, such as international institutions, which are sometimes referred to as parallel institutions.

state institution. We restrict our focus to state institutions to provide clarity in the terms being discussed and their practical application.

Comparing state institutions

In this book, we are concerned with how state institutions affect political stability and economic performance (and vice versa). In fact, abundant literature exists examining these very relationships. Researchers have argued for some time that one of the key factors that accounts for why developed states are often more politically stable and economically prosperous than their counterparts in the developing world is that their institutional landscapes are very different. At the heart of this line of inquiry, then, is a comparison of state institutions, identifying how they differ from one another and which differences are most important for explaining key political outcomes of interest.

In some cases, researchers compare how states that have certain types of state institutions differ from those in which they are absent. As an example, a number of studies have looked at how states with political parties differ from those without them.[27] In other cases, researchers compare how the same type of state institution is configured differently across states. As an example of this, a number of studies have examined how states with organizationally strong political parties differ from those in which parties are organizationally weak.[28] What all of these analyses share in common is an emphasis on comparing states' institutional landscapes.

Researchers have identified a number of dimensions along which state institutions can be compared, the most notable of which are offered by Samuel Huntington.[29] According to Huntington, for societies to develop in a harmonious fashion, the state must develop along with them. The strength and scope of the state's political institutions are critical to this endeavor. State institutions can differ, therefore, along both of these dimensions, which we briefly review here.

We note that in this book, we hold the position that the institutional dimensions that matter for outcomes vary depending on the *type* of institution in question, a subject we discuss in some detail later in this chapter. We highlight these dimensions, however, because they provide some background for thinking more deeply about the relationship between state institutions and key political outcomes.

---

[27]Gandhi (2008).
[28]See Magaloni (2006).
[29]Huntington (1968).

Institutional strength

Strong institutions are important, in Huntington's view, because they enable states to "curb the excesses of personal and parochial desires."[30] To assess whether a state's institutions are strong or not,[31] Huntington looks at four factors: autonomy, coherence, adaptability, and complexity.

Autonomy

Autonomy refers to the extent to which institutions are shielded from outside influences. In states with autonomous institutions, "political systems have an integrity" that is lacking elsewhere because their institutions are "insulated from the impact of non-political groups and procedures." Greater autonomy protects state institutions from being taken advantage of to suit one actor's or one group's needs. By contrast, when a state's institutions are not autonomous, they are "highly vulnerable to outside influences" and more likely to be corrupt.[32] Such institutions function as the political instruments of a particular social group—whether it be a family, clan, or class.

Coherence

Coherence has to do with the extent to which there is a consensus on the boundaries of the institution and the procedures for resolving disputes that arise with them. According to Huntington, institutions that are coherent function in a similar fashion to professionalized military institutions. He writes: "The problems of creating coherent political organizations are more difficult but not fundamentally different from those involved in the creation of coherent military organizations."[33] Huntington argues that greater institutional coherence reduces the likelihood of instability, since the procedures that exist are considered fair to all.[34]

Adaptability

Adaptability deals with the extent to which institutions are easily molded to fit the changing needs of society. According to Huntington, this is an acquired trait, meaning that it is a function of an institution's age and the

---

[30]Ibid., 20.
[31]In this passage, Huntington argues that these dimensions are critical to "institutionalization." For consistency, we use the term "strength" here instead.
[32]Huntington (1968: 403).
[33]Ibid., 23.
[34]Ibid., 403.

environmental challenges it has faced in the past. Adaptable institutions are important because "the needs of one age may be met by one set of institutions; the needs of the next by a different set."[35] States with institutions that are adaptable are more stable because they can adjust to different contexts.

Complexity

Complexity refers to the extent to which institutions are internally variegated. It may involve "both multiplication of organization subunits, hierarchically and functionally, and differentiation of separate types of organization subunits."[36] When institutions are complex, they are better able to secure and maintain the loyalty of their members, ensuring stability. The number of actors with an interest in preserving the institution increases. As Huntington puts it: "The simplest political system is that which depends on one individual. It is also the least stable."[37]

Scope

State institutions also can be differentiated by their scope. According to Huntington: "Scope refers simply to the extent to which the political organizations and procedures encompass activity in society."[38] Institutions are limited in scope when only a small elite group belongs to them and abides by their procedures. They are great in scope when the opposite is true. Institutional scope captures the degree to which a central authority incorporates an entire geographical area within the state's territorial boundaries.[39] For example, some state institutions only extend to the capital or urban areas, whereas others reach virtually all of the populated areas within a state's borders. Greater institutional scope is important because it ensures that institutions and the society they operate in are mutually engaged.

Here we have discussed one of the most prominent ways in which researchers have differentiated the key dimensions of state institutions, offered by Huntington. As mentioned earlier, in this book we posit that, though it is important to think about different institutional dimensions, those that matter for understanding outcomes in behavior vary based on the *type* of institution in question, a subject to which we now turn.

---

[35]Ibid., 397.
[36]Ibid., 18.
[37]Ibid.
[38]Ibid., 12.
[39]Bratton and Chang (2006: 1067).

Types of state institutions

In this book, we disaggregate state institutions into four types: political institutions, administrative institutions, judicial institutions, and security institutions.[40] We choose these four types because they encompass the majority of the key institutions of the state. Taken together, they provide a solid portrait of a state's institutional landscape.

We disaggregate state institutions for a number of reasons. The first reason is that how state institutions shape political behavior varies depending on the type of institution in question. Some types of institutions may be crucial to understanding political stability, but not economic growth, for example, while others may affect both. The nuances of the relationships between state institutions and particular outcomes vary according to which type of institutions we are referring to.

The second reason we disaggregate by type is that states differ markedly in the extent to which they have developed some types of institutions versus others. For example, both South Africa and Botswana have institutions in place that enable them to collect taxes, but they lack institutions for coping with the HIV/AIDS epidemic. Colombia has institutions that protect private property, but it has lacked strong institutions to ensure public order. For North Korea, the reverse is true. These patterns come to the surface once we look at how states fare with respect to different types of state institutions.

Disaggregation is also desirable because it allows for greater specificity, which in turn lends itself to the provision of more precise policy guidelines. If, for example, we know that weak security institutions cause terrorism, then policy makers can focus on institutional design as it pertains to strengthening the state's security institutions. By being very clear about the particular type of institution that is of interest, we can better inform the debates over institutional design.

Last, we disaggregate state institutions by type because each maintains its own framework of inquiry. How researchers conceptualize security institutions, for example, differs markedly from how they conceptualize administrative institutions. Different types of institutions have different dimensions that are meaningful, as mentioned above. In some cases, researchers focus on the "quality" of institutions, in other cases their "strength," and in yet other cases, whether they exist at all to begin with. In some frameworks, "strong" institutions lead to desirable outcomes, while in others the opposite is true. In yet other frameworks, institutional strength is not the focal

---

[40]To derive these categories, we draw from Tobias Debiel, who breaks institutions into these same four categories, plus an additional two: social institutions and economic institutions. We do not use these latter two categories because in our conceptualization they are covered by the other four categories. See Debiel (2006: 1–14).

point of interest at all. Thus the framework of inquiry and the dimensions that are meaningful within it are contextually dependent on institutional type.

We should add that for this reason, we do not offer a universal definition regarding what these adjectives mentioned mean with respect to state institutions. We provide greater definitional specificity in our individual chapters dedicated to each type of state institution.

The chapters that follow provide an in-depth discussion of the four types of state institutions that we emphasize. Here we briefly summarize what we mean by each of these types:

- *Political institutions*: Institutions of the state engaged in decision-making and articulating policy and in the selection of public officials. These include political parties, legislatures, and elections.

- *Administrative institutions*: Institutions of the state engaged in implementing policy, as well as regulating and delivering services. These include state ministries and bureaucratic agencies.

- *Security institutions*: Institutions of the state engaged in law enforcement, border control, protection of citizens, and defense. These include the police and military forces.

- *Judicial institutions*: Institutions of the state engaged in interpreting and enforcing laws, distributing punishments, and conflict mediation. These include the courts. Property rights regimes and the rule of law are also considered to be important components of judicial governance.

We note that there is some overlap in the functions accorded to each type of institution. Both the security and judicial institutions, for example, play a role in law enforcement. In addition, there are some state institutions that fall under multiple types. For example, the Ministry of Justice is both an administrative institution and a judicial institution, just as the Ministry of Defense is both an administrative institution and a security institution. In the chapters that follow, we use great care to identify the specific institutions and functions of interest in the individual studies we summarize.

Conclusion

State institutions are a critical component of the state. They play a key role in shaping how politics work in a society and are, in turn, shaped by political dynamics. In this chapter, we reviewed the basic theoretical approaches to the study of institutions and defined what it is that we mean by them. We also discussed the four types of institutions that we feature throughout the rest of this book: political, administrative, security, and judicial institutions.

Our emphasis on state institutions is intended to provide a way to move forward beyond the concept of state failure, given the limitations and drawbacks associated with this line of inquiry. We argue that exploring how specific types of institutions affect political stability and economic performance (and vice versa) provides us with greater analytical leverage than is offered by the failed states literature. This is more useful than focusing mostly on the challenges (internal conflict, coups, crime, terrorism, and poverty) to the developing world and assuming that the "state" is somehow linked to these issues. This narrower focus should improve our efforts to understand some of the central challenges in the developing world and in what ways institutions are important.

CHAPTER THREE

Challenges to institutional development in the developing world

This book argues that rather than focusing on the concept of state failure it would be more valuable to examine the various institutions of the state, such as the administrative, judicial, security, and political institutions, and how they affect instability and economic (under)performance. But what explains why and how these institutions became effective or ineffective in the first place? Robert Bates, a prominent scholar in the failed state literature, writes that little empirical research has focused on the *causes* of state failure as most of the literature has emphasized the indicators of state failure.[1] This chapter analyses the *challenges* to state building and provides an overview of the *causes* of why these key institutions have been so weak in the developing world.

Waves of state failure

Before World War II, there was little scholarly focus on state failure. In fact there were very few states that existed, with only 50 countries signing the UN Charter in 1945 compared to over 190 members today. Instead, the focus in the past was entirely on state building and development. Scholars have noted that there have been four waves of independence movements and state building, each following the collapse of empires.[2] The first wave took place

---

[1]Bates (2008a: 1–12).
[2]Chazan (1991).

in South America in the *nineteenth century* with the collapse of the Spanish Empire. The second wave took place in Europe *after World War I*, with the collapse of the Austria-Hungarian and Ottoman Empires. The third took place in Asia and Africa *after World War II* with the collapse of the Belgian, Dutch, French, British, and Portuguese Empires. The final wave took place in the *late 1980s* in the Caucasus, Central Asia, and Eastern Europe with the collapse of the Soviet Union and the end of the Cold War. In most cases, these systemic transitions led to the abrupt creation of new states in very hostile environments.[3] While the first wave was relatively less conflictual, the second, third, and fourth waves have been riddled with problems.

Historical macro-level perspectives

Some scholars have used long-term perspectives to understand the causes of institutional weakness.[4] Many scholars have argued that the global system, dependency, and colonialism are to blame for the weakness of institutions in the developing world. These perspectives claim that the colonial background of states or the peripheral positioning of states in the global economy helps explain why state capacity has been so weak. This perspective claims that developing state capacity is not a linear process. This perspective emphasizes that the behavior of developed states with strong institutions affects the capacity of developing states with weaker institutions.

What are the effects of colonialism?

Many scholars have noted the tragic consequences of colonialism particularly in Africa.[5] Colonialism wrecked havoc on the process of state formation that was taking place in many developing countries and the process of *nation building*—or creating a national identity.[6] The colonial experience heightened ethnic identities, which complicated efforts to instill a national identity (see Box 3.1). Borders were also arbitrarily drawn, paying no attention to ethnic boundaries. Furthermore, efforts to build institutions during the colonial period were mixed. In Africa, especially, all countries with colonial backgrounds faced numerous challenges since gaining independence.[7] In addition to giving a heavy focus on Africa, we also highlight the main challenges to Asia, the Middle East, Latin America, and the post-Soviet republics.

---

[3]Carment (2003: 407–27).
[4]Ibid., 410.
[5]Alao (1999); Gros (1996: 455–72).
[6]Ignatieff (2002: 114–23).
[7]Esty et al. (1998).

BOX 3.1 Nation building

Nation building describes the efforts of a society to come together and form a united identity.[8] The process of nation building involves the development of a common behavior, values, and language.[9] In countries with populations that are not homogenous, nation building involves the construction of an identity, which can accommodate ethnic, linguistic, and religious pluralism.

Nation building is often integrated with state building—and many scholars argue that the state plays a strong role in the nation-building process, particularly for late developers.[10] The creation of a national identity is shaped by the state's ability to exercise control, not just over territory but also by penetrating society and reaching a greater number of people. As a result of regular contact, the government and citizens are linked by daily bonds.[11] The state also plays a role in shaping the nation through the use of rhetoric and creating cultural symbols. Nation building takes place through a "complicated educational process."[12] Education is often an important tool of nation building because it is used to socialize the population about the goals and accomplishments of the country and the common destiny shared by all. The state plays a role in creating *civic* conceptions of nationalism. According to Jack Snyder, diverse states with weak institutions are likely to see *ethnic* conceptions of nationalism prevail instead.[13]

Colonialism has posed many challenges for nation building. Colonialism brought together people from different ethnic, political, and religious groups, which made forming a common sense of citizenship very difficult.[14] The record of achieving a sense of citizenship has been particularly weak in Africa and parts of the Middle East. Kwame Anthony Appiah writes: "Europe left Africa at independence with states looking for nations."[15] In Iraq and Lebanon, clan loyalties and sectarian rivalries are stronger than state institutions or national solidarity.

Citizens in states with weak national identities are connected more strongly with cultural and ethnic groupings rather than being confined to state borders. Not only does national loyalty to the state remain low, but

(Continued)

[8]Bendix (1996).
[9]Deutsch and Foltz (1963).
[10]Hill (1995: 2).
[11]Ibid., 21.
[12]Alter (1989: 21).
[13]Snyder (1993: 5–26).
[14]Alao (1999).
[15]Kwame Anthony Appiah, *In My Father's House: Africa in the Philosophy of Culture* (Oxford, UK: Oxford University Press, 1992), 162.

BOX 3.1 *Continued*

so does tolerance for others. Scholars note that states with weak national identities and poorly demarcated borders are more conflict prone.[16] For this reason, it is critical that states with diverse societies, cultivate a national identity that can supersede clan, ethnic, or sectarian divisions.[17]

Arbitrary borders, divide and conquer strategies

Until the twentieth century, borders in Africa were changing constantly and political systems were diverse. The Berlin Conference of 1884 eliminated any form of African autonomy as the European powers carved up Africa under the direct jurisdiction of France, Great Britain, and, to a lesser extent, Spain, Germany, Belgium, Italy, and Portugal. Frontiers were designed to suit the needs of the colonial powers and seemed illogical given the ethnic make-up of the territory. These borders were quickly and badly drawn up and were incompatible with their populations. National borders cut across communities and ethnic groups, and thus across established corridors of social interaction. Scholars have noted that "little attention was paid to the implications of colonial borders for Africans. They negated the realities of African identities and autonomous African perceptions of the world."[18] Other parts of the developing world dealt with similar fates such as in South Asia (India, Pakistan, Bangladesh, and Sri Lanka), which was colonized by Great Britain in the mid-nineteenth century until 1945, and Indonesia, which was colonized by the Netherlands from 1602 until 1945. Hundreds of ethnic groups were cobbled together in the process to serve the interests of the colonial powers.

To maintain control over the indigenous populations, colonial powers often used *divide and conquer policies*, which heightened ethnic identities. Many scholars have claimed that colonial experiences have a direct effect on the extent of communal tensions that have impacted state institutions.[19] Colonial policies often exacerbated social fragmentation to serve the interests of colonial powers. For example, certain groups were deliberately used as tools of the colonial administrations as in the case of Rwanda with the Belgian's exclusive use of the Tutsis over the Hutus or in Sri Lanka with the British use of the Tamils over the Singhalese. Exclusionary policies were followed that involved a narrow coalition of elites who provided

---

[16]Reilly (2008: 28).
[17]Kaplan (2008). Some of these societal divisions may be due to colonialism when borders are drawn up arbitrarily.
[18]Prah (2004: 6).
[19]Esty et al. (1998: 14); Gros (1996); Horowitz (1985).

only exclusionary access to state structures and resources. Because a single ethnic group was encouraged by the colonial power to dominate, this led to direct challenges from other groups later on.[20]

In Sudan, for example, divide and rule policies were used that heightened the ethnic identities of Christians and Muslims. In the south of Sudan, Christian missionaries were allowed free rein and Christian education was provided. In the north, Arabs were prevented from extending their influence. In Syria, French colonists emphasized the distinctiveness of the Alawites and the Sunnis. French policies were designed to create political fragmentation.[21] In Lebanon, Christian Maronites were favored by the French over Sunnis and Shiites. These exclusive identities directly weakened state institutions.[22]

Rapid emergence with little preparation

Colonial governments were also not focused on preparing their colonies for independence and sustainable statehood. Many states that achieved independence after colonization emerged with little more than an empty shell and did not qualify for statehood by the criteria in use in the 1930s.[23] They lacked effective political institutions with centralized administrative organs. They lacked judicial institutions and professionalized security forces. Because of this, many of these states were not politically or economically viable. Compounding this problem, many of these states also lacked a national identity, a shared common language, and common culture. Moreover, many of the new states were not connected to society.[24]

The political, administrative, judicial, and security institutions lacked the capacity to provide an efficient and functioning political order, sustained economic growth, a strong sense of citizenship, and a national identity. People in these newly created states had little understanding of what the state was and what they could expect from it. The UN was mostly focused on self-determination, ignoring whether or not these states were well equipped to deal with independence. Thus, the first waves of state failure took place in the 1960s after independence, since newly independent states were unable to survive in the global system without strong and capable institutions.[25]

The effects of colonialism have varied by region, the timing of independence, and what the goals and needs were of the colonial power. States that

---

[20]Carment (2003: 411).
[21]Cleveland (1994).
[22]Esty et al. (1998: 15).
[23]Herbst (2000).
[24]Ibid., 97–136; Reno (1995).
[25]Zartman (1995).

were granted independence more recently such as in Africa have had a higher risk of political instability and poor economic performance, compared to states that received their independence over a century ago such as in Latin America and many parts of Asia. In Asia, in contrast to Africa, more state building took place during the colonial period, which created foundations for an eventual transformation into real statehood.[26] In Africa, the colonial period was focused more on the extraction of valuable resources than on state building. Robert Jackson notes that following independence "quasi states" emerged, which were incredibly weak, vulnerable to collapse, and completely dependent on foreign aid.[27] Quasi states enjoyed juridical sovereignty but did not exercise total security over their borders. After independence many of these states were on their own, but not well prepared for statehood. The following section provides an overview of the various effects of colonialism on the political, administrative, judicial, and security institutions in the developing world.

Colonialism also did little to build effective *political institutions*. In the case of Africa, the few institutions that were built during the colonial period were instruments of coercion and domination. Political parties were built around charismatic personalities. Legislative organs were weak. Ghana (known as the Gold Coast) was given the most political responsibility but even this was only labeled as "semi-responsible government."[28] No other governments in Africa were given much experience at all with political institutions. In most cases, political activity was banned.[29] Colonialism also gave Africa little experience with elections.[30] One of the few exceptions was Senegal (one of Africa's more democratic countries today), where four Senegalese communes were given the right to vote for a deputy in the French National Assembly after 1848.[31] In the final years of colonialism more participation in elections was permitted and some fledgling parliamentary systems were erected by the British colonists.[32]

Little investment went into developing political institutions in Latin America as well. Both the Spanish and Portuguese governments believed that their survival depended on preventing the rise of potential challengers from the colonies.[33] The colonies in Latin America were given a centralized

---

[26]Some perspectives argue that the quality of institutions was also affected by who colonized you. Though Japanese colonization was equally brutal as elsewhere, Japan invested much more in the infrastructure of its colonies, namely Korea (1910–45) and Taiwan (1895–1945). The Japanese invested in infrastructure and destroyed the traditional states. In its place, Japan introduced efficient administrations (Sindzingre).

[27]Jackson (1987).

[28]Meredith (2005: 17).

[29]Ibid.

[30]Golder and Wantchekon (2004: 401–18).

[31]Ibid.

[32]Ibid.

[33]Coatsworth (2008: 562).

political system led by a governor who then answered to the crown without any independent legislature or judiciary. Spain and Portugal also never allowed limited self-rule. Once independence was achieved settler elites in much of Latin America (Bolivia, Peru, Ecuador, Colombia, Guatemala, El Salvador, and Nicaragua, notably) were resistant to institutional change. Superimposing new political institutions to replace the colonial system of domination often led to violent battles between political factions.[34]

With few exceptions, colonialism in Asia "left a legacy of only rudimentary governmental institutions and even less-formed political party and interest group organizations."[35] Speaking specifically of the case of Indonesia under Dutch colonial rule, personal rule developed due to the lack of any sort of political structure. Under Japanese colonialism, Korea was also given no concessions to develop its political institutions. Korea was ruled by a governor-general who was appointed by the Japanese emperor and was empowered to rule by decree. In 1910, the Central Advisory Council of 65 council members was established to assist the governor-general. Only a few Koreans who had been deemed loyal to Japanese rule were given the opportunity to participate in the council.[36]

India, on the other hand, was one of the more notable exceptions. Under British colonialism, political parties in India emerged in the late nineteenth century. By 1885 the Indian National Congress was established. Because of this, India gained many years of experience with parliamentary practices. By the time India achieved its independence, the Congress party was one of the more institutionalized parties to emerge from colonialism. Samuel Huntington referred to the Congress Party at the onset of its independence as "one of the oldest and best organized political parties in the world."[37]

In the Middle East, the provinces under Ottoman rule were given little opportunity to develop political structures. Egyptians had the most experience with parliamentary politics, but other provinces in the Ottoman Empire had little exposure to parliamentary practices. This situation improved very little when the European powers took over and carved out their own mandates (1920–46). Many Lebanese and Syrian politicians had gained some experience in constitutional parliamentary government under the Young Turk regime. Nevertheless, under the French, supreme power rested in nonelected officials who stood above the law—in this case the French high commissioner had the power to rule by decree and dismiss the parliament. The parliaments were so weak that the French viewed them as "noisome window dressing."[38]

---

[34]Oszlak (1981: 3–32).
[35]Liddle (1985: 68).
[36]Khaled (2002: 11).
[37]Huntington (1968: 84).
[38]Thompson (2000: 53).

In the newly formed countries that once were a part of the Soviet Union, the Soviet legacy has been very important. One of the biggest issues for these post-Soviet countries is to overcome the legacy of years of having the party fused with the government. The Soviet legacy also led to weak institutions that were overly dependent on the executive. During the Soviet era, people deferred to their leaders and power was personalized.

In most cases (with the exception of Kyrgyzstan), the first presidents after independence rose to power through the Communist Party and held high office during the Soviet era. Thus, the executive institutions have merely supplanted the old Communist Party institutions. Many of the staff executive institutions were recruited from the former party apparatus and many of the members of the staff of the Central Committee have remained in positions of power, as there have been very few changes to personnel.[39] President Islam Karimov and President Sapamurat Niyazov (of Uzbekistan and Turkmenistan, respectively) were particularly repressive Communist Party bosses prior to 1991 and continue to regularly crush or exile any political opposition, just as they had in the past. The Communist parties have simply been renamed, with the ideological content eliminated in order to fit the needs of the leader.

The post-Soviet states are also dominated by patrimonial power structures inherited from Soviet rule. Informal patronage style politics gained strength during the post-Soviet transition as the formal institutions of the state weakened.[40] Instead of political parties, in countries such as Tajikistan and Azerbaijan, patronage networks remained the most cohesive institutionalized structures.[41] This extensive system of patronage networks re-established authority and consolidated authoritarian regimes in countries like Kyrgyzstan, Kazakhstan, Uzbekistan, and Turkmenistan.[42]

The *administrative institutions* were also especially weak after colonialism. Most states in Africa emerged into patron-client fiefdoms. The state was not seen as an agency to provide public goods, but as a "fountain of privilege" for the small elite.[43] Moreover, the indigenous population was rarely given an opportunity to gain administrative experience. Most of the staff of the administrative institutions was of European descent.

In the Middle East, under Ottoman rule, the administrative institutions were also poorly developed. While large investment went toward security institutions, the Ottoman administrative institutions were plagued by patrimonialism (i.e. recruitment methods were not based on merit), nepotism, and corruption.[44] The prime focus of the leadership during the Ottoman

---

[39]Franke et al. (2009: 114).
[40]Ishiyama (2002: 42–58).
[41]Rubin (1998).
[42]Grzymala-Busse and Luong (2002a).
[43]Jackson (1987: 527–8).
[44]Owen (1992: 9).

era was to defend itself from European encroachment. More than two-third of the expenditure of the state budget went to security-related spending during this period as building administrative institutions was considered a low priority.[45] Weak administrative institutions persisted during the French mandate period for Lebanon and Syria. The French deliberately never gave the Lebanese or the Syrians much administrative responsibility to keep them dependent on the French.[46]

In contrast, India's indigenous population was given more opportunity to work in the administrative institutions under British rule. Though the British only recruited Indians who were fluent in English, Indians did gain administrative experience during the colonial period.[47] In the mid-nineteenth century, examinations were set up to recruit qualified candidates.[48] By the time India achieved its independence, the Indian Civil Service was hailed as "one of the greatest administrative systems of all time."[49]

Latin American administrative institutions should be stronger compared to their counterparts in other countries in the developing world because they have existed longer, having achieved independence much earlier.[50] The problem is that the historic legacy of Spanish colonialism has been difficult to overcome.[51] The colonial powers invested very little in public services or human capital.[52] Most of the resources went toward defense. The administrative institutions were patrimonial during the colonial period and rarely utilized the indigenous population.

However, by the 1920s and 1930s, many of these institutions in Latin America were better developed. By the 1930s numerous development banks were created. By the 1960s a variety of public sector agencies to promote development were established. A new class of technocrats appeared with skills in management, engineering, and planning. They set up developmental agencies and financial institutions. Some of these would later lose their original rationale but others remained strong such as the Brazilian Economic Development Bank (BNDE) in Brazil, mentioned in Chapter Four.[53]

The dominance of the Communist Party over state institutions undermined the administrative institutions during Soviet rule. The Communist

[45]Ibid., 10.
[46]Cleveland (1994).
[47]Guha (1997: 167).
[48]Khaled (2002).
[49]Braibant (1963: 373).
[50]Administrative institutions in Latin America have existed for hundreds of years under Spanish and Portuguese colonial rule. The problem for these institutions is that the colonial period fostered a culture of non-compliance. Due to the distance between the colonial powers and the colonies obedience was pledged, but noncompliance was the norm; Farazmand (2009: 364).
[51]Hanson (1974: 199).
[52]Coatsworth (2008: 562).
[53]Evans (1992: 168).

Party usurped state functions, leaving the administration in many of the post-Soviet republics inexperienced and underdeveloped. The centralization of decision making in Moscow also meant that state institutions in the republics had no opportunity to exercise such functions.[54] Thus the post-Soviet republics inherited "proto-states" that were never designed to perform the functions of a sovereign state and lacked the institutional capacity required to manage an independent state.[55]

Additionally, administrative institutions during Soviet rule were actually much weaker than previously thought, with low levels of legitimacy.[56] Decision making was opaque.[57] Institutions were regularly subordinated to powerful individuals. Many post-Soviet states inherited networks of patronage and kinship instead.[58] The institutions were built on loyalties rather than merit. Having connections was how administrative positions were filled and how one rises up the ranks.[59] Traditional loyalties and patronage ties have survived from the pre-Soviet period and were incorporated into the system.[60]

Judicial institutions were also affected by colonial penetration. Africa's colonial history played an important role in causing individuals to lose trust in the law. For example, countries in Africa under French rule were subjected to colonial officials punishing them on the spot for up to two weeks in prison as well as a cash penalty, for anything that was deemed an offence.[61] With the exception of Senegal, the French colonies had two sets of codes, one for French citizens and one for Africans.[62]

African countries colonized by the British faired a little better in that local Africans were trained and employed to adjudicate disputes between themselves. Thus there was a cadre of experienced legal practitioners within

---

[54]Whitmore (2005: 3).

[55]Ibid., 4.

[56]Lewis (2008). However, the administrative institutions during the Soviet era also provided services, much more extensive than in Latin America, Africa, or the Middle East. The new states of Central Asia inherited the administrative structure of Soviet socialism with virtually no changes. Some of the remnants from the Soviet era included the military organizations, the bureaucracies, economic networks of supply and production, physical infrastructure of communications, pipelines, railroads, and water supply; see Rubin 1998: 6; Beissinger and Young 2002. The Soviets also invested in a comprehensive health and education system. The problem, however was that the reach of the state was uneven. Moreover, infrastructural investment and maintenance in the post-Soviet world has been weak or nonexistent in some parts of the region.

[57]The problem with opaque decision-making is that because the process of making decisions is not clear, this leads to large information gaps between state and society, which handicaps the administration's ability to implement sound policy.

[58]Bach (2011: 33–41).

[59]Franke et al. (112).

[60]Grzymala-Busse and Luong (2002a: 532).

[61]Joireman (2001: 579).

[62]Ibid.

British colonies.[63] However, the judiciary was more or less controlled by the colonial administration. There was little distinction between the judiciary and the executive during the colonial period, in countries such as Ghana. The judiciary was easily infiltrated by the objectives of the executive. The colonial courts could not review decisions or decrees by the colonial governors. Anyone seeking to challenge a legislative or executive act by the colonial administration was denied access to the courts.[64] The unfairness of the colonial courts system has led to low levels of societal trust in the judiciary.

Thus the legitimacy of the judicial institutions in Africa is undermined by its weak position as a holdover from the colonial period. For example, judges in South African District Courts are not perceived to be independent because of their past status under apartheid rule.[65] Nigeria's judiciary also continues to be regarded poorly due its colonial connection.[66] It has been deemed by much of the public as an institution created only for implementing colonial goals. As a result, many citizens are unaware of what constitutes citizens' rights. Leaders have further de-legitimized the institutions by weakening its power vis-à-vis the executive.[67]

The legacy of colonialism has also affected judicial institutions in Latin America. The judicial institutions under Iberian rule were ineffective and overly rigid. In Latin America, having inherited the Iberian legal system, the laws were incredibly cumbersome.[68] Another problem with the Iberian legal system is that the law was applied by judges rather than *interpreted*. This has made the power of judicial review weak to nonexistent.[69] The Spanish legal system was also incredibly weak.

Many of the countries in Asia inherited more effective judicial institutions from colonial powers. These systems were more extensive and complex than the judicial institutions inherited in other regions of the developing world. The colonial imprint was especially strong for those countries in Asia that were colonized by Great Britain. In the case of Malaysia, the "judiciary and the entire judicial process operated and are still operating under the profound influence of British common law, judicial precedents, principles, ideas and concepts."[70]

Judicial institutions in the Middle East have been negatively affected by the legacy of Ottoman rule.[71] Under Ottoman rule, powerful leaders

---

[63]Ibid.
[64]Prempeh (2006: 25).
[65]Dung (2003).
[66]Yusuf (2009: 680).
[67]Ibid.
[68]Coatsworth (2008).
[69]Domingo (1999: 161).
[70]Woo-Cummings (2001: 26).
[71]Kuran (2004).

exercised little respect for contracts and as a result, the rule of law has been arbitrary and property tights have been weak. Many communities endured expropriation of property, which created an environment with few incentives for investment. As there were few rich merchants, there were also few with a stake in improving property rights.[72]

The Middle East historically has also lacked the judicial institutions to manage the contracts for more complex partnerships.[73] Under Ottoman rule, Islamic contracts remained more ephemeral. This made it difficult for commercial or financial enterprises to materialize. Court systems did not recognize rules that were suitable for business enterprises. As a result partnerships remained small. In the absence of corporate structures, "Islamic law recognized only individuals. Partners could sue one another, of course, as parties to a contract."[74]

For the post-Soviet states, the Soviet legacy has impacted their judicial institutions. Under the USSR, political ideology and patron-clientelism were more important than qualifications.[75] A hierarchy formed where party professionals controlled appointments to the best jobs. Attaining a job was not based on merit but on loyalty to a patron. Laws were also purchased, and there was no effort placed in passing effective laws and regulations. The rule of law had little meaning. Thus the laws that do exist today in many of the former Soviet states are arbitrary, contradictory, and arbitrarily enforced.

In comparison to administrative, judicial, and political institutions, the *security institutions* were often built up more during the colonial period. Nevertheless, these institutions were primarily geared toward internal control rather than repelling external attacks or providing professionalized training. In Africa, troops were rarely stationed on frontiers. Instead cantonments were erected near major cities, more readily to control the populace. Thus, the early development of the security institutions in Africa was shaped by the security needs of foreign actors rather than the mass population.[76] Early recruitment methods were based on reliability and unquestioning loyalty. Recruitment was often based on ethnicity as well. Most African officers were recruited from ethnic groups that hailed from coastal regions.[77]

Patrimonial styles of recruitment were seen outside of Africa as well. In Lebanon, due to France's close ties to Christian groups, all of the troops recruited were Christian Maronites. In the case of Indonesia, the Dutch

---

[72]Ibid.
[73]Ibid.
[74]Ibid., 76.
[75]Jowitt (1983: 275–97).
[76]Wendt and Barnett (1993: 331).
[77]Welch (1975).

mainly recruited the Ambonese for the military in order to counter powerful Javanese groups.[78]

The security institutions in Latin America received most of the Crown's attention during colonial rule. Comparatively speaking, security institutions in Latin America were well developed. Originally only soldiers from the mother countries were used to defend the colonies. No one born in the colonies was allowed to join the military. However, by the mid-eighteenth century, locals were recruited into the military and the officers received the same rights and privileges as those in the regular Iberian armies. The military acquired a prestigious standing in society. The military was also not subject to regular courts and had their own judicial system, which increased its appeal to potential recruits.[79]

The military apparatuses in the post-Soviet states have been inherited from the Soviet era and have had varying degrees of strength. Russia and Kazakhstan emerged with strong institutions, while countries like Tajikistan and Georgia emerged with weak security institutions. In addition to the military, the police were also mostly inherited from the Committee for State Security (KGB) and most of the post-Soviet regimes have relied on the former KGB and the police apparatus to maintain power.[80]

Wrong model for former colonies

Among the scholars that have been critical of colonialism and external factors, some such as Jeffrey Herbst (and other Africanists) argue that the question should be raised whether or not the state is the right model for countries in the developing world.[81] Herbst argues that for countries in Africa this is particularly salient since most of the cases of state failure and weakness are in the African continent. Herbst argues that Africa's demography and sparse population, its geography, political culture, social structure, and heritage of political control and order over people rather than land with multiple layers of sovereignty make the imposition of the European model of the nation state a bad fit. Sovereignty was bestowed on Africa after years of colonial rule, but the alternative to colonialism may not have been a great idea. This challenge has been supported by other scholars who treat the state as an impediment to development.[82]

---

[78]Hack (2006).
[79]Rouquié (1989: 45).
[80]Collins (2009: 249–81).
[81]Herbst (2000).
[82]Keohane (2003: 276–7); Milliken and Krause (2002: 763).

What are the effects of the global international economic system?

Macro and global perspectives also focus on the role of the international system in weakening new states. From this perspective, the *unfair terms of trade* make it impossible for states in the developing world to build up the revenues they need to build strong institutions. Dependency perspectives see *economic equity* issues at the center of state failure.

Dependency theory was one of the first challenges to *modernization theory* to gain mass attention. It originated from the UN Economic Commission on Latin America (ECLA), which formed in 1948.[83] ECLA scholars argued that colonization had left regions like Latin America at a distinct disadvantage. These scholars argued that the plunder that took place during the Spanish and Portuguese colonial periods has persisted in the post-independence age as well, as Latin America continues to be exploited by the United States and other rich countries in Europe.

Scholars argued that one could not ignore the historical factors of when a country was inserted into the global economy. Those inserted later became involved in dependent relationships with industrialized countries, which produced manufactured and high-value goods, while great powers oriented the economies of the colonies around the production of primary products for export.[84] Developing countries were at a structural disadvantage due to their entrenched position as producers of only primary products and raw materials.

These primary products generated unfair terms of trade, making it difficult to generate enough revenues. Economies centered around the production of primary products and raw materials were vulnerable to fluctuations in the production of these goods and the inelasticity of demand. Efforts made to catch up by producing domestically made high-end goods were thwarted by the competition from more efficient industrialized countries that had already created economies of scale. Any later development that took place was dependent, since most of the capital was controlled by foreign sources.[85] As a result, the state was weakened and left persistently dependent upon the developed world. The state was left permanently impotent to generate capacity.

---

[83]Some of the more noteworthy dependency scholars include: Paul Baran, Raul Prebisch, Fernando Henrique Cardoso, and Andre Gunder Frank.

[84]Colonial governments also extracted resources from their colonies, stripping them of valuable assets.

[85]Noted dependency scholar Fernando Henrique Cardoso (who would later become the president of Brazil in 1997) believed that development was possible in developing countries but that the linkages between elites in developing countries and foreign capital would preclude independent development for developing countries, instead leading to associate dependent development.

Key figures in the ECLA such as Raul Prebisch argued in favor of Import Substitution Industrialization (ISI), where infant industries would receive subsidies, state support, and protection from foreign competition. This process had already begun in some countries such as Argentina, Mexico, and Brazil, which had large internal markets. However, when industry stagnated, this left many of these countries in more debt than before. The pattern of industrialization that developed was not focused on sustainable development, but on a showcase of modernity. Consumption patterns were skewed in favor of elite groups at the expense of the poor and lower income majorities.[86]

Many scholars have attacked the dependency theory for failing to examine *the internal causes* of underdevelopment and stagnation.[87] In the case of Argentina, which has experienced some economic success but has underperformed given its resources, populist (see Box 3.2) leadership and weak institutions have had a negative effect on economic development.[88] Chile, on the other hand, reduced poverty by investing in research and infrastructure when it received a boom in the prices of copper.[89] Thus dependency theory would be more useful if it focused on exactly how institutions have been underdeveloped by late insertion into the global capitalist system and unequal terms of trade.

For many states in Latin America, the flip-flopping back and forth between an ISI approach and neoliberal strategies has not improved the capacity of the state to generate economic development. Guillermo O'Donnell illustrates this point well in the case of Latin America. He writes that "the long agony of the state-centered, import-substitutive pattern of capital accumulation has left us with a dinosaur incapable even of feeding itself, while the 'solutions' currently under way lead toward an anemic entity which may be no less incapable of supporting democracy, decent levels of social equity, and economic growth."[90]

BOX 3.2 Populism

Populism is an amorphous concept, most often used by scholars of Latin American politics to describe a style of leadership that has characterized many Latin American leaders such as Juan Perón in Argentina, Getúlio Vargas in Brazil, Alberto Fujimori in Peru, Carlos Menem of Argentina, or more recently Hugo Chávez in Venezuela. Though the term is often thrown at politicians with charisma, populism does not necessarily denote a charismatic style of leadership. A populist leadership can be charismatic, but the

(Continued)

---

[86]Woo-Cummings (1999: 22).
[87]Harrison (1988).
[88]Ibid.
[89]Ibid.
[90]O'Donnell (1993: 18).

BOX 3.2 Continued

more necessary condition is that the populist leader is both *personalistic* and *paternalistic* (in contrast to a *personalist dictator*, the populist enjoys more genuine widespread popular support and does not need to resort to repression). Populist leaders hone in on societal needs and demands and exacerbate the problems that society faces.[91] More importantly as far as this chapter is concerned, populism is a style of leadership that *weakens state institutions*.

Populism usually emerges when political and intermediary institutions, which are supposed to aggregate and channel societal demands, are already weak. When political parties and labor unions have failed to mediate between the citizens and the state, populist leadership is more likely to arise. Populism is also more likely to emerge when the state is in crisis, both economic and political. This is demonstrated in the rise of Alberto Fujimori of Peru in 1990. Fujimori emerged at a time when the alternative seemed unattractive. He made few concrete promises and presented himself as an outsider with no links to the establishment.[92]

Populist regimes and leaders have important implications for institutional development. Populism encompasses a type of political mobilization that "*bypasses institutionalized forms of mediation* or at least subordinates them to more direct linkages between the leader and the masses."[93] *Political institutions* such as political parties and legislatures are often weakened. For example, Hugo Chávez has led various political parties, such as MVR and MBR-200. MVR was later disbanded in favor of forming a larger and more amorphous coalition of 23 parties. The institutional structure of the parties led by Chávez diminished. None of these political parties constitute "a disciplined organization with ongoing societal links."[94] Under Fujimori, the party system also deteriorated with programmatic differences being overshadowed by personal characteristics. Furthermore, the legislature was left impotent after a self-imposed coup.

Populist leaders may also try to weaken the *judicial institutions* by packing the courts with judges that are politically pliable. The courts may also be a source of patronage for the populist leader to deliver goods to his supporters. In the case of Argentina under President Carlos Menem, the courts were undermined by his deliberate selection of politically loyal judges. This ensured that court rulings were always friendly towards his regime. As a

(Continued)

---

[91]Roberts (1995: 88).
[92]Crabtree (2000: 163–76).
[93]Roberts (1995: 88).
[94]Ellner (2003: 153).

BOX 3.2 *Continued*

result, the rule of law was weakened, and a host of scandals and government abuses took place with impunity.

Populism may also lead to the weakening of *administrative institutions*. The economic policies of a populist regime or populist leader are focused on the *distribution of patronage* to a wide array of clients in order to ensure popular support.[95] From this perspective populist leaders are not focused on economic growth through stimulating entrepreneurship but on nationalization of industries in order to keep employment levels high.[96] Because the policies are distributional, there is no urgent need for an effective bureaucracy. The bureaucracy becomes a large resource that the populist leader can use to distribute patronage to his or her constituents and main support groups. For example, Chávez weakened the state by appointing a large number of military officers to top government and party positions.[97]

The populist leader also tries to circumvent the administrative institutions in order to deliver goods directly to people; as a result, the linkages between the leader and his or her constituents are also stronger. For example, Chávez has skirted state institutions in order to create more direct linkages with the population. Fujimori eliminated the state's role in distribution as well, preferring to make more direct contact with his constituents. All of the strategies of the populist leader have the effect of elevating the popularity of the populist leader at the expense of the state's institutions.

What are the effects of the Cold War?

In addition to the collapse of the colonial order, the Cold War and its end also led to the weakening of many young states. The entire Cold War period was particularly damaging to states in the developing world, as they became pawns in the hands of the superpowers, the United States and the USSR. Economic assistance was provided without a clear strategy. Instead of fostering economic growth, corruption and overdevelopment resulted.[98]

During the Cold War many proxy wars were fought within the developing world. During these proxy wars military assistance given by the superpowers (the United States and the Soviet Union) was channeled to *violent non-state actors* and to *weak and corrupt regimes*. Many of the countries in the developing world were fed military aid by the superpowers in order to maintain a balance of power in the international system. Weak

---

[95]Roberts (1995: 88).
[96]Dornbusch and Edwards (1990).
[97]Ellner (2003: 149).
[98]Dorff (1996: 17–31).

and corrupt regimes were propped up if they vocalized their partisanship for one superpower. Military aid was pocketed directly by kleptocratic rulers (see Chapter Eight) and doled out to maintain their elite support groups. Warlords, criminals, and other non-state actors who claimed to be on the right side of a superpower were also supported with military aid. Compounding this problem, during this period the proliferation of small arms challenged the state's ability to maintain a monopoly over the legitimate use of force (see Box 3.3). Instead of state-building efforts, non-state actors were gaining more and more power, enabling them to directly challenge the state.

BOX 3.3 Small arms

Small arms are weapons that are intended for individual use and include pistols, rifles, submachine guns, assault rifles, and light machine guns. Light weapons are designed for use by two or more people that may serve as a crew and include heavy machine guns, grenade launchers, mortars, antiaircraft guns, and antitank guns, which must all be less than 100 mm in caliber.[99] Both small arms and light weapons are easily available, widely produced, cheap, easy to use, easily transportable and diffused, difficult to trace and monitor, have a long shelf life, and are easily maintained.

There are over half a billion small arms (640 million) and light weapons available, causing 15,000 to 20,000 casualties per year. More than 8 million small arms circulate around West Africa alone. There are 8 million new guns being manufactured every year by at least 1,249 companies in 92 countries. Producing small arms requires little technical know-how, and due to demand, there are well over 600 suppliers around the world.

Small arms are *hard to monitor* and are easily stolen. Every year at least 1 million firearms are stolen or lost worldwide. The weapons can easily end up in countries that have weak security institutions, or controls regarding how the weapons will be used. In particular, war-torn countries or countries with poor border security are flooded with surplus weapons. Small arms are frequently recycled from country to country, and their ownership is transferred to violent non-state actors.[100]

Effective security institutions play a role in ensuring that arsenals of small arms are not stolen, illegally flooding the market. Unprofessional

(Continued)

---

[99]United Nations Institute for Disarmament (2006: 1–30).
[100]"Small Arms and Light" (2008: 25).

BOX 3.3 *Continued*

militaries can loot weapons from official sources and then ship them into conflict zones for a profit.[101] Recently, a parliamentary commission in Ukraine revealed that, between 1992 and 1998, some US$ 32 billion worth of weaponry (a third of the country's stocks) had been stolen from national armories.[102]

East Asia has strong control over small arms and other weapons. North Korea and South Korea have not been adversely affected by increased arms trafficking. In Singapore gun control laws are extremely tight and are based upon a presumption of guilt if any person is found to be in possession of two or more unlicensed weapons. In Japan it is virtually impossible to own a firearm legally and there appears to be little demand for illegal weapons, except from organized criminal gangs.[103]

Southeast Asia has more trouble controlling the flow of weapons—there has been huge flows of weapons into Cambodia (where one in 263 is an amputee).[104] Vietnam is still awash with light weapons and ammunition. South Asia, however, is much worse. In South Asia, the proliferation of weapons has risen significantly. This started with the arms pipeline that was set up in the 1980s after the Soviet invasion of Afghanistan that sent $8 billion worth of light weapons from Karachi to Rawalpindi.[105] The Pakistani government has claimed that over 3 million Kalashnikov rifles were hidden along the Pakistan–Afghanistan border.[106] Virtually anyone can acquire weapons in the North West Frontier Province and routes in the entire region are very porous.[107]

The availability of small weapons has had the most devastating effects on Africa, however.[108] Small arms have been particularly damaging in Sudan, Uganda, Sierra Leone, Rwanda, Angola, the Democratic Republic of Congo, Somalia, and Liberia. In Liberia, Charles Taylor was able to sell $8 million a month in natural resources to buy light weapons to fund the conflict there.[109] The main suppliers to the Samuel Doe regime (president

(Continued)

---

[101]Musah (2002b: 244).
[102]Ibid.
[103]"Small Arms and Light" (2008: 14).
[104]Ibid.
[105]Ibid., 17.
[106]Ibid., 18.
[107]Ibid.
[108]With the exception of South Africa, over the past decade, spending on arms in Sub-Saharan Africa increased by 15 percent at a time when the region's economic growth rose by less than 1 percent in real terms.
[109]"Small Arms and Light" (2008: 24).

BOX 3.3 *Continued*

of Liberia from 1986 to 1990) and rebel army led by Charles Taylor were the United States, Nigeria, Ivory Coast, South Korea, Libya, Taiwan, and Israel. Subsequently, Charles Taylor was able to continue to supply weapons to rebel forces in Sierra Leone.[110]

During the Somali conflict, most of the heavy weapons in Somalia were inoperable. However 30,000 people were killed by light weapons in 1991 and 1992. About 500,000 weapons that were abandoned by the Somali army fell into the hands of General Mohamed Farah Aideed and Ali Mahdi. Weapons also flooded into Somalia after the collapse of the Mengistu regime in Ethiopia.[111] Further, the United States also donated 5,000 M-16 rifles and 5,000 handguns to the Somali police, which was seen at the time as a maladroit gesture in a country already flooded with weapons. Soon after, brand-new M-16s were sighted in the hands of criminals.[112]

In region such as Africa, at independence it was not originally burdened by the problem of small-arms proliferation. Even in countries such as Ethiopia and Somalia, arms were generally under the state's control.[113] This all changed as the Cold War proxy wars heated up in the region. Arms started to diffuse in the 1960s. There were 10 manufacturers of small arms in the former Soviet Union in the 1960s; by 1999 this figure had grown to 66 in the ex-Soviet territories. Globally, corresponding figures stood at 99 and 385 respectively.[114] From sales of around US$ 3 billion per year during the Cold War, global private-arms sales were estimated to have exceeded $25 billion in 1996.

The proliferation of small arms has had a long-lasting effect on human security, and once the proliferation has become large scale, control is difficult. In countries considered to be at peace, the level of violence due to small arms is considered to be as high as in war zones. In 90 percent of conflicts since 1990, small arms and light weapons have been the primary weapons used in fighting, and have contributed to the increased proportion of civilian deaths in those conflicts.[115] Given the high number of battle deaths due to small arms, their role in exacerbating the casualties inflicted during conflicts is important.

Conflicts have had an especially high cost for Africa. Oxfam claims that conflict has cost Africa $300 billion from 1990 to 2005. Today Africa loses

(Continued)

---

[110]Ibid.
[111]Ibid., 26.
[112]Ibid., 27.
[113]Lefebvre (1992).
[114]Musah (2002b).
[115]Bourne (2007).

BOX 3.3 *Continued*

about $18 billion a year. Wars, civil wars, and insurgencies have shrunk African economies by 15 percent and conflicts have weakened the capacity of the state to function. Transit routes are blocked, national industries cannot function, businesses halt, and foreign investors leave. Schools cannot operate, basic services are disrupted (e.g. a water project that aimed to connect a pump to a nearby school in Kenya was derailed due to bandits in Northern Kenya), health care cannot be provided, food cannot be harvested, the population is displaced, disease spreads, and sexual violence is more easily carried out.[116]

To deal with this issue, state institutions need to develop the capacity to remove surplus and obsolete weapons, strengthen export controls, enhance stockpile security, improve law enforcement capabilities, increase transparency, and foster parliamentary oversight.[117] This requires strengthening not only laws, but also the capacity of security, judicial, administrative, and political institutions.

Not all countries, however, were badly affected by the Cold War. While Africa was undermined by foreign involvement, East Asia thrived. East Asia was seen as an area of strategic importance to both superpowers, but particularly the United States. This led to significant amounts of aid and investment from the United States to countries such as Taiwan, South Korea, and Japan. Educational systems were overhauled to improve human capital and create a more skilled work force. Land reform was enacted (most successfully in Japan). Security was provided on a massive scale. This contrasts with Africa, which more or less served as a theater for various internal conflicts and proxy wars. Most of the assistance came in the form of military aid, which was used to purchase weapons.

Many scholars have argued that the *end* of the Cold War and the collapse of the Soviet Union led to the emergence of many weak and failing states.[118] During the Cold War, many weak states were propped up with foreign aid, enabling them to survive. When the Cold War ended, economic and military aid stopped completely. Leaders at the helms of weak states no longer had the resources to distribute to their followers or to maintain the military. States that had been losing the monopoly over violence were now completely unable to exercise control and order.[119] More violent conflicts

---

[116]Alagappa and Inoguchi (1999: 93).
[117]Stohl (2005: 75).
[118]Rosh (1989); Ayoob (1996); Holm (1998); Dorff (1996); Ignatieff (2002); Zartman (1995).
[119]Dorff (1996: 18); see also Gros (1996: 455–72).

broke out while existing conflicts intensified.[120] This explains why the peak of global incidence of instability took place around 1992 following the end of the Cold War.[121] The end of the Cold War led to an environment that was overall hostile to state building.[122]

The end of the Cold War also coincided with the collapse of the Soviet Union and the emergence of multiple new states in Eastern Europe, Central Asia, and the Caucasus. Many of these states only had "marginal capacities to function politically and economically."[123] The Central Asian republics and the states in the Caucasus were particularly weak. In some cases these new states also had to contend with break away regions that hoped to gain their own independence. These break away regions, referred to as de facto states, directly challenged the stability of these newly independent states (see Box 3.4).

BOX 3.4 De facto states

A de facto state is a geographic entity, usually consisting of a particular ethnic group, which wishes to secede from the parent state that it is a part of and be recognized as a de jure state by the international community.[124] In some cases de facto states may have an organized political leadership, some administrative capacity to provide services, popular support, and control over a specific territory. De facto states often go unrecognized by the international community for fear that this would deteriorate its relationship with the sovereign state and that it could set a precedent that would lead to more cases of secession around the world.

De facto states usually have very low functioning institutions. Political institutions are most always personalized with opaque decision-making and little pluralism.[125] Corruption and patron-clientelism is also high (see Chapter Eight). Potential threats are often neutralized through repression or co-optation rather than accommodation and compromise.[126]

(Continued)

---

[120]Conflict has hit Africa particularly hard. About 60 percent of the deaths from armed conflict in the contemporary world have occurred in the region. Arms exports to the region nearly doubled over the year as different factions fought not only over territory but also for valuable mineral resources. During the past ten years, over half of the countries in Sub-Saharan Africa have been engaged in armed conflict or confronted by a significant threat from armed groups at one point or the other. In March 2003, Komla Siamevi, of the WHO Regional Office for Africa, Brazzaville, put the economic losses due to wars in Africa at $15 billion per year (OCHA 2003).
[121]Zartman (1995).
[122]Moss et al. (2006: 1–28).
[123]Dorff (1996: 18).
[124]Pegg (1998: 26).
[125]Lynch (2002: 836).
[126]Ibid., 842.

BOX 3.4 *Continued*

In security matters, the ability of de facto states to provide security varies considerably. The Pridnestrovyan Moldovan Republic (PMR) in Moldova and Nagorno Karabakh in Azerbaijan exercise considerable control, and have "clear armed force structures, police agencies, border troops and customs posts."[127] In contrast, both South Ossetia and Abkhazia in Georgia are much weaker. In Abkhazia the state has been "unable to provide law and order" and NGOs and other international organizations "have become the pillars of social security in Abkhazia."[128] In some cases, security has to be outsourced—as Russia, for example, has provided security for Abkhazia and South Ossetia. Security institutions in Abkhazia, South Ossetia, and Transnistria are often headed by Russians or officials who are "de facto delegated by state institutions of the Russian Federation."[129]

In administrative matters, de facto states also vary considerably in their abilities. In Abkhazia, the government "maintains the daily operations of legislative, executive and judicial institutions, but performs very few services for the population."[130] Any revenues collected often go into the hands of private pockets. De facto states have systems with very little transparency and very high levels of crime.[131]

For most de facto states, the parent state offers little motivation to remain. For example, Dov Lynch writes that parent states such as Moldova, Georgia, and Azerbaijan "have not become magnets sufficiently attractive to induce the separatist areas to compromise in order to benefit from the restoration of political and economic relations. The authorities of the de facto states believe that the economic situation in Moldova, Georgia and Azerbaijan is just as bad as theirs, if not worse."[132]

De facto states pose great challenges for state building. They often perpetuate frozen or active conflicts with the sovereign state. These conflicts tend to be intractable with settlement near impossible.[133] De facto states also weaken the sovereignty, capability, and security of the parent state as resources are diverted from providing services to competing against the de facto state.

Moreover, in de facto states, severe *economic difficulties* are common and often spill over.[134] The economies of the parent states and sometimes

(Continued)

---

[127]Ibid., 838.
[128]Ibid., 836.
[129]Popescu (2006: 11).
[130]Lynch (2002: 836).
[131]Kolsto (2006).
[132]Lynch (2002: 843).
[133]Ibid., 838.
[134]Ibid., 841.

BOX 3.4 *Continued*

neighboring states suffer as investment slows down due to potential threats to instability. Moreover, because de facto states cannot legally trade with the outside world and usually face blockades, this encourages illegal business activity.[135] There are huge economic costs to nonrecognition, which persist since the de facto state is completely closed off to the outside world.[136]

Other complex processes took place that had profound implications for the region. The withdrawal of Soviet troops from Afghanistan led to a mad rush to capture what was left of the central Afghan state by various warlords and factions. The effects of the Soviet war with Afghanistan and the subsequent civil war led to a massive flow of refugees, which put pressure on existing developing states in the region such as Pakistan and Iran.

The end of the Cold War also ushered in a wave of regime change, with many authoritarian states trying to make the transition to democracy. The combination of weak institutions coupled with fledgling democracies was a recipe for instability. In this environment, "relatively weak democratic institutions and processes can easily fall prey to the forces of uncertainty and fear."[137] As the "failed state" literature has emphasized, weak democracies are more prone to instability than strong authoritarian regimes.

What is the neoliberal perspective?

The specific policies espoused by globalization proponents, including policy makers, economists, and some political scientists are best described as neoliberal; they were collectively known as the *Washington Consensus* after the term was coined by John Williamson in 1989. The neoliberal perspective argues that good governance (which equates less government and policies of nonintervention) is the key to ensuring poverty reduction and ensuring economic growth.

Neoliberals claim that free markets, instead of governments, are the most efficient means of resource allocation. They assume that individuals are rational and self-interested, which allows markets to operate best. Development, as they see it, can only take place when markets are given

---

[135]Kolsto (2006).
[136]Ibid.
[137]Dorff (1996: 25).

the freedom to operate freely. The "state" (administrative institutions) is viewed with disdain because the state is seen as an instrument of interference with the market. Neoliberals disagree with any political interference in the market that distorts prices. They argue that the state's involvement in the market encourages *rent seeking* (see Box 8.2, Chapter Eight) and leads to inefficiency and waste.

Most specifically in Latin America in the 1990s, neoliberal policies targeted state institutions with the advice that the government privatize businesses, deregulate the economy, stop public spending, ensure competitive exchange rates, and open up their economies to imports in order to attract foreign direct investment. Scholars have argued that the neoliberal agenda weakened state (administrative) strength rendering most states more fragile than ever before.[138]

The implementation of the neoliberal agenda (primarily in the late 1980s and 1990s) came in the form of structural adjustment programs (SAPs) by international financial institutions (IFIs) such as the International Monetary Fund (IMF), the World Bank (WB), and the World Trade Organization (WTO).[139] These organizations (known as the Bretton Woods institutions) were originally constructed to help the major powers prevent the economic hardships that took place during the Great Depression, possibly leading to World War II. In efforts to prevent war and to increase economic interdependence, the IMF was constructed to give out loans to deeply indebted countries of the developed world. The policies prescribed to the developed countries in need of loans were Keynesian style prescriptions of import substitution industrialization (ISI), managing domestic supply and demand through taxing and spending. By the 1970s, almost all of the loans were being doled out to developing countries.

These loans were not delivered without conditions, known as SAPs. Aid recipient countries had to adopt free market policies. National industries were privatized. Public spending was curtailed. The number of civil servants was supposed to be reduced. However, instead of tying aid to reforming the bureaucracy through meritocratic recruitment methods and by streamlining the bureaucracy, salaries eroded. This was a way for governments in developing countries to evade domestic conflict. But the result was an even more poorly performing public sector with an underpaid and unqualified staff.[140]

IFIs were blamed for granting loans to illegitimate and inept governments and dictatorships and were also accused of imposing conditions that had no chance of being followed. Finally, IFIs were critiqued for triggering a *fallacy of composition*. By encouraging the production of single commodities

---

[138]Boege et al. (2009).
[139]The WTO was formed in 1995 and was preceded by the General Agreement on Trade and Tariffs.
[140]Fritz and Menocal (2007: 542).

this created a decline in prices due to the excess of supply and the inelasticity of demand. For example, in Africa, countries were encouraged to focus on the production of commodities such as coffee. Unfortunately, this led to overproduction and a decline in coffee prices, rather than leading to a comparative advantage.[141]

Scholars critical of the Washington Consensus have argued that the neoliberal policies ignore the role of the *developmental state* (see Box 4.1, Chapter Four) in helping developing countries navigate the global economy.[142] Cuts in foreign aid and economic conditionality (such as mandating that administrative budgets be slashed) cut at the heart of the administrative institutions in developing countries.[143] Critics claim that "bad policies" are not the sole cause of economic stagnation in the developing world.[144]

Thus, the Washington Consensus ignores the role of the state *administrative institutions* in the economy.[145] Many of the policies only work for states that have already established a sophisticated system of taxation and redistribution, not for states that are weakly developed and cannot perform these functions yet. As these states are already short of important revenues from taxation, the inability to use other means to gain revenues makes it difficult for the state to provide much (such as food subsidies or cheap housing). Many states that were forced to follow these policies became weaker and less able to regulate transactions, while non-state actors tapped into resources and gained revenues for insurgencies.[146] Modes of authority of the state weakened, mechanisms of social regulation were dismantled, and the bond between state and society was threatened.[147]

Changes took place in the late 1990s when some IFIs realized that just relying on markets was not working well to prevent instability and poverty. More attention was placed on the institutional quality of states (making the circular argument that aid is most effective to states that already have good governance). Neoliberal institutionalists, who have their roots in neoliberal economics, look at effective institutions such as independent central banks, property rights (see Chapter Five), and the rule of law, which are all concerned with the functioning of the market. More recently, institutions such as the World Bank have looked at the strength of administrative institutions and the ability to provide social capital and social safety nets.[148] These perspectives also argue that state administrative institutions provide conditions

---

[141]Sindzingre (2007: 615–32).
[142]See also Clapham (2002), Reno (1995), Duffield (2007); Bilgin and Morton (2004).
[143]Stedman (1996: 243).
[144]Sindzingre (2007).
[145]Clapham (2002b: 792).
[146]Ibid., 793.
[147]Bilgin and Morton (2004: 175).
[148]World Bank (2001).

that are hospitable (or not) to integration into the global economy.[149] Since these perspectives believe that globalization should not necessarily have a negative impact on state institutions, they see poor governance, not international factors, as the cause of instability and poverty.[150]

In line with this viewpoint, economists and some international organizations such as the IMF, the World Bank, and the OECD argue that instability and poverty are the result of poorly conceived policies and not globalization.[151] Therefore states that have been able to take advantage of technological possibilities and export goods and services that have favorable terms of trade have grown. States that are *more open* not only attract more FDI but also are more stable and less impoverished. Moreover, the OECD argues that low levels of economic production and little investment in manufacturing are the root causes of poverty and instability. Finally, states that have more international linkages and higher levels of trade have stronger infrastructure and lower levels of corruption.

However, attracting FDI is not easy for small economies that are primarily *dependent on single commodities*, with deteriorating terms of trade. Many countries in the developing world have small domestic markets, which may explain why investment levels are so low. FDI has also been uneven not just across countries but within them as well. Africa has been the hardest hit by low levels of FDI.[152] But, creating larger domestic economies does not happen overnight. Developing countries often have to deal with low purchasing power, poor infrastructure to transport goods, and expensive transport costs. There are also fewer incentives for developing countries to remain open with regional partners when countries are dependent on single commodities. Rather than complementing one another, these economies compete with one another.[153] Critics of neoliberalism have charged that small economies are especially in need of strong state institutions in order to prevent being swallowed up by market forces.

What are the effects of globalization?

Critics of neoliberalism argue that the international political economy, external interference, and transnational forces that have accompanied globalization have directly weakened state *administrative institutions*.[154]

---

[149]Hameiri (2007: 126).
[150]Ibid., 128.
[151]Economists understanding of failed state differs from political science. Economists argue that persistent shortfalls in growth rates compared to comparable countries are what cause states to fail. Thus, from the economic perspective states like Argentina could be listed as failed after its economic breakdown.
[152]Sindzingre (2007).
[153]Ibid.
[154]Raemakers (2005: 4).

Globalization encompasses a global market, with a free flow of goods, services, and information. States interact and trade at unprecedented levels, with market forces often making important decisions instead of states. Because of this, some scholars argue that institutional weakness should be considered to be in tandem with globalization.[155]

Globalization is a powerful force. It can promote growth but also large inequalities and poverty. It can lead to achievement but also frustration. Globalization can lead to turbulent financial markets and capital flows. It can destroy traditional social structures, and lead to more protests and instability. It can lead to growing unemployment and debt. Non-state actors (such as multinational corporations) have grown in power.[156] Foreign aid has disappeared, while the prices for global commodities produced in the developing world have decreased.[157] Though the modern nation state is not going to wither away because of globalization, for weaker states globalization presents many challenges and demands and causes states to become more vulnerable.

Globalization places pressure on the state (namely the administrative institutions) to contract and allow the logic of the market to take control. The administrative institutions are no longer autonomous and able to provide public goods for its citizens. Welfare is no longer distributed due to pressures on the state to cut its budgets. Subsidies and price controls are also eliminated. There are also more economic crises and external shocks (such as spikes in food and oil prices), which states with weak administrative institutions have a difficult time dealing with.[158] Globalization has made maintaining of administrative institutions more difficult.[159] It reduces administrative capacity, when the state is needed more than ever to deal with constant threats to stability.

Situational micro-level perspectives

Micro-level perspectives of state failure focus on the endogenous factors that put pressure on state institutions and make it more difficult for them to function. Robert Rotberg refers to these as the situational causes of state failure.[160] These causes include environment, resources (for an explanation of the effects of resources on the state see Box 3.5) and population demographics. These perspectives argue that there may be internal factors that pose unique challenges to state-building efforts.

---

[155]Ignatieff (2002: 114–23).
[156]Reilly (2008: 28).
[157]Dorff (1996).
[158]Doornbos (2006).
[159]Doornbos (2002: 804).
[160]Rotberg (2003).

Environment

Some states have a physical and geographical legacy that make their institutions inherently ineffective, such as being prone to terrible droughts, extreme temperatures, natural disasters, diseases, having difficult borders to monitor, overly rugged terrain. Adverse environments with poor soil quality and unreliable rainfall undermine agricultural production. This is all the more problematic given that agriculture constitutes 25 percent of the region's GDP.[161] Many states in Sub-Saharan Africa have faced numerous droughts. The countries in the Sahel region face extreme temperatures making it more difficult to produce food. Countries like Chad and Niger have faced numerous droughts that have led to famine. In Niger, since the drought of 2010, 2.4 million of 3.6 million people are considered highly vulnerable to food insecurity. Countries in Eastern Africa have suffered as well. Only 2 percent of Somalia's land is arable. The lack of arable farmland increased the competition between farmers and placed pressure on an already weak state to resolve these disputes. For other countries, strong earthquakes and hurricanes make them particularly vulnerable, such as Haiti. All of these types of natural disasters disrupt economic activity and make it nearly impossible for the state to collect revenues to function.

For other countries their geography is difficult to manage, posing challenges to the *security institutions*. Indonesia has to control over 17,000 islands. The Philippines also has to control over 7,000 islands. Afghanistan is so mountainous that maintaining control over the borders is near impossible. Neighbors matter as well. Being surrounded by other expansionist or meddlesome states makes state building more difficult, such as Lebanon and its constant interference from Israel and Syria. Geography can also be a problem for generating revenues, which directly impact *administrative institutions*. Countries that are landlocked often suffer economically. Africa's population is atypically landlocked. A high proportion of the population is remote from the coast or navigable waters. Being landlocked reduces a nation's annual growth rate by around half of 1 percent.[162] Countries that are landlocked such as Chad are some of the poorest countries in the world. This in turn provides the administrative institutions with few sources of revenue.

The "curse of the tropics" is also cited as a problem for states, many of which are in Africa, which challenge the *administrative institutions* by adversely affecting the economy.[163] A propensity for diseases, such as malaria, reduces life expectancy and lowers productivity levels. Diseases such as malaria, yellow fever, African sleeping sickness (known officially as

---

[161]Sachs and Warner (1999: 43–76).
[162]Ibid.
[163]Sachs and Warner (1997: 335–76).

African trypanosomiasis), and chagas disease (in Latin America) to name a few, all directly challenge state capacity. Not only are there fewer sources of revenue for the state due to lower productivity levels, but the health problems associated with tropical diseases strain any public health institution.

Resources

Many scholars have pointed to the historical role that resources have played in the institutional development of states that have been colonized.[164] The argument follows that during the colonial period certain types of resources (referred to as endowments) undermined the fostering of stable institutions, which can persist decades afterward.[165] Endowments include crops, resources, labor supply, and settler mortality rates. Colonies that had high settler mortality rates and an abundance of natural resources were more likely to be extractive colonies and colonies that had low levels of settler mortality rates were more likely for form settler colonies. From this perspective, the quality of *judicial and administrative institutions* was directly affected by whether or not the colonies were extractive or settler.[166] Settler colonies that had large settler populations such as in South Africa, Rhodesia (Zimbabwe), and Botswana had more demand from settlers to build up administrative institutions and property rights that would help them govern the colony. Extractive colonies typically did not have large settler populations and were primarily focused on the extraction of resources, not the development of stable institutions.

The types of resources available may have affected the quality of the *political institutions* as well. To illustrate this point, Latin America is abundant in natural resources that required high levels of low skilled labor. As a result, extractive colonies developed as well. Crops such as sugar, coffee, and cocoa were grown on large plantations, which demanded the importation of slaves further exacerbating large divisions of wealth. In contrast to much of North America where there were small farms and a middle class pushing for representation, landed elites in Latin America were able to amass great personal fortunes and resist democratic reforms. The only colonial institutions that developed were exploitative, and these institutions of exploitation persisted after independence was achieved. The institutions only protected the rights of a small group of elites. As Stanley Engerman and Ken Sokoloff put it, "the relatively small fractions of their populations composed of whites, as well as their highly unequal distribution of wealth, may have contributed to the evolution of political, legal, and economic

---

[164]See Acemoglu et al. (2001); Engerman and Sokoloff (2002).
[165]See Coatsworth (2008); Acemoglu, 2004; Rodrik, 1999; Isham 2005.
[166]Acemoglu et al. (2001); Acemoglu et al. (2004: 1–111).

institutions that were less favorable toward full participation in the commercial economy by a broad spectrum of the population."[167] In contrast, in North America and other colonies of low settler mortality, institutions were created to protect a broad spectrum of the population.[168]

Even for states that have not been penetrated deeply by colonization, national resource abundance still affects the quality of state institutions. Resource abundance may give the government a false sense of security and allow the state to not prioritize bureaucratic efficiency, institutional quality, and sustainable development.[169] States that rely on resources are not forced to develop capable institutions that are necessary for encouraging growth in manufacturing and services (for more on this see Box 3.5). For example, Russia and Mexico export oil because this generates huge revenues for the government. On the other hand, due to the weakness of their institutions, they are not able to generate wealth from other means.[170] Financial institutions for savings and investment are underdeveloped.

BOX 3.5 Rentier state

Political scientists, and more specifically area specialists, have argued that certain natural resources undermine administrative capacity and economic development. An abundance of resources may impact the way a state gains revenues. Terry Lynn Karl argues that the "revenues a state collects, how it collects them, and the uses to which it puts them define its nature."[171] States that rely predominantly on resources for revenues are often referred to as *rentier states*.

Rentier states do not rely on extracting the domestic population's surplus production; instead they're reliant on external revenues known as *rents* (usually derived from oil or the exploitation of other natural resources). These rents are easily captured by the state through exports, and because of this the state makes few attempts to encourage production and manufacturing. Instead the state focuses on allocation and distribution of these rents. Much of this allocation and distribution often comes through patron-client networks, which can give the state a certain measure of stability due to the dependence that forms between the clients and patrons.[172] (For more on patron-clientelism, see Box 8.1, Chapter Eight.)

(Continued)

---

[167]Engerman and Sokoloff (2002: 552).
[168]Coatsworth (2008: 554).
[169]Gylfason and Zoega (2002).
[170]Isham et al. (2005: 141–74).
[171]Karl (1997: 13).
[172]Benjamin Smith, "Oil Wealth and Regime Survival in the Developing World, 1960–1999," *American Journal of Political Science*, 48, no. 2 (2004): 232–46.

BOX 3.5 *Continued*

In spite of the appearance of stability, resources affect the quality of state administrative institutions. The rentier state is not "Weberian" (see Chapter Four) and is often times bloated and inefficient, as there is little incentive to create successful industries and hire the best and the brightest when the state can rely on rent to keep itself afloat. Rentier states are also "particularly vulnerable to the problems of patronage and corruption as well as bribery and nepotism."[173] This again is due to the lack of incentives to hire individuals to work for the state based on merit, hard work, and expertise.

Furthermore, as mentioned before, because rentier states can gain resources from revenues they do not need to *develop extractive institutions*. A number of scholars have argued that raising income tax revenue requires administrative institutions possessing *Weberian features*.[174] The necessity to extract income may force states to develop capable administrative institutions, with a competent, experienced, well-paid, and autonomous staff.

The extractive capabilities of states in the developing world vary considerably possibly due to the prevalence of resources. States with foreign rents in the form of foreign aid, resources, or loans, often have underdeveloped extractive institutions because they have little need to develop them. Administrative institutions have never developed extensively in the Middle East in particular, and the state has never had to be effective in collecting taxes. Many states in the region have been aided by external revenues in the form of foreign aid, oil, or loans. The state's security institutions grew in power but administrative capacity did not.[175]

Growth rates have been correspondingly unimpressive in the region as a whole. After a better-than-average showing between 1960 and 1975, the Middle East recorded the lowest rate of growth in the world between 1975 and 1990, and lost nearly all the ground that it had gained earlier.[176] States in the Middle East with a steady flow of foreign rents have been afforded with the luxury to make huge investments in state-owned enterprises with low levels of productivity. The result has been economic underperformance.

Many of the post-Soviet states' economies have been reliant on natural resources. Because of this, the extractive institutions are underdeveloped. Taxation is viewed as strange. There is little transparency of the budget. It is unclear as to how much revenue goes to each of the state

(Continued)

---

[173]Gawrick et al. (2011: 6).
[174]Hydén et al. (2003: 7).
[175]Bellin (2004: 139–57).
[176]Owen (1992); Said (2000: 5–18).

BOX 3.5 Continued

bodies.[177] Moreover, high levels of corruption in the tax administration cause the private sector to avoid tax and other regulatory burdens of government. Thus tax evasion is pervasive. Because the state can generate some rents from natural resources, there is no urgency to resolve this problem.

Afghanistan has also never developed a system of extraction. Instead of collecting formal taxes directly, Afghanistan relied on foreign aid, rents from gas, and collecting customs revenues. In Afghanistan, by 2002 it was estimated that tax collection in the villages amounted to around US$40 million in the whole of Afghanistan, as opposed to between US$500 and US$600 million collected in custom revenues.[178]

Many states in Latin America have also chosen to rely on resources, customs revenues, and tariffs rather than directly extract its national wealth. Compared with other countries, the state taxes a much smaller share of the national wealth, roughly one-third of the tax rate of countries in the G7.[179] States in Africa have almost exclusively relied on resources, customs, and foreign aid to fill their coffers. In Africa, not only have extraction rates been low but so has capacity.[180]

Other studies have focused on the role of *resources in affecting economic policies.* Not needing to tax the citizens also has economic consequences because it shapes government behavior.[181] The government can embark on large spending programs where the incentive to be effective and efficient is low.[182] The state often spends money on prestige-oriented projects that may only deliver profits to elites involved in them.[183] The state also lacks the capacity to promote developmental policies. When states are aided by external rents, this leads to low levels of domestic production. Though the state may grow, it remains uneven in its capabilities. Rentier states can ensure security, but are less effective at collecting any sort of taxes or developing strong economic policies. The necessity to extract income from individuals and corporations helps build the capacity administrative institutions need to perform other vital functions as well.

---

[177]Franke et al. (2009: 109–40).
[178]Giustozzi (2003b: 6).
[179]O'Donnell (1993: 1372).
[180]Lundahl (1997: 47).
[181]Bates (2001).
[182]Moore (2004).
[183]Beblawi and Luciani (1987: 63–82).

Since resources tend to employ a small segment of the population but generate a lot of revenues, the state may also neglect to invest in human capital, which would be needed to foster non-resource based industries. Studies have also shown that school enrolment at all levels is inversely related to natural resource abundance, as measured by the share of the labor force engaged in primary production.[184] Public spending on education is also lower in countries that have resource abundance.[185] The abundance of resources may cause governments to neglect investment in educational institutions and reduce incentives to accumulate human capital.[186]

States that are abundant in resources also have a tendency to neglect other industries, such as manufacturing. This scenario is known as *Dutch Disease*, referring to the decline in Netherlands' manufacturing sector after it discovered a natural gas field in 1959. Dutch disease neglects the quality and quantity of manufacturing exports and incentives to save and invest, in favor of concentrating on resource extraction.[187] Countries where a large proportion of the population benefits from a high-level, non-wage income (from high levels of social spending, low taxes) are unlikely to invest and save.

Resource abundance can also facilitate kleptocracy (see Chapter Eight) and the politics of plunder.[188] Countries with weak institutions can fall prey to dictators and their entourage who plunder resources to fill their own pockets. Resource abundance can lead to myopic policies by facilitating policies based on distribution and spending rather than saving and investment. Resources may also be used to bankroll inefficient developmental projects that were patronage-doling machines but did nothing to provide a source of long-term economic growth. The government may lose sight of the need for economic management.

Huge natural resource rents may create opportunities for rent seeking (see Box 8.2, Chapter Eight) on a large scale, which diverts more resources away from productive economic activity. High resource abundance makes it easier for rent seeking to take place because resource rents are easily captured

---

[184]Gylfason et al. (1999).
[185]Ibid.
[186]School enrolment at all levels is inversely related to natural resource abundance, as measured by the share of the labor force engaged in primary production; Gylfason et al. 1999.
[187]Gylfason (2001: 847–59). A natural resource boom also increases the real exchange rate of a currency, which reduces the appeal of manufactured goods and other exports. The recurrent booms and busts that are associated with resources increase exchange rate volatility (Gylfason et al. 1999). Booms in primary exports can also increase wages for that sector which then raises wages in other sectors making the production of manufactured goods more expensive. Through all of these mechanisms, Dutch disease can reduce the total exports relative to the Gross National Produce (GNP).
[188]Acemoglu et al. (2004: 162–92).

by the state, leading to monopolistic behavior. However it's important to note that the prevalence of resources, in itself, does not *cause* rent seeking. Countries that have well-defined property rights and the rule of law and later discover natural resources have not been adversely affected.[189]

Resources may also play a role in indirectly sapping state strength by facilitating *conflict*. Some scholars have argued that economies whose export earnings are dependent on natural resources (such as oil, gems, minerals) are vulnerable to disorder and violent competition to lay claim to these resources.[190] Accordingly, most of the states in Africa that are experiencing conflict or internal strife were dependent upon the export of oil or some other mineral export for revenues.[191] Many countries in Africa (and North Africa) that have experienced conflict, also have a high dependence on resources: Algeria (with 98 percent of foreign exchange earnings from oil exports), Angola (83 percent of its export earnings in 1998 came from oil exports), Nigeria (96 percent from oil), Sierra Leone (96 percent from titanium ore and diamonds), and Democratic Republic of Congo (78 percent from copper and cobalt).[192]

Paul Collier and Anke Hoeffler empirically show how natural resources increase the probability of civil war.[193] Collier and Hoeffler claim that natural resources provide opportunities for rebels to fund conflicts, and, therefore, the presence of resources helps explain why some countries are more conflict prone.[194] According to Paul Collier: "It does not really matter whether rebels are motivated by greed, by a lust for power, or by grievance, as long as what causes conflict is the feasibility of predation."[195]

Michael Ross explains why this is the case and argues that the degree to which a commodity is linked to conflict depends on its lootability, obstructability, and legality.[196] Resources that are lootable are easy for any persona to extract using basic tools. Resources such as alluvial diamonds, which are easily lootable, can perpetuate conflicts when the government is not able to monitor their sale.[197] Ross claims that they especially perpetuate non-separatist conflicts such as opportunistic rebel activity.[198] Resources that are obstructable are difficult to transport and there may be more obstacles for rebels to use them to fund a conflict. Therefore resources such

---

[189]Gylfason and Zoega (2002: 1–52).
[190]Reno (2000a: 219–35).
[191]Ibid.
[192]Ibid.
[193]Collier and Hoeffler (1998: 563–73).
[194]Collier and Hoeffler (2004: 563–95).
[195]Collier, "Economic Causes of Civil Conflict and their Implications for Policy" (April 2006): 3.
[196]Ross (2004: 337–56).
[197]Snyder and Bhavnani (2005: 563–97).
[198]Ross (2003).

as drugs are likely to fund war efforts. Compared to gas, oil, and timber, which require more time and complicated enterprises to loot and transport them, drugs are relatively easy to move around. Finally resources that are illegal also benefit non-state actors because they tend to be more valuable on the market and non-state actors are not affected by international sanctions. Illegality also has important implications for the duration of conflicts. According to James Fearon, conflicts where rebels relied extensively on contraband financing had a mean duration of 48.2 years, compared to just 8.8 years for other conflicts.[199]

Nevertheless one cannot assume that the presence of resources such as diamonds *cause* conflicts. The top four diamond producing countries in the world, Botswana, Russia, Canada, and South Africa have not experienced conflicts that were funded by the diamond trade. Though resources may *prolong conflicts*, they are not the cause.[200]

The literature on the effects of resources very convincingly argues that resource rich countries have fewer incentives to develop high functioning administrative, judicial, and political institutions. Developing effective institutions is simply not a necessity for their survival. Resource may also have indirect effects on the state by sapping the manufacturing sector, which affects economic performance, and by making kleptocracy, rent seeking, and conflict more feasible. Thus the role of resources poses interesting challenges for state building, as they can help the state develop the revenues needed for the state to be strong, but they can also reduce incentives for the state to develop capacity.

Demographics: Population density and ethnic antagonisms

Population density can also be a factor impacting the capacity of state institutions. States have a more difficult time maintaining authority when population density is higher.[201] Security institutions may be strained to provide security for such a large population. Population density may also make it more difficult for the state to provide goods and services. For example, Haiti is densely populated with 756 people per square mile and the security, administrative, political, and judicial institutions barely function.[202] Bangladesh's population density is 2,676 per square mile and illustrating the weakness of its administrative institutions, it ranks number 120 on the corruption index (Transparency International).

---

[199]Fearon (2004: 275–301).
[200]See Fearon (2004) ; Ross (2004).
[201]Herbst (2000).
[202]Gros (1996: 464).

Population density however may be more important in leading to *conflict* than weak institutions. Population density may lead to more competition over scarce resources. Rwanda is the most densely populated state in Sub-Saharan Africa (601 per square mile). In the 1980s, 60 percent of its population was under the age of 30. It is currently one of the stronger and more efficient states (both in administrative capacity and military/police strength) in Africa even though it faced both a civil conflict and genocide in the mid-1990s. Thus, though population density may make a state more prone to protracted conflicts, population density may not directly affect the state's ability to govern.

Scholars are in disagreement about the impact of ethnic diversity on institutions. In general homogenous countries may have an easier road to *nation building* (see Box 3.1), which generally leads to an easier road to *state building*. However, even a state without a cohesive national identity can overcome this problem by building effective power-sharing institutions, such as has been the case in Malaysia, which comprises Malays, Chinese, and Indians.[203] In Malaysia, power is shared between these different ethnic groups as part of the Barisan National Coalition, which forms the dominant coalition.[204]

The issue may not be how diverse a society is but how the ethnic mix is managed and what policies are pursued. Cameroon is one of the most ethnically diverse countries in Sub-Saharan Africa with over 250 different ethnic groups.[205] René Lemarchand argues that a state's legitimacy is connected to the nature of the political institutions.[206] Exclusionary ethnic policies can erode the state's legitimacy when they favor one group over another. L. P. Singh claims that in the absence of strong political institutions such as secular political parties, ethnicity can become the focus for understanding institutional decay. The state's administrative institutions may also pursue national policies that lead to backlash from minority groups. When these differences are also exacerbated by economic inequalities, which are sustained over decades, this can further aggravate long-standing ethnic or religious fault-lines dividing a society and lead to instability and conflict, which may in turn sap state strength.[207]

---

[203]Horowitz (1989: 18–35).
[204]Ibid.
[205]US State Department, Country Profile, Cameroon.
[206]Lemarchand (1997: 173–93).
[207]See also Acemoglu et al. (2001).

PART TWO

Institutions in the developing world

CHAPTER FOUR

Administrative institutions

Administrative institutions are the institutions of the state in charge of implementing policy and regulating and delivering services. Administrative institutions are synonymous with what is often referred to as "the bureaucracy."[1] They include both state ministries and bureaucratic agencies. In this chapter, we discuss the role of administrative institutions in the functioning of the state. We delineate the defining features of high-quality (versus low-quality) administrative institutions and offer examples comparing and contrasting administrative institutions to illustrate these points. Last, we examine how variations in the quality of administrative institutions affect key outcomes of interest.

The role of administrative institutions in the state

Administrative institutions are charged with administering the policies of the state.[2] They carry out and enforce government-mandated regulations and are responsible for providing basic goods and services to citizens in areas such as infrastructure development, education, and healthcare.[3] They

---

[1]We use the term "administrative institutions" instead of the term "bureaucracy" because, in the Weberian sense, bureaucracies imply a set of administrative institutions that are well organized; see, for example, Evans and Rauch 1999: 749. (We discuss this in more detail in the section that follows.) Doing so also enables us to maintain consistency in the terminology used throughout the book.

[2]For more on the importance of administrative institutions and its functions see Goldsmith, who writes that "societies need a capable administration to keep order, collect revenue, and carry out program" (Goldsmith 1999: 531).

[3]Schneckener (2006: 24).

are responsible for delivering mail, collecting garbage, providing utilities. In this way, administrative institutions are essential to ensuring that government policies are translated into actions and outcomes.

In addition, administrative institutions are tasked with extracting resources from citizens on behalf of the state (i.e. collecting taxes). Because states cannot function without sufficient extraction, the ability of administrative institutions to efficiently carry out this task is particularly critical.[4]

Administrative institutions are therefore important because without them states lack regulatory capacity and revenue, both vital to the proper functioning of the state, and citizens are denied access to public goods, which is a key element of the state's ability to provide for its citizens and satisfy their expectations. Administrative institutions "make a difference when it comes to the legitimacy of the regime and policy outcomes."[5]

We should note that officials in administrative institutions, often referred to as civil servants, are not elected to their positions. They gain office either through appointment or a traditional hiring process. In this way they differ from their counterparts in political institutions, who are typically elected. In addition, administrative officials do not directly play a role in policy making, like political officials do, but instead are responsible for carrying out the laws and guidelines stipulated by policy makers.

Last, we note that the quality of state policies, as in the appropriateness of regulatory choices, public good allotments, and taxation levels differ significantly across states and do not fall into the domain of the state's administrative apparatus. In other words, the state may fail to meet the expectations of citizens, even with effective administrative institutions, if the state's policy choices are poor. Though poor state policy choices often go hand and hand with incompetent administrative institutions, here we examine administrative institutions assuming that the quality of state policies is consistent across states.

Categorization

Administrative institutions vary markedly in their capacity to execute key tasks and the efficiency with which they do so. High-quality administrative institutions are professionalized and insulated from politics; low-quality administrative institutions, by contrast, are poorly organized, inefficient, and serve as the pawns of political actors. The former are often referred to as *Weberian administrative institutions* and the latter as *patrimonial administrative institutions*. States with Weberian administrative institutions are competent at meeting their responsibilities and serving society, while states

---

[4]Whitmore (2005: 5). Moore (1997).
[5]Hydén et al. (2003: 3).

with patrimonial administrative institutions are not. In this section, we discuss what these two poles of the administrative institutional spectrum mean in practice and the various features that differentiate them.

High-quality administrative institutions

High-quality administrative institutions mirror the ideal bureaucratic type identified by Max Weber. For this reason, they are often referred to as *Weberian administrative institutions*. It is important to note that, in Weber's view, the bureaucracy consists of a set of competent and professionalized administrative institutions, which stand in stark contrast to patrimonial government administrations.[6] To Weber, a bureaucracy is the ideal type of administrative institutional structure in a state. Though today we often conceptualize bureaucracies as administrative institutions that can vary in their organizational strength and capacity, Weber uses the term bureaucracy to reference organizationally strong and capable administrative institutions.[7] To mitigate confusion, throughout this chapter we use the term "administrative institutions," where possible, in lieu of the term "bureaucracy."

In his foundational book *Economy and Society*, Weber emphasizes the importance of administrative institutions in providing the state with the structure required for capitalist growth.[8] Ideally, administrative institutions consist of a formalized, standardized, hierarchical, and specialized bureau with professional staff who enjoy merit-based, lifelong employment and careers. These officials are concerned with "carrying out their assignments and contributing to the fulfillment of the goals of the apparatus as a whole."[9] The action of administrators should be predictable, transparent, based on objective methods and follow uniform procedures.[10] They are hired and promoted based on their levels of expertise and competence, rather than their political affiliations or connections. The state provides them with long-term career rewards and high salaries to give bureaucrats incentives to maintain their positions within the state apparatus, establish

---

[6]Evans and Rauch, (1999: 749).
[7]In addition, Weber saw "patrimonial bureaucracy" as a particular form of bureaucracy staffed with unfree officials such as "slaves or ministeriales," as opposed to administrative institutions that are incompetent and organizationally weak. From Erdmann and Engel (2006), www.giga-hamburg.de/dl/download.php?d=/content/publikationen/pdf/wp16_Erdmann-engel.pdf.
[8]Weber (1978); Evans (1992: 146). Of this, Goldsmith writes that "countries that fail to bring their public bureaucracies closer in line with Weberian precepts are going to have a hard time meeting their populations' economic and social needs" (1999: 546).
[9]Evans (1992: 146).
[10]Brinkerhoff and Goldsmith, (2002). Studies have shown that bureaucratic efficiency is improved by having clear guidelines, clear assignments, and clear feedback for bureaucratic performance; Anwaruddin (2004: 305).

consistent norms within it, and minimize the lure of engaging in corrupt activities, such as trying to supplement their salaries with bribes. The result is an administrative institutional structure that is capable of fulfilling its responsibilities, carrying out the mandates of the state, and meeting the needs of citizens.[11]

Low-quality administrative institutions

Low-quality administrative institutions, by contrast, lack these features. They are often referred to as *patrimonial*.[12] According to Weber, patrimonial administrative institutions are based on "personal relations of subordination . . . instead of bureaucratic impartiality."[13] In states with patrimonial administrative institutions, personal considerations, favors, promises, and privileges dominate.[14]

With patrimonial administrative institutions, there is *no separation between the "private" and the "official" spheres*, making the state's administrative apparatus easily politicized. The administration of the state is viewed as a "purely personal affair of the ruler, and political power is considered part of his personal property which can be exploited by means of contributions and fees."[15] This makes it difficult to understand when corruption is taking place.[16]

Personal and political connectivity drive hiring and promotion decisions, such that civil servants lack the competence of their peers in Weberian administrative institutions. Recruitment is often based on kinship or loyalty.[17] For example in Liberia under Samuel Doe (1980–90), jobs were distributed solely based on whether or not one belonged to his fellow Krahn tribe. One in ten Egyptian civil servants polled claimed that they received their job through a personal connection.[18]

In contrast to Weberian institutions (where the purpose of administrative institutions is to implement policy), the purpose of patrimonial institutions is to *supply jobs and dole out patronage*. Many of those hired have

---

[11]The achievements of successful countries "have been built on a base of impartial, professional bureaucrats," indicating that "Weberian insights are correct" (Goldsmith 1999: 525).
[12]The patrimonial bureaucracy is often referred to as a type of administration where civil servants are responsible and loyal to a particular leader, and not to the state. Corruption levels tend to be high as government jobs are treated as income producing assets rather than positions of public service. We use the term patrimonialism synonymously with neo-patrimonialism. The key difference between the former and the latter is that the latter is a patrimonial system and also has a *rational-legal veneer*.
[13]Weber, as quoted in Hutchcroft (1991: 415).
[14]Ibid.
[15]Weber (1978: 128–9).
[16]Bøås (2001: 700).
[17]Weber (1978: 343–7, 351–2).
[18]Palmer et al. (1988: 26).

few skills to offer. Even in the face of budgetary pressure, public employment is maintained.[19] For many years the Brazilian state was referred to as a massive *cabide de emprego* (source of jobs). Jobs were given on the basis of connections rather than competence.[20] Governments in Africa have also been accused of being more preoccupied with securing public employment than ensuring the quality of the civil service.

In many cases, civil servants are *underpaid* and can be *dismissed for no reason*. Moreover, civil servants in patrimonial administrative institutions also have *"staccato" careers*.[21] Rapid turnover of personnel makes it difficult for any one group to gain experience and knowledge. Regularly rotating positions of civil servants may prevent anyone from developing their own power base, but it also prevents the emergence of an "esprit de corps" in the workplace.[22] In Brazil in the 1980s, civil servants shifted agencies every 4–5 years.[23] Long-term commitment to their agency was weak as a result.

In addition, because civil servants are often underpaid and lack job security, they are easily enticed by bribes and prone to corrupt activity and arbitrary behavior (see Chapter Eight). As a result, patrimonial administrative institutions are incompetent, ineffective, and incapable of fulfilling their duties.

In some extreme cases patrimonial institutions can become *predatory*. Administrative institutions are referred to as predatory when they extract resources from society without providing any public benefits.[24] Peter Evans defines predatory administrative institutions as ones that prey on its citizens and provide no services in return.[25] Evans continues that the predatory administrative institutions fail to provide even the most basic prerequisites, such as minimal infrastructure, health, and education.[26]

Not only are civil servants poorly trained and underpaid, but the system is so unstable and uncertain that civil servants are encouraged to engage in theft.[27] Market transactions dominate the public realm and the state degenerates into a "perverse form of public enterprise."[28] Administrative corruption takes place on a massive scale. Government services are sold to the highest bidder.

Of predatory institutions Crawford Young writes: "Institutions of rule lose their capacity to translate public resources into sustenance of

---

[19]Hydén et al. (2003: 8).
[20]Evans (1992: 167).
[21]Evans (1995).
[22]Bratton and van de Walle (1994: 463).
[23]Taken from a 1987 survey of 281 Brazilian bureaucrats from Evans (1992: 167).
[24]North (1981: 22); Kocher (2010: 141–2).
[25]Evans (1995: 45).
[26]Evans (1992: 151).
[27]Lundahl (1997: 33).
[28]Derek and Goldsmith (2000: 17).

infrastructures or valued amenities. A pervasive venality surrounds most public transactions. As a consequence, the subject comes to experience rule as simple predation; the aura of the state as powerful and nurturant protector vanishes."[29]

In Zaire under Mobutu a 1980 analysis concluded that the administrative institutions were almost completely nonproductive. Instead they had become completely privatized, and converted into an instrument for self-enrichment. The report claimed that "those at the top of the bureaucratic hierarchy have institutionalized corruption and locked their subordinates into corrupt practices in a systemic way."[30] The president and prime minister also confirmed that "two-third of the country's civil servants were fictitious, representing a budgetary loss of half of the annual budget deficit for that year."[31]

The Philippines under Ferdinand Marcos is another example of the politics of plunder. Together with his wife Imelda and his cronies, the Marcos family amassed US$5–10 billion by milking state enterprises.[32] Monopolies were created in the sugar and coconut industries with funds being channeled directly to himself, members of his family and friends (for more on this see Chapter Eight).[33]

In extreme cases when the administrative institutions are not functioning at all, they are referred to as *collapsed*. Scholars such as William Zartman refer to administrative collapse as cases where the "basic functions of the state are not longer performed. The state is paralyzed and inoperative."[34] There is not even a façade of a bureaucracy. Thus citizens would have no idea where to go to obtain a passport. All services that would normally be provided by the state are either not provided at all or are provided by sub-state or non-state actors.[35]

In the case of Sierra Leone, the leadership saw the functioning of the administrative institutions as a threat to their own power base. As a result, administrative institutions stopped offering services.[36] Toward the end of Mobutu's (1965–97) rule in Zaire and Siad Barre's (1969–91) rule in Somalia, any semblance of administrative rule had completely disappeared.[37] Of Somalia under Barre, Daniel Compagnon writes that "not a single public service was working effectively" — the administration was

---

[29]Young (1997: 2).
[30]Gould and Amaro-Reves (1983: 10).
[31]Ibid.
[32]Quimpo (2009: 339).
[33]Ibid.
[34]Zartman (1995: 6).
[35]Hastings (2009).
[36]Brinkerhoff and Goldsmith (2002).
[37]Young (1994).

completely paralyzed.[38] Currently the administrative institutions in the Democratic Republic of Congo are barely operating.

Pockets of efficiency

Few administrative institutions in the developing world fit the Weberian ideal, and yet there are many states in the developing world that cannot be categorized as entirely patrimonial as well. Peter Evans refers to these cases as "intermediate" in that they have elements of Weberian and patrimonial institutions. Because the bureaucracy is not a monolithic entity and comprises many different agencies, it is possible that some agencies may function in a Weberian fashion, acting autonomously and efficiently while others do not. This point is echoed by other scholars. Daniel Gingerich writes that "the fact that a country's national-level score for bureaucratic capacity and the actual capacity of particular state agencies contained within that country may differ drastically is important for both students of development and policymakers."[39]

In the case of Brazil, some agencies of the administration act with the same esprit de corps of their counterparts in Weberian bureaucracies. This is referred to by Barbara Geddes as "pockets of efficiency" (bolsoes de eficiencia). The National Development Bank (BNDE) was cited as a case in point. Since 1956, the BNDE started a system of public examinations for recruitment. Most directors were recruited internally and the agency offered a clear career path.[40] As a result, the BNDE fulfilled 102 percent of its targets while other bureaucratic agencies fulfilled only 32 percent.[41]

Key features of high-quality administrative institutions

High-quality administrative institutions have three features that define them:[42]

1 *Meritocratic recruitment and promotion*: civil servants are hired and promoted based on their competence and the needs of the state (as opposed to their political or elite ties).

2 *Salary competitiveness*: civil servants are paid sufficiently to deter their propensity to engage in corrupt behavior.

---

[38]Compagnon (1992: 9).
[39]Gingerich (2009: 1–64).
[40]Geddes (1990); cited from Evans (1992: 168).
[41]Evans (1992: 168).
[42]Dahlström et al. (2011: 1–13).

3 *Autonomy*: civil servants have career stability, lifelong tenure, and special laws that cover the terms of their employment.[43]

States with all three of these features have high-quality (i.e. Weberian) administrative institutions, while states that have none of them have low-quality (i.e. patrimonial) administrative institutions. In practice, many states have some, but not all, of the features identified and fall somewhere in between.[44] We discuss the three features in more detail in what follows.

Meritocratic recruitment and promotion

Meritocratic recruitment and promotion refers to hiring and promotion decisions that are driven by an individual's qualifications, as opposed to personal and political affiliations. The fundamental principles of merit in administrative institutions are: competitive examinations; selection and promotion based on purely functional, technical points; the absence of partisan political pressure; and the prohibition of firing except for cause.[45] Administrative institutions that use meritocratic recruitment and promotion are sometimes referred to as professionalized.[46]

States have a number of tools at their disposal to ensure that merit underlies hiring decisions and promotions, as opposed to other considerations, like loyalty or kinship. States, for example, can require that candidates meet certain educational levels to qualify for positions. They can also subject candidates to civil service examinations. These tactics not only provide consistency in recruitment and promotion standards, but also ensure that the staff possesses certain levels of expertise. As Göran Hydén et al. write: "Competence, and thus better performance, [stems] from competition based on merit rather than personal contacts or illicit payments."[47] Objective entry and promotion requirements, like these, therefore increase the likelihood that civil servants will be competent.[48]

Beyond raising the competence levels of civil servants, meritocratic recruitment and promotion also help to generate institutional coherence and esprit de corps, which can increase the motivation of individual officials.[49] When officials believe that they and their colleagues have attained

---

[43]Ibid. refer to autonomy as "closedness"
[44]Hall (1968); Dahlstrom et al. (2011).
[45]Emrich-Bakenova (2009: 717); Weber (1978).
[46]Dahlstrom et al. (2011), www.qog.pol.gu.se/digitalAssets/1358/1358366_2011_6_dahlstrom_lapuente_teorell.pdf.
[47]Hydén et al. (2003: 8).
[48]Evans and Rauch, (1999: 752).
[49]Ibid.

their positions because they share similar abilities, "they are more likely to internalize shared norms and goals than are those who know they owe their office to the favor of a particular kinsman or patron."[50] This can foster allegiance to colleagues and the organization itself.

Scholars examining administrative institutions have tended to generalize about Asia, arguing that a merit-based bureaucracy played a key role in stimulating rapid economic growth.[51] Japan was often studied as an ideal case for the positive role of the state in the economy. The administrative institutions were noted for having the "greatest concentration of brainpower in Japan."[52] Citing the cases in East Asia, scholars have argued that building credible administrative institutions served as instruments to achieve sustained economic growth.[53]

China embarked on reforms of its bureaucracy under Deng Xioaping's guidance in 1978. Modernization of the administrative institutions was a key priority in order to implement market-oriented reforms and ambitious new policies. Merit-based entrance exams were introduced. Performance-based incentive schemes also reinforced incentives for the administrative institutions to work to improve economic development.[54] Regulations and guidelines have become more transparent. Bureaucratic decisions are more predictable, which has reduced uncertainty.[55]

In Japan, Taiwan, and South Korea, meritocratic civil service exams were institutionalized as a method for recruiting members to the civil service. The most talented members of the most prestigious universities apply. In South Korea only 2 percent of those who take the exam are accepted.[56] This contrasts greatly with how civil servants were recruited under Syngman Rhee (1952–60). Rhee's administration did away with civil service examinations, and as a result the administration was mired in corruption and suffered from low levels of productivity. Once Park Chung Hee came to power in 1961, he dismissed more than 35,000 civil servants and replaced them with those who were able to pass a rigorous entry exam.[57] During this period South Korea's growth rates were astronomical.[58]

---

[50]Ibid.
[51]Hydén et al. (2003: 1). For more details on the history and accomplishments of the developmental states, see Box 4.1.
[52]Evans (1992: 152).
[53]Ghani et al. (2005: 19).
[54]Li and Lian (1999: 161–90).
[55]Nee et al. (2004: 9).
[56]Evans (1992: 155).
[57]Evans (1998: 73).
[58]Johnson (1987).

BOX 4.1 Developmental state

The developmental state is one whose mission is aimed at ensuring economic development, by means of "high rates of accumulation and industrialization."[59] Its legitimacy is derived from its promotion of *sustained development*, which is understood by achieving economic growth and structural change in the productive system both domestically and in its relationship to the international economy.

The most recent experiences with successful transformations generated by developmental states have been those in East Asia between the 1960s and 1980s. Over a period of 30 years, a set of city-states and countries including Hong Kong, Singapore, South Korea, and Taiwan underwent rapid economic growth and radical socioeconomic change, moving from being poor agrarian societies in the 1960s to producers of high technology and high value-added goods by the 1990s.[60]

In order to accomplish these types of achievements, developmental states are often characterized by a leadership that is strongly committed to developmental goals, and that places national development ahead of personal enrichment and/or short-term political gains.[61] However elite commitment is not sufficient on its own. The state must have the capacity to transform the vision into reality.

Thus, developmental states have a high level of administrative capacity, not just political will to push through the developmental projects. Developmental states typically have strong bureaucracies that recruit highly talented people. The administrative institutions are relatively cohesive, disciplined, and based on merit. More than just providing basic services, these bureaucratic agencies are charged with the enormous task of industrial transformation.[62]

(Continued)

---

[59]Mkandawire (2001: 290). The concept of the developmental state was made popular by Chalmers Johnson, specifically in his work on Japan. See Johnson (1982). The roots of the idea of a developmental state reach back to Gerschenkron (1962), who looked at the role of the state in rapid "late" industrialization in continental Europe.
[60]Fritz and Menocal (2007: 531–52). These countries may have benefited from Japanese investment. South Korea and Taiwan may have also benefited from the investment in the state and infrastructure that took place during the Japanese colonial period.
[61]Ghani et al. (2005: 1–20).
[62]Chalmers' construction of the state was one that was neither socialist nor totally in favor of free markets. It was a state that conjoined private ownership with *state guidance*. In the case of Japan, links between business and bureaucratic elites were institutionalized in order to improve the exchange of information. This helped to promote the cooperation of key industries and improve decision making and policy making on industrial targeting.

BOX 4.1 *Continued*

In contrast to patrimonial bureaucracies, in developmental states, economic growth and production is emphasized over consumption and distribution. States such as Japan encouraged or directed companies into higher value-added and more technologically intensive forms of production. The state invested heavily in the creation and refinement of new technologies. The state also set up research and development facilities and then transferred the information directly to private companies. World markets were researched by the state in order to figure out the best export opportunities and identify new demands that domestic companies could be encouraged to fulfil. The state also played a heavy hand in protecting industry. Domestic markets were protected to ensure that infant industries could compete. Price controls were also used initially to ensure stability. However to minimize inefficiencies, developmental states such as Japan have subjected companies receiving state guaranteed credits to performance standards in order to minimize nonproductive investments or corruption.

The developmental state illustrates the importance of *administrative institutions* in guiding economic development. There is increasing consensus that "the orientation and effectiveness of the state are the critical variables explaining why some countries succeed whereas others fail in meeting development goals."[63] World Development Reports have been dedicated to rethinking the role of the state. Even market-based economies require functioning capable states in order to operate and grow.[64] Thus the question of how institutions function is a key component of developmental states.[65] What types of institutions can transcend personal power and prevent a personalized spoils system from developing? What types of institutions can limit clientelistic practices? These are particularly important questions for states that are interested in economic development.

Thus there was a lot of *policy coordination* between the administrative agencies and the business community. In developmental states there exists a concrete set of *social ties* that bind the state and society together in order to continuously negotiate goals and policies. In spite of these close ties, policy networks were still *insulated* from the day-to-day special interest pressure groups that might make demands that would be compromising to long-term economic growth. Economic policies were devised that were unencumbered by the claims of myopic private interests. For more on this see Evans (1995).

[63]Fritz and Menocal (2007: 543).
[64]Fritz and Menocal (2007).
[65]Sindzingre (2007).

In Singapore, though exams are not used, the best and brightest are identified based on their performance in school and are given scholarships to further their education in return for a commitment to work in the administrative institutions. Taiwan also selects civil servants for key economic and planning agencies who have both graduated from the prestigious Taiwan National University and have completed graduate training abroad.[66]

When recruitment is based on kinship or loyalty, by contrast, civil service examinations are not used. In addition, whether a candidate meets hiring criteria (should they exist) is rarely verified. The staffing of administrative institutions is instead viewed merely as a vehicle for governments to distribute patronage. Additional positions are created solely to give governments greater opportunities to reward supporters.

Like many states in Southeast Asia, the administrative institutions in the Philippines have retained a *patrimonial character.*[67] Administrative institutions were filled with cronies, relatives, and former classmates who were loyal to Marcos. He only promoted those close to him.[68] Being skilled was unnecessary. Competitive entrance exams were not utilized. Important and lucrative positions were given to family members. For example, the head of Import Control was Marcos' relative. As a result, corruption reached flagrant proportions during the Marcos years.[69] To gain more support, the bureaucracy expanded to give out more jobs. Unfortunately, the legacy of patrimonial rule left by Ferdinand Marcos' (1965–86) rule is still felt. Today in the Philippines, jobs in administrative institutions are still determined by personal connections over merit.

In Indonesia during Suharto's (1967–98) rule, merit played almost no role in recruitment of staff. Only 6 percent of the Indonesian bureaucracy has a university degree.[70]

Many governments in Africa, for example, have been accused of expanding administrative institutions solely to increase their ability to distribute patronage.[71] They do so by creating additional positions at lower skill levels. Maintaining high levels of public sector employment has been prioritized over any delivery of services.[72] Instead of recruiting the most capable staff, many states in Africa have preferred to use the administrative institutions as a source of patronage. The World Bank echoes this point, arguing that "[African] governments have become employers of last resort

---

[66]Evans (1998: 71).
[67]Hutchcroft (1991: 424).
[68]Aquino (1997: 4).
[69]Ibid.
[70]Anwaruddin (2004: 305).
[71]Hydén (2003: 8).
[72]Collier and Gunning (1999b: 10).

and dispensers of political patronage, offering jobs to family, friends and supporters."[73]

In Uganda when Idi Amin (1971–79) came to power, experienced civil servants were replaced by unqualified cronies. In Zaire, only the most trusted kinsmen of Mobutu occupied bureaucratic positions.[74] Most of the staff came from a small ethnic group, the Ngbandi in the Équateur province.[75] In Somalia under Siad Barre (1969–91) effective and committed civil servants were seen as a threat and removed.[76] Barre had total power to appoint, transfer or sack, anyone he pleased.[77] As a member of the Darod clan, Barre used favoritism as a method of bureaucratic appointment.

In the post-Soviet states, there is little professional recruitment and competitive examinations are not used to fill administrative positions. Instead personal and family ties are emphasized. In Azerbaijan, "family, associates, clans and patronage" determine the make-up of the administration.[78] In some local administrative institutions in Kazakhstan hiring is based on clan membership. In the Zhambyl region, 80 percent of civil servants were replaced by members of the same clan of regional leader Amalbek Tshanov, while mass purges took place to make room for them.[79] The administrative institutions in Ukraine have also been captured by ruling clans.

Georgia which suffered from administrative collapse following independence embarked on measures to improve the quality of its administrative institutions under the leadership of Mikheil Saakashvili. Competitive exams were introduced for both the educational system and the bureaucracy and this has had a profound impact on Georgia's corruption ratings.[80]

---

[73]Hydén et al. (2004: 8); World Bank (1997: 95). Given the poor quality of African administrative institutions, that state has failed to provide basic infrastructure such as telecommunications, roads, ports, rail service, and electricity. Telecommunications networks have been inadequate and the poor state of African telecommunications was estimated to reduce African growth rates by 1 percent (Collier and Gunning 1999a: 1–35, 10–11). Railway investment has also been low. In Africa, railway stations serve only 8 percent of all localities (Bratton and Chang 2006: 1067). In many countries roads have also badly deteriorated. In Zaire under the leadership of Mobutu, he boasted that he never once built a road (Englebert 2002: 135). In the case of the Republic of Congo, roads are so poor that local youth have set up roadblocks and demanded bribes to maintain the road (Englebert and Ron 2004: 68). Many roads in Uganda were totally impassable by 1986 (Lundalh 1997: 47). Shortages in electricity have also been a problem in Africa. Shortages of electricity in Uganda were cited as the single most important constraint in impeding the growth of businesses (Collier and Gunning 1999a). Poor infrastructure investment can also affect education.
[74]Evans (1992: 150).
[75]Acemoglu et al. (2004: 169).
[76]Menkhaus (2006/07: 80).
[77]Compagnon (2010: 9).
[78]Franke et al. (2009: 118).
[79]Emrich-Bakenova (2009: 722).
[80]Nasuti (2011: 1).

Efforts to improve the civil service in Russia started under President Vladmir Putin in 2001. The main objective was to improve the qualifications of staff and the stability of professional advancement. However, the curriculum for schools training bureaucrats has not changed much and professional standards for bureaucrats remain much lower than in the past.[81] Rules for demanding qualifications are widely violated and many civil servants lack higher education.[82] Thus, the current system is viewed as "fairly distant from the Weberian model of rational bureaucracy." Patronage is still widespread and as a result corruption remains extremely high.[83]

The administrative institutions in the Middle East have been characterized as overstaffed, unproductive, excessively centralized, corrupt and incompetent.[84] Recruitment methods are still based on kinship and loyalty. Systems of "cronyism and nepotism permeated recruitment throughout the governance structure."[85] In Syria under the Assad family (1970–), Alawites were favored over Sunnis for administrative positions. In Iraq

---

[81]Brym and Gimpelson (2004: 105).
[82]Ibid.; Emrich-Bakenova (2009: 719).
[83]Gaman-Golutvina (2008: 42).
[84]Jreisat (2009: 583–5).
[85]Ibid. 582. The Arab Human Development Report 2002 claimed that "reforming public administration is a central and urgent task for Arab countries; it lies at the core of the wider agenda of institutional reform" (UNDP 2002 cited in Common 2008: 180). Administrative institutions in the Middle East have generally suffered from low levels of capacity, especially given the amount of revenues that is often generated by foreign rents (Jabbra 1989: 2).Due to low functioning administrative institutions the state in the Middle East has mostly distributed by providing little investment. Infrastructural investment is badly needed for road networks in Egypt (Said 2000: 15). There has been almost no government effort to alleviate traffic problems and to ensure that traffic rules are adhered to. Though huge apartment high rises were constructed in Beirut in Lebanon, there has been little effort to improve public transport in Lebanon.Human capital in the region is well below its potential given the region's access to foreign rents. The gulf monarchies of Saudi Arabia, Oman, the UAE, Bahrain, Qatar, and Kuwait have performed better in this regard. Governments have provided healthcare and education. Many citizens with advanced degrees are entitled to lucrative government jobs (Byman and Green 1999: 20–37). However the quality of education offered does not correspond with the needs of Gulf societies. There are too many graduates in the humanities and not enough in science and math. The educational system needs to be updated and huge gaps still exist between men's and women's educational opportunities (Baghat 1999: 127–36). Outside the gulf monarchies, the educational situation is also dire for women. For example in Egypt, literacy rates are 63.5 percent for women compared to 80 percent for men. In Morocco only 43.9 percent of women are literate compared to 68.9 percent of men. In Yemen, only 46.8 percent of women are literate compared to 81.2 percent of men. Though the region has received plenty of foreign rents, education has not been emphasized, making most of the workforce unskilled. This has left many private sector jobs to be filled by foreigners, and has resulted in high levels of domestic unemployment.Public service employment has been used as a strategy to disguise unemployment (Baghat 1999: 5). In Egypt the bureaucracy grew rapid from 350,000 people in 1951 to 1 million by 1965, which is far in excess of the growth of general employment. The number of government ministries doubled (Owen 1992: 24). In Egypt, the state still employs 25 percent of the labor force. The productivity level of these

under Saddam Hussein (1979–2003), Sunnis were favored over Shiites and Kurds. In Lebanon, bureaucratic appointments are entirely based on sectarian connections.[86] In Libya under Muammar Qaddafi (1969–2011) certain tribes were favored for administrative positions over other tribes. A study on Egypt's bureaucracy found that only 45 percent entered the civil service after taking an exam.[87] Posts in Lebanon are also not filled by merit. Merit-based recruitment is difficult to implement not only because of political interference but also because of the absence of job descriptions for administrative postings and a clear classification system. Moreover, there is a general lack of qualified personnel because education and training has not been prioritized enough.[88]

In Afghanistan the quality of civil servants is also extremely low. It has had a difficult time attracting and retaining qualified professionals with administrative experience. Warlords have pushed for coveted appointments within the administrative apparatus. Most have no experience in government and are illiterate. Incompetent individuals with money or connections continue to dominate the state's key industries in Afghanistan.[89]

When administrative institutions lack meritocratic recruitment and promotion, favoritism and patronage dominate, leading to an unprofessionalized administrative apparatus. As Saule Emrich-Bakenova argues, "the "extension of political appointees deep down the hierarchy distances top echelons of political power from rank-and-file civil servants, complicates the flow of information in both directions, disturbs continuity, and creates instability in the reform process."[90] Because personal and political ties pervade the state's administrative institutions, officials are less apt to use their positions to perform public service, instead viewing them as vehicles to attain personal wealth and status.[91] This is magnified by the fact that governments in these contexts often opt to pay civil servants through "privileges," that is, access to rents, as opposed to stable and predictable annual salaries. Such privileges vary in magnitude depending on the particular official's loyalty to the government.[92]

---

jobs is very low, if at all (Said 2000: 13). Syria also experienced bureaucratic expansion. The number of Ba'ath party employees grew from 34,000 in 1960 to 170,000 in 1975 (Owen 1992: 25). In Iran, the number of civil servants doubled between 1963 and 1977 (81). In the Gulf monarchies, public sector employment is particularly high. In Qatar 88 percent of Qataris work in the public sector, while this number is as high as 85 percent and 82 percent in the United Arab Emirates and Kuwait respectively.
[86]Norton (1995).
[87]Ali et al. (1985: 353).
[88]Jabbra (1989: 2).
[89]Suhrke (2007: 1302).
[90]Emrich-Bakenova (2009: 717).
[91]Bratton and van de Walle (1994).
[92]Weber (1972: 342–7, 351–2).

Though *pockets of efficiency* exist, Latin America administrative institutions continue to be plagued by patrimonialism because there are no codified rules for recruitment.[93] Mexico, Argentina, Chile, and Venezuela have made use of technical specialists, but (illustrating the problems of not investing enough in education) all of these countries suffered from a shortage of administrative specialists. Many posts have had to be filled by foreigners. Though in some cases standards of achievements are honored in the selection of civil servants, these standards coexist with nepotism and clientelism. As a result, levels of professionalism are uneven and arbitrary practices are still the norm.[94]

There are some exceptions in Latin America, however. Chile has enacted a series of reforms aimed at improving the efficiency of the bureaucracy in the 1990s. Though the reforms have been incremental by 2003 Chile had implemented competitive examinations. The civil service in Costa Rica also established a competitive selection process for administrative staff. Posts

---

[93]Some scholars argue that in Latin America, patrimonialism may be due to the legacy of the three centuries of Spanish and Portuguese presence.

[94]O'Toole (2007: 174). Scholars of Latin American politics have argued that there is a clear link between the quality of public sector institutions and economic and social development. Latin America has a legacy of weak, although extensive, over-bureaucratized states. Though the state is "over-bureaucratized" it has little redistributive capacity, little transparency, and little mechanisms of accountability (Domingo 1999: 151). Many Latin American bureaucracies have been characterized by corruption, instability "inefficiency, job insecurity, high staff turnover rates, an inadequate use of expertise, poor communication, a lack of coordination between departments, and nepotism" (O'Toole 2007: 174). Administrative weakness has been cited as an explanation behind persistent inequality levels. The inequalities that plague the region are the worst in the world. The institutions have not eliminated inequalities, effectively targeted poverty, or created a cohesive society. Some institutions of the state provide a wide range of services, while other institutions of the state are beset by corruption, mismanagement, and inefficiency. Even countries like Chile that perform well in terms of economic growth, inflation, per capita income, and literacy rates still record high rates of income inequality. Brazil, Argentina, and Peru have done no better than Chile at alleviating inequalities.Miguel Angel Centeno writes that Latin American states have "performed badly with regards to health, education, housing or transportation and communications infrastructures" (2002: 2). Centeno continues that the distribution of goods and services across classes, races, genders, and regions is "distorted" (2). Education is unevenly applied. While universities are strong institutions of learning, primary schools are lacking funding. The wealthy can have access to the best healthcare at private institutions, but the poor have to deal with sub-par standards in some cases.In contrast to many states in Sub-Saharan Africa, there has been more investment in infrastructure, giving the appearance in some parts of Latin America of high levels of development. "The state played the leading role in expanding the economic infrastructure that facilitated both industrialization and overall growth. Construction of roads, telephone networks, energy supply at reasonable costs and other public utilities allowed the consolidation of an effective domestic market. A number of administrative agencies were created to promote specific sectors such as industry, forestry, agriculture and mining, depending on the country" (Thorp 1998: 143). Nevertheless, though major cities boast impressive highways and public transport systems, outside urban centers

are distributed based on suitability and merit.[95] Merit and professionalism are also used as criteria for promotion.[96]

Salary competitiveness

Salary competitiveness refers to civil servant salaries that are sufficiently high enough to attract and retain highly skilled employees.

Competitive salaries ensure that talented applicants are attracted to public sector positions. By paying civil servants reasonable wages, valuable candidates are incentivized to enter as well as remain in the civil service. When public salaries rival those offered in the private sector, the number of applicants for the state's administrative positions increases.[97] Competitive salaries therefore expand the size of the pool of talent contending for positions. Hydén et al. point out, for example, that this has been an effective strategy in East Asia, where "adequate compensation of civil servants has been used as one means of attracting and retaining competent staff."[98]

Beyond offering competitive salaries, states can also offer *incentive payment schemes* to encourage good performance. Doing so incentivizes civil servants to work harder to meet the organization's goals.[99] The provision of monetary incentives for positive performance aligns the interests of the individual employee with the interests of the organization.

Japan, South Korea, and Taiwan all pay their civil servants competitive salaries. Singapore ensures that civil servants are better paid than individuals working in the private sector.[100] Hong Kong civil servants are some of the best paid in the world, and senior staff members enjoy generous perks.[101] Incentive payment schemes also exist in order to motivate staff.

In comparison, salaries are incredibly low in countries such as Bangladesh, the Philippines, and Indonesia. Civil servants are so poorly paid that they must supplement their incomes by either holding second jobs or resorting to petty corruption.[102] For example a 1990 study in Indonesia showed that the salaries for civil servants only covered one-third of an official's household

---

travel can be hard and dangerous. Many states in Latin America have not invested enough in the telecommunications sectors. Telephone service can be spotty, which explains why Latin America was an early leader in the cell phone boom because of the absence of adequate public telecommunications (Centeno 2002: 2).
[95]Echebarría and Cortdzar (2006: 144).
[96]Ibid.
[97]Cho and Porumbescu (2011: 5).
[98]Hydén (2004: 8).
[99]Cho and Porumbescu (2011: 5).
[100]Evans (1998: 71).
[101]Painter (2006: 340).
[102]Quah (2006: 176).

needs.[103] Today wages for civil servants continue to lag behind the rise in the costs of living.[104] India's high levels of corruption may also be due to the low salaries of civil servants.[105]

Patronage needs in Africa may swell the ranks of the civil service, but *salaries have fallen* considerably. Salaries for civil servants in Africa are very low and benefits are kept to a minimum. Civil servants can barely survive on the salaries that they are given. In Tanzania, for example, salaries in the civil service were allowed to fall by an incredible 90 percent in real terms during the first two decades of independence, even as the size of the civil service more than tripled over the same period.[106]

Low pay makes it difficult for managers to motivate staff. Because promotion is based on social connections rather than skill, this also undermines the ability of the administrative institutions to deliver services.[107] In Somalia under Siad Barre, low salaries of civil servants led to chronic absenteeism.[108] Payment has not always been assured in countries like Nigeria and the Democratic Republic of Congo. The "absence of pay raises, the lack of connection between effort and reward, the missing basic supplies were all highly unmotivating."[109] In these conditions the best workers flee to the private sector. Those who continue to work are forced to take second jobs.[110] In many cases, civil servants resort to using "ghost workers" or retired, deceased, or nonexistent people who draw paychecks, which current civil servants can use to supplement their own incomes.[111]

Higher salaries for the ministries responsible for the collection of taxes and overseeing customs resulted in improvements in performance in the case of Ghana. After salaries were raised to be on par with the banking sector and financial incentives were given for high performance, tax and customs revenues almost doubled as a share of GDP.[112]

In the Middle East, it is hard to attract qualified employees because of *low pay*. Salaries for public servants in many states in the Middle East (with the exception of the oil-rich monarchies) are inadequate.[113] Yemen has great difficulty paying civil salaries. Salaries are incredibly low in Morocco and Lebanon as well. In Egypt salaries of civil servants were "remarkably low"

---

[103]Robertson-Snape (1999: 590).
[104]Suharto himself agreed that corruption was due to low wages (Robinson-Snape 1999: 590). During his predecessor Sukarno's rule, civil servants were impoverished by the rising inflation (592).
[105]Quah (2006).
[106]van de Walle (2000).
[107]Collier and Gunning (1999b: 10).
[108]Menkhaus (2006/07: 80).
[109]Goldsmith (1999: 543).
[110]Ibid.
[111]Ibid., 525.
[112]Ibid., 545
[113]Jabbra (1989: 4).

during the regime of Gamal al-Nasser, but after liberalization took place under the leadership of Anwar Sadat, salaries compared to the private sector became "wholly inadequate."[114] Because salaries were so low, 89 percent of civil servants acknowledged that they held second jobs. Productivity is lowered because civil servants are forced to divide their time and energy in more than one position.[115] In a survey in Egypt, senior administrators complained that it is difficult to retain their best employees due to low salaries.[116] In the Middle East, the low pay for civil servants has also led to petty corruption, in addition to low levels of commitment to public service.[117]

In the post-Soviet states, wages in the public sector are entirely too low, which forces civil servants to extract bribes in order to make a living. At the top of the scale, wages represented only a fraction of the wages offered for similar jobs outside the government.[118] Many of the most qualified civil servants in Russia have left to enjoy alternative jobs in the private sector since salaries still remain too low.[119] Tajikistan's administrative workers were not paid any salary at all during the latter half of 1993 and most of 1994. Though Kazakhstan's civil service is generally stronger than its counterparts in the region, anyone who occupies an administrative post could not be expected to live on the salary alone as civil servants are poorly paid.[120] In Kyrgyzstan civil servants receive $10–40 a month, which means that they can only survive on bribes.[121] Turkmenistan's administrative workers maintained their posts mainly based on bribes they could extract for public services. Other means of dealing with low salaries include the practice of "intentionally not filling vacant positions or filling them with ghost workers."[122] This enables civil servants to increase their wages by belonging to more than one payroll.

In Latin America, public employees are also not paid well and falling salaries have led to a decline in status. There are no codified rules for salaries, remuneration, promotion, or dismissal. Many of the most capable individuals in Latin American countries have either left the region or have left for the private sector.[123] There are some exceptions however. Salaries in Chile and Uruguay (for more on this see the case study on Uruguay in this chapter) continue to be more competitive after a series of reforms were enacted in the early 1990s.

---

[114]Ali et al. (1985: 353).
[115]Ibid., 360.
[116]Ibid., 354.
[117]Jabbra (1989: 4).
[118]World Bank 1996.
[119]Brym and Gimpelson (2004: 91).
[120]Emrich-Bakenova (2009: 721); Gleason (1995).
[121]Thomas and Kiser (2002: 11).
[122]Emrich-Bakenova (2009: 722).
[123]Chaudhry et al. (1994).

Competitive salaries for civil servants, therefore, increase the competency and performance of staff, increase their retention rates, and may prevent corruption.

Autonomy

Autonomy refers to the extent to which there are guarantees of career stability and internal promotions for civil servants. Administrative institutions that are autonomous offer civil servants long-term careers and give them protection in their employment.[124]

A consequence of autonomy is that it reduces the turnover of staff within administrative institutions. When employees know that there are rewards for working for the organization long term, they have an incentive to maintain their posts. One such reward is *tenure*, or the provision that after a set number of years employees are protected from dismissal. Tenure not only helps to attract high-quality individuals to civil service positions, but also gives them motivation to continue working for the organization. Other rewards, such as laws that protect the terms of employment, serve a similar purpose. They reduce staff turnover, which in turn increases corporate coherence.[125] For example, in Singapore, Taiwan, and Hong Kong there is a clear career path for those who want to work in the civil service.

Many African governments, however, have not provided a long-term career path for civil servants. In the case of Zaire under Mobutu (1965–97), individuals were completely dependent on Mobutu for selection into the administrative institutions. Positions were frequently rotated, leaving civil servants constantly feeling uncertain and vulnerable.[126] Many who worked for Mobutu were sent to prison only to be released and appointed to posts once again. The impact of these strategies was deemed "catastrophic" for Zaire's economy.[127]

In the post-Soviet states, bureaucratic careers can also be very unstable. Leaders are free to move bureaucrats around at their whim. In Kazakhstan, many high-level civil servants are also constantly rotating positions, never getting the chance to develop expertise and experience.[128]

In Latin America, because administrative jobs are often based on connections to a particular leader, jobs are fleeting and circulation is high,

---

[124]Peter Evans claims that the strength of autonomous institutions is that they are "embedded" with society and able to work with society to achieve collective goals, while not being captured by particularistic interests (1992).
[125]Evans and Rauch (1999: 752).
[126]Acemoglu et al. (2004: 169).
[127]Leslie (1993: 6).
[128]Emrich-Bakenova (2009: 736).

making it difficult to gain expertise or to develop organizational loyalty. State jobs are often viewed with suspicion since there is little career advancement. Other studies of Latin American administrative institutions have commented that most Latin American bureaucrats actually manage to have long careers. The problem however is that their careers are not orderly or stable and are characterized by constant movement.[129]

For example, in the case of Brazil (with the exception of some of the agencies, such as the BNDE and the foreign service) Peter Evans writes that "instead of being tuned to the long term gains via promotions based on organizationally relevant performances, Brazilian bureaucrats face staccato careers, punctuated by the rhythms of changing political leadership and periodic spawning of new organizations. They shift agency every 4–5 years."[130] In a survey from 2009, 40 percent of Brazilian civil servants responded that it was "highly probable" that they would lose their jobs in the near future.

Careers are even more fleeting however in Bolivia. The same 2009 survey revealed that 68 percent of respondents in this country believed that it was "highly probable" that they would lose their jobs in the near future.[131] This contrasts starkly with the case of Chile. The Chilean bureaucrat enjoys more career stability. The same survey demonstrated that only 18 percent of respondents believed that they would lose their jobs.[132] The Costa Rican bureaucrat also enjoys a long career. There are also many opportunities for training to help staff advance in their careers.[133]

A key feature of autonomy is the use of *internal promotion*. With internal promotions, high-level positions in an organization must be filled by either current organization employees or other members of the civil service.[134] These promotions are based on a set of clear standards and guidelines. This practice has a number of positive consequences. For one, it gives staff incentives to operate in the long-term interests of the organization (both because their own time horizons within the organization are long and because doing so increases their chances of moving up the organization's career ladder.[135] Internal promotions also increase the bond among civil servants, such that a "sense of commitment to corporate goals and 'esprit

---

[129]Farazmand (2009: 365).
[130]Evans (1992: 168).
[131]Many bureaucracies in Latin America have suffered from uncertain careers. In the Dominican Republic under Rafael Trujillo, administrative positions were constantly being shuffled around. One could never be certain of the permanence of one's position (Acemoglu et al. 2004). The result of such shuffling was confusion and inefficiency (167–75).
[132]Gingerich (2009).
[133]Echebarría and Cortdzar (2006: 144).
[134]Rauch and Evans (2000: 52).
[135]Cho and Porumbescu (2011: 5).

de corps' develop," increasing the long-term stability of the organization.[136] These practices help improve performance of the administrative institutions as it's been noted that "insecure people do not perform well."[137]

In Hong Kong and Singapore, promotions are controlled internally and are entirely based on merit and performance. In most of the developing world, internal promotions are not utilized, however. Chile has more recently also made use of internal promotions. The Costa Rican administration is also very autonomous; the General Civil Service Department in Costa Rica controls the selection of personnel. This agency is able to make all of its hiring decisions without interference.[138]

Autonomy in administrative institutions also protects these bodies from *politicization*. When it is difficult to dismiss civil servants (either due to laws protecting them or tenure) and when promotions for certain positions are done internally, political leaders and elites are less able to intervene in staffing decisions. In such contexts, civil servants cannot be dismissed based on their lack of political loyalty, and political officials cannot use their positions as a tool for punishing opponents and rewarding supporters. Many leaders, for example, regularly rotate positions to prevent rivals from developing a power base; autonomous administrative institutions put limits on such a practice.[139]

In Singapore and Hong Kong there is less political tampering with the administrative institutions. For example, Hong Kong's civil servants have been accustomed to relatively high levels of insulation from political and societal forces.[140] Civil servants in Singapore also enjoy considerable autonomy in financial, personnel, and other managerial matters.[141]

Administrative institutions in Africa are also plagued by political interference. Though Kenya had an independent public service commission, this was soon rendered to a rubber stamp, with the president retaining authority over the civil service after constitutional provisions. The same fate happened to the public service commissions in Tanzania and Zambia, enabling the leadership to exercise control through clientelistic relationships. In these systems getting ahead was due to connections rather than performance. Gaining expertise is not encouraged because it threatens the power structure.[142] Ivory Coast, Ghana, and Nigeria all have civil services that have been politicized. As a result they have been "rendered inefficient."[143]

---

[136]Rauch and Evans (2000: 52). Cho and Porumbescu (2011: 5).
[137]Wilder (2009: 21).
[138]Echebarría and Cortdzar (2006: 144).
[139]Bratton and van de Walle (1994: 463).
[140]Painter (2006: 335).
[141]Haque (2004: 232).
[142]Goldsmith (1999: 540).
[143]Ibid., 539.

Political interference has also been commonplace in the Middle East usually due to overly powerful executives, but in some cases this has been caused by the persistence of sectarian identities. In Lebanon, sectarianism has led to political interference in the administrative institutions.[144] Political affiliations (often based on sectarian identities) dominate the appointment process, with those appointed remaining loyal to their political patrons rather than to the state agency that they work for. Civil servants who enjoy the support of influential political figures cannot be controlled by their superiors. Higher-level administrators also do not delegate authority to subordinates who do not share their political views.[145] Political interference also affects promotions in the Middle East. For example, in Morocco in spite of efforts to reform, pay is not based on performance incentives but affected by political loyalties.[146]

The administrative institutions in the post-Soviet states also suffer from too much political interference from the executive. The bureaucracy is "beholden to the president" and positions are usually based on their loyalty to the president not their level of competence.[147]

In Latin America bureaucratic autonomy is low because many administrative positions are *appointed*. The Brazilian state is known as a massive source of jobs based on connections rather than competence.[148] Under the military regime (1964–85) the Brazilian federal bureaucracy expanded from 700,000 jobs to 1.6 million jobs, many of which were appointed. The president of Brazil has the power to appoint over 50,000 jobs, making it difficult to implement meritocratic recruitment procedures.

Political interference in the administrative institutions in Latin America has made these institutions more bloated and inefficient than streamlined and focused. When a new regime comes to power, civil servants that are not viewed as politically loyal or personally connected to the new regime must move over to make way for those who are connected. Displaced administrators are given minor and pointless tasks, which causes more inefficiency.[149]

In sum, meritocratic hiring and promotion, salary competiveness, and autonomy are three defining features of high-quality, Weberian administrative institutions. In low-quality, *patrimonial* administrative institutions, by contrast, all three of these features are lacking. In the section that follows, we offer a few case studies to illustrate these points, before examining how differences across states on these fronts help to explain variations in state performance.

---

[144]Iskandar (1997: 37).
[145]Ibid.
[146]World Bank (2009: 2).
[147]Starr (2006: 16).
[148]Evans (1995).
[149]Farazmand (2009: 365).

Case studies

India presents an interesting case of *institutional decay*. At the time of independence, India had a "venerable" bureaucracy.[150] It was referred to as the "steel frame of the empire."[151] Entry into the civil service was competitive via nationwide examinations.[152] Slowly however, the administrative institutions began to erode. By the mid-1960s, the autonomy of the bureaucracy was increasingly interfered with by politicians.[153] Once the agencies became penetrated by political tampering, the quality of the administrative institutions deteriorated. Politicians would use the administrative institutions to create jobs and revenues for friends and supporters.[154] Careers were short and characterized by rapid rotation of people. The average tenure in some agencies was not more than 15 months.[155] Due to the short span of careers, the bureaucracy lacked corporate coherence. Individuals had no long-term ties to the administrative agency that they worked for. Because jobs were based on political connections, civil servants had no incentives to acquire expertise or to be productive and efficient.[156] Political tampering also meant that there were no disciplinary sanctions for misconduct.[157] The civil service became pervaded by corruption, bribes, overstaffing, wastefulness.[158] India's high levels of corruption may also be due to the low salaries of civil servants. The starting salaries in India are relatively much lower than in Japan, Singapore, and Thailand.[159]

Like India, Pakistan's bureaucracy was once an institution of prestige— based on education and professionalism.[160] The bureaucracy retained control over the selection, training, and posting of members.[161] One of its biggest challenges today is that it does not recruit talented candidates.[162] Though Pakistan has used a Federal Public Service Commission exam process, it has come under criticism for not being very difficult. The recruitment process is not transparent.[163] Once hired, training has not been rigorous. There

---

[150]Evans (1992: 172).
[151]Ibid.
[152]Ibid., 173.
[153]Sondhi (2000: 11).
[154]Ibid., 4.
[155]Evans (1992: 173).
[156]Ministries created to train civil servants and deal with public grievances were undermined by frequent cabinet reshuffling (Dwivedi 1989: 263).
[157]Dwivedi (1989: 265).
[158]Quah (2006: 241). The legal system that the Indians inherited from the British provided provisions for delays and evasion, which offers many opportunities for bribes (Sondhi 2000: 11).
[159]Quah (2006: 243).
[160]Shafqat (1999: 997).
[161]Wilder (2009: 20).
[162]Ibid., 23.
[163]Ibid., 25.

is little career development and civil servants are not paid well.[164] Instead of equal opportunities, a tradition of giving preferential treatment is still used.[165] There are no performance appraisal mechanisms to reward strong performance. Promotions are based on loyalty and not merit. Senior positions in the civil service are given to members of the military rather than to specialists.[166]

Early on in Pakistan, there was little political interference from politicians with the administrative institutions, and the bureaucracy maintained its autonomy. Political interference became commonplace in Pakistan by the time Zulfikar Ali Bhutto (1971–7) came to power. Over 1,300 civil servants were purged including some of the elite civil servants. A professional work ethic was not emphasized. Safeguards against dismissals were eliminated. The civil service was quickly filled with close relatives and associates of Bhutto. It has become "increasingly difficult for civil servants to get postings, transfers or promotions without the support of a political patron."[167] These practices continued under successive civilian governments.

Subsequent military leaders such as General Muhammad Zia-ul-Haq (1978–88) and General Pervez Musharraf (2001–8) dictated that at least 20 percent of the administrative institutions were filled with members of the armed forces. Members of the military who were inducted at the captain level were placed in positions of seniority regardless of their administrative qualifications or experience. As a result, the administrative institutions were not professionally competent.[168] The ineffectiveness of the administrative institutions in Pakistan has seriously undermined the welfare of its citizens, and the ability of the state to provide social services and the rule of law.[169]

In contrast, in Botswana and Mauritius the administrative institutions resemble more closely the Weberian prototype. Civil servants are recruited on the basis of merit and qualification. Administrative jobs require a rigorous entrance exam.[170] The bureaucracy is independent of political interference and political neutrality is expected.[171] The president in Botswana is only allowed to make a few senior appointments.[172] In Mauritius, the Public Service Commission was set up in 1953 to serve as an agency for meritocratic recruitment of civil servants. Public sector ethics have been clarified

---

[164]Ibid., 23.
[165]Ibid., 25.
[166]Islam (1989: 279).
[167]Wilder (2009: 21).
[168]Ibid., 22; Shafqat (1999: 1003).
[169]Wilder (2009: 19).
[170]Sebudubudu (2005: 82).
[171]Goldsmith (1999: 539).
[172]Ibid.

and enforced.[173] Administrators in Botswana and Mauritius are also relatively well paid and advancement is strictly based on merit, not connections. There are also transparent standards for promotion. Employees also have the right to appeal personnel decisions.[174] As a result, corruption and patronage politics in Botswana and Mauritius have been relatively absent.[175] Botswana and Mauritius have also experienced sustained economic growth and have fared better than other states in Africa on the human development index.

Uruguay also presents an interesting case of administrative reform. Prior to 1997, Uruguay's administrative institutions could be characterized as *patrimonial*, in that a significant amount of positions were appointed and based on political affiliation.[176] The bureaucracy was considered to be bloated and inefficient. There were no stable career patterns for civil servants. There were also no meaningful evaluation and promotion procedures, no job descriptions and job specification, no objective criteria for evaluation and qualification.[177] To remedy this, Uruguay embarked on a series of administrative reforms from 1997 to 2000. Efforts were first made to streamline the bureaucracy and make it more efficient by cutting thousands of jobs but creating more specialized jobs with very competitive salaries and better financial incentives.[178] New senior management posts were created. More qualified candidates with specialized knowledge were recruited. Moreover, a new training strategy was offered to improve the technical expertise of its staff.[179] A new system of evaluation of personnel based on measurable performance indicators was introduced. As a result, pay has become more related to performance. A new body, the Executive Committee for the Reform of the State, was set up to oversee its implementation. The objectives of the reform program have exceeded the government's expectations.[180]

Measuring the quality of administrative institutions

There are only a handful of measures available that assess the quality of states' administrative institutions. Most of these measures are based either directly or indirectly on the three features discussed in this chapter. For

---

[173]Kiiza (2006: 13).
[174]Goldsmith (1999: 539).
[175]Sebudubudu (2005: 84).
[176]Panizza and Philip (2005: 673).
[177]Panizza (2004: 1–28).
[178]Panizza and Philip (2005: 676).
[179]Echebarría and Cortdzar (2006: 135).
[180]Chaudhry et al. (1994: 135).

example, though researchers may not use the term "autonomy," they will include in their measure of bureaucratic quality the extent to which opportunities for internal promotions exist.

The primary measure of administrative institutional quality comes from Political Risk Services' International Crisis Research Group (ICRG). This organization offers a variable called Bureaucracy Quality, which captures whether administrative institutions are autonomous from political pressures and have established mechanisms for recruitment and training, among other things.[181] The variable enables researchers to evaluate how the overall quality of states' administrative institutions affects outcomes of interest.

Because the ICRG does not offer measures of the specific *features* of a state's administrative institutions, however, researchers cannot use these data to disentangle which of them drives relationships. Aggregate data can inform us about how the quality of institutions as a whole bear on outcomes, but reveal very little in terms of the particular institutional characteristics that are critical to these relationships.[182] For this reason, a handful of scholars have conducted detailed and extensive surveys of the quality of administrative institutions in various subsets of the world's countries that explicitly capture these underlying features.

We should note that the World Bank's Worldwide Governance Indicators project (WGI) offers a measure of government effectiveness that includes an assessment of the quality of administrative institutions. This measure, however, also includes indicators of the outcomes these institutions produce (such as public goods provisions). Because the WGI government effectiveness measure does not isolate institutions from outcomes, it is less useful in studies concerned with assessing how administrative institutions, specifically, work to shape outcomes.[183]

Key findings

The literature on administrative institutions suggests that high-quality administrative institutions (as in Weberian administrative institutions) have a number of positive consequences for states. In this section we synthesize existing findings on this subject to evaluate these claims. We should note that this literature is less abundant than that devoted to other types of state institutions, primarily due to the lack of data measuring administrative institutional quality. That being said, there are a handful of studies that have taken up this topic. These studies primarily look at how the quality

---

[181]More information on this variable is available at International Country Risk Guide: www.prsgroup.com/ICRG_methodology.aspx.
[182]Evans and Rauch (1999).
[183]World Bank Governance Indicators Project http://info.worldbank.org/governance/wgi/pdf/ge.pdf.

of administrative institutions affects corruption and economic growth. For this reason, we organize this section around these themes.

Economic performance

Economic growth

Economic growth is the outcome that has perhaps received the most attention in the literature on administrative institutions. Indeed, the relationship between administrative institutions and economic growth is at the core of Weber's analysis. He argues that capitalism cannot work unless a state has competent administrative institutions (which he refers to as bureaucracies); the two go hand and hand. As Weber puts it: "Capitalism and bureaucracy have found each other and belong intimately together."[184] Weber claimed that patrimonial systems are detrimental to capitalist development because they are subjective and changeable.[185] A number of researchers have echoed this theme. Evans argues, for example, that the state is dependent on its administrative institutions to support markets and capitalist accumulation.[186] The World Bank has argued that poor administrative performance causes declines in general welfare.[187]

There are a number of mechanisms through which administrative institutions can affect growth. For one, autonomy of states' administrative institutions gives civil servants longer time horizons, both by making them less likely to be subjected to arbitrary dismissals and more likely to be enticed to stay with the organization for the long term due to the rewards associated with doing so. Such long-time horizons should increase the likelihood that administrative institutions will advocate for public-sector infrastructure investment (which helps growth) as opposed to consumptive expenditures (which harm growth).[188] In addition, because the returns on public infrastructure investments depend on how widely and deeply they are implemented, the internal cohesion of the bureaucracy (a function of both meritocratic recruitment and promotion and autonomy) should make them more effective.[189]

High-quality administrative institutions may also bolster economic growth indirectly, by increasing levels of private investment. Private investment is known to be critical to fostering the growth of a state's economy. Investors, however, are more likely to be reluctant to invest when they face

---

[184]Weber (1978). Vol. 1, cited from Evans (1989: 567).
[185]Brinkerhoff and Goldsmith (2002: 9).
[186]Evans (1992: 146).
[187]World Bank (1997: 30).
[188]Evans and Rauch (1999: 752).
[189]Ibid.

significant amounts of "red tape" in their transactions. When administrative institutions are full of incompetent staff, they are more likely to function inefficiently and deter private investment. In addition, higher-quality administrative institutions could indirectly lead to higher growth rates by decreasing the likelihood of corruption (this mechanism is discussed in the prior section).

The consensus expectation, then, is that higher-quality administrative institutions improve a state's ability to grow its economy. The most comprehensive study to evaluate this expectation comes from Peter Evans and James Rauch.[190] The authors collect a new data set for 35 developing countries that places them on a "Weberianness Scale" based on the extent to which major state agencies use meritocratic recruitment and offer predictable and rewarding long-term careers for civil servants.[191] They find strong evidence that this measure is positively related to economic growth: states with Weberian administrative institutions have higher growth rates than states without them. Their findings are robust to controls for levels of development and human capital. They argue that Weberian administrative institutions are a significant factor in explaining regional differences in growth rates. They state that their findings support interpretations of East Asia's economic successes that emphasize the important role of competent and cohesive administrative institutions, as well as analyses of Africa's economic disasters that emphasize the problem of governance.[192]

The findings of Evans and Rauch are supported by other studies in the literature.[193] A number of case studies, primarily from East Asia (see Box 4.1), have shown that Weberian administrative institutions in that region account for its strong economic performance in the 1970s and 1980s.[194]

In addition, there have been quite a few cross-national studies on the subject. Unfortunately, most of these cross-national studies do not measure administrative institutions explicitly, but rather look at broader measures of governance, of which the quality of a state's administrative institutions is but one component. This generally occurs because such studies are concerned with the larger concept of governance, as opposed to the caliber of the administrative apparatus specifically. Steven Knack and Phillip Keefer, for example, find that the quality of governance is positively associated with economic growth.[195] Though their measure of governance quality includes the ICRG indicator of bureaucratic quality, it is aggregated with a number of other measures, including corruption in government and rule of law. Because studies such as theirs do not isolate administrative institutions from other components of governance, we do not review them here.

---

[190]Ibid.
[191]Evans and Rauch (1999: 749).
[192]Ibid., 760.
[193]See Hydén et al. (2003: 5) for a review of this literature.
[194]See Evans and Rauch (1999) for a review of these case studies.
[195]Knack and Keefer (1995).

We should note that some scholars have pointed out that it is possible that the causality runs in the other direction, in that positive economic performance could pave the way for high-quality administrative institutions. Alberto Chong and Cesar Calderon find some evidence that this is true. In their study, the evidence indicates that the quality of administrative institutions both affects and is affected by economic performance.[196]

Regardless, the general consensus among researchers is that high-quality Weberian administrative institutions are positively associated with economic growth. Additional research on the subject is needed to identify the particular features of the administrative apparatus that are important in this regard.

Corruption

One aspect of improving economic performance is reducing corruption, which is why it is an important goal for most states (for more on the different types of corruption, see Chapter Eight). Not only does widespread corruption lessen the state's legitimacy in the eyes of citizens, but it also hurts the economy. High levels of corruption have been shown to decrease levels of investment and reduce economic growth.[197] Though most observers agree that corruption has pernicious political and economic consequences for states, the impact of administrative institutions on corruption is often ignored. This is true despite the fact that theoretically there is reason to expect that the quality of administrative institutions bears on levels of corruption: Weberian administrative institutions should be associated with less corruption than patrimonial institutions.

For one, meritocratic recruitment and promotion increase organization coherence (as discussed above), which in turn has the potential to lower corruption. In such contexts, civil servants should be more likely to view corrupt activities as subverting the goals of the organization and engage in effective intra-organizational monitoring.[198] Meritocratic recruitment, in particular, also separates civil servants from elected officials.[199] By hiring individuals based on merit, agencies end up selecting individuals who have separate interests from their elected counterparts. This results in "two groups with different chains of responsiveness and subsequently with different careers."[200] Meritocratic recruitment ensures that there are two groups of individuals in office (civil servants and politicians) whose interests are divergent.[201] As a result, whistle blowing is more likely because individuals

---

[196]Chong and Calderon (2000).
[197]Mauro (1995).
[198]Evans and Rauch, (1999: 752).
[199]Dahlström et al. (2011: 4).
[200]Ibid.
[201]Ibid.

from one group do not have as much to lose in exposing the corrupt activities of individuals from the other group.

Offering high salaries to civil servants also has the potential to lessen the temptation to engage in corruption.[202] It's been argued that very large increases in wages are needed to reduce corruption, and this strategy appears to have been successful in some countries.[203] Singapore, for example, is one of the least corrupt countries in the world. One reason for this may be the government's belief that "an efficient bureaucratic system is one in which the officers are well paid so the temptation to resort to bribes [is] reduced."[204] When employees are well compensated, they should be less likely allured by opportunities for corruption.

Last, autonomy should lower corruption rates too. In autonomous administrative institutions, officials are more insulated from the political sphere; their fates are not determined by their political loyalties. This should make them more open to whistle blowing because they do not fear political reprisal for doing so. The use of internal promotions, specifically, also has the potential to disincentivize corruption. The prospect of future promotion reduces the lure of the quick return that corrupt activities offer. As Evans and Rauch argue, "careers that provide the expectation of a series of promotions related to performance and conformity to organizational norms create disincentives to corrupt behavior, especially if such behavior undermines organizational goals."[205]

Though there are a number of reasons to expect that Weberian administrative institutions will reduce corruption rates, only a few studies have examined this relationship. We highlight three of them here, all of which use specially designed surveys to capture features of states' administrative institutions.

Julius Court et al. examine the relationship between administrative institutions and corruption using a sample of 20 countries in Africa.[206] They find that *autonomy* in the administrative institutional structure decreases levels of corruption, particularly the extent to which top civil service positions are insulated from political leadership changes.

Evans and Rauch do the same using a sample of 35 developing countries. They find that *meritocratic recruitment* decreases the incidence of corruption.[207] Though internal promotion and career stability (i.e. autonomy or closedness) also matter, they are of secondary importance.

---

[202]Becker (1974).
[203]Van Rijckeghem and Weder (2001: 307).
[204]Rahman (1986: 151).
[205]Evans and Rauch, (1999: 752).
[206]Court et al. (1999).
[207]Evans and Rauch (1999).

Carl Dahlström et al. also look at this relationship.[208] Their study is based on a sample of 52 countries, most of which are in the developed world (the exceptions being Russia and a handful of countries in Eastern Europe and elsewhere). They, too, find that high-quality administrative institutions decrease corruption, but that this relationship is driven solely by the use of *meritocratic recruitment* procedures. They do not find evidence that salary competitiveness or autonomy affect corruption.

All three of these studies reveal a relationship between the quality of administrative institutions and levels of corruption. They differ, however, in terms of the particular feature of the administrative institutional structure driving the result. The first finds that meritocratic recruitment and promotion matter, the third finds that autonomy matters, and the second finds that both do. It is worth noting that none of the three studies finds evidence that salary competitiveness plays a role, but many case studies have shown otherwise.

The results of these studies may differ due to the different samples used. The first study uses African countries exclusively, for example, which typically lie at the lowest echelon of the development rung. The second study also looks at developing countries, but uses a more wide-ranging sample. The third study, by contrast, is primarily based on developed countries. It is possible, then, that the particular way in which administrative institutions affect corruption varies based on the level of development of the country under examination (i.e. an interactive effect). Regardless, in all of these studies, higher-quality administrative institutions are associated with lower levels of corruption.

It is worth pointing out that this relationship may also be affected by the behavior of the political leadership. As Hydén et al. point out: "If the elected politicians are not corrupt, they tend to set an example that is emulated in the bureaucracy. If, on the other hand, they are corrupt, this tends to spread to the civil service too."[209] The authors base this statement on the experiences of the Philippines and Russia, where cronyism and political patronage created an atmosphere in which civil servants used their offices to get rich, rather than promote the interests of the public. This occurred even though merit-based recruitment procedures were used. In other words, though high-quality administrative institutions in general lessen the pervasiveness of corruption, these institutions do not operate in a vacuum. The propensity for civil servants to engage in corruption, therefore, may increase when such activity is observed in other spheres, particularly the political.

---

[208]Dahlström et al. (2011).
[209]Hydén et al. (2003: 21).
[210]Collier and Hoeffler (2006: 11).

Conflict

Though few studies have evaluated the relationship between administrative institutions and conflict, it is theoretically possible that such a relationship exists. There is evidence, for example, that the inability of governments to extract revenue is associated with a greater risk of conflict.[210] Paul Collier and Anke Hoeffler argue that governments have a higher incidence of conflict when they cannot defend themselves from rebel groups, a situation that is far more likely when governments are incapable of extracting revenue. Without sufficient income to invest in defense, governments are prey to rebel group predation and conflict erupts. Because administrative institutions play a critical role in revenue extraction, it is possible, then, that higher-quality administrative institutions lessen incidences of internal conflict. Future research is necessary, however, to evaluate this expectation.

Some studies have also indicated that when low-quality (patrimonial) administrative institutions deliver goods based on ethnic loyalties this may make minority groups feel excluded and lead to challenges to the state.[211] In the Ivory Coast, unity of the different ethnic groups and nationalities had been expertly maintained under President Felix Houphouët-Boigny (1960–93) as the administrative institutions never favored one ethnic group over the other. When he left power, the practice of discriminating against Burkinabé immigrants from Burkina Faso led to rising tensions and eventually conflict in 2002. In Kenya, people of Luo origin are ten times more likely to say that their impoverished economic condition is due to systematic discrimination by the state.[212] The practice of ethnic favoritism is a sign of low levels of state legitimacy.

Terrorism

The terrorism literature had originally argued that state weakness was connected to terrorism. Newer scholarship has investigated this relationship empirically and found that this is not the case.[213] For example, many of the most "failed states" according to the rankings made by the Failed State

---

[211]Many groups have internationalized their demands and received support from international actors. See also Lipschultz and Crawford (1996).

[212]Bratton and Kimenyi (2008: 8).

[213]Hehir argues that the "strength of institutions does not have a relationship with international terrorism" (2007: 308). Newman (2007: 483).

Index do not have a high number of terrorist organizations.[214] Countries like the Democratic Republic of Congo, Chad, Haiti, and Liberia have incredibly low performing administrative institutions, yet they are not hot-beds for terrorist groups. The quality of the administrative institutions may not have a huge impact on the number of terrorist organizations and terrorist activity. For terror-ist groups to operate, some administrative goods must be provided such as infrastructure, telecommunications, and technology.[215] Because terrorists need to be able to move, organize, and operate easily, adequate infrastruc-ture is very important. States with deteriorating infrastructure are not an attractive locale for terrorists to set up a base.[216] Al-Qaeda also tried to infiltrate the weakest states in the Horn of Africa, but was unable to do so because they found the lack of infrastructure and terrain to be too difficult. There were not enough flights and the roads were too bad and too remote. Though al-Qaeda had to contend with a much more hostile government, the increase in infrastructure, air connections, communication, and inte-gration of the economy made Kenya a more attractive option to set up a base.[217]

Because terrorism involves high-level planning, electronic connectivity is also important.[218] States must have strong internet services and other telecommunications infrastructure in order to maintain the networking to connect with different cells. The technological constraints have made European states seem like more suitable bases of operations for cells of al-Qaeda.[219] Improved information technology allows terrorists to com-municate, organize, gather information, recruit, and proselytize their agenda. Media coverage provides a bigger audience. There are many states with weak institutions, poor service delivery, and poverty whose territory has not become a terrorist haven and who have not experienced terrorist activity.[220]

---

[214]For example, Somalia also lacks the administrative infrastructure for groups like al-Qaeda to house and train its members, and these facilities would have to be reconstructed at a serious cost. It would also be harder for terrorist groups to hide out in Somalia (Menkhaus 2003a). Due to the flat terrain in Somalia, it would also be easier for foreign states to destroy bases and much harder for terrorist groups to hide (Menkhaus 2002: 109–23). Moreover, Somali society is very open with few secrets. It's a very oral society that does not like hiding people (109–23). Reports surfaced that bin Laden visited Somalia in 1999 but dismissed it as an option because he believed he would be betrayed. For al-Qaeda, Somalia also was not Islamic enough (Menkhaus 2002). More fundamentalist interpretations of Islam are foreign, and viewed as an alien doctrine of Gulf Arabs (Menkhaus 2002).

[215]Menkhaus (2003a).

[216]Menkhaus (2004b).

[217]Hehir (2007).

[218]Sageman (2004).

[219]Hehir (2007: 328). The planning for the September 11 attacks took place in European locations as well as Afghanistan.

[220]Newman (2007).

In contrast, countries like the United Kingdom have been attractive to international terrorist groups. The attacks of homegrown terrorists in Madrid and London also demonstrate that strong states can provide terrorist havens. Furthermore, al-Qaeda may be present in over 70 countries including strong states such as Switzerland, Belgium, and Ireland.[221]

Organized crime

Some studies have shown that organized crime is linked to corruption in the administrative institutions.[222] One important finding has emphasized that administrative institutions with higher levels of political intervention in the appointment, dismissal and promotion process, and poor pay are correlated with higher levels of organized criminal activity.[223] In particular, states with high-quality administrative institutions are better able to prevent illicit activities that are common amongst organized criminal groups such as tax evasion and they may be better at monitoring money-laundering activities. A well-trained administrative sector is better able to ensure that financial regulations that organized criminal groups try to circumvent are more consistently enforced.[224]

Moving forward

Administrative institutions, though often overlooked, fulfill a critical role in the functioning of the state. Charged with administering the decisions of the state, it is the duty of administrative institutions to ensure that state policies are translated into tangible actions for citizens. Administrative institutions are also responsible for enforcing state regulations, which are often created to protect the public from undesirable activities, and for collecting revenues, which are often vital to the state's ability to distribute goods and services. Administrative institutions are therefore important because without them states cannot execute their policy choices, regulate society, or extract resources.

In this chapter, we reviewed the key purposes of administrative institutions in the state. We also discussed the particular features that can be used to define high-quality versus low-quality administrative institutions.

---

[221]Hehir (2007: 321).
[222]Buscaglia (2008); (2003).
[223]Buscaglia (2003).
[224]When institutions such as the banking system are more transparent with higher standards of regulatory enforcement, this also decreases organized crime. It is also helpful for businesses to have access to financial services within a regulatory framework (see studies by Edgardo Buscaglia). Anti-money laundering legislation is also important.

In high-quality administrative institutions, which we refer to as Weberian, meritocratic recruitment and promotion procedures are used, civil servants' salaries are competitive, and civil servants' positions are insulated from politics and full of long-term rewards. In low-quality administrative institutions, which we refer to as patrimonial, the opposite is true.

To illustrate these differences, we provided numerous examples and case studies from the developing world. These examples highlight the extent to which the quality of administrative institutions can vary across states and the consequences of these differences.

Last, we examined how administrative institutions affect key outcomes of interest. Though the literature on this front is somewhat sparse, a number of central findings come to the fore. Specifically, high-quality administrative institutions have been shown to decrease levels of corruption and increase economic growth. Given the centrality of both of these outcomes to improving a state's level of development, it is clear that improving the quality of administrative institutions merits our attentions.

At the same time, to be able to offer more precise policy advice for states, it is essential that we disentangle the particular features of administrative institutions that drive outcomes. In what ways (if at all) do the three features discussed here—meritocratic recruitment and promotion, salary competitiveness, and autonomy—shape key outcomes of interest? Future research in this area is needed to inform this discussion. A major obstacle to such an undertaking, however, is the paucity of cross-national data available that measures them. Hopefully, as the international and development communities gain awareness of the importance of administrative institutions in the functioning of the state, greater resources will be dedicated to such efforts.

CHAPTER FIVE

Judicial institutions

Judicial institutions are the institutions of the state engaged in interpreting and enforcing laws, distributing punishments, and mediating conflicts. They are primarily the courts. Officials in judicial institutions can be either appointed or elected to their positions. This chapter discusses the role judicial institutions play in the functioning of the state. We examine the defining features of high-quality (versus low-quality) judicial institutions and provide detailed examples and case studies to highlight our main points. We then discuss the relationship between judicial institutions and the rule of law and enforcement of property rights, before assessing the state of the literature on judicial institutional quality on other outcomes.

It is important to note at the onset that this field is very much in its infancy. Few studies have been devoted to discussing the particular features of judicial institutions that make them high or low in quality. And even fewer studies have assessed how these features affect state performance. Instead, the bulk of the literature examines how the rule of law and property rights protection—two concepts that are closely related to but not synonymous with judicial institutional quality—affect outcomes of interest. Existing research simply tells us very little about the relationship between the consequences of high- versus low-quality judicial institutions. Unpacking the mechanics that underlie the relationship between judicial institutions and state performance therefore remains an important task, one that is critical to our ability to understand how developing countries can better structure their judicial institutions.

The role of judicial institutions in the state

Judicial institutions are responsible for interpreting and enforcing state policies. In this capacity, they play a role in mediating conflicts that arise between citizens, between citizens and the state, and between competing state institutions.[1] Judicial institutions also determine appropriate punishments when state policies are breached.

Without judicial institutions, state policies exist in name only. Policies that are implemented can be easily ignored by the citizenry and/or manipulated in ways to satisfy individual interests. Conflicts that arise over the interpretation or enforcement of state policies also lack a means of arbitration. No formal third party exists that can mediate disputes. By taking dispute resolution out of the hands of individuals, judicial institutions reduce the potential for violence.[2]

Judicial institutions are therefore important to ensuring that state policies are properly and consistently enforced in an unbiased and just fashion, meaning that the law is consistently applied regardless of the nature of the parties involved.[3] In doing so, they provide order in society and help to ensure social peace.[4] As Daniel Webber writes: "There has been increasing recognition in recent years by the World Bank and other development institutions that, to be successful, the development process must be comprehensive and supported by an effective judicial system."[5] Other scholars echo these points arguing that high-quality judicial institutions are critical to the survival of the state.[6]

We note that in this chapter we discuss solely the formal judicial institutions of the state. We recognize that informal judicial institutions often operate in states, particularly in those that lack formal dispute resolution mechanisms.[7] Occasionally, these informal institutions resolve disputes in a manner superior to formal institutions.[8] Though we acknowledge the importance of informal judicial institutions, we restrict our discussion in this chapter to those that are formal.

We also note that the capacity for the state's judicial institutions to interpret and enforce laws in a consistent manner is often influenced by the quality of the state's policies. When governments enact laws that are contradictory or unclear, for example, it is difficult (if not impossible) for the judicial system to fulfill its role. In addition, state policies themselves may be unfair or discriminatory. It is not the duty of the state's judicial institutions to ensure that policies are fair, however, but rather to make certain that they are interpreted and enforced in an equitable and just manner. We return to this point briefly in our discussion of the rule of law.

---

[1]Whitmore (2005: 5).
[2]World Bank Group Work in Low Income Countries under Stress: A Task Force Report (2002).
[3]World Bank (2002: 120).
[4]Ibid., 117.
[5]Webber (2007).
[6]Chang (2006); Kaufmann et al. (1998).
[7]Buscaglia and van Dijk (2003: 1–32).
[8]Messick (1999: 117–36).

Last, we we group law enforcement institutions (i.e. police forces and corrections facilities) with the state's security institutions. We do so primarily because law enforcement institutions, like security institutions, primarily exist to enforce state policies and judicial decisions. They play little role in the interpretation of laws or the distribution of judgment.

Categorization

Judicial institutions differ significantly in the extent to which they issue rulings in a fair and equitable manner that is consistent both with the law and across cases. High-quality judicial institutions give fair and impartial decisions; their judges (and other officials) are capable of making choices independent of the desires of the government and other actors. These officials are protected from retaliation for their judgments, but are also held accountable if they engage in unethical behavior. Cases are managed in a transparent fashion. Moreover, the judicial institutions are accessible to all. Low-quality judicial institutions, by contrast, give rulings that are politicized and arbitrary, with little adherence to existing laws or legal precedent. Officials within them face the very real risk of retribution for unpopular decisions. At the same time, these officials are often able to violate procedures and codes with impunity, as there are few means for holding them accountable. In this section, we discuss what these two types of judicial institutions look like in practice and the various features that differentiate them.

High-quality judicial institutions

High-quality judicial institutions consist of a set of well-trained officials and staff who receive their appointments and positions based on their merit. The assignment of judges to cases is also driven by qualifications, as opposed to political affiliations or leanings. A sophisticated case management system exists, such that the method for assigning judges to cases, the expenditures involved in cases and proceedings, and the logic underlying judicial decisions are publicly available and easy to monitor. Judicial decisions are rooted in legal guidelines and precedents and are consistent from one case to the next. The judicial apparatus is properly funded, such that it has sufficient resources at its disposal to efficiently and adequately handle cases. Salaries are also competitive to minimize the lure of bribery, and disciplinary procedures exist and are enforced for officials who behave unethically. In states with high-quality judicial institutions, citizens have trust in "the system" and its ability to arbitrate in a fair and consistent manner.

Low-quality judicial institutions

The opposite is true of low-quality judicial institutions. In states with these institutions, political interference in the judicial process is the norm. Judicial officials can engage in unethical behavior with few repercussions, yet have little protection from political retaliation should they deliver unpopular decisions. Insufficient and/or erratic financial resources are dedicated to the judiciary, and budgets are often tampered with for political goals. Existing laws or legal precedents do not drive decisions, but rather political motivations and/or bribery. When similar cases are heard, judgments issued by one official may differ dramatically from those issued by another. Case management systems, should they exist, are unclear and unsophisticated. Information such as why a particular judge was assigned to a case, how much expenditure was involved in the case and the reasoning behind the judge's ultimate decision is essentially unavailable for public consumption. As a result, citizens cannot rely on the state to enforce laws in an unbiased and consistent fashion, giving laws little de facto significance and making judicial decisions seem arbitrary.

Low-quality judicial institutions are also characterized by high levels of political interference. "Telephone law" is a term used to describe the "legal framework" of countries where party and government leaders would habitually contact the judges to direct the outcome of a case. Judges, like others in official positions, had to be party members and they could not ignore the advice/instruction dictated by the party line. Judges were appointed for fixed terms, usually for five years, and the office could be terminated at any time. How long judges were kept in office, and whether their terms were extended, depended on how well they executed their decisions in light of given instructions. The judicial budget was a part of the government budget, and all benefits for judges, ranging from the houses/apartments to tuition fees for their children, were subsidized by the executive. The judiciary was not perceived as an independent and impartial body accessible by the public to seek justice and protect their legitimate rights. Instead, the people used the courts only when they had no alternative. All these factors have set a foundation for the *dependence of the judiciary* in many transitional countries.[9]

Key features of high-quality judicial institutions

There are a number of key features that define high-quality judicial institutions, most of which we draw primarily from the United States Agency for

---

[9]Dung (2003: 8).

International Development (USAID)'s assessment of judicial institutions. They include:

1 *Independence*: the government and other sectors of society do not affect how cases are decided; instead, judgments are made based on well-qualified judges' understanding of the law. Budget allocations are not politicized and officials are protected from political retaliations for their decisions.[10]

2 *Integrity and accountability*: ethical standards of conduct for judicial officials exist and are enforced.[11]

3 *Transparency and efficiency*: sophisticated case management systems are in place that ensure standards are adhered to in the assignment of cases to judges and other officials, allocation of financial resources, and logic underlying judicial decisions and that the judicial process is swift and minimizes costs.[12]

4 *Equal access*: the judicial system is equally accessible and available to any citizen regardless of their income or geographic location.[13]

States whose judicial institutions have all these features have high-quality judicial institutions where citizens can expect laws to be interpreted and enforced in a clear and consistent manner.[14] States whose judicial institutions lack them have low-quality judicial institutions, where arbitrariness dominates the legal system. We now turn to discussing each of these features in greater detail.

Independence

Independence means that judicial decisions are rooted in the law and legal precedent; they are not affected by the government or other sectors of society. Independent judicial institutions are free from political interference: individual judges make their decisions based on their interpretation of the law rather than political pressures or considerations. Samuel Huntington writes that a "judiciary is independent to the extent that it adheres to distinctly judicial norms and to the extent that its perspectives

---

[10]US AID (2009: 4).
[11]Ibid.
[12]Ibid.
[13]Prillaman (2000); Staats et al. (2005).
[14]See Prillaman (2000) and Messick (1999) for a discussion of similar features identified as critical to a high-quality judiciary. Though we do not explicitly include access as a key feature here, as these researchers do, we note that transparency is a related concept given that it serves to increase the system's accessibility.

and behavior are independent of those of other political institutions and social groupings."[15]

Independence is perhaps the most critical feature of high-quality judicial institutions.[16] It helps to ensure that judicial rulings are consistent across cases, giving citizens (as well as foreign investors) trust in the legal system. Regardless of whether they agree with the laws in place, they at least know what to expect out of the legal process. Without judicial independence, there can be no rule of law.[17] When political actors influence judicial decisions, by contrast, how laws are interpreted will vary from one case to the next. In such a context, judicial decisions seem arbitrary, and individuals lose faith in the legal system itself as a result. The average citizen should have confidence that the justice system can enforce basic regulations, which may be difficult without judicial independence.[18]

Independence also allows judicial institutions to curb the power of other state institutions. It prevents the expansion of political powers by other government bodies, particularly the executive.[19] Freedom from political interference enables judicial institutions to call attention to unconstitutional efforts on the part of government actors and keep their behavior in check. For example, in many countries in Africa, as executive power became unaccountable, the courts have been powerless to limit governmental power or protect individual rights.[20]

Historical roots of the Latin American legal systems were characterized by a deep involvement of the executive powers interfering with the courts and controlling judicial nominations.[21] The executive has played a significant role controlling the court system in Colombia. The president has discretion to veto decisions by the Supreme Court if a criminal can be extradited or not.[22] In Mexico, for over 80 years under the Partido Revolucionario Institucional (PRI) regime, the judges served at the discretion of the president.[23] The judges lacked jurisdiction over politically salient cases. In Honduras in 1998, the Supreme Court was packed with lawyers who were close to both the military and to officials embroiled in corruption.[24]

---

[15]Huntington (1968: 20).
[16]See Asian Development Bank; World Bank.
[17]See Asian Development Bank.
[18]Fernández-Kelly and Shefner (2005: 35).
[19]Prillaman (2000: 2). Of course, judicial independence requires governments that agree to respect the law. As the World Bank writes: "Forcing rulers to follow the law is a problem as old as government itself" (World Bank 2002: 118). This underscores the fact that governments may not want to develop high-quality institutions in the first place, a problem that lies outside the scope of this study.
[20]Widner (2001).
[21]Ibid., 12.
[22]Bibes (2001: 254).
[23]Helmke and Rosenbluth (2009: 345–66).
[24]Berkman (2005: 10).

In the post-Soviet states, the courts and judges are absorbed into the executive branch. With the exception of Georgia, which has made dramatic improvements in its judicial system, the presidents in the regimes in Central Asia, Azerbaijan, and to a lesser extent in Armenia can directly influence the justice system.[25] In Belarus the judicial institutions are completely under the control of President Alexander Lukashenko (1994–). Any Justice that did not appear to be politically pliable has been removed, such as was the case with the removal of Belarusian Justice Pastukhov in 2002. Illustrating the judiciary's role, the president stated: "Under the Constitution, the judiciary is in essence part of the Presidency. Yes, the courts are declared to be independent, but it is the President who appoints and dismisses judges. Thanks to that, it is easier for the President to pursue his policies through the judiciary."[26] In Kyrgyzstan, international observers noted during the 2000 election that the judicial branch was biased against opposition candidates and used their power to selectively harass strong opposition candidates. When Askar Akayev (1990–2005) was in power, he relied on the courts to make decisions that were in his favor.[27] In some cases judicial institutions are simply eliminated. In Kazakhstan in 1995, a constitutional court was eliminated in favor of a constitutional council, whose decisions are subject to presidential veto.[28]

Presidents in Africa also retain too much power and face few checks from the judiciary. Kwame Nkrumah (1960–6) of Ghana and Kenneth Kaunda (1964–91) of Zambia faced no opposition from their respective judicial institutions.[29] Nkrumah packed the courts with loyal judges after the constitution was amended in 1964 to allow him to remove judges at his own will.[30] Kenya under Jomo Kenyatta (1964–78) utilized a similar strategy by packing the court with British "contract judges" who were loyal to his regime. Those that exhibited an independent streak were terminated or punished.[31] In Kenya today the president still selects the most important judicial commission in the country without any sort of oversight or input.[32] The courts are treated like any other agency of the executive and appointed through patronage and expected to carry out the wishes of the executives if they want to keep their jobs.[33] In Zaire (DRC) under Mobutu, the judiciary functioned at the pleasure of the executive. Most of the time, it never functioned at all.[34] This situation has not changed significantly.

---

[25]Kachkeev (2012: 1255–75).
[26]Dung (2003: 14).
[27]Cokgezen (2004: 91).
[28]Kachkeev (2012).
[29]Prempeh (2006).
[30]Ibid., 33.
[31]Mutua (2001: 109).
[32]Ibid., 102.
[33]Ibid., 105.
[34]Savage (2006: 6).

Judges were mostly reverential to the decisions made by politicians.[35] The judicial institutions are supposed to support the president rather than challenge him. In most cases, they have done whatever necessary to accommodate the wishes of the executive in exchange for financial and political rewards.[36] In many cases in Kenya, the president has given the Supreme Court justices "circulars" instructing them on how to rule.[37] Justice Derek Schofield of Kenya illustrates this point: "the Chief Justice and some of the judges saw it as their duty to assist the President [Moi] and the government [KANU government] . . . Thus the superior courts tended to support the government and particularly the President [Moi] grew to expect compliance with his wishes."[38]

When the first Ugandan chief justice, Benedicto Kiwanuka, refused to comply with the wishes of Idi Amin's regime, he was murdered.[39] In Zimbabwe, the chief justice and senior judges were harassed and forced to resign for the upholding of a law that respected citizens' rights and the rule of law with respect to the seizure of white farms by the Mugabe regime. The judiciary is routinely harassed if it does not adhere to the wishes of the executive.[40] In Swaziland, judges were harassed for the way that they handled a case involving relatives of the king. The judges were warned that they either follow his instructions or resign.[41]

In some cases the independence of the judiciary is undermined by the presence of parallel courts. In the Middle East, for example, responsibility has often been delegated to alternative courts, religious courts, or extra legal authorities such as the military.[42] The judiciary in Saudi Arabia is controlled by the Wahhabi religious establishment. The courts are subject to judicial decisions based on the Wahhabi interpretation of the Koran. Any reforms proposed have been met with resistance.[43] In the case of Egypt, under President Gamal Abdel Nasser (1952–70) a series of exceptional courts were created throughout the 1950s including the Court of Treason, the Court of Revolution, and the People's Courts. These courts had wide mandates, few procedural guidelines, no appeals process, and were staffed mostly by the military or other loyal supporters of the regime.[44] Nasser removed members of the court at will. Positions were sometimes transferred or forcibly retired. Military courts provided a venue where the regime could

---

[35]Prempeh (2006).
[36]Mutua (2001: 113).
[37]Ibid., 115.
[38]Ibid., 110.
[39]Rugege (2006: 413).
[40]Ibid., 414.
[41]Ibid.
[42]Owen (1992: 29).
[43]Ghadyan (1998: 246).
[44]Moustafa (2003: 888).

try its opponents. All judges are military officers appointed directly by the minister of defense and the president for two-year renewable terms.[45]

The Egyptian judiciary faced constant *political interference* under Nasser. In 1969, the courts were completely subordinated to the executive with the creation of a new Supreme Court. Members would only serve three years and needed to be appointed by the president. This gave the regime more control over judicial appointments, promotions, and disciplinary action.[46]

Judicial autonomy in Egypt improved in 1972, when Anwar Sadat embarked on a strategy to increase foreign direct investment and please international donors. The new law gave the judiciary more power of appointment. The chief justice was now selected by the president from the most senior justice already serving on the Supreme Constitutional Court (SCC).[47] The SCC has control over its own financial and administrative matters and was able to perform judicial reviews.[48] Judges in Egypt had remained the one area that tried to retain a strong sense of independence and distance from the regime.[49]

When Mubarak took power, judicial independence waned. Ruling by presidential decree, he amended the law of the SCC in 1998. He appointed Fathi Naguib, a former assistant minister of justice who helped engineer laws to restrict civil society, to serve as the head of the court. The SCC was a political pliable companion for Mubarak.[50]

Measuring judicial independence

Though judicial independence may seem like an immeasurable concept, there are ways of capturing it. As USAID writes: "Independence involves issues of the selection of judges, security of tenure, promotion and transfers . . . and safeguards against interference through manipulation of budgets, salaries, or working conditions."[51] In light of this, we derive three indicators of independence: meritocratic selection, assignment, and promotion; career safeguards; and sufficient budgets.

Meritocratic selection, assignment, and promotion procedures mean that officials are hired, assigned to cases, and promoted based on their qualifications rather than their political leanings or affiliations.[52]

---

[45]Ibid., 905.
[46]Brown (1997).
[47]Moustafa (2003: 893).
[48]Ibid., 894.
[49]Brown (1997).
[50]Brownlee (2002: 9).
[51]US AID (2009: 7).
[52]Berkowitz and Clay (2006).

There are a variety of ways in which judges can be selected for their positions, ranging from meritocratic appointments on one end to partisan elections on the other. Scholars have noted that a *merit-based appointment* leads to the most independent judiciary, while partisan elections lead to "the least independent judiciary."[53] As the legal scholar Roscoe Pound argued in 1906: "Putting the courts into politics and compelling judges to become politicians, in many jurisdictions has almost destroyed the traditional respect for the bench."[54] With meritocratic selection, independent screenings are used to assess the qualifications of candidates, making for less politicized judicial institutions.

In most of the post-Soviet republics, originating from the Soviet period, political leanings are more important in selecting judges than qualifications. Georgia, in contrast, has adopted an examination-based selection procedure to ensure the transparent and merit-based process of judicial appointments. This process was widely regarded as fair and clear, and encouraging for talented lawyers, since it displays qualifications without bias. In contrast in Russia, due to low salaries, very few were graduates came from a law faculty.[55] Most new judges came from law enforcement or only had experience as a court secretary.

There are few mechanisms in Latin America to ensure that appointments to High Court positions are reliable and face more public scrutiny. The selection of judges in Honduras is done without much attention to training, procedures, and merit. The hiring process is politicized by the influence of important political and economic figures.[56] Judges are then easily pressured by their superiors to make decisions conforming to the political beliefs of those in power, disregarding the law.[57]

In Vietnam numerous improvements have taken place in terms of the qualifications for judges. Vietnam requires that judges obtain an academic degree. However there is still need for a more merit-based nomination process to ensure that the best-qualified lawyers are chosen to become judges. The selection process needs to become still more transparent.[58]

In China, appointments and promotions are now also more merit based, with a greater role for the higher-level courts in the decision-making process. New graduates must generally start in lower courts, and work their way up. Supreme and High Court judges must have at least five years experience, and all come from a competitive academic background. Political background is not as important as legal skills and qualifications.[59] This has

---

[53]Ibid., 416.
[54]Pound (1906: 748). From Berkowitz and Clay (2006: 417).
[55]Solomon (2008).
[56]Berkman (2005: 11).
[57]Ibid.
[58]Dung (2003: 38).
[59]Peerenboom (2002: 11).

improved the stature and respect of the judicial institutions, which has in turn led to higher enforcement rates for judgments.[60]

Some other cases in Asia have suffered from non-meritocratic selection methods. For example, the selection process in Mongolia is very politicized. Family connections and loyalty is more important than qualifications in the selection of judges.[61] In the Philippines under Ferdinand Marcos, he was able to control the judiciary through his power to appoint the judges as he personally saw fit. After Marcos' regime fell in 1986 Corazon Aquino accepted the resignation of all the Supreme Court members and then reconstituted it with judges in line with her own ideological preferences. Subsequent politicians have treated the judiciary as a source of reciprocal exchange. Nominations are filled by those who are most loyal to the current leader.[62]

Pakistan's judicial organs have had a history of political interference though this initially was not the case. At independence, Pakistan's judicial institutions were venerable and impressive. Members were appointed through the bureaucracy using a merit-based process, requiring government confirmation. Starting with General Ayub Khan (1958–69) appointments started to take place under political affiliations. More and more judges were appointed based on familiar considerations as well. The system deteriorated further under Zulfiqar Bhutto (1971–7). Bhutto made appointments entirely based on political affiliation, favoritism, and nepotism. Under General Muhammad Zia (1977–88), unknown lawyers who were considered politically pliable were appointed to high positions in the judiciary. Once taking the position, judges had to take an oath of loyalty to General Zia.[63] This pattern became even more blatant and widespread under Benazir Bhutto as political considerations mattered more than experience, competence, and criminal record. One judge appointed was on trial for murder. Another was completely inexperienced. Another had lost three elections as a member of the Pakistan People's Party (PPP) and was given the position as patronage.[64]

Beyond using merit to drive the selection of officials, it is also important that officials are assigned to cases and promoted for the same reason. *Meritocratic case assignment* means that judges and other staff are allotted cases because of their qualifications; political motives do not play a role.

Case assignment in many countries in Asia is still deliberate rather than random. The problem with deliberate assignment of cases is that it leaves more room for corruption and political intervention.[65] China has

[60]Ibid., 9.
[61]White (2009).
[62]Haynie (2000: 15).
[63]Tate (1993: 322).
[64]Newberg (2002).
[65]Dung (2003: 34).

implemented reforms to ensure that case assignment is done randomly and impartially.[66] Though politically sensitive cases are referred to a party controlled political-legal committee for consideration, in most cases the judiciary is given autonomy.[67] In the Philippines under Marcos, judges were not able to handle cases by public officials or crimes of public disorder. The military was given jurisdiction to try almost any criminal case.[68] In Pakistan, parallel religious courts and military courts were created under General Zia, which handled cases deemed to be politically sensitive by Zia.[69]

In many states in Africa cases are assigned due to political considerations. When justices do not make the correct rulings, they can be immediately removed from a case, as has been the case in Kenya. It is unclear how cases are assigned and there is often little public knowledge of proceedings.

Similarly, meritocratic promotion implies that there are *clear career paths* in place for existing officials. Promotion decisions are based on officials' records, as opposed to political considerations. In order to recruit the best-qualified candidates there must be transparency in the judicial appointment process, both in the criteria and the procedures. A transparent appointment process would also ensure that the appointment does not undermine judicial independence. Judicial vacancies should also be widely announced or advertised.

In many states in Africa, career paths and promotions are affected by political interference. This was not always the case, however. After Kenya received its independence, the constitution provided a complex process to remove judges that insulated them from executive power. Judges could only be removed after a tribunal made recommendations to the president. The regimes of Kenyatta and Moi changed this, and judges were removed at their will.[70] Lower court judges are treated like civil servants in need of strict supervision. Their selection, promotion, and dismissal are not based on merit and performance but on how closely they adhere to the objectives of the executive.[71] Many of those appointed and promoted are either "mediocre or flatly incompetent."[72]

A second indicator of judicial independence is the establishment of *career safeguards* for judicial officials. Career safeguards refer to procedures that protect judicial officials from negative repercussions should they deliver a ruling that is politically unpopular or controversial.

---

[66]Peerenboom (2002: 8).
[67]Dung (2003). A 1993 study on the Chinese judicial system indicated that 8 percent of the Supreme Court cases received political interference (Peerenboom 2002: 15).
[68]Tate (1993: 326).
[69]Newberg (2002); Tate (1993: 323).
[70]Mutua (2001: 101).
[71]Ibid., 106.
[72]Ibid., 113.

One of the most effective career safeguards is the security of tenure. According to the UN Office of the High Commissioner for Human Rights (OHCHR), "unless judges have some long-term security of tenure, there is a serious risk that their independence will be compromised, since they may be more vulnerable to inappropriate influence in their decision-making."[73] Security of tenure means that judges are guaranteed long terms of office upon their appointment or soon after. In the latter case, decisions about tenure are made by independent commissions, as opposed to political actors.

Only four countries in Latin America use lifetime appointments (Argentina, Brazil, Chile, and Paraguay). The other countries in Latin America have appointments that range only from 4 to 15 years, which makes these positions more easily affected. In Mexico under the PRI, the average tenure was just ten years from 1934 to 1994, and 40 percent served five years or less.[74] Supreme Court justices in Guatemala have to seek reappointment after each five-year term. In El Salvador, judges only have nine-year terms, which is an improvement from the past usage of five-year terms.[75] In Honduras, there is a high turnover for judges. Those who are deemed "no manejables" (unmanageable) are removed. Judges are biased in their decision making as a result.[76]

While lifetime appointments are important, it is also important that judges feel secure. In Mexico, Colombia, and Brazil, judges have to hide for their own safety. Making the wrong decision could result in being assassinated. In Colombia between 1979 and 1991, 278 judges were killed.[77] In 1987 alone, 53 members of the judiciary were assassinated.[78] Colombian judges have had to hide their faces to avoid being targeted.[79] In Brazil in 2003, Judge Antonio Jose Machado Dias was assassinated possibly due to his presiding in a case involving a drug cartel.[80] In Honduras, judges who assert themselves in human rights cases have faced death threats and violent attack.[81]

In Pakistan, security of tenure was not guaranteed in the past as judges were removed at the will of the executive. Under Zulfiqar Bhutto, judges who tried to assert their independence were fired as lifetime appointment was removed based on changes made to the 1973 constitution.[82] Under Zia,

---

[73]OHCHRC (2003: 127).
[74]Helmke and Rosenbluth (2009).
[75]Dung (2003).
[76]Berkman (2005: 10).
[77]Knoester (1998).
[78]Max Manwaring, "Non-state Actors in Colombia: Threat and Response," *Strategic Studies Institute* (May 2002): 13.
[79]Knoester (1998: 12).
[80]Coelho (2007: 75).
[81]Berkman (2005: 10).
[82]Newberg (2002: 139).

Chief Justice Yaqub Ali Khan was removed and quickly replaced.[83] In the Philippines under Marcos, judges were worried that ruling against Marcos would lead to their dismissal.[84] As a result, not one decision by the Supreme Court posed a threat to Marcos' rule. In Vietnam there are also issues with *length of tenure* for judges. Judges are appointed for five-year terms and can be removed for different reasons, with the grounds of removal and procedures being unclear.[85]

Though judicial appointments in Saudi Arabia tend to be long and judges cannot be removed without cause, the king still has the power to remove any judge: the highest-ranking judge has been removed by the king in the past.[86] They are at his will as he is the supreme authority on all judicial matters.[87] In contrast, due to pressures from the European Union, Turkey has embarked on numerous measures to strengthen its institutions and the courts are one such area that has been fortified. Currently judicial institutions have remained mostly autonomous in Turkey. Fifteen of the court members are permanent while five serve as substitutes.[88]

Most judges in Africa do not enjoy security of tenure. Security of tenure for Supreme Court judges was removed in Kenya in 1988.[89] Though it was reinstated in 1990, the executive can "easily circumvent the procedures."[90] In the Democratic Republic of Congo, 315 judges have been unilaterally removed.[91]

In many of the countries in the post-Soviet sphere, the constitution stipulates that the president has the authority to fire members of the judicial branch. This has made the courts and judges fully subordinated to the president. In 2011, the Kazakh president eliminated six Supreme Court judges at his own will. Tenure for judges in Azerbaijan is only ten years, while in Belarus tenure is only eleven years.[92] In Russia under Vladmir Putin, improving judicial tenure has been an area targeted by reform. Judges gained lifetime appointments after a probationary stage with release only if there was due cause.[93]

In addition to tenure guarantees, *salary guarantees* also constitute a career safeguard. With salary guarantees, officials are assured a salary that falls within a predetermined range based on their position. Salary decisions

---

[83]Tate (1993: 322).
[84]Tate and Haynie (1993: 707–40).
[85]Dung (2003: 35).
[86]Ghadyan (1998: 15).
[87]Ibid., 45.
[88]Shambayati and Kirdiş (2009: 775).
[89]Mutua (2001: 102).
[90]Ibid., 106.
[91]Liwanga (2012: 200).
[92]Dung (2003).
[93]Solomon (2008).

(including pay raises and cuts) affect entire ranks, rather than particular individuals. In the most extreme form, salary guarantees consist of laws that prohibit salary reductions of any sort for judicial officials. Salary guarantees help to ensure that individual judicial officials (as well as the judicial apparatus as a whole) are protected from negative financial repercussions should they issue controversial decisions. Salary guarantees also make judges less susceptible to accepting bribes.[94]

In many states in Africa, the judiciary does not have any control over its salaries and must depend on the legislative and executive branches for the resources with which to operate. As result, justices must constantly seek attention from influential politicians for resources to run the courts.[95] In the Democratic Republic of Congo, as of 2012 the judges have no control over their budget.[96] In most countries in Africa, judges and staff are severely underpaid and pensions cannot even cover the cost of living.[97]

In the post-Soviet republics, salaries are also too low to encourage strong candidates to join the judicial institutions. A typical judicial salary in Kyrgyzstan and Tajikistan is as low as US$30 per month.[98] A typical judicial salary in Russia was as low as US$140 per month, but recent changes under Putin have seen salary increases of up to $1,000 a month. Nevertheless, though salaries of judges rose, salaries of court staff remained the same.[99]

In many countries in the Middle East, judges are also *poorly paid*. This is especially true at the lower levels. Salaries of judges are so low in Lebanon that better qualified individuals have gone to private practices to earn a living.[100] In Egypt judges are not paid particularly well, but what's been more problematic has been the low pay for court employees. Court employees have such low salaries that they have stopped performing key functions in order to exact bribes from the public. Court employees have been accused of "losing key documents, delivering papers to the wrong address, forging signatures to indicate that papers were served when they were not."[101]

In contrast, some countries in Asia have undertaken reforms to improve judicial salaries but there is still room for improvement. In Vietnam, judges enjoy higher salaries than other public servants but they are still consistently underpaid. It is difficult to live off of their own incomes, and many judges in Vietnam are forced to rely on the incomes of other family members or find other sources of incomes, which impedes their ability to perform their

---

[94]Buscaglia et al. (1995).
[95]Prempeh (2006: 68).
[96]Liwanga (2012: 201).
[97]Prempeh (2006: 67); Dung (2003).
[98]Dung (2003).
[99]Solomon (2008).
[100]Mallat (1997).
[101]Brown (1997: 193).

duties. Judges in the Supreme Court in China are paid very well. Judges working in major cities such as Shanghai and Beijing are also paid high salaries in order to attract and retain the highest qualified judges. However, judges in remote areas are paid poorly and are overstretched, which has led to many parties withdrawing their lawsuits.[102] In Pakistan, both the salary and prestige of judges has decreased—so much so that a position in the lower courts is considered a last choice for law graduates in Pakistan.[103] In Mongolia the situation is even worse; a judge in Mongolia makes between $33 and $51 a year. A third of the judges in the countryside are homeless due to low pay.[104]

A third indicator of judicial independence is *sufficient budgets*.[105] According to Webber, the size of the judiciary's budget is important because effective judiciaries genuinely require resources.[106] Sufficient budgets refer to those in which the state's judicial institutions receive adequate funds to carry out their duties. This means that budgets are not reduced for political purposes, but rather fluctuate in line with overall state budget reductions and/or changes in the judiciary's case loads. In some states, this is assured by dedicating to the judicial apparatus a fixed percentage of the government's annual budget.[107] Performance management analysis can also be used, such that budgets are based on the volume of case flow and the efficiency with which cases are managed.[108]

Sufficient budgets allow for the provision of competitive salaries for judicial officials.[109] This potentially reduces the likelihood that judicial officials will be enticed by bribery or other forms of corruption for financial gain. It also helps judicial institutions attract and retain a capable staff. According to USAID, adequate budgets are important for judicial independence because they "contribute to an environment conducive to continuity and consistency in judicial employment."[110]

Without sufficient budgets, a state's judicial institutions cannot afford decent facilities, equipment, and staff support. Salaries are too low and officials are overworked. As the OHCHR points out: "Without adequate funds, the Judiciary will not only be unable to perform its functions efficiently, but may also become vulnerable to undue outside pressures and corruption."[111]

---

[102]Peerenboom (2002: 7).
[103]Newburn (1999).
[104]Quah (2006: 176).
[105]Berkowitz and Clay (2006).
[106]Webber (2007: 5).
[107]Buscaglia and Dakolias (1999: 13).
[108]Ibid.
[109]Court et al. (2003: 11); Carothers (1998: 164); Moore (1985: 313–18).
[110]US AID (2009: 16).
[111]OHCHRC (2003: 121).

Sufficient budgets are therefore another key indicator of judicial independence. They signal that political forces are not reducing budgets for political purposes and that the judicial apparatus as a whole is well funded. Indeed, higher budgets are associated with better-performing judicial institutions.[112]

Overall, the resources available for judicial services remain very low in the post-Soviet states as well due to a shortage of funds. In most of the countries in the region, courthouses are drab and unwelcoming. Buildings are dilapidated. Waiting areas are unappealing. Many courthouses lack modern equipment such as photo copiers. In Russia, budgets for the courts have always been very small. Many courts had little money left to pay salaries and were forced to accept funding from private firms. Under Putin, budgetary increases have improved the courts' infrastructure but the courts are still shabby and in need of repairs.[113]

The judicial budget in Mongolia is also not adequate to deal with judicial issues. The court buildings do not provide a respectable environment to dispense justice, lacking both office space and courthouses.[114] Pakistani courts have been notoriously understaffed and lack trained administrators. Their physical infrastructure is also grossly inadequate and of poor quality.[115]

In a handful of countries in Latin America, such as Costa Rica, the budget for the judiciary is guaranteed through the constitution as a percentage of the national budget. Other countries have also worked on increasing their judicial budgets. Argentina has increased its budget by more than 50 percent since 1997. Chile doubled its budget for the courts in a five-year plan in 2003.[116] In most Latin American countries, however, funding levels for the judiciary are quite low. Judges in Latin America also generally have to work in poor working conditions.[117] Due to low levels of funding for the judicial institutions, there are also increasing backlogs and delays.[118]

The judicial institutions in most of Africa are sufficiently underfunded, leaving it with "inadequate and outmoded technology, dilapidated and overcrowded courthouses and offices."[119] Countries like Liberia that are recovering from years of war lack the funding and resources to staff and train a capable judiciary. The judicial institutions are also severely underfunded in Ghana. There is little available office space, not enough courtrooms, and

---

[112]Moore and Buscaglia (1999).
[113]Solomon (2008).
[114]White (2009: 226). The judicial budget is 1 percent of the national budget (ibid., 209–76).
[115]Diamond (2000: 101).
[116]Dung (2003: 17).
[117]Buscaglia et al. (1995: 11).
[118]Ibid., 2.
[119]Prempeh (2006: 67).

insufficient budgetary allocations.[120] The courts are also under-resourced in Uganda. To illustrate, backlogs caused by shortages of stationary were alleviated in Ugandan courts after donations of paper came in.[121] In the DRC, the infrastructure of the judicial system has collapsed with judges and lawyers lacking resources as simple as basic legal texts. There continues to be little commitment to rebuilding a strong and independent judicial system. In 2004 the administration devoted a mere 0.6 percent of the total budget to the needs of the judicial system.[122]

In sum, judicial independence is a critical feature of high-quality judicial institutions. It can be captured by three indicators: meritocratic selection, appointment, and promotion; career safeguards, and sufficient budgets.

Integrity and accountability

Integrity means that there are ethical standards of conduct in place for judicial officials, whereas accountability means that these standards are enforced and the actions of judicial officials are monitored and reviewed. We discuss the former concept before turning to a discussion of the latter.

Integrity implies that judicial officials are behaving in an ethical manner, as defined by the state. It can be assessed in a number of ways, including the frequency with which judicial officials participate in ethics training and/or recuse themselves from cases on ethical grounds, the percentage of judicial officials who comply with requirements for public disclosure of their assets and income, and the existence of ethical and disciplinary programs and performance standards for officials.[123]

The existence of ethical standards alone, of course, is not enough to ensure compliance. It is also critical that judicial officials are held accountable for their actions. Accountability means that ethical standards are enforced through internal controls and nonpolitical disciplinary commissions.[124] In accountable judicial institutions, judicial decisions are subject to appellate review and budget allocations within the judiciary are audited. At the same time, to maintain judicial independence, judicial officials have the right to a fair hearing or review process and decisions on ethical violations are available for public consumption.[125] Disciplinary commissions also operate autonomously from the political sphere.

Accountability provides for more consistent and fair legal judgments, while also ensuring that judicial resources are not being wasted or dedicated to corrupt activities. The evidence indicates that accountability helps

---

[120]Mangu (2009: 15).
[121]Botero et al. (2003: 68).
[122]Matti (2010: 47).
[123]US AID (2009).
[124]Buscaglia and Dakolias (1999: 4).
[125]Ibid., 11.

to increase the efficiency of the legal system, as well. According to the World Bank, for example, "greater accountability of judges to the users of the judicial system has been more important in increasing its efficiency than the simple increase in financial and human resources.[126]

Beyond their clear potential for reducing corruption, integrity and accountability improve the quality of the state's judicial institutions by increasing the likelihood that judicial officials will deliver judgments based on existing laws and legal precedents, as opposed to their own individual biases. This, in turn, makes it more likely that similar cases will be decided upon in a consistent manner, rather than varying in outcome depending on the particular official(s) assigned to them.

Integrity and accountability also enhance the overall self-image of the judiciary, contributing to a set of institutions where honesty and ethics are valued. According to USAID, experience indicates that "judges, court personnel, and lawyers respond positively to thoughtful efforts to establish high standards of ethical conduct, create expectations of behavior in conformity with those high standards, and maintain systems to motivate compliance."[127] This development of a positive and cohesive esprit de corps, in turn, can reinforce standards of ethics and officials' adherence to them.

Survey research shows that Latin Americans have low opinions of the judicial system. Many believe that judges apply the law in an arbitrary manner.[128] Often the public tries to avoid the formal judicial system. Checks on corruption of the judiciary would help to improve public opinion of the courts, such as by using investigatory commissions.[129] Judges in Latin America also still need to be better trained as to what their jobs entail and the importance of their positions in the functioning of society.[130] Judges in Chile are now required to undergo a short-term training course to instill stronger ethics.[131]

In most countries in Africa, judicial accountability is "hampered by a dearth of professional and academic commentary on judicial decisions."[132] There needs to be continuing judicial education for judges, better library and research facilities, internet access, and seminars.[133] The case of Rwanda, however, illustrates how reforms to maintain integrity and accountability can be successful (see case study of Rwanda in this chapter).

The judicial institutions in the Middle East have suffered from issues of integrity. Judicial corruption is considered rampant because of the ease

---

[126]Court et al. (2003: 12) quoting the World Bank (2002: 118–19).
[127]US AID (2009: 4).
[128]Ibid., 6.
[129]Buscaglia et al. (1995: 12).
[130]Ibid., 6.
[131]Dung (2003).
[132]Prempeh (2006: 70).
[133]Ibid., 147.

with which people are able to personalize exchanges involving the courts.[134] Lebanon's judiciary is considered corruptible and unprofessional. The reputation of judges in Lebanon is very poor due to farcical prosecutions and judicial anomalies. All of these inconsistencies and cases of corruption have led to low levels of trust in the judicial institutions in Lebanon.[135] In Saudi Arabia, the Sharia courts in particular were viewed as susceptible to corruption.[136] Though there is a judicial committee that has the power to discipline the judges on the court, there is no clear criterion as to what constitutes misconduct.[137]

Nevertheless, Saudi Arabia has employed some mechanisms to enhance judicial integrity. Judges appointed are on probation for their first year, and any judge that receives a below average evaluation in his efficiency reports will be transferred.[138] Efforts were also made to improve judicial integrity in Egypt under Anwar Sadat. During the Nasser era, lucrative consulting positions were distributed by the state to better control judicial decisions. When Sadat took over, judges were forbidden from holding lucrative consulting positions.

Judicial integrity is low in India because judicial corruption is rarely punished. If judicial corruption is addressed, it is handled in the most "inefficient and lethargic manner."[139] The situation is even worse in Bangladesh. A survey in Bangladesh revealed that 82 percent of the public believed that the judicial institutions were the most corrupt.[140]

There is more oversight of judicial integrity in countries like Hong Kong and Singapore (for more information on Singapore see case study in this chapter). Judges have the power to complain if state institutions, public organizations, officials, or individuals infringe on their rights or interfere in particular cases.[141] By the same token, there are judicial bodies to monitor the judiciary and judicial misconduct or negligence is sanctioned.[142]

Efforts have also been made in Vietnam to improve judicial integrity. Judges in Vietnam are required to undergo a short-term training course and professional skills are enhanced through these training sessions. However, corruption in the judiciary still persists with many judges being caught for taking bribes, which lowers public confidence. Nevertheless, in an effort to clean up the judiciary, judges who have been exposed have been sentenced to jail.[143]

---

[134]Timur (2004: 106).
[135]Mallat (1997: 34).
[136]Brown (1997: 62).
[137]Seznec (2002: 43).
[138]Ibid., 45.
[139]Sondhi (2000: 12).
[140]Khan (1998: 11).
[141]Peerenboom (2002: 10).
[142]Ibid.
[143]Dung (2003: 36).

The judicial institutions in the Caucasus also suffer from low levels of integrity. It is perceived that court decisions are up for sale and that judges can be easily bought. Immunity for important political figures has been common as has impunity for transgressions. A BEEPS survey revealed that businesses believe that the courts are corrupted.[144] The situation is worrisome in Armenia and Azerbaijan. In contrast to most of the regimes in the Caucasus, great strides have been made in Georgia to eliminate judicial corruption. When President Mikheil Saakashvili came to power in 2004, he made it his mission to clean up the state and improve judicial corruption. Saakashvili arrested high-level officials and ended the climate of impunity.[145]

Under Putin, Russia has enacted judicial reform to make the courts stronger and more legitimate in the eyes of the public. The prestige of judges in Russia was always very low. Measures were enacted to ensure the accountability of judges. A Judicial Qualification Commission was established with two-thirds of the members of this Commission comprising judges. Judges have to undergo review by their peers on the Judicial Qualification Commissions. Judges were also forced to declare all sources of income and assets, and were asked to keep diaries of meetings with members of the public outside of trials. Also in efforts to improve public trust in the judiciary, more information has been provided about how the courts work and information is further diffused through the use of press secretaries.[146]

Surveys have indicated that the reforms have led to an increase in the public's trust of the courts. According to a June 2007 survey by the Russian Academy of State Service, around half of the public believes that the judicial system is fair "now and then," with only 26 percent reporting that they trusted the courts.[147] In spite of the low levels of trust, many more Russian citizens have relied on the courts than in the past. The number of civil cases heard in 2006 was more than 7.5 million, compared to 3.04 million in 1996 and 1.65 million in 1990.[148] Furthermore, 68 percent report that they would seek help from the courts if their legal rights were violated.[149]

Transparency and efficiency

Transparency means that there is public access to how cases are managed, while efficiency means that cases are processed in an effective and economical manner. *Sophisticated case management* systems are critical to both;

---

[144]Anderson and Gray (2006).
[145]Kukhianidze (2009: 215–34).
[146]Solomon (2008).
[147]Ibid.; see also Dung (2003).
[148]Solomon (2008).
[149]Dung (2003).

they open the judicial system up to public scrutiny and reduce transaction costs. Sophisticated case management systems aggregate information regarding the assignment of judges and other officials to cases, the allocation of financial resources within the judicial apparatus, and the logic underlying judicial decisions and make it available for public consumption.[150]

Providing the public with *information* about judicial assignments decreases the likelihood that these assignments will be based on political leanings or affiliations. In addition, making judicial salaries and assets public makes it less likely that there will be conflicts of interests in cases officials are assigned to, while offering information regarding how judicial resources are spent (including the costs of cases) helps to ensure that these resources are used efficiently.

Research from the World Bank has found also that overly complicated procedures that are unclear and simplified procedures are critical for the judicial institutions to function effectively.[151] Procedures that are overly complex give more opportunities for officials to elicit bribes to move a case forward. *Simplifying procedures* decreases time and costs.[152] Studies in Latin America have revealed that the judicial procedures are often too cumbersome. For example, in Brazil, court decisions are hard to enforce.[153] Laws are formally upheld and then defied in practice.[154]

By making so much information transparent, sophisticated case management systems have the potential to deter judicial corruption. They help to ensure that judges and other officials are randomly assigned to cases and that there are clear records of case proceedings, which are two frequent areas of abuse in corrupt judicial systems. As USAID points out, "where clerks of individual judges maintain case files in insecure environments there is a substantial risk that documents, or even entire files, might disappear . . . [eliminating] a potential source of corrupt manipulation of judicial records."[155]

Studies by the World Bank have argued that introducing computer systems or other mechanization helps to reduce delays and corruption. Computerized case inventories are easier to handle and are more accurate. When compared with paper-based procedures, computerized inventories are harder to manipulate making it less likely that judges will "lose" case files in order to extract bribes.[156]

---

[150]US AID (2009: 5).
[151]Botero et al. (2003).
[152]Ibid.
[153]Rule of Law Index in The World Justice Project.
[154]Larrain (1999).
[155]US AID (2009: 10).
[156]Botero et al. (2003: 63).

According to USAID, the evidence suggests that most delays in litigation "are attributable to lax management by the judge in keeping the case moving toward decision."[157] With sophisticated case management systems in place, it is easier to identify and address the causes of judicial delays. Sophisticated case management citizens therefore allow cases to be processed in a more expeditious manner.[158] This, in turn, increases citizen confidence in the judicial system by reducing the extent to which they are subject to judicial holdups. It also may ensure that everyone has equal access to justice, and not just those with political connections.

In Serbia, for example, the country's notoriously corrupt commercial courts introduced an automated case management system in 2004. This system randomly selects judges, charges litigants standard fees, and enables citizens to monitor the progress of cases online. This change led to a 24 percent reduction in the inventory of pending cases in 2006.[159]

Sophisticated case management systems offer citizens a record on which they can hold the state's judicial institutions accountable: because citizens are privy to judicial institutional activities, like the productivity of judges and court personnel, they can monitor whether the judicial system is in fact functioning effectively. The courts in Central Asia and the Caucasus suffer from problems of transparency in that information about court activity is not readily known nor is it provided on court websites.[160] In Georgia, however, in an effort to curb corruption, reforms were made to make the system more transparent.[161] In Russia under Putin serious efforts were also made to improve the efficiency of the courts. Courts were computerized, and court websites and databanks were developed in order to make courts more open, transparent, and efficient. More simplified procedures have been extended to serious crimes. Civil cases have also improved. In order to deal with backlogs of cases, more court employees were hired and new positions were created such as judicial assistants and clerks. The legal time frame for most civil cases is three months.[162]

In Latin America, the system of record management of cases, case flow, and case load is inefficient and unclear. Case statistics and archives are also not well maintained.[163] The courts lack a professional class to administer the court system, which may limit time spent on cases.[164] Another problem is that the system in Latin America is centralized where the number of

---

[157]US AID (2009: 11).
[158]World Bank (2002: 118).
[159]US AID (2009: 2 11).
[160]Solomon (2008). For example, it is unclear where and how to file cases.
[161]Kukhianidze (2009).
[162]Solomon (2008).
[163]Buscaglia et al. (1995: 12).
[164]Domingo (1999: 168).

staff assigned to different courts is fixed without reference to the case load that the court must deal with at any specific time. The number of staff is not affected by the volume of cases. This is inefficient because sometimes there are surplus case workers, while other times there are shortages.[165] The effect is that in most countries in Latin America the courts are over-burdened and their proceedings are often delayed for years at a time.[166] Though Latin America has taken steps to reform their judicial institutions, inefficiencies remain.[167]

The judicial institutions in Egypt are also overburdened.[168] There are huge delays in the Egyptian court system due to corruption, incompetence, and improper case management.[169] Documents and notices for litigants do not appear often causing further delays.[170] In Lebanon there is no computerized system to handle cases. Cases also accumulate because of the misuse of the procedural codes. Moreover, delaying tactics and loopholes are easily used and there are no pretrial proceedings.[171]

Several countries in East and Southeast Asia have efficient judicial systems. In China, great improvements have taken place in developed areas such as Shanghai, Beijing, or Guangdong to improve resources and necessary technological infrastructure. So much investment has taken place that cases move efficiently and quickly.[172] Other important reforms have also prevented backlogs. The judiciary has encouraged the use of more simplified procedures for both civil and criminal trials. Roles have been streamlined to make the process more efficient. In the past the same judge was in charge of accepting a case, carrying out pretrial investigation, and trying the case. All of these responsibilities have now been allocated to different positions.[173]

In contrast, the judicial system in India is beset by delays. Corruption cases take years to be decided, and as such those that are accused often escape punishment. The result of inordinate delays and conviction rates of only 6 percent is that justice is often denied and public trust and confidence in the judicial institutions are low.[174]

---

[165]Buscaglia et al. (1995: 14).
[166]Domingo (1999: 165).
[167]Ibid., 168.
[168]Brown (1997: 1).
[169]Ibid., 192.
[170]More delays are caused by those who refuse to accept judgments involving payment. Egyptian judicial institutions have been lenient to those who delay making payments in civil cases and there is little enforcement (ibid., 193).
[171]Mallat (1997: 34).
[172]Peerenboom (2002).
[173]Ibid.
[174]Sondhi (2000: 12).

The inefficiency of the Indian judiciary also has had a negative effect on the business environment and entrepreneurship. The average time of adjournment is 4–6 months, the trial dates are not available for at least 2 years with the average law suit settlement time taking place over 15 years.[175] The backlogs in the judiciary led to more breaches of contract, which discourage firms from making investments and impede access to financial institutions for new firms, which lead to shortages of capital.[176]

With the help of the Asian Development Bank, Pakistan has worked to improve judicial efficiency by improving case flow management. Case flow management techniques were taught to judges in pilot districts with the objective of speeding up case disposal. The result of the reforms created better conditions for business and entrepreneurship. The increased speed with which cases were handled led to more individuals willing to arrange for financial resources or apply for loans. More people were also confident that they could obtain credit, which led to more people seeking to buy land, machinery, or buildings to establish businesses. The reforms implemented in 2002 cost Pakistan 0.1 percent of its GDP but led to a 0.5 percent jump in its GDP.[177]

Equal access

Judicial institutions are also measured by their accessibility.[178] Accessibility means how much the judicial system is "equally available to citizens regardless of socio-economic status or geographic location."[179] Thus, accessibility to the courts should not be dependent on income and influence. Accessibility is often measured by examining the legal aid and public defender systems and examining hours of access. Access is also measured by the time it takes to get a case heard and adjudicated and the direct and indirect costs of litigation.

In many countries in Latin America, few people living in rural areas have access to the courts. Edgardo Buscaglia claimed that peasants living in Peru had to travel more than 50 km to reach a court, making it difficult to access formal channels of justice.[180] According to a UNDP 2004 survey of 19 countries in Latin America only 18.1 percent claimed that poor people have their rights respected by the court system.

The slow pace of the justice system also affects accessibility in Latin America. Those with money can pay bribes to expedite matters, which

---

[175]Chemin (2009: 113).
[176]Ibid.
[177]Ibid., 115.
[178]Prillaman (2000).
[179]Staats et al. (2005: 79); Prillaman (2000: 18).
[180]Buscaglia (1998).

leads to uneven access to justice.[181] For many citizens in Latin America, accessing the courts is difficult. There is often no access to translators and no help for illiterates. In Guatemala's case, there are language barriers for disadvantaged groups. In many Latin American countries, there are also few public defenders and court costs are prohibitively high for people from lower economic groups.[182] The poor accused are forced to await their trial languishing in jails. Many prisoners "disappear into the morass of an administrative apparatus that cannot track their whereabouts much less ensure a prompt trial."[183]

Accessibility to the courts in Africa is another pressing problem all around Africa. In Ghana, many citizens could not get access to justice because they could not afford it.[184] In the DRC only 20 percent of the population had access to the formal judicial system.[185] High legal costs and confusing rigid procedures keep poor litigants out of court. South Africa has addressed this problem by creating special courts, called Equality Courts, which are designed to be accessible to all South Africans. The problem is that they still remain unknown and underutilized.[186]

The procedures, formalities, and languages used by the courts disconnect them from the majority of Africans.[187] The procedures resemble "a game conducted in a foreign language."[188] The few instances where Africans interact with the courts systems are only as a criminal defendant or witness in a criminal trial.[189]

While great efforts have been made to improve accessibility in Singapore (see case study), other countries, such as Cambodia, Vietnam, and Indonesia, have many barriers due to little access to information and high costs of legal services. In the Philippines, only 5 percent of people who had a debt collection dispute went to court, and none of those surveyed had their conflict resolved in less than a year.[190]

For most of the countries in the region, the hours of court access are limited. Moreover, the system of legal aid, which was among the world's best in Soviet times, has declined in states like Russia. There is no legal aid available for complaints against government officials. Though legal aid is available to veterans and the disabled, legal aid is only available to

---

[181]In cases such as Argentina, Brazil, Ecuador, and Venezuela, the bribes offered to the courts constitute an additional cost of 8–12 percent (Buscaglia 1998: 11).
[182]Buscaglia et al. (1995: 9).
[183]Centeno (2002: 8).
[184]Mangu (2009: 15).
[185]Savage (2006: 6).
[186]Kaersvang (2008: 4–9).
[187]Ibid., 31.
[188]Ibid., 64.
[189]Ibid., 61.
[190]Rule of Law Index, in The World Justice Project.

low-income persons in criminal cases and a small group of civil cases. In Russia, Putin has tried to make the courts more accessible by ensuring that information about the courts is readily available and by making the courts user-friendly.[191]

In sum, independence, integrity and accountability, transparency and efficiency, and equal access are the key defining features of high-quality judicial institutions. They help to improve the impartiality of the judicial system and ensure that laws are interpreted and enforced in a just manner that is consistent across cases. Judicial institutions that lack these features are of low quality. Citizens cannot expect that they will be treated in an unbiased manner nor that existing laws and legal precedents will drive decisions. In the section that follows, we offer a few case studies to illustrate these points, before turning to the relationship between judicial institutional quality, the rule of law, and property rights enforcement.

Case studies

The judicial institutions in Singapore represent an ideal case in terms of integrity, accountability, efficiency, transparency, and equal access. Though the autonomy of the courts has been questioned, Singapore has ensured that the rule of law is adhered to as consistently as possible. There are several features of the judicial institutions in Singapore that are worth providing further detail.

Singapore has prioritized creating high-quality judicial institutions by ensuring that the staff is qualified and well taken care of. The recruitment process for the judicial institutions in Singapore is rigorous and judges are regarded with high esteem in society. Judges are recruited that have already amassed years of experience working in the public sector. Though judges must tread carefully when ruling on politically sensitive matters, they do not face constant political interference, and usually have long careers.[192] Judges in Singapore are also *well paid*. A Supreme Court judge earns US$500,000 a year.[193]

Singapore, in particular, has made great strides in improving the integrity of its judicial institutions through its adoption of a set of ten "commandments," which detail its approach to judicial integrity. This includes tenets such as "clear ethical markers and guidelines for judges" and "performance standards for the judiciary and the judges."[194]

---

[191]Solomon (2008).
[192]The impeachment process for judges is a lengthy one, but the president does exercise discretionary power. Worthington (2001: 498).
[193]Dung (2003).
[194]US AID (2009: 8).

The judiciary regularly monitors its own performance to assess how the judicial institutions can be improved. The courts use a research and statistics unit to gather information about "emerging trends in crimes, the causes of criminal behavior, and the effectiveness of sentencing options."[195] Other court programs and rehabilitation programs are also evaluated.[196]

The judiciary in Singapore is also committed to ensuring that judges continue to be trained after they've been appointed. Seminars are held that emphasize judicial skills and professional knowledge. Training has been provided in mediation and negotiation. Since the judicial institutions in Singapore use the latest technology, all those in the legal profession are offered free workshops to provide awareness of the new technologies being used.[197]

Singapore is also the model state in terms of judicial efficiency. Reforms have taken place focusing on aggressive case management and alternative dispute resolution. Cases are heard within weeks of being filed.[198] All of these reforms have been aided through using technical innovation.[199] Since 1995, case information is publicly available online. Technology is used to videotape testimonies for foreign witnesses, to record oral testimonies, and to file and manage cases. Electronic kiosks are used to pay certain fines to avoid court appearances.[200]

The judiciary in Singapore also receives high marks for access and fairness. Survey research indicated that 97 percent of the people interviewed agreed that the courts administer justice fairly to all.[201] As many as 80 percent felt that the court fees are affordable and 95 percent agreed that mediation services have made it more affordable to access justice.[202]

Singapore has consistently received high marks on the rule of law index and it also registers as one of the countries with the lowest scores on the corruption index. This has translated into higher levels of foreign investment and economic growth. Singapore ranks high on the ease of doing business index, and much of this is due to the quality of its judicial institutions, to

---

[195]Blochlinger (2000: 606).
[196]Ibid., 607. Surveys of the judiciary have indicated that it is well respected. As many as 97 percent surveyed claimed that they have full confidence in the fair administration of justice, regardless of language, race, religion, or class and 98 percent agreed that the courts independently administer justice according to law (Subordinate Courts of Singapore, Research Bulletin No. 23: Survey on Public Attitudes & Perceptions of the Singapore Subordinate Courts; from ibid., 615).
[197]Ibid., 607.
[198]Ibid., 601.
[199]Ibid., 593.
[200]Ibid., 602.
[201]Ibid., 614.
[202]Ibid. citing the Subordinate Courts of Singapore, Research Bulletin No. 23: Survey on Public Attitudes & Perceptions of the Singapore Subordinate Courts.

provide certainty to the business community that contracts are honored, and that any conflict will be adjudicated in a fair and timely manner.

One of the modest success stories in Africa has been the judicial reform that took place in Rwanda from 2003 to 2004. Several important improvements were made to the judicial institutions, which bear noting. There is now lifetime appointment for Supreme Court justices, who are appointed by the president after consultation with the cabinet and election by the senate. The executive does not have a role in the appointment of the other judges.[203] All potential judges have to be legally qualified. Judges also enjoy security of tenure until retirement unless they are found guilty of serious misconduct or incapacity.[204]

To maintain integrity and accountability, the Office of Ombudsman can submit complaints received to the courts about the behavior of some judicial officers, delays, and hearing of cases.[205] Judges also have to be persons of integrity and cannot have a record of misconduct or corruption. There is now a Code of Ethics for judges that requires impartiality, integrity, and diligence

Judges and court personnel with a record of corruption are dismissed.[206] Judges cannot be involved in business activities that may compromise their independence.[207] Skills have been enhanced through various training programs, which have received support from the international community. Efforts have also been made to make proceedings quicker. The procedure is simplified to make cases move faster.[208] Though judicial independence in Rwanda is still a work in progress, it is undeniable that important changes have taken place for the better. This has all contributed to the perception that Rwanda has a high regard for the rule of law, and correspondingly high growth rates have ensued since the end of the conflict.[209]

High-quality judicial institutions and the rule of law

High-quality judicial institutions are often associated with the rule of law. Because of the frequency with which the two concepts are conflated, it is worth discussing briefly what the rule of law means and how it differs theoretically from the quality of a state's judicial institutions.

---

[203]Rugege (2006: 417).
[204]Ibid., 424.
[205]Ibid., 419.
[206]Ibid., 420.
[207]Ibid., 421.
[208]Ibid.
[209]Ibid.

The rule of law is a concept that is promoted as critical to development and stability by multiple international organizations, including the United Nations and the World Bank, as well as the state-building literature.[210] As Thomas Carothers writes, "one cannot get through a foreign policy debate these days without someone proposing the rule of law as the solution to the world's troubles."[211]

The rule of law is defined as the following:

> A principle in governance in which all persons, institutions and entities, public and private, including the State itself, are accountable to laws that are publicly promulgated, equally enforced and independently adjudicated, and which are consistent with international human rights norms and standards. It requires, as well, measures to ensure adherence to the principles of supremacy of the law, equality before the law, accountability to the law, fairness in the application of the law, separation of powers, participation in decision-making, legal certainty, avoidance of arbitrariness and procedural and legal transparency.[212]

This definition makes clear that it is impossible to have the rule of law without high-quality judicial institutions, which are vital to ensuring that judicial decisions are unbiased and transparent and that judicial officials have integrity and independence from political meddling and are accountable for their actions.

The definition also illustrates, however, that high-quality judicial institutions cannot by themselves ensure the rule of law. For example, the definition states that laws must conform to international human rights norms and standards. Though a consequence of high-quality judicial institutions is that existing laws are interpreted and enforced in an unbiased manner, the *content* of these laws falls outside of the domain of the judicial apparatus. Law-making is the responsibility of the state's political institutions. The same is true regarding the requirement of participatory decision-making. It is up to the state's political institutions, not judicial institutions, to ensure that decisions reflect the viewpoints of more than a single individual.

This distinction holds even if we rely on different definitions of the rule of law. Lawrence Solum, for example, identifies seven requirements of the rule of law.[213] Many of these pertain to judicial institutions, such as the requirements that "arbitrary decisions by government officials must not serve as the basis for legal verdicts" and "similar cases must be treated in an equivalent manner." Another requirement, however, is that "legal rules must be

---

[210]See, for example, Ottaway (2002: 1001–23).
[211]Carothers (1998: 95).
[212]United Nations, Rule of Law, www.un.org/en/ruleoflaw/index.shtml.
[213]Solum (1994: 120–4).

stated in general terms and not aimed at particular individuals or groups," which clearly is not up to the state's judicial apparatus to assure.[214] Julius Court et al. indirectly get at this distinction when they write that the role of law is to subject human conduct to the governance of rules.[215] They add that this entails not only the rules themselves (which we argue fall into the domain of the state's political institutions), "but also the ways in which these rules are applied in society" (which we argue falls into the domain of the state's judicial institutions).[216]

The prevalence of the rule of law has a "significant positive impact on growth."[217] The rule of law index averages the indicators of government commitment to its contractual engagements, risk of expropriation, and quality of institutions (including the judiciary).

Despite the fact that high-quality judicial institutions and the rule of law are concepts that are often discussed interchangeably, a high-caliber judiciary is but one requirement of the rule of law. While reform of the judiciary is essential to promoting the rule of law, it does not ensure it.[218] Because we seek to isolate the components of states' institutions that matter for political stability and economic performance in this study, we focus on the factors that underlie the quality of states' judicial institutions, as opposed to those that promote the rule of law.

High-quality judicial institutions and property rights

Property rights refer to the authority to determine how a resource is used. (In practice, the term typically refers to private property rights, as opposed to governmental property rights.) With property rights, individuals have the exclusive right to the services of the resource, as well as the right to delegate, rent, or sell it.[219] Property rights are typically viewed as a precondition for the rule of law, the idea being that demand for the enforcement of these rights leads to the development of the rule of law.[220] Whether property rights *exist* is a decision that is up to the state's political institutions, as are decisions regarding the legality of government expropriations of property. Whether property rights are *enforced*, by contrast, is largely up to the state's judicial institutions.

---

[214]Ibid.
[215]Court et al. (2003).
[216]Ibid., 5.
[217]Englebert and Tull (2008).
[218]Webber (2007).
[219]Alchian (2008).
[220]Hoff and Stiglitz (2005).

Property rights enforcement is often touted as a sign of high-quality judicial institutions and of judicial independence, in particular.[221] The argument is that when judicial institutions are not subject to political interference they are more capable of protecting private interests.[222] Therefore, whether property rights are enforced is an *indicator* of the quality of judicial institutions (namely judicial independence), but not necessarily a *direct* measure of it. It is quite possible, for example, that a state's judicial institutions are able to enforce property rights, but are subject to political intrusion in other spheres. It is also possible that property rights enforcement is nonexistent, not due to the politicization of the judiciary, but because these rights do not exist in the first place.

Like the rule of law, property rights enforcement falls into the domain of both the state's political and judicial institutions. Because both spheres are involved, emphasizing property rights' enforcement, as opposed to the specific features of the judicial apparatus, is less conducive to the provision of specific policy guidance for judicial reform.

Because in this study we are interested in the relationship between specific features of state institutions and the outcomes they produce, we do not focus on property rights here. We simply note that disentangling the relationship between the state's judicial institutions and the likelihood of property rights enforcement remains a fruitful area for future research.

Measuring the quality of judicial institutions

To our knowledge, cross-national measures of the quality of judicial institutions are largely unavailable to researchers.[223] The vast majority of existing measures either: (1) do not isolate judicial institutions from the outcomes they produce, or (2) do not isolate judicial institutions from other state institutions. To be fair, this is primarily due to the fact that these measures are not intended to capture judicial institutional quality, but rather other similar concepts, the most notable being the rule of law. We review these existing measures here.

The first measure we discuss comes from the United Nations, which, through its World Governance Survey, aggregates governance information from surveys conducted in a cross-section of developing countries. One of

---

[221]Although independent judicial institutions are not the only types of institutions that can help provide credible commitments to property rights, they are among the most important (see Moustafa (2003: 888)).

[222]World Bank (2002: 129); Collier and Gunning, (1999a).

[223]For example, Business International compiled an index for judicial reliability that was used in Paulo Mauro's 1995 study on corruption, but to our knowledge this index is not publicly available.

the areas the survey targets is the judiciary. Assessments of the judiciary deal with "how easily members of the public have access to justice, how transparently justice is being administered, how accountable judges are, how open national rights regimes are to international legal norms, and what the scope is for non-judicial forms of conflict."[224] Though the first three components explicitly capture features of judicial institutions, the last two do not. The survey's assessments of the judiciary therefore appear to be more suitable proxies for the rule of law than for the quality of states' judicial institutions.

Political Risk Services' International Country Risk Guide (ICRG) also offers a variable, law and order, that captures the strength and impartiality of the legal system.[225] Though the concept of law and order is conceptually similar to the quality of the state's judicial institutions, practically speaking, the variable measures both outcomes and institutional features. Countries are given low rankings on this variable, for example, if they have high crime rates, which are themselves a potential consequence of low-quality judicial institutions. Issues such as these make this variable a poor measure of judicial quality, as some researchers have noted.[226]

Another major indicator available to researchers is the World Justice Project's Rule of Law Index. The index assesses (in a cross-section of countries) the extent to which states adhere to the rule of law, defined as "a system in which no one, including the government, is above the law; where laws protect fundamental rights; and where justice is available to all."[227] It comprises country scores on eight factors: Limited Government Powers, Absence of Corruption, Order and Security, Fundamental Rights, Open Government, Effective Regulatory Enforcement, Effective Civil Justice, and Effective Criminal Justice.[228] Most of these factors, however, do not exclusively capture features of the state's judicial institutions; all of them either blend features of judicial institutions with those of other state institutions or with the outcomes they produce.[229] This is not surprising, given the organization's goal in producing the index: "For the most part, our focus is

---

[224]Court et al. (2002: 27).

[225]"International Country Risk Guide Methodology" (2012).

[226]Staats et al. (2005: 81).

[227]Note that because this definition of the rule of law includes the provision that laws protect citizens' rights, it also encompasses more than what a state's judicial institutions could be expected to provide. The World Justice Project, Rule of Law Index, http://worldjusticeproject. org/rule-of-law-index/.

[228]Botero and Ponce (2011: 1–120).

[229]As examples of this, Limited Government Powers includes a measure of the freedom of the press, Open Government includes a measure of the clarity of state laws, and Effective Regulatory Enforcement includes a measure of whether the government expropriates private property (an outcome of the absence of judicial independence, but not a feature of the state's judicial institutions).

on the rule of law *outcomes;* as opposed to the institutions means or *inputs . . .* to attain them" (italics in original).[230]

The factor Effective Civil Justice is perhaps the exception. This factor is intended to capture whether "ordinary people can resolve their grievances through formal institutions of justice in a peaceful and effective manner."[231] It is measured using a number of sub-indicators, including the public's general awareness of available remedies and whether there are procedural hurdles or other impediments to access to formal dispute resolution systems. Though this factor does not directly measure the features of judicial institutions discussed here, it serves as a reasonable proxy for the overall quality of the judicial apparatus. To our knowledge, no studies have used country scores on this factor to evaluate how the quality of judicial institutions affects outcomes of interest.

In addition, the World Bank's Worldwide Governance Indicators project (WGI) offers a measure of the rule of law as part of its cross-national indicator of governance. This measure is intended to capture "perceptions of the extent to which agents have confidence in and abide by the rules of society, and in particular the quality of contract enforcement, property rights, the police, and the courts, as well as the likelihood of crime and violence."[232] As this description makes clear, features of the state that could potentially affect key outcomes of interest (like the quality of the courts) are grouped together with these very outcomes (like the quality of contract enforcement and the likelihood of crime and violence). Though this measure is useful for capturing the rule of law, it is of limited utility for researchers interested in capturing the quality of judicial institutions.

The Heritage Foundation also has a measure of property rights protection (as part of its Index of Economic Freedom) that includes an assessment of judicial independence.[233] This measure captures the extent to which laws exist that protect private property and the degree to which they are enforced. Though judicial independence is part of this measure, it cannot be used in isolation from it. A further problem is that judicial corruption (an outcome) is also part of the measure, lumping together outcomes with features of the judiciary.

In sum, few cross-national indicators exist for researchers interested in assessing the quality of states' judicial institutions and their underlying features.[234] Part of the problem is that gathering the data to do so is not an easy task. As Joseph L. Staats et al. point out, "accumulating data sufficient to measure judicial performance across all its dimensions for a

---

[230]Botero and Ponce (2011: 16).
[231]Ibid., 14.
[232]Kaufmann et al. (2009: 6).
[233]2012 Index of Economic Freedom, www.heritage.org/index/property-rights.
[234]See Staats et al. (2005).

single country is difficult enough, but the generation of data across multiple countries poses an even greater challenge."[235] Yet, at the same time, the task is not an impossible one. A number of studies have compiled judicial quality data for specific regions, for example.[236] There are also studies that have identified potential models for surveys in this area. USAID, for one, has compiled a fairly exhaustive list of sample questions.[237] These questions are intended to be used by within-country development officials to assess levels of judicial corruption, but many of them would be suitable for capturing the quality of the state's judicial institutions. The majority lend themselves well to measuring specific features of the judicial apparatus, including all of the features identified in this chapter. William C. Prillaman also identifies ways to measure the quality of judicial institutions, including assessments of case management methods and the duration of trials, as do Edgardo Buscaglia and Maria Dakolias, who create a methodology to assess judicial efficiency.[238]

Perhaps the greater roadblock to compiling measures of judicial institutional quality is that doing so is not the current focal point of the development community, which primarily funds such large-scale data collection efforts.[239] Instead, the emphasis is on the broader concept of the rule of law. We argue, however, that because the rule of law blurs together the political and judicial domains, it is less informative for providing policy guidance.[240] Though we can examine how the rule of law affects key outcomes, when we focus on the rule of law as opposed to the quality of judicial institutions, it is far more difficult to offer concrete suggestions regarding where states should direct their reform efforts. Should resources be devoted to changing the types of laws that are implemented, increasing the quality of the judicial apparatus, or both? The same issues arise when the focus is on property rights enforcement. A more narrow focus on the judicial institutions of the state, as opposed to the rule of law, would enable more precise policy guidance regarding the features of judicial institutions that are particularly important for improving state performance.

---

[235]Ibid., 79.
[236]See, for example, ibid.
[237]See appendix B in US AID (2009).
[238]Buscaglia and Dakolias (1999).
[239]The World Bank (2002: 120) notes that an additional problem is most governments do not monitor the performance of their judiciaries.
[240]Prillaman (2000) notes that judicial reform efforts should not isolate a single feature and improve it independently of others, as "one positive reform does not inevitably lead to another" (6). Yet at the same time, it is possible that some features matter very little for government performance and should therefore not be targeted in the first place. Until we have a better understanding of which features matter for outcomes, we will lack a starting place for carrying out efforts at judicial reform.

Key findings

Because cross-national measures of the quality of judicial institutions are largely unavailable to researchers, few studies have examined how judicial institutional quality (explicitly) affects key outcomes of interest. Even fewer have looked at how the underlying features of these institutions factor in. The overarching focus instead has been on the rule of law, property rights enforcement, and governance more generally and their consequences.

Economic performance

Those studies that have taken up the topic of judicial institutional quality have primarily used small-scale surveys of public perceptions of the strengths and weaknesses of the judicial system to capture the concept.[241] Most of these studies have been devoted to the impact of these institutions on economic outcomes.

This is perhaps unsurprising given the strong research tradition that exists examining the relationship between property rights enforcement and the rule of law. Theoretically, the argument is that if property rights are insecure due to the risk of government expropriation, people will work less and invest little, hurting the growth of the economy.[242] The basic idea is similar with the rule of law: when investors are concerned about the maintenance of law and order they will be less likely to invest, and the economy will suffer as a result.[243] A number of studies have empirically examined these relationships and found evidence that supports the expectations.[244] Property rights enforcement and the rule of law are shown to contribute to development, economic growth, and the welfare of citizens.[245,246]

Though property rights enforcement and the rule of law are not synonymous with the quality of judicial institutions (as discussed above), there are a number of reasons to expect judicial institutional quality to affect economic performance as well.[247] As Richard Messick points out, there are two main hypotheses that have been put forth to explain this relationship.[248] The first hypothesis is that high-quality judicial systems increase

---

[241]World Bank (2002: 120).
[242]Barro (2000).
[243]Ibid.
[244]There are, of course, a handful of studies that question this relationship. See, for example, Hewko (2002).
[245]See, for example, North and Thomas (1970); North (1981); Knack and Keefer (1995); Engerman and Sokoloff (2002).
[246]See also Joireman (2004).
[247]Indeed, this relationship is often alluded to in the literature (see, for example, Messick 1999).
[248]Ibid.

economic growth because they lead to property rights enforcement, checks on government abuses of power, and the upholding of the rule of law. The second hypothesis is that they do so by enabling economic exchanges between private actors.

According to Messick, there is tentative, indirect support for both hypotheses. The problem is that most studies examining this subject rely on questionable measures of the quality of judicial institutions, do not adequately address the potential endogeneity of the relationship (in that positive economic performance could also impact judicial quality), and do not rule out competing explanations.[249] For reasons such as these, the consensus among researchers is that the evidence supporting the expectation that high-quality judicial institutions improve economic performance is still uncertain.[250] As Court et al. conclude, "research on the impact of the judiciary on human development remains thin and more work is required."[251]

The lack of empirical work devoted to the relationship between the quality of judicial institutions and key outcomes of interest is perhaps even more surprising given the abundance of international development resources devoted to judicial reform.[252] A host of international organizations, such as the World Bank and USAID, have spent millions of dollars to modernize the judicial branches of governments, so much so that the "the majority of developing countries and former socialist states are receiving assistance of some kind to help reform courts, prosecutors' offices, and the other institutions that together constitute the judicial system."[253, 254] This is occurring despite the fact that more information needs to be known about the impact of judicial institutions on economic performance.[255] As Prillaman writes, "it is difficult if not impossible to determine whether a judicial reform program is having success without a clear sense of what one is measuring, what variables serve as indicators, and whether and how those factors affect other

---

[249]This is noted in ibid.
[250]Prillaman (2000); Court et al. (2003). There are, of course, a few exceptions to this. Burnetti et al. (1998), for example, examine how uncertainty over the judicial process affects economic growth. Using a survey of representatives in the private sector in Latin America and Southeast Asia, they find that in countries where respondents do not feel the judicial process was transparent, economic growth is lower. Specifically, the extent to which private actors expect judicial proceedings to be vague and arbitrary explains 23 percent of per capita growth rates in the countries surveyed. They argue that this finding is due to the fact that lack of transparency in the judicial system deters investment, which in turn lowers growth.
[251]Court et al. (2003: 9).
[252]Messick (1999).
[253]Ibid., 117.
[254]The World Bank has stated their position on the matter very clearly. As they see it, well-functioning courts boost economic performance by upholding the rule of law and controlling government abuses.
[255]Ibid., 117.

aspects of the judiciary."[256] Clearly there is a strong need for future studies to investigate the relationship between the quality of judicial institutions and economic performance.

Other studies have argued that there is a direct link between the quality of judicial institutions and economic growth.[257] Scholars have reasoned that since judicial independence is based on the law, it is the most reliable guarantor of protection of economic measures and their enforcement.[258] For example there are many repercussions when commercial courts are weak. This makes contract enforcement difficult. Businesses thus must restrict themselves to long-standing clients rather than risk contracts being repudiated by new clients.[259] Scholars have noted that "unreliable courts" can have an impact on economic growth.[260]

One study examined the influence that judicial independence has on GDP growth per capita. Looking at a sample of 57 countries, it was argued that countries that benefit from de facto judicial independence experience higher levels of economic growth.[261] Judicial independence reassures investors and others involved in economic activities that their property and investments will be safe and that economic activity will not be disrupted.[262] If a government reneges on a promise, an investor can take the case to court. The predictability provided by the government leads to higher levels of investment and higher levels of growth.[263] For example, in the case of Egypt, some scholars have noted that the lack of judicial autonomy has led to a dearth of investment and an estimated $20 billion being held abroad in the 1960s.[264]

Aside from economic performance, a handful of studies on judicial institutional quality have looked at the relationship between the quality of judicial institutions and the likelihood of *judicial corruption*. To do so, these studies rely on case studies and their own survey data. The central finding to emerge from them is that corruption is more likely when procedures are numerous, complex, and lack transparency and when uncertainty exists over existing laws and regulations due to things like the absence of a legal

---

[256]Prillaman (2000: 5).
[257]Chemin (2009). Institutions may also exert a fundamental impact on the contracting behaviour of firms as countries with better judiciaries may have more complicated contracts (Chemin 2009; Knack and Keefer 1995).
[258]Rugege (2006: 416).
[259]Widner (2001).
[260]Collier and Gunning (1999a: 10).
[261]Feld and Voigt (2003: 497–527).
[262]Rugege (2006: 425).
[263]Feld and Voigt (2003).
[264]Moustafa (2003: 888).

data base.[265] In addition, one study has shown that perceived judicial independence is correlated with the perceived extent of judicial corruption, as well as levels of organized crime.[266]

Because of their specificity, these studies lend themselves to fairly clear policy guidelines for reducing judicial corruption. For example, Buscaglia writes that Chile and Uganda have reduced judicial corruption by enacting a simple procedural code.[267] Singapore and Costa Rica did the same by creating additional administrative support offices to support the courts in areas such as budget and personnel management and case and cash flows.[268]

One other area that has been addressed in the literature is *credit market performance*. Tulio Jappelli et al. examine the relationship between judicial efficiency, as measured by the length of trials and the number of backlogs of pending trials, and the performance of credit markets.[269] They do so using data collected across the provinces of Italy. They find that greater judicial efficiency leads to a higher volume of lending and fewer credit constraints. Their conclusion is that "judicial inefficiency has high economic costs in credit markets."[270] Another study looking at India argues that poor and inefficient judicial institutions may lessen the amount of credit available by increasing opportunistic behavior in borrowers. As borrowers anticipate that creditors will not be able to recover their loans easily and cheaply via courts since they move too slowly, borrowers are more tempted to default. Creditors respond to this strategic behavior by reducing credit availability.[271] In contrast, judicial reform may improve access to credit for entrepreneurs. It may make individuals more confident in obtaining loans, which may lead to more entrepreneurship.[272] We note, however, that because the evidence here used is restricted to Italy and India respectively, it is possible that this relationship does not hold when applied elsewhere to the developing world.

Low-quality judicial institutions may also be slow and inefficient, which may then be associated with *firm performance*. In Pakistan and India, slow and inefficient judicial institutions lead to more breaches of contract and a preference for family ownership of firms. All of these factors lead to poor firm performance.

---

[265]Buscaglia and Dakolias (1999); Buscaglia (1997).
[266]Buscaglia and van Dijk (2003: 1–32).
[267]Buscaglia (2001).
[268]Ibid.
[269]Jappelli et al. (2005: 233–49).
[270]Ibid., 240.
[271]Chemin (2009).
[272]Ibid., 117.

Organized crime

Other areas of study have examined the connection between weak judicial institutions and *organized crime*. Scholars have argued that "organized crime thrives in a society with weak (judicial) institutions."[273] Therefore, to deal effectively with crime, government must strengthen their judicial institutions."[274]

Analysis "shows that judicial independence is strongly related to levels of organized crime."[275] It was argued that "independent judges were less vulnerable to corruption and better able to implement repressive actions against organized crime, even when the political system and other areas of the state had been captured by organized crime."[276] Unpredictable judicial rulings have been linked to higher levels of organized crime. When judicial institutions are independent, judicial rulings are more consistent.

Among the factors making it possible for organized crime to capture the court system, the most significant are procedural complexity and abuses of substantive judicial discretion. The present analysis verified those links (e.g. that higher degrees of procedural complexity were linked to judicial corruption and to higher levels of organized crime). The link between the abuse of substantive judicial discretion on the one hand and judicial corruption and increases in organized crime on the other was confirmed through another analysis. Moreover, lack of predictability of judicial rulings was linked to higher levels of both court corruption and organized criminal activities. Rulings are also more consistent when the case management system is uniform and transparent.[277]

The World Bank claims that organized crime persists due to high rates of impunity.[278] Criminals who commit crimes once are more likely to commit crimes again with low frequency of punishment.[279] Therefore, it is critical that judicial institutions convict criminals when crimes are committed and offer adequate punishment. If the judicial institutions are not autonomous, upright, and accountable, judges may be easily bought off and organized crime will persist.

In Colombia, weak judicial institutions have enabled organized crime to thrive. Judicial decisions are heavily influenced by political considerations, intimidation, and bribery.[280] Criminals have gone

---

[273]Bibes (2001: 255).
[274]Ibid., 256.
[275]Buscaglia and van Dijk (2003: 12).
[276]Ibid.
[277]Buscaglia et al. (1995: 2).
[278]Fajnzylber et al. (1998: 31).
[279]Davis (1988).
[280]Buscaglia et al. (1998: 2).

unpunished and the justice system was unable to produce any results. The conviction rate was only 5 percent. Criminal organizations operated with impunity. Laws were even rewritten to suit the needs of drug kingpin Pablo Escobar. Sentences were reduced and criminals who surrendered to authorities were offered level benefits. Rulings have also favored those with power. Drug lords have been given light sentences while peasants involved in the cultivation of drugs are given 12-year sentences. In Mexico, there are high levels of impunity for those who are able to buy their way out of jail.[281] In most cases only the poor and the weak are punished.[282] It's therefore not surprising that Latin America's criminal investigation and adjudication systems rank among the worst in the world.[283]

Moving forward

Judicial institutions clearly fulfill an important function in the state. They play a key role in the arbitration of disputes, helping to ensure that a formal third party exists to mediate conflicts, enforce laws, and distribute judgments. Without them, states would lack social order.

In this chapter, we reviewed the main responsibilities of judicial institutions. We also discussed the particular features of judicial institutions that make them high or low in quality. With high-quality judicial institutions, judicial decisions are delivered in a fair and unbiased fashion based on existing laws or legal precedents. The opposite is true with low-quality judicial institutions. High-quality judicial institutions give citizens confidence in the state itself; low-quality judicial institutions, by contrast, lead to a disillusioned citizenry that lacks faith in the system.

To highlight these differences, we discussed multiple examples and case studies to illustrate the extent to which judicial institutional quality varies across states and affects state performance.

Last, we discussed key work that remains to be done in this field. We assessed that few cross-national measures exist for researchers interested in examining the consequences of high-quality judicial institutions. As a result, few studies have been carried out in this area.

Gaining a better understanding of the particular features of judicial institutions that affect key outcomes of interest, therefore, remains an important task. This is particularly true given evidence indicating that, in

---

[281]Bergman (2006: 218).
[282]Ibid.
[283]Rule of Law Index in The World Justice Project.

comparison to other institutions of the state, the quality of judicial institutions is particularly low in many developing countries.[284] Surveys point to the fact that the administration of justice is slow and often corrupt and citizens lack trust in the system itself. To be able to better guide efforts at judicial reform, future research on judicial institutional quality is clearly needed.

---

[284]Court et al. (2003).

CHAPTER SIX

Security institutions

Security institutions are the institutions of the state engaged in defense, the protection of citizens, control of borders, and law enforcement. They encompass any organization or agency authorized to threaten or use violence in order to protect the states and its citizens.[1] These include the military forces, police, paramilitary forces, militias, and, in some cases, the intelligence services.[2] The ministries of interior and defense are also typically part of the state's security institutions (as well as part of the administrative institutions). In this chapter, we examine the purpose of security institutions in the functioning of the state. We discuss what high-quality and low-quality security institutions look like in practice and outline the key features that differentiate them. We then offer examples and brief case studies to illustrate these points, and provide an overview of an array of violent non-state actors that challenge low-quality security institutions before turning to a discussion of how the quality of security institutions impact key outcomes of interest.

The role of security institutions in the state

Security institutions are responsible for providing public security. They have "a formal mandate to ensure the safety of the state and its citizens

---

[1]Ball and Brzoska (2002); Pion-Berlin (1992).
[2]Ball and Brzoska (2002: 8).

against acts of violence and coercion."[3] Their primary task is to guarantee the internal and external security of the citizenry.[4] Security institutions are necessary to provide order within the country's borders and to protect them from outside attacks.

These institutions have other tasks, as well. Like judicial institutions, security institutions are responsible for enforcing laws (as opposed to formulating them, which falls into the domain of the state's political institutions). Unlike judicial institutions, however, they do not interpret laws or distribute judgments. In a similar fashion, like administrative institutions, security institutions are responsible for helping to carry out state policies, but unlike administrative institutions, they are authorized to use force to do so.

In sum, security institutions are in charge of defending the state against external and internal threats, ensuring the control of the state's borders, protecting citizens from violence or harm, and enforcing the state's laws. What makes security institutions unique is their ability to use force to carry out these tasks.

Security institutions therefore provide a very distinct role for the state. Without them, the state is unable to fulfill its end of the social contract with its citizens. Citizens want protection. Therefore when security institutions are absent, non-state actors will emerge to fill this need instead (see section on Warlords).[5] For citizens, these alternatives are often lesser evils rather than preferred alternatives.[6] Because the provision of security is one of the primary responsibilities of the state, the performance of the state's security institutions heavily factors into citizens' perceptions of the state's legitimacy and performance.

We note that though law enforcement institutions are a component of the security apparatus, the bulk of the literature devoted to this sphere of the state focuses on military institutions. As a consequence, the discussion here primarily focuses on the military, though much of the same criteria apply to the police as well.

In addition, as with judicial institutions, security institutions are responsible for enforcing the law, but they do not play a direct role in shaping it. Because of this, they are not responsible for the quality of state laws. It is not up to the security apparatus to ensure that laws are respectful of human rights, for example. Security institutions are tasked with following the orders of the state's government (i.e. the political apparatus), even if these orders entail the use of force against citizens in ways that violate basic human rights.

---

[3]Ghani et al. (2005: 9).
[4]Wulf (2004).
[5]Bøås (2001); Reilly (2008: 17–32).
[6]Goldsmith (2002).

Categorization

Security institutions differ significantly in the extent to which they fulfill their key tasks. High-quality security institutions provide for internal order in the state and effectively defend it against external threats.[7] They ensure that the state exerts full control over its territory. High-quality security institutions also do not interfere in policy-making or try to govern. Instead, they focus their efforts on enforcing policies enacted by the state, always heeding orders by the state's political institutions.[8] This contrasts starkly with low-quality security institutions, which allow for societal disorder. Low-quality security institutions leave citizens vulnerable to harm and violence and are impotent in the face of threats from internal and external actors. They also breach the division between the political and the security spheres and seek to influence policy, either by disregarding orders from the state's political apparatus or by actively pursuing its overthrow. In rare and extreme cases, low quality security institutions can deteriorate and become collapsed. In this section, we discuss what these two institutional poles refer to in practice and the specific features that set them apart.

High-quality security institutions

High-quality security institutions are not necessarily characterized by their size, but rather their structure and the types of functions that they perform.[9] They are professionalized, meaning that they are well trained, well organized, well funded, and internally cohesive.[10] Professionalized security institutions are successful in war and other military encounters, protecting the state from external and internal threats. They are also effective in law enforcement, ensuring that protocols are followed and standards are adhered to.

In addition to being professionalized, high-quality security institutions are also accountable to civilians. This protects citizens from abuses of power by the security forces, while also restricting these forces from interfering in the political sphere. They should avoid being involved in civilian affairs such as entrepreneurship since this distracts the military from its prime objective of protecting the nation.

---

[7]MacDonald (1997).
[8]Lee (2005).
[9]Janowitz (1988: 7).
[10]Brzoska (2003); Huntington (1957).

Low-quality security institutions

Low-quality security institutions operate very differently than those high in quality. Their members lack proper training and, as such, are recruited not due to their qualifications but due to their social and/or ethnic backgrounds. These institutions receive inadequate funding (which leads to ungoverned spaces), hampering any efforts to improve training and adequately arm personnel. Low salaries are the norm, and members are often disgruntled. In other words, they lack professionalization.[11] As a result, low-quality security institutions perform poorly in combat and are ineffective at protecting citizens from threats. They enforce laws in an arbitrary manner, ignoring protocols and standards for law enforcement, should they exist.

Low-quality security institutions do not possess a monopoly over the legitimate use of force. The centralized regular army is counterbalanced by a parallel military unit, which has the responsibility of preventing the centralized military from staging a coup. Security institutions that face counterbalancing see their resources in both equipment and personnel being drained elsewhere.[12] Low-quality security institutions are also poorly organized, with an ambiguous and ever-changing internal hierarchy and structure. This contributes to an environment where members do not share a common sense of purpose.

Low-quality security institutions are also largely free from civilian accountability. They can engage in abuses of power with impunity, as their behavior largely goes unchecked.[13] The boundaries between the political and security spheres are not respected and interventions in politics, such as coups, are the norm.[14]

Collapsed security institutions

In rare cases, the low-quality security institutions have completely collapsed and a condition known as *warlordism* ensues. In these cases, the central security institutions no longer provide basic security and are replaced by armed non-state actors or "rule of the strong."[15] The security forces are no longer present in large swathes of the territory. In some cases, the military is longer being paid a salary and are given the go-ahead to fend for themselves.

---

[11]Perlmutter (1974). Some researchers (see, for example, Perlmutter 1974; Lee, 2005; and MacDonald 1997) refer to low-quality security institutions as praetorian. We do not use this term here because of the wide-ranging ways in which it is defined.
[12]Quinlivan (1999).
[13]MacDonald (1997).
[14]Perlmutter (1974).
[15]Zartman (1995).

For example in Zaire under Mobutu, the soldiers were so poorly paid that he gave them a blank check to ransom and loot to compensate for their low salaries. Troops were encouraged to plunder and pillage.[16] As revenues grew slim, financially pressed rulers in Sierra Leone directed soldier to figure out ways to pay themselves. "Operation Pay Yourself" gave soldiers the go-ahead to use force to shake the population for money. Government soldiers turned into rebels. Warlordism also developed in Somalia toward the end of Siad Barre's rule. Armed groups replaced the central security apparatus leading to anarchy.

Warlordism also developed in Afghanistan. When the Taliban government collapsed in late 2001, the interim Afghan government did not have the strength to establish much control over any territory outside of Kabul. Warlord armies after the fall of the Taliban numbered 750,000.[17] The rural areas of the south, east, west, and north were particularly dangerous. Because of the lack of law and order the border lands developed a *kalishnikov culture* of every man for himself.[18]

Warlordism also took over in Tajikistan. The government was only able to project power in selected parts of the country. In vast areas of the country, there was no government at all and the "state lost its meaning."[19] Warlords became incredibly powerful and President Emomali Rakhmononov (1992–) had to buy their support just to maintain himself in power.[20] Russia has subsequently had to be the guarantor of security in Tajikistan.[21]

Key features of high-quality security institutions

There are three features that set high-quality institutions apart:

1 *Professionalization*: Rigorous training requirements exist, promotions are based on merit, and budgets are sufficient allocated. This lowers the likelihood of corruption, disincentivizes political interference, increases performance in combat, and ensures effective law enforcement.

2 *Centralized military command structure*: The centralized military should have a monopoly over the legitimate use of force. It should not be forced to compete with parallel armies or personal security units. The creation of parallel armies, in particular, severely undermines the legitimacy and effectiveness of the central armed forces. A centralized military should also have a clear internal chain of command.

---

[16]Acemoglu et al. (2004).
[17]Giustozzi (2003: 4).
[18]Riedel (2008).
[19]Rotberg (2003: 245).
[20]Nourzhanov (2005: 109–30).
[21]Rotberg (2003: 16).

3 *Civilian accountability*: The security sector answers to the state's political institutions, reducing the likelihood of rogue behavior and protecting the boundary between the security and political spheres. The security sector should avoid involving itself in activities that can be accomplished by the civilian sector.

States that are characterized by these features have high-quality security institutions. States that possess one or neither of them, by contrast, have low-quality security institutions. This is because security institutions that are professionalized but not accountable to civilians can easily interfere in politics and stage coups.[22] As a well-organized and effective body, they possess all the tools to do so. Security institutions that are accountable to civilians but not professionalized, by contrast, are incapable of providing security. They are largely impotent and, as a result, leave their citizens vulnerable to threats and unprotected. Security institutions that compete with parallel armies do not possess a monopoly over the legitimate use of force and their resources are siphoned off to units that are assigned with *regime* protection not state protection. Professionalism, centralization, and civilian accountability are therefore needed for security institutions to be considered high in quality.[23] We discuss these three features in more detail in what follows.

Professionalization

Professionalization refers to the organization and expertise of the security apparatus as a whole. It has four components—rigorous training requirements, a clear internal chain of command, merit-based promotions, and sufficient budgets—each of which we examine in depth here.

Professionalization requires "specialized knowledge" and "established paths of recruitment," which can only be accomplished through the use of military colleges and/or special training programs as barriers of entry to the security forces.[24] Rigorous training requirements are therefore a key part of professionalization. They ensure that security personnel have the proper knowledge to carry out their responsibilities and are prepared for combat. They entail: (1) the use of an intense, high-caliber training program and (2) the requirement that members must pass this program before entering or moving forward within the security forces.

---

[22]Perlmutter (1969); Moran (1999).

[23]This need for a security apparatus that is strong enough to execute the orders of civilians, but not so strong that it ignores them, is referred to as the civil–military challenge (Feaver 1996).

[24]Moran (1999: 45); Bellin (2004: 146).

Proper *training programs* use modern curricula that emphasize physical and psychological preparation, technical expertise, morale building, and organization.[25] They focus on organizational integrity and fighting effectiveness.[26] They provide members with the skills necessary to work effectively, exposing them to new technology, increasing their proficiency with weapons, and helping them to coordinate tactical movements. They also improve their ability to adapt to new environments by exposing members to potential environmental changes and training them in ways to respond appropriately.[27]

Rigorous training programs also indoctrinate trainees with the values of the security apparatus, particularly its subordination to civilians. They seek to "replace the inductee's individual or civilian identity with a corporate spirit, or esprit de corps."[28] This contributes to a "sense of organic unity and consciousness of [trainees] as a group apart from laymen."[29] Trainees develop a corporate identity that is distinct from civilians.[30] This process increases the internal cohesion of the security apparatus, which in turn enhances its effectiveness.[31]

Many of the countries in Latin America have also received proper training, with national war colleges set up to provide more extensive programs for educating soldiers. The Brazilian military invested millions of dollars in giving its troops proper training. In contrast, while François Duvalier was in power in Haiti, he closed down the only military academy in Haiti.[32]

Because completion of a high-caliber training program is required to enter the state's security institutions, personnel bond quickly through their shared training experiences. According to Edward Shils and Morris Janowitz, for example, solidarity with comrades helped to motivate members of the German military: "as long as [the German soldier] felt himself to be a member of his primary group . . . his soldierly achievement was likely to be good."[33]

The militaries in Africa have also been poorly trained to deal with their specific security objectives and have suffered from low levels of morale.[34] Crawford Young and Thomas Turner write that the military under Mobutu had "legendary indiscipline" and demonstrated a "repeated incapacity" "to defeat even small and poorly armed foes."[35] Zairian troops under Mobutu were so poorly trained that they were unable to fight off a small group of

---

[25]Moran (1999).
[26]Shils and Janowitz (1948: 280–315).
[27]Huntington (1957).
[28]Lee (2005: 85).
[29]Huntington (1957: 26).
[30]Bellin (2004).
[31]Shils and Janowitz (1948).
[32]Pion-Berlin (1992: 151).
[33]Shils and Janowitz (1948: 281).
[34]Titley (2002: 44).
[35]Young and Turner (1985: 248).

1,500 mercenaries from Angola during 1978–9 even though Mobutu had received millions of dollars in military aid.

In Iraq, the elite Republican Guard received better training than the regular army, which made it difficult for the regular army to be effective in offensive operations.[36] The military had never received proper training, since it was forbidden to use live ammunition during training and no military exercise was allowed above the company level.[37] The Libyan military was also unable to coordinate its activities due to lack of training. As a result, Libya under Qaddafi performed terribly in Chad in the 1980s.[38]

This entry requirement also ensures that members of security institutions are *selected based on merit*, rather than on their political ties, social status, or ethnic group. This is important because it helps to prevent the security institutions from using their strength to discriminate against individuals who do not share their views or background.[39] Because only individuals who have completed the training program can enter the security apparatus in the first place, those individuals who lack the proper skills and aptitude are weeded out, increasing the caliber of the state's security institutions as a whole. Samuel Huntington writes, for example, that the Ottoman Ruling Institution retained its vitality and coherence only so long as entry was restricted and recruits subject to "an elaborate education, with selection and specialization at every stage."[40]

Many nonprofessionalized militaries recruit based on family, clan, ethnic, religious, and regional ties. Communal recruitment methods interfere with the quality of the troops.

Syria has had a long history of exploiting communal ties, dating back to the mandate period (after World War I) when French officers privileged religious minorities in the security apparatus. In Syria under the current Assad family, the Alawite groups are favored by the regime when it comes to military recruitment. Though only 10–12 percent of Syrians are Alawite, they account for 90 percent of the Syrian officer corps.[41]

The Bahraini military is also not a national army. It is composed completely of Sunni Muslims even though 70 percent of the country is Shiite. This may explain why Bahrain's Sunni army quickly confirmed its support for the Sunni monarchy of Bahrain, by suppressing the Shiite revolt in 2011.[42]

---

[36]Quinlivan (1999: 157).
[37]Pollack (2002).
[38]Black (2000: 1–30).
[39]Brzoska (2006: 1–13).
[40]Huntington (1968: 23).
[41]Rubin (2001: 119).
[42]Barany (2011).

Jordan and Morocco also have relied on tribal and Bedouin loyalties and male relatives have held key military posts.[43] In Jordan, Palestinians cannot rise above the rank of major or lieutenant colonel in combat units.[44] Though Palestinians constitute a majority of the population, there is a very limited number of Palestinians in the military.[45] Recruitment methods in the Lebanese military were also hampered by clear favoritism toward Maronite Christians since the military chief was always a Christian.

Military recruitment in Iraq under Saddam Hussein was based on loyalty and personal ties. In contrast to the original policy of the Ba'ath Party, Saddam Hussein retained access to party dossiers that carefully recorded the tribal associations of each member of the Ba'ath Party in order to serve as a method of recruitment. Family ties were deemed most important followed by tribal ties.[46] In addition, an overwhelming number of elite units in the military were Sunnis.

In Libya, Qaddafi recruited security and intelligence personnel primarily from the Margariha and Werfella clans. He relied on cronies and family members rather than individuals with experience. Family members were given key positions in the military and certain tribes were favored over others.[47] In contrast, in Egypt, Turkey, and Tunisia recruitment patterns are not entirely based on kinship and tribal affiliations. Turkey in particular has worked to create a professionalized military force that could be effective in battle against aggressive neighbors and be effective in guerrilla warfare against the Kurdistan Worker's Party (PKK) in the southeast.

In Africa, recruitment methods have often been based on loyalty and kinship ties. Troops were recruited in Zaire based on ethnicity. Mobutu personally controlled the military and primarily filled it with officers from his own region, Équateur (46 percent of the officer corps came from this region).[48] It was only close relatives, cronies, and members of the Ngbandi tribe that were granted the most important positions in the armed forces, making the military structure highly politicized.[49]

In Pakistan, recruitment and promotion was historically based on regional considerations with more than 75 percent of the military's recruits coming from five districts in Punjab.[50] This contrasts with Singapore, which has multiracial conscription.[51]

---

[43]Herb (1999: 159).
[44]Bellin (2004: 149).
[45]Rubin (2001: 52).
[46]Quinlivan (1999: 139).
[47]Black (2000: 11).
[48]Snyder (1992: 393).
[49]Acemoglu et al. (2004: 169).
[50]Talbot (2002: 53).
[51]Tan (2009: 1–32).

The second component of professionalization is *merit-based promotions*. According to Amos Perlmutter, professionalized security institutions have "established paths for career advancement," such that "promotion is based on performance not politics."[52] With merit-based promotions, clear guidelines exist stipulating the criteria used for promotion decisions; career advancement is based on individual qualifications above all else. In addition, there are standards in place for pay and benefits, career trajectories, and internal resource allotment.[53]

Beyond the obvious implications of merit-based promotions for increasing the caliber of the security apparatus, these guidelines also help to increase bonding among personnel. This occurs because there is a "dependable exchange between the service members and the institution, [such that] service member effort, loyalty, and continuous performance are traded for a sense of elevated purpose, compensation . . . and career progression."[54] Such bonding increases the effectiveness of the security institutions (as mentioned above), while also potentially deterring rogue behavior among members of the security forces.

With merit-based promotions, career advancement is driven by qualifications, as opposed to shared political ties, ethnicity, or social class. This makes it more difficult for the security apparatus to develop its own narrow base of societal support, decreasing its propensity to represent only particularistic interests.[55]

The existence of clear merit-based guidelines for promotions also deters political actors from intervening in the internal hierarchy of the state's security institutions. As Risa Brooks writes, "the tinkering of chains of command for political reasons significantly inhibits the effectiveness of Arab armies."[56] In addition, political interference with internal military promotions is known to be a major cause of military coups.[57] The establishment of clear rules dictating the criteria for promotions helps to limit this type of political involvement, thereby reducing the chances of a response from the security sector.

Merit-based promotions are therefore important because they increase the overall quality of security personnel, limit the development of security institutions that bias a single ethnic or other social group, and reduce the likelihood of civilian interference in the promotion process.

African militaries have often been weakened by arbitrary methods of promotion and dismissal. To create a sense of fear among members of the

---

[52]Perlmutter (1969: 388).
[53]Bellin (2004).
[54]Siebold (2007: 290).
[55]Feld (1975); Fields et al. (1998).
[56]Brooks (1998: 46).
[57]Nordlinger (1977); Geddes (2003).

military, Mobutu of Zaire purged over 10 percent of the most promising officers in 1978. Mobutu was particularly threatened by his elite advisers, such that he set in place a number of provisions to ensure that their competence was limited.

In Somalia under Siad Barre, promotions were also based on clan affiliation as the Mareehaan clans and to a lesser extent the Darood clan officers benefited at the expense of others. Family members were also given important military appointments. Loyalty was considered a more important attribute than merit and experience.[58]

In the Central African Republic, Jean-Bédel Bokassa preferred to surround himself with sycophants, and made sure that key security positions were held by his most loyal kinsmen.[59] Individuals viewed as remotely threatening were fired or reassigned if they were lucky; many simply disappeared.[60] For instance, in 1966 when Commander Martin Lingoupou proved to be too skilled and well liked, Bokassa fired him and he disappeared soon after.[61] Bokassa felt threatened by more qualified personnel; he craved "adulation and constant glorification."[62]

In Uganda, the officer corps was purged and soldiers loyal to Idi Amin have been promoted, in several cases from the rank of sergeant to colonel.[63] Promotions in the military were given to individuals who had little experience or education, and uneducated military officers were assigned important positions in the government.[64] Amin often chose illiterate advisers, as he resented any individuals who were better educated.[65] At one point, Amin even complained that some of his aides were "too competent."[66] For Amin, an individual's qualifications were unimportant; sycophants were preferred. Military strategy was often crafted with the help of his drinking buddies.[67]

In Togo, Gnassingbé Eyadéma allocated the majority of officer positions to his fellow ethnic Kabye group, even though they only comprise about 20 percent of the population. Senior commanders also came from his own village.[68]

In Pakistan under Zulifqar Bhutto (1971–7), drastic changes took place that affected the level of military professionalism. Under criticism by Islamists, Bhutto wanted to project an image of being a faithful adherent

---

[58]Compagnon (1992: 9).
[59]Titley (2002: 50).
[60]Ibid., 34, 39.
[61]Ibid., 45.
[62]Decalo (1985: 222).
[63]Decalo (1973: 113).
[64]Gertzel (1980: 470); Decalo (1985: 222).
[65]Ravenhill (1974: 248).
[66]Frantz and Ezrow (2009).
[67]Decalo (1985: 227).
[68]Decalo (1989).

to Islam. He sacked military officers who appeared not to be loyal enough to him. He replaced the chief of staff and several generals with those who were considered to be more politically pliable and surrounded himself with yes-men.[69]

In Saudi Arabia entire branches of the military and security forces are members of the royal family. Political reliability, nepotism and favoritism supersede merit in promotions as well.[70] Saudi Arabia has not adapted to the fact that a "modern military training and promotion must be based on performance and merit, not on birth, family and politics or social custom."[71] Saudi recruitment methods have led to a privileged class of the military that was entirely ineffective in battle.[72] Though the Saudi force is becoming more professionalized through more rigorous training methods, it still suffers from the patrimonial lines of promotion that encumber its capacity to defend itself.[73]

In Syria, loyalty is also an important consideration when it comes to military promotions. For example, a trusted friend of Hafez Assad was appointed to be the Syrian Air Force commander though he was not even a pilot. The elder Assad's son Bashar Assad has continued this tradition, purging anyone suspected of opposing his rule and rewarding those who are fiercely loyal.

In Iraq, Saddam Hussein never appointed any commander that had a military background.[74] Loyal but incompetent soldiers could be promoted whereas capable but possibly disloyal officers were demoted and put on long-term assignments (where they could lose their qualifications). Worse yet, they could be fired altogether or executed.[75]

Though most of the militaries in Latin America used a merit-based process for promotion, there have been a few exceptions. The military in the Dominican Republic under Rafael Trujillo also faced constant political interference. Promotions were entirely based on loyalty over merit and experience.[76] Rafael Trujillo's son was made a full colonel at the age of four and

---

[69]Khairan (2004: 61).

[70]Cordesman (2009: 106).

[71]Ibid., 144.

[72]Owen (1992: 180–93).

[73]Cordesman (2009: 106). Though Saudi Arabia still employs patrimonial methods of recruitment and promotion, the Saudi government has spent billions of dollars to upgrade its military and increase its training. Billions have been spent in Saudi Arabia to improve the quality of the military's equipment. From 1990 to 2006, the Saudi military received $62.7 billion in weapons and equipment (see Cordesman 2009: 4). The Saudis have ensured that their regular frontline forces routinely have the best equipment available in the Saudi arsenal (Quinlivan 1999: 158). Saudi Arabia has invested in a comprehensive system of military education starting from the cadet academy to the staff college (Cordesman 2009: 152).

[74]Hosmer (2007).

[75]Owen (1992).

[76]Wiarda (1968).

brigadier general at the age of nine, highlighting "the fact that the morale, autonomy and abilities of the armed forces were affected by nepotism." In Haiti, under François Duvalier, only those that he trusted were promoted.[77] He allowed poorly trained but highly loyal noncommissioned officers to rise quickly through the ranks, while depriving highly trained officers of career opportunities.[78]

The third component of professionalization is *sufficient budgets.* Sufficient budgets mean that the security institutions are allocated enough financial resources to adequately compensate and equip personnel and carry out operations and maintenance.[79] Budgets to pay for adequate security personnel on the ground have often been thin in many countries in Africa. Afrobarometer surveys in 2003 revealed that only 28 percent and 11 percent of localities recorded a visible police or army presence respectively.[80]

It is important for members of the state's security institutions to receive appropriate *salaries*, regardless of how serious the fiscal circumstances of the state are, because failure to do so can prompt decisions to intervene politically (i.e. stage coups) and increase the likelihood that personnel will engage in rogue behavior. As Robert Bates writes with respect to Mobutu of Zaire "When Mobutu was no longer able to pay his security forces in 1993, they rebelled and turned to looting . . . when left unpaid by their governments, specialists in violence can then pay themselves."[81]

This point is illustrated in Uganda. In the 1980s, "any soldier who needed money . . . would just pick an isolated . . . part of the road, put logs or chains across and wait for unfortunate travelers. These twentieth century highwaymen would rob anyone of anything they fancied: cash, watches, cassette radios, clothes, and the like."[82]

The Russian military, once one of the most professionalized military forces, has since the dissolution of the Soviet Union suffered from eroding levels of professionalism and institutional decay—something that scholars have noted may explain Russia's poor performance in its conflict against Chechen rebels.[83] Salaries are now too low to attract high-quality recruits.

---

[77]Pion-Berlin (1992: 151).
[78]Ibid.
[79]MacDonald (1997).
[80]Bratton and Chang (2006: 1067).
[81]Bates (2005: 3).
[82]Ibid., 26.
[83]Moran (1999). The decline in professionalism is also due to lower levels of training and expertise. The military was starved from the funding necessary to take on technological development and innovation. The lack of funding affected military readiness. One survey found that only 41 percent of all military officers felt that they were improving their skills, while 55 percent felt that they did not have the opportunity to do so (Moran 1999: 62). From 1992 until 2000, the military did not have combat training due to lack of funding. In May of 2003 it was reported that Russian pilots only received 6–8 hours of combat training per year, which is far below the 150 hours or more required by NATO pilots (Herspring 2005: 138). Senior military officers in Russia have also complained about the weapons systems and equipment that they have to work with (138).

One survey found that between 1989 and 1993 the number of those who said that they were willing to serve as conscripts declined from 82 to 31 percent.[84] Many soldiers that enlist do not have high levels of education. About 7 percent have only primary education, over 30 percent do not have secondary education, and 40 percent had not worked or studied before they joined the army.[85] The military claims about 5,000 desert every year."[86] Low wages have forced many to quit.[87]

In contrast, military salaries in Egypt, Singapore, and Malaysia are relatively very high.[88] In Egypt, the military enjoyed access to the best salaries, housing, and health care in the country.[89] In Singapore not only are salaries high, but welfare benefits and scholarships for higher education are also given out. As a result, a career in the military is not looked upon as "employment of last resort."[90]

Others have noted that insufficient budgets provide incentives for security personnel to get involved in commercial endeavors, distracting them from their duty to protect and defend the state and its citizens.[91] (For more information on this see Box 6.1 Military Entrepreneurship.)

BOX 6.1 Military entrepreneurship

Many militaries both in the developed and the developing world have become involved in military entrepreneurship. The military can become involved in a host of economic activities including the production of military equipment to the production of nonmilitary products as well. The military often becomes involved in business enterprises in order to give the military a vested interest in the regime. Military entrepreneurship is an important perk that can keep the military happy, and less likely to confront the leadership. When the military rules directly (or at least shares power), it almost always becomes involved in economic activities, as evidenced by cases in Egypt, Thailand, Pakistan, Syria, Nigeria, Brazil, Peru, and Turkey, to name a few.

(Continued)

---

[84]Moran (1999: 82).
[85]Herspring (2005: 130).
[86]Ibid., 139.
[87]Russian President Vladmir Putin claims he is tackling these problems by increasing funding for the military and upgrading its status in society.
[88]Ghoshal (1986).
[89]Harb (2003).
[90]Cunha (1999: 466).
[91]Mani (2011).

BOX 6.1 *Continued*

Military entrepreneurship affects the quality of military institutions, however. Military entrepreneurship makes it easier for the military to not be accountable to civilian governments. The military is so empowered due to its economic activities that it becomes completely autonomous. Military entrepreneurship may also affect professionalism because it may distract the military from training and providing security for the nation. Its judgment may become clouded by business activities that it loses sight of what its key responsibilities are. Military entrepreneurship can also lead to rent seeking (see Box 8.2). When the military starts to monopolize key industries, this makes it near impossible for civilian-run businesses to compete. The playing field is never level, and the military may benefit from lucrative contracts that could be given out to more deserving companies. Moreover, the combination of power and involvement in the economy has often led to large-scale corruption. By involving itself in the economy, the military opens up more and more opportunities for graft, which are often unaccounted for by weak civilian governments.

The military in many countries in the Middle East has played a large role in the economy.[92] In Syria, the military was encouraged to use their own resources to develop factories and repair shops to maintain the large arsenals of weapons they owned. They also ventured out into manufacturing weapons themselves. By the mid-1980s, the military was in control of the two largest enterprises in Syria, housing and construction.[93] In Egypt, the military has been incredibly involved in economic activities, representing half of Egypt's manufacturing capabilities. The Egyptian military is also involved in water management, electricity generation and reclamation and other public utilities and public works. By the year 2000, the military employed 75,000 workers tasked with making products such as cars, televisions, videos, and electric fans.[94] Some sources claim that the military accounts for up to 40 percent of Egypt's economy.[95]

The military in Pakistan is so involved in business activities it is often known as Military Inc.[96] The military owns all major businesses, such as sugar mills, chemical plants fertilizer factories, gas companies, power plants, education institutions, hospitals, construction, and telecommunications. The military is also involved in real estate, insurance, the media,

(Continued)

---

[92]Owen (1992).
[93]Ibid.
[94]Ibid.
[95]Masoud (2011: 25).
[96]Siddiqa (2007).

BOX 6.1 *Continued*

shipping, private security, and banking.[97] Because of this, the military has a big stake in maintaining the "existing structures of the state and political economy."[98] The other problem is that any civilian firms that try to compete have been pushed into bankruptcy, as rent seeking has benefited the military primarily.[99]

Military entrepreneurship has been commonplace in Thailand as well. The military believes that it has the right to intervene in domestic politics, given that there is little that the civilian government can do about it. The military in Thailand has controlled Thai Airways and the Thai Military Bank. After the 2006 coup it added to its arsenal other key state enterprises in areas such as telecommunications and transport.[100]

In Indonesia, under the leadership of both Sukarno and Suharto, the military was given the chance to expand its business operations in return for support. The military established more than 20 different foundations that served as holding companies through which individual businesses operated from.[101] However, more recently the military has been barred from running its own businesses. It also no longer oversees domestic security, which is now under the jurisdiction of the police. As a result, the military's influence has waned and it is now more accountable to the civilian government.[102]

The Chinese military is also more accountable to the civilian government. Though the military was once involved in different enterprises, the Communist Party decided that the military's business activities were not in the interest of the country.[103] The military never protested this decision, and has continued to engage in a rigorous training routine instead. The military in China respects the chain of command and understands its role and responsibilities.[104]

Sufficient budgets are also important because they ensure that the state's security apparatus has enough resources to be able to defend the state and its citizens from threats. An underfunded security sector cannot ensure the security of the population.[105] As Larry Diamond and Marc Plattner point out, militaries can completely disintegrate due to "the failure of the

---

[97]Mani (2007: 599).
[98]Ibid., 598.
[99]Ibid., 599.
[100]Tambunan (2007: 108).
[101]Ibid., 106.
[102]Bayuni (2012).
[103]Mani (2007: 596).
[104]Ibid., 603.
[105]Wulf (2004: 5).

leadership to properly feed, pay, clothe, and generally care for the army."[106] The provision of security requires that resources are devoted to this effort. In some cases states that have poorly funded security apparatuses allow paramilitary groups to "do the dirty work or occupy the spaces created by the de-legitimization of the legal order."[107] Up until recently the security budget in Colombia was too small to tackle its guerrilla conflict. There were only 20,000 professional soldiers in 1998, which was smaller than the total number of leftist guerrillas.[108] Colombia had been relying on right-wing paramilitary groups to offset the emergence of left-wing guerrilla groups. The problem is that this leaves the state permanently fragile and constrained in its ability to consolidate territorial control.[109]

To summarize, professionalization is a critical feature of high-quality security institutions. It entails rigorous training requirements, a clear internal chain of command, merit-based promotions, and sufficient budgets.

Centralized military command structures

The second criterion of high-quality security institutions is that they are *centralized*. The national army should be the most well-trained, well-paid, and well-equipped security unit in the country. Often leaders in nondemocratic countries are obsessed with their own personal survival. Because of this, leaders have often tried to coup proof their regimes, by creating a parallel ground security force that could offset the power of the armed forces. With high-functioning security institutions, the military should not be forced to compete with other *parallel armies*.[110] We note that institutional multiplicity is just one coup-proofing strategy, among many. Other coup-proofing strategies are described in Box 6.2. Another component of a centralized command structure is a clear chain of command. High-functioning security institutions have hierarchical structures, with clear guidelines for who reports to whom. The presence of parallel security forces with overlapping jurisdictions and countervailing chains of command undermine the effectiveness of the security institutions to serve their functions.

The creation of parallel military armies undermines the quality of the regular security institutions because parallel armies weaken the capacity of the centralized armed forces and undermine their effectiveness.[111] These parallel groups are only concerned with providing *regime security*, not state security.[112] While providing some short-term security for rulers, the

---

[106]Diamond and Plattner (1996: xxxii).
[107]Koonings and Kruijt (2004: 7).
[108]Felbab-Brown (2009).
[109]Koonings and Kruijt (2004: 7).
[110]Quinlivan (1999).
[111]Bratton and Chang (2006: 1060–1).
[112]Musah (2002a: 921).

long-term impact has been to distribute weapons and military expertise more widely in societies.[113] This strategy also risks creating autonomous centers of violence, despite a ruler's best efforts to balance and divide these agencies. Parallel armies have often gained a life of their own, eroding state control.[114]

Moreover, resources that should be spent on the centralized military are wasted elsewhere. For example, Liberia's government reported a budget of 65 million for all official operations in 1999, most of which was spent on the Special Security Unit, Security Operations Division, "Demon Force," Joint Security Forces, National Bureau of Investigation, Anti-Terrorist Brigade and Anti-Terrorist Unit, and irregular personal forces such as "Charlie's Angels."[115]

Many countries in Africa have created parallel armies that have been detrimental. In the Republic of Congo, the Cobras led by General Sassou Nguessou threaten the authority of the state.[116] In Zaire, Mobutu created a 10,000-man Guarde Civile under the command of one his closest associates, General Kpama Baramato.[117] Sierra Leone under Siaka Steven created a parallel military force to terrorize his own people.[118] Parallel units were created in Somalia under Siad Barre, which were exclusively drawn from the Mareehaans, which undermined the national army.[119]

Some states in the Middle East have also made use of parallel security units. Saudi Arabia makes use of a tribal-based "White Army" that is close to the regime. This army is used to fight off regime opponents who may come from a different religious or ethnic background.[120] Syria has also made use of parallel military formations. For example, Hafez Assad created a parallel military organization and put his brother Rifaat in command.[121] Because resources have been stretched by parallel military units, the Syrians have been unable to bring their best units and best equipment to battle with other states.[122] In Iraq under Saddam Hussein, parallel organizations were created with overlapping responsibilities.[123] Resources were often used up by parallel units, which caused the regular military to face

---

[113]Reno (1998).
[114]Bratton and Chang (2006: 1060–1).
[115]Reno (2002: 840).
[116]Musah (2002a: 922).
[117]Reno (1998).
[118]Rotberg (2003: 12).
[119]Compagnon (1992: 9).
[120]Gause (2011).
[121]Quinlivan (1999: 148).
[122]Ibid., 158.
[123]Ibid., 144.

severe limitations. While the parallel units were given training, the regular military was also was given little training, guidance, or equipment. When forced to face Iranian attacks during the Iran-Iraq war, the regular army frequently collapsed.[124]

In the case of Haiti, François Duvalier worked to remove the threat of the military by fragmenting the armed forces and creating his own personal security forces.[125] These included the presidential guard (Garde Presidentielle) and the private, rural militia known as the Tonton Macoutes (Volontaires de la Sécurité Nationale or VSN). Both were designed to serve as counterweights to the military, which was deliberately kept down.[126] The VSN comprised primarily of young illiterate men from the countryside who were fiercely loyal to Duvalier. It acted as a security police in Haiti, detecting and punishing any subversive behavior.[127] The VSN eventually grew to be twice as powerful as the army, since Duvalier had also purged any influential officers or commanders from army ranks.

The VSN were free to disregard human rights and were not made accountable to any institution other than their leader, "Papa Doc."[128] This created a chaotic environment were young men were armed and dangerous with little fear of retribution from the state. This left a legacy of "paramilitary violence and . . . brutality" and spawned more paramilitary groups.[129] In the decades that followed, a series of massacres by paramilitary groups took place.[130] As a result, Haiti still remains plagued by violence.

In contrast, the security institutions in countries such as Brazil and India have not been "coup proofed" (see Box 6.2). Militarized shadow networks have not been deliberately created to protect the leaders from disloyal military units. Though some violent non-state actors have emerged, which have weakened the strength of central authority, the state has not deliberately created parallel units. The military structures have remained centralized, strong, and capable.[131]

---

[124]Ibid., 145.
[125]Ferguson (1988: 39).
[126]Lundahl (1997: 17).
[127]Ferguson (1988: 40).
[128]Aponte (2010).
[129]Ibid.
[130]The Revolutionary Front for the Advancement and Progress of Haiti—FRAPH emerged in the 1990s and was reportedly just as "sadistic" as the Tonton Macoutes (Aponte 2010).
[131]Riedel (2008).

BOX 6.2 Coup proofing

Coup proofing is an institutional strategy of survival, most often used by authoritarian regimes, to minimize the possibility of the military from seizing power.[132] Coup proofing includes interfering in the recruitment, promotion, and assignment procedures of the military, providing low levels of unified training for the regular army, creating parallel organizations, multiple monitoring, and surveillance agencies with overlapping jurisdictions and a loyal presidential unit to personally guard the leader.[133]

Leaders who fear coups undermine the professionalization of the military by engaging in *recruitment,* and *promotion* patterns that are based on ethnicity, kinship, or other sectarian ties.[134] Recruitment takes place along communal lines in order to ensure loyalty. Coup proofing also entails providing *little unified training* for the regular army.[135]

Coup proofing also involves *creating parallel armed forces* to counterbalance the regular army. Leaders will divide up the military manpower by creating a small rival organization in order to counterbalance the central military and create competition. Any military unit that wanted to stage a coup would possibly be balanced by another military unit that was loyal to the political leadership.[136] Parallel armed forces are often better trained and given better equipment. Because they are supplied with better weapons and superior training, they are usually more confident in their military abilities as well.[137] In contrast, the regular military feels inferior and less confident due to weaker training and older weapons.

Another coup proofing strategy is to create a *presidential guard* that is designed exclusively to protect the leader and his elite entourage. This elite unit is usually heavily recruited from a tribe, ethnic group, or region tied to the leader. In some cases the presidential guard is the best-equipped unit in the nation. In Gabon, Omar Bongo established a presidential guard that served under his direct control to suppress a possible coup. The presidential guard was bigger and better equipped than the regular army.[138] The presidential guard in Haiti proved valuable to François Duvalier, as he survived several coup attempts during his tenure. The first, for example, took place on June 28, 1958. Major mistakes on the part of coup plotters—such as

(Continued)

---

[132]Quinlivan (1999). A coup is the rapid infiltration of a small segment of the state apparatus to remove the existing government from its control and seize power. This is thus much more ambitious then just assassination of a regime's leader (see Luttwak 1968).
[133]Quinlivan (1999).
[134]Pilster and Bohmelt (2011).
[135]Quinlivan (1999: 133).
[136]Ibid.
[137]Ibid., 155.
[138]Pilster and Bohmelt (2011).

BOX 6.2 *Continued*

their uncertainty regarding the location of needed weapons—undermined their coup effort.[139]

A final coup-proofing tactic is to create *multiple security agencies with overlapping jurisdiction* that can monitor and serve as informants to help uncover coup plots before they occur. This includes the creation of intelligence or counterintelligence agencies to monitor the activities of the military. Along with parallel militaries and presidential guards, these monitoring agencies enjoy a chain of command that is distinct from the regular military and have direct contact with the regime. In Syria, Hafez Assad would call the heads of the various intelligence agencies directly. Other informants were also used to ensure that the military was not being disloyal.[140]

Coup-proofing techniques were effective for many years in Syria under the Assad family regime and in Iraq under Saddam Hussein. Neither military has been particularly effective in battle but neither regime was ousted in a coup, as of yet. In Syria, the military is not professionalized. Junior officers and commanders are mainly selected by religious affiliation. As a result, they were incompetent and incapable during the Syrian offensive operation on the Golan Heights in 1973 and have had great difficulty in dealing with rebel forces attempting to overthrow the regime.

Most scholars claim that the biggest problem facing developing states is establishing security and a monopoly over the use of force.[141] Yet coup-proofing strategies prevent the security institutions from being effective. Interfering with recruitment, promotion, and assignment procedures discourages the development of leadership qualities.[142] Low levels of training, poor supervision, and competence of commanders makes it difficult to carry out complex commands and deliver information.[143] Coup proofing a regime can often lead to a loss of the monopoly over the legitimate use of force in the long term. Moreover, because the security institutions have been deliberately weakened, regime transitions are more prone to chaos and instability.[144]

The second component of centralization is a *clear internal chain of command*. This means that the hierarchy and structure of the security apparatus is well defined and obvious to personnel. Members of the security institutions know who their superiors are and whose orders they are required to follow. A clear internal chain of command is important because it increases

---

[139]Ferguson (1988: 41).
[140]Quinlivan (1999: 141).
[141]See Zartman (1995).
[142]Pilster and Bohmelt (2011).
[143]Ibid.
[144]Driscoll (2008: 1–56).

the security sector's effectiveness; it enhances its ability to perform well in combat.[145]

African militaries have often not enjoyed a clear chain of command. In Zaire under Mobutu, there was no institutionalized and hierarchical command structure in the military.[146] Mobutu rotated officers' positions frequently and encouraged them to report any suspicious activity directly to him.[147]

The chain of command in Libya was also intentionally confusing. Ranks and titles had little meaning and it was unclear what each individual's responsibilities were. Captains, for example, occasionally reported to individuals with no rank.[148] The goal of this setup is to ensure that "ambitious underlings" were kept in check by being played off one another.[149] As Craig Black writes: "No one outside Libya—and perhaps even inside— knows for sure who controls exactly what. The vagueness and obscurity of this system was Qaddafi's own design, intended to confuse potential competitors within the regime."[150] The chain of command in Iraq under Saddam Hussein was also confusing and bewildering. Hussein rotated generals from post to post so that no one could build up a personal following.

In contrast, the Brazilian military has a clear chain of command and is a hierarchical yet unified organization. The army remained relatively cohesive even during 20 plus years of military rule. The military was able to institutionalize the succession of leadership to ensure that one individual never became too powerful.[151] In stark contrast, the chain of command was completely interrupted in Haiti under François Duvalier by his creation of a dual hierarchy that permitted slightly lower-ranking officers to keep tabs on the activities of superiors and report directly to Duvalier in return for increased incomes and other privileges.[152]

Civilian accountability

The third critical feature of high-quality security institutions is civilian accountability.[153] Civilian accountability means that the security institutions must answer to civilians, whether this means the state's political or judicial institutions.[154]

---

[145]MacDonald (1997).
[146]Afoaku (1999: 10).
[147]Ibid., 11; Acemoglu et al. (2004: 172); Snyder (1992: 393).
[148]Black (2000: 10).
[149]Ibid.
[150]Ibid.
[151]Hunter (1997: 27).
[152]Pion-Berlin (1992: 151).
[153]See, for example, Howe (2001), who argues that, in addition to transparency and meritocracy, accountability helps elevate security institutions.
[154]Ottaway also claims that "accountability of the military and the police to civilian authorities" is critical to stability (2002: 1006).

Civilian accountability is characterized by a number of factors.[155] The first is the existence of a constitutional and legal framework that separates the powers of the security apparatus from those of other spheres. Such a framework delineates institutional checks on the security forces, while also clearly stating their responsibilities. Regardless of whether these checks are respected in practice, without them lack of accountability is assured.

The second factor is civilian control over the security sector, as reflected in the placement of civilians in top positions of security-related ministries, like the Ministry of Defense and the Ministry of Interior. Within these ministries, civilians control the direction of policies. This ensures that, though security institutions can maintain their own internal hierarchy, the upper echelon, where decisions are made, is dominated by civilian actors.

The third factor is legislative oversight of the state's security institutions. This means that the legislature has the power to approve security budgets, implement laws pertaining to security, play a role in security strategy and decisions over troop deployments, and hold inquiries and hearings related to security activities. Legislative oversight provides another institutional check on the security institutions, subjecting them to monitoring and keeping in line any efforts they might engage in to interfere in politics.

The last factor is judicial oversight of the security institutions. This means that the behavior of security personnel is subject to the civilian justice system. Judicial oversight is important because it can help to deter rogue behavior on the part of security personnel.

Taken together, these four factors enable civilian accountability. Civilian accountability is primarily important because it reduces the likelihood of political interference by the state's security institutions, namely the military, which is dangerous for the stability of the state.[156] Frequent coups are both politically and economically disruptive. Such interventions also blur the lines between the security and political spheres, which is detrimental to democracy.[157] As evidence of this, a large number of international institutions have resolutions stating that accountability of the security sector to civilians is a critical feature of democratic governance.[158]

In addition, civilian accountability lessens the chance that security institutions will engage in rogue behavior, given that members are subjected to oversight. It ensures that the security institutions are brought into the realm of the rule of law.[159] For example, there are questions about the loyalty of the security institutions in Pakistan to the civilian leadership.

The military in Africa has had a history of not being accountable to the public. Military coups have been a common occurrence in Africa. In the

---

[155]Hänggi (2003: 17–18).
[156]Perlmutter (1969).
[157]Hänggi (2003: 17–18).
[158]Ibid.
[159]Brzoska (2003).

absence of institutions, the coup has become the "institutionalized method for changing governments"[160] Previous studies of coups in Sub-Saharan Africa have reported that coups have been so prevalent that 41 out of 48 states (85.4 percent) have experienced a coup or coup attempt.[161] From 1956 to 1984, 55 percent of all coups and a third of all attempted coups were reported to have taken place in Africa.[162]

The military has also had little respect for civilian rule in Pakistan and Thailand. In the former, the military took over in 1958, 1977, and 1999. The military has often involved itself directly in the government. After Zia took power in 1977, 10 percent of all government posts were taken by retired army officers. After the 1999 takeover there were over 1,000 military officers taking civilian posts in different ministries and divisions in Pakistan. In the case of Thailand, military intrusion has been a constant and the military has staged coups over 12 times. In contrast, in the case of India, the Indian military inherited a tradition of civil supremacy over the military apparatus from the British. The military is isolated from civilian government and is discouraged from participating in politics.[163]

Civilian accountability is also important in preventing an inefficient use of funds and engaging in corrupt procurement practices. In the case of Singapore, the People's Action Party (PAP) controls defense spending and procurement. The government encourages the military to use its allocated resources in a productive and efficient manner.[164]

In contrast, in countries where procurement practices are not monitored, the military can profit from kickbacks on expensive and unnecessary military equipment (see the section "Military corruption" in Chapter Eight). For example, the Nigerian military has purchased weapons and aircraft procurement, most of which was completely unnecessary such as battle tanks and fighter jets, and surface to air missiles. Most of the equipment being procured required sophisticated educational and technical training and could not be operated by the soldiers themselves.[165] In the 1970s, Nigerian military officers received $3.6 million from Lockheed Corporation when they purchased 6 transport planes worth $45 million. Officers were more likely to receive a large kickback when they procured large-scale items instead of training and replacement material. As a result of these corrupt procurement practices, the Nigerian military was unable to contain low intensity conflicts. The country needed a well-trained and mobile infantry unit with riverine training. The US offers to provide this sort of training, but was declined.[166]

---

[160]Kposowa and Jenkins (1993: 126).
[161]McGowan and Johnson (1986: 546).
[162]Agyeman-Duah (1990: 547–70).
[163]Chari (1977).
[164]Tan (2009: 28).
[165]Howe (2001: 42).
[166]Ibid., 41.

In sum, professionalization, centralized military structures, and civilian accountability are the three defining features of high-quality security institutions. When these features are in place, citizens are secure, order is maintained within the state, and the security sector does not interfere in political affairs. When one, two, or all three of these features are lacking, by contrast, the state's institutions are of low quality. Citizens are vulnerable to attack or harm, the state's territory is insecure, and coups are a frequent occurrence.

Case studies

Much of the international community has focused on the process of rebuilding Afghanistan's military. This case study illustrates the challenges involved in building security institutions that have eroded considerably.

The Afghan military has never been professionalized, centralized, or accountable to the government. Early on, efforts to conscript troops have always met with resistance. Recruits have been poorly paid, and soldiers have resisted working under a centralized command. The military prior to the Soviet invasion was badly factionalized with a tense divide between officers and troops. Poor pay is still a problem today. The Ministry of Defense does not pay the salaries to the troops and only guarantees an irregular supply of food. Even the best units suffer from chronic under-supply. As a result, discipline is low and desertion levels are very high, some saying as high as 50 percent.[167]

Recruitment methods of the military have often been patrimonial. Prior to 1963, the military was filled with primarily Pashtuns. Efforts were made to reform the recruitment methods by enlisting more troops from other ethnic groups with limited success during the 1960s and 1970s. Any merit-based recruitment has been since abandoned. The military is now very Tajik heavy, particularly at the top levels, which is unsurprising given that the former minister of defense Mohammed Fahim (2002–4) is an ethnic Tajik.[168] All Pashtun recruits have been dropping out in high numbers, accusing the Tajiks of mistreatment. The Pashtun belt is particularly sensitive to the fact that the army is dominated too heavily by Tajiks.[169]

Military appointments have also been strictly based on political considerations not merit.[170] Most of the commanders are politically allied to the minister of defense. To illustrate, 37 of the 38 generals chosen were Tajiks.

---

[167]Giustozzi (2003a: 25–8). The Ministry of Defense had been paying the commanders, but Giustozzi argued that most of the money spent by the Ministry of Defense is pocketed directly by the commanders (25).

[168]Though Tajiks constitute 25 percent of the Afghan population, 40 percent of the army is Tajik.

[169]Giustozzi (2003a: 28).

[170]Ibid., 25.

More problematic is the fact that most of these new generals have no professional army background at all.[171]

The Afghan army has also lacked the equipment and training to secure the national territory, and this is still the case today. Moreover, even if the military receives more sophisticated equipment (as it had in 1978), the military still lacks the human resources to operate it.[172] For example, it has been difficult to recruit pilots or technicians.[173] Training programs have also been cut short.

Due to the low allure of the military, troops have not wanted to leave their homes; this is why it has proven easier for the Afghan state to rely on local militias to spontaneously defend their own territories rather than on a national professionalized army.[174] The Afghan military never attempted to seriously disband these local militias. Due to recruitment problems, private militias have been absorbed into the national army, but they have remained loyal to local warlords and commanders.

Additionally, the military still contends with many militias that operate outside of the national army structure but are supposedly part of the Afghan National Army. This has also made the chain of command confusing. These units are exempted from being trained by the United States because they may have patrons other than the Ministry of Defense.[175]

As a result of all of these problems, the military capabilities of the Afghan National Army are "abysmal."[176] Even chasing small guerrilla units is beyond their capability. Building a professionalized Afghan military is considered one of the most important tasks for state builders (see Chapter Nine), but one that appears to be insurmountable.

Cuba under Fidel Castro represents a case where the security institutions are of high quality. The Cuban military enjoys high levels of esteem and respect and it has earned a reputation for diligence. Military training has been rigorous in Cuba. The military is well paid and corruption in the military is very low.[177] Recruitment is not based on communal ties; the recruitment process is uniform and based on merit.[178] Cuba has been primarily focused on recruiting high-quality troops.[179] Promotions are also based on expertise not political loyalty. The Cuban military has seen a rise in more experienced and professional officers who are less "infatuated" with Fidel Castro's leadership.[180]

---

[171] Ibid., 28.
[172] Ibid., 23.
[173] Ibid.
[174] Barfield (2005: 8).
[175] Giustozzi (2003a: 27).
[176] Ibid., 28.
[177] Mani (2011: 42).
[178] Suchlicki (1989: 14).
[179] Ibid., 17.
[180] Ibid., xv.

The military is also well organized and retains its hierarchical structure.[181] It has worked on eliminating military factionalism and is unified and cohesive. As a result, the Cuban military has been particularly effective in global conflicts such as when it sent troops to Angola to support the People's Movement for the Liberation of Angola (MPLA).[182] Of Cuba's involvement in the Angola, the US State Department noted Cuba's "tactical finesse" and successful "projection of power on the ground."[183]

In addition to being effective in battle, the Cuban military is also committed to the Cuban Communist Party and supports the regime. While under former Cuban leader Fulgencio Batista, allegiance to the military was low (which explains why it quickly fell apart during the revolution in 1959), the current military under Castro is respectful of civilian rule. There have been no coups or coup attempts in Cuba.

Police

Though we have not chosen to focus on the police extensively, it is important to comment on the key aspects of a high functioning police force, as highlighted by the literature. Studies have argued that proper training, funding, salaries, rigorous recruitment methods, a long-term career path, and civilian accountability are all important components of a high functioning police force.[184] Low budgets, in particular, make it difficult for the police to perform their job. In the case of Mexico, in violent cities like Tijuana, the police are often required to purchase their own "basic equipment, such as bullets, firearms, uniforms and bulletproof vests."[185]

Moreover, some studies have shown that in developing countries where salaries may be very low, the police are more likely to resort to bribes as has been the case in India and Bangladesh.[186] Low salaries and poor training have been cited as a problem in Mexico as well. The average salary of a Mexican police officer is $375 a month, which is well below the $660 that the Mexican government claims is the bare minimum required to feed a family and cover basic needs.[187]

---

[181]Mani (2007).
[182]The MPLA was a Marxist-Leninist party that had fought for independence against Portugal and then later had to fight for control of the Angolan state against anti-communist parties.
[183]Joseph and Spenser (2007: 128).
[184]See Walker (1977); Goldsmith (2002).
[185]De la Torre (2008: 80).
[186]Verma (1999: 264–79); Quah (2006).
[187]De la Torre (2008: 80).

But high salaries are not enough to promote effectiveness. Recruitment methods should be just as rigorous as in the military.[188] Full screenings should be used to recruit candidates. Candidates with higher education experience should be sought after and those who continue their education should be rewarded. Promotions should be based on merit.[189]

In addition to more stringent recruitment methods, studies have argued that proper training also is important. Ethics training has been cited as critical to reducing police corruption.[190] In the case of Mexico, though some reforms are taking place in terms of training the police, prior to 2007 the government indicated that "the vast majority of Mexico's police forces had received little or no formal training prior to putting on their uniforms."[191] In fact, the great majority of police surveyed did not have basic knowledge of the operation of the criminal justice system.

Case studies

The case of Nigeria illustrates how the professionalization of the police force poses a challenge to achieving security. Nigeria spends most of its security budget on the military and military equipment, most of which has rarely been used. Little attention has been paid to building a professional police force. The police forces in Nigeria have had difficulty with recruitment and training. The police service does not attract high-quality applicants because the conditions of service are poor and police salaries are low. Recruits have been paid a national minimum wage, with no overtime. Many recruits were barely literate because the age of recruitment was lowered to 17 and 70 percent were unemployed before joining. Training facilities and police headquarters have left much to be desired. Dormitories were not equipped with mattresses, ventilation, electricity, windows, and sometimes toilets.[192] Recruits in Nigeria also have received poor training.[193] Many were given weapons before having experience firing them. Nigerian police training was "at least 20 years behind what it should have been."[194] This is particularly important given how prevalent violent crime is in Nigeria.

---

[188]Newburn (1999).
[189]Sarre et al. (2005: 12).
[190]Newburn (1999: 28).
[191]De la Torre (2008: 83).
[192]Hills (1996: 289).
[193]Ibid.
[194]Ibid. The South African police force is also very weak and ineffective. Training offered to the South African police force is inadequate. Resources are poor, which makes them ineffective in dealing with crime. Pay is low, which leads the police to collaborate with criminals (Baker 2002: 35). The police service is uneven as certain sections of the public feel neglected compared with others (33). The weak security sector has led to the emergence of privatized security, which does not offer public protection (34).

In Colombia, the police have also been poorly trained to deal with the challenges the country has faced. Historically, the police were recruited from followers of local political bosses. Though recruitment methods have improved somewhat, the government has lacked the resources or the will to expand law enforcement coverage to the entire country. More than 80 percent of the police are stationed in urban areas, though much of the conflict in Colombia has taken place in rural areas. In the 1990s, in 15 percent of Colombia's municipalities that happen to be rural, there was no police presence at all. Due to a lack of training and funding, the police have resorted to turning the other way in the face of criminal activity and violence. A Human Rights Watch report in 1997 stated that while paramilitary violence was taking place in Miraflores, Colombia, over a four-day period, the police never ventured out of their barracks, never patrolled the town, and never investigated the killings.[195] There are other problems related to poor allocation of personnel. Only 10 percent of the police in Colombia are devoted to criminal investigation compared with 20 percent in Japan.[196] Moreover, because the police received meager salaries they were highly prone to corruption.

Some improvements have taken place in the last decade with regard to Colombia's police force. First the average salary has been raised from $190 a month to $700 a month. Second, all police officers must receive a minimum of six months of training. Third, the training programs have been reformed to also include ethics training to prevent police corruption and promote good conduct.[197] Overall, Colombia has seen a rapid decrease in homicide rates and is no longer the most violent country in the world, in that category.

Weak security institutions played a role in expediting the complete breakdown of the Solomon Islands, an archipelago located in Oceania. Tensions between residents of the islands of Guadacanal and Malaitian were so high that the country erupted into a civil war from 1998 to 2003, followed by a collapse of the state.[198] Though corruption has been cited as the primary *cause* of the conflict, it is interesting to examine how the weakness of the security institutions may have expedited a complete breakdown.

When the British departed the islands in 1978, the Solomon Islands were not equipped with strong institutions, particularly in the security sector. By the late 1990s, the security sector in the Solomon Islands was anemically funded. The police were understaffed. Stations were left unattended.

---

[195]Goldsmith (2002: 16).
[196]Llorente (2005).
[197]De la Torre (2008).
[198]Residents of one of the islands, Guadalcanal, resented the recent immigration of Malaitans from the neighboring island of Malaita, due to the perceptions that economic gains were being made by the latter at the former's expense.

Officers were forced to go long periods without pay. Officers also received little in terms of training. There was a total absence of basic supplies at stations. For example, pens and paper were nonexistent at many police stations. Rosters and payrolls were years out of date. No one knew the number of officers stationed at locations throughout the islands.[199] There were also limited communication capabilities between stations.[200] When rioting broke out, the police were completely unable to maintain any semblance of control. Peace was not restored until Australia staged an intervention in 2003, but rebuilding the security institutions has been a large task even for a country of only 450,000.

In Afghanistan, the police have been cited as the key obstacle to achieving stability.[201] The police force is still incredibly ineffective and incompetent in spite of efforts to reform it. Several reasons have been laid out for why this problem persists. First, there has been very little to work with. The security programs were severely underfunded. The police had no uniforms, pens, paper, boots, cars and armed vehicles, ammunition, police stations, police jails, and communications equipment. There was also no national command and no intelligence sharing.[202] Second, the policemen that have been recruited lack even rudimentary education; more than 70 percent of police recruits in Afghanistan are illiterate.[203] This makes it more difficult to train the police force. Third, training methods have been poor. The police are trained by foreigners using interpreters who are completely unfamiliar with security sector terms. Fourth, the police have trouble attracting and sustaining high-quality personnel because salaries are very low. Salaries are so meager that those who don't desert are forced to rely on bribes.[204] For example, the average policeman only earns $16–24 a month, which is difficult to live off of in Afghanistan.[205] The police-building efforts in Afghanistan still have a monumental task ahead of them.

Georgia represents an interesting case of *police reform*. In Georgia in the early 1990s, the police were so weak that they were unable to keep order on the streets of the capital, let alone in the separatist areas of Abkhazia, Ajaria, and South Ossetia.[206] Parts of Georgia, such as the Pankisi Gorge region in north-central Georgia, were a no-go zone for most of the late 1990s. Armed groups and criminal networks were able to base themselves there and act with impunity. Georgia sent no police to the Pankisi

---

[199]Peake and Brown (2005: 522).
[200]Ibid., 522.
[201]Murray (2007: 113).
[202]Sedra (2003: 33); Wilder (2009).
[203]Giustozzi (2004: 1–19).
[204]Perito (2009: 119).
[205]Murray (2007: 113).
[206]Fairbanks (2001: 49–56).

Gorge region for years. Law enforcement capabilities were nonexistent and large sections of Georgian territory were captive to organized crime. When Mikheil Saakashvili came to power in 2004, sweeping reform of the nation's police agency, at that time considered the most corrupt institution in the country, were enacted. Saakashvili fired the vast majority of the country's policemen and then gave the remainder a significant raise in pay. This caused bribe-taking virtually to disappear from the police force, and by 2011 the police had become one of the most trusted organizations in Georgia.[207] Moreover, the once unstable Pankisi Gorge is now under Georgian control.[208]

Violent non-state actors

There are many non-state actors that pose great challenges to the security institutions. These include warlords, political insurgents, opportunistic rebels, terrorist groups, private security companies, and organized criminal groups. Many of the goals and functions of these groups have become blurred. Though making distinctions is becoming increasingly difficult, we highlight the key differences here and explain the ways in which they challenge the state.

Warlords are leaders of armed groups that control local territory locally. They are also able to act "financially and politically in the international system without interference by the state."[209] Warlords command and exercise power in a geographical area where allegiance to the national government is low. Warlords are distinct from insurgents—insurgents draw support from the population, whereas warlords *prey* on the population and recruit from the local community.[210] The warlord does not depend on any popular support and the only service they provide is security. Waging military campaigns may be necessary to maintain some legitimacy, but overall they are not committed to a higher cause. Warlords are motivated by greed—and aim to acquire territory, money, and resources, doing so through the use and threat of violence. Warlords aim to maximize the profits from state disorder.[211]

Warlords are more likely to exist in environments where the state is absent, and where the *security institutions* are weak to nonexistent. They fund themselves by usurping functions typically reserved for the state such as taxing goods in transit. They also generate revenue through involvement

---

207Nasuti (2011: 1).
208Fairbanks (2001: 51).
209Duffield (1998: 81).
210Mackinlay (2000: 56).
211Mair (2005: 14).

in illicit trade and extortion. In chaotic environments such as conflict zones, warlords are likely to emerge. The warlord appears to provide security, but they also manufacture insecurity to justify their existence. In most cases, the warlords provide very little in the form of public goods. Any goods that the warlord provides only cement their clientelistic networks.[212] Their main motivation is self-enrichment, not state building. Jean-Germain Gros writes that they have the "emotional immaturity of teenage fighters."[213]

Warlords in Africa have operated by exploiting areas under their control through looting and taxation. They have also benefited financially from seizing key assets and developing export trades with foreign firms. Much of the earnings go toward their own personal enrichment and toward the purchasing of patronage and arms. The rank and file soldiers were encouraged to loot what was left.[214] Charles Taylor emerged as a powerful warlord in Liberia. He controlled not only parts of Liberia but also parts of Sierra Leone, referred to as Taylorland. Taylorland had its own currency, banking system, and TV station. He supported himself through his involvement in the illicit trade of diamonds and timber.[215] Through the vast links he created he was able to net himself an income of over $400 million per year, benefits which he passed on to no one.[216]

Warlords in Afghanistan have been particularly powerful in threatening the sovereignty of the state. As the state has rarely exercised a complete monopoly over the legitimate use of force, opportunities have abounded for non-state actors to take control over small territories and provide protection in an insecure environment. Warlords have undermined the capacity and legitimacy of the state in Afghanistan because they have usurped revenues that could be collected by the government. For example, all of the revenues from the transit trade in the region of Herat (one of the richest regions in the country) have gone directly to warlord Ismail Khan. This undercuts the state's ability to collect revenues and weakens the fiscal power of the state.[217]

Scholars have found that policy makers wishing to reconstruct security institutions in states that have been captured by warlords face numerous challenges. Efforts by the West and the Economic Community of West African States (ECOWAS) to rebuild security institutions in Somalia and in Liberia have been difficult because this involves forcing warlords to give up control and profess allegiance to a state that has little power.[218] Often

---

[212]Giustozzi (2004).
[213]Gros (1996: 459).
[214]Allen (1999).
[215]Reno (1995a: 28).
[216]Ibid., 10.
[217]The Hamid Karzai government has incorporated warlords in key positions in the government, regardless of their expertise or experience. According to a delegate, "in the Loya Jirga, 85% of the elected were with the warlords or were warlords" (Kolhatkar 2003).
[218]Gros (1996: 459).

these warlords earn their large sums of money through exploiting valuable resources and through their involvement in trade of illicit material. Thus, warlords pose one of the biggest challenges to state-building efforts, and to the legitimacy of the security institutions specifically.

An insurgency is a group of non-state actors usually concerned with undermining a constituted authority through violence, gaining more autonomy, seceding or overthrowing the incumbent regime. The political goals of insurgents are more concrete, and are often more national and ideological. The main target of political insurgents is almost always the state. Though civilians may be victims of insurgencies, they are not the prime target. The main strategy used by insurgents is armed struggle against the state's military. As such, a political insurgency is less likely to emerge in states that have strong security institutions because the insurgency will not have the capacity to challenge it. Thus, insurgencies emerge in cases where the power of the state and the insurgency is more or less equal. Effective insurgencies can choose the tactic of directly contesting the state because they have the capability to do so. In some cases, insurgents may be able to seize a sizable amount of territory and exercise de facto control over it. The insurgency may also receive a sizable amount of support from the public. Because a successful insurgency relies on public support, this can also moderate their behavior.

In resource rich countries, rebel groups may emerge that wish to thwart or challenge the state in protest of how resources are distributed. Rebels may emerge due to real political grievances, but as they begin to fund their war effort through the sale of lootable resources, their motivations may mutate into purely economic ones. Rebels may also begin to prey on the public and have very little interest in state building.

Terrorist groups are non-state actors who wish to challenge the state by targeting civilians. As a strategy, terrorism constitutes a nonconventional form of violence.[219] Terrorism is a strategy of intimidation and is a form of signaling. The terrorist group hopes to signal to civilians (by inflicting terror) to pressure the government to change its policies. Terrorist groups are not strong enough to compete against the state they are targeting. For this reason, they are resigned to use impactful terrorist tactics of signaling instead of engaging in a more conventional form of armed struggle against the state. Therefore the strength of the security institutions may not help explain why terrorist groups emerge. Terrorist groups almost always operate in secret and do not enjoy high levels of public support. Any support they may have will wane as civilian casualties rise.

Organized crime is most interested in controlling or subverting legal structures to be able to maintain their operations unbothered. In comparison to

---

[219]Tilly (2004).

the state, the power of organized crime varies. Organized criminal groups usually have no political goals and are more concerned with profits. In some cases they can infiltrate the state institutions in order to ensure that policies are enacted that ensure their viability and preclude them from having to adhere to the law. In these cases, the state has been captured by organized crime at every level and in every institution.

Private security companies have no political goals. Their goals are only economic in nature, but they are not concerned with undermining the state by circumventing the law. They aim to provide security in states that are highly insecure. They can also be used to fight conflicts and protect businesses. One of the more notable private security companies (it has since been disbanded) was Executive Outcomes (EO) in South Africa. EO was operational in more than 20 countries in Africa.[220] EO had access to helicopters, gunships, fighter jets, and Boeing 727 transport aircraft. The decentralization and privatization of security ultimately undermines the legitimacy of the state to provide security, creating a more insecure environment and less trust in the state's security institutions.

With the exception of terrorist groups, the prevalence of violent non-state actors is a clear indicator that the security sector is not functioning well. High-quality security institutions should be able to effectively deal with violent non-state actors. The security institutions should be the most powerful actor in the state.

Measuring the quality of security institutions

Existing measures of the quality of security institutions primarily capture various facets of professionalism, specifically with respect to the military. To our knowledge, there are no publicly available measures of civilian accountability. We briefly review here the ways that researchers have measured the components of professionalism.

By far the most common aspect of professionalism that has been empirically addressed in the literature is sufficient budgets. This is mainly because decent data exist to capture this. To measure this, researchers have used data on military expenditures. Significant military expenditures are an indicator that members of the security apparatus are receiving adequate salaries and have the equipment they need to carry out their responsibilities. Sources for these data include the "World Military Expenditures and Arms Transfers" reports published by the US Arms Control and Disarmament Agency, the Stockholm International Peace Institute, and the Correlates of War data

---

[220]Shearer (1998).

set.[221] Researchers use these data in a number of ways to capture whether budgets are sufficient, including looking at military expenditures as a percentage of GDP, percent changes in military expenditures from one year to the next, and military expenditures per solider.[222]

The second aspect of professionalization that researchers have derived measures for is rigorous training requirements. In their study on the relationship between military professionalization and political instability, Tomislav Z. Ruby and Douglas Gibler capture professionalization by looking at the attendance rates of international attendees to US Professional Military Education programs.[223] These programs provide foreign military officers with extensive education and training at the elite level. Though all US officers are required to complete these programs, foreign military personnel are also invited to do so. Ruby and Gibler tabulated the summary counts of US Professional Military Education graduates by country during a span of five years. This is an indirect, though reasonable, proxy for the caliber of training received by the elite in foreign militaries.

Beyond sufficient budgets and rigorous training requirements, however, few measures exist (to our knowledge) that capture the quality of security institutions. This is partially due to the fact that some of these characteristics are difficult to assess. For example, the easiest way to measure meritocratic promotions is most likely through surveys of members of the security apparatus. Yet, members may be reluctant to participate in such surveys, particularly if the security institutions are internally cohesive, out of sensitivity of relaying unflattering information about these institutions to outsiders.

Multiple scholars have also commented on the structuring of parallel militaries as a method of coup proofing. James Quinlivan spells out the criteria for measuring them.[224] The parallel military does not have to be as large as the regular armed forces and does not need to be able to defeat them in war. However, it must be large enough that it may be able to defeat a small group of disloyal forces. The parallel military also reports directly to the leader and not through the Ministry of Defense. Furthermore, the parallel military is also always a ground combat force. The International Institute for Strategic Studies has provided information on the number and size of parallel armies around the world. To our knowledge, few studies have examined clear internal chains of command. Similar to measuring meritocratic promotions, the easiest way to measure this would be through surveys of members of the security institutions, which may be difficult to do.

---

[221]Singer et al. (1972: 19–48).
[222]Data on the size of the military needed for the latter measure are also available in the Correlates of War data set.
[223]Ruby and Gibler (2010: 339–64).
[224]Quinlivan (1999).

Measuring civilian accountability should also be somewhat less difficult. For example, most constitutions are publicly available, enabling researchers to capture the existence of a constitutional framework separating the security apparatus from other spheres. Data are also available for most countries regarding the identity of cabinet members through sources like the CIA World Leaders directory. With this information, researchers could assess whether civilians are in control of the top positions of security-related ministries. Last, capturing the extent to which the legislative and judicial branches of government have oversight over the security institutions could be done through surveys. Researchers could gather information about perceptions of oversight capabilities using a sample of participants from the legislative and judicial sectors, respectively.

In sum, measures exist for researchers interested in capturing whether security institutions have sufficient budgets, rigorous training requirements, parallel armies, and civilian accountability. Measures in other areas pertaining to security institutional quality, however, are largely lacking. Filling this void therefore remains an important task.

Key findings

The bulk of the literature devoted to security institutions and their implications focuses on their consequences for political instability, most notably coups. In this section, we review the major findings in this area. We also touch briefly on the relationship between security institutional quality and terrorism.

Coups

Coups refer to forced seizures of power, typically carried out by members of the military. Deterring the onset of coups is often a central goal of development agencies and state governments given their negative consequences for economic performance, as well as the negative implications they have for democracy.[225] For this reason, a number of studies have examined the relationship between the quality of security institutions and the likelihood of coups.

Most of the research in this area has emphasized the role of professionalization, specifically. Theoretically, researchers disagree over the direction of this relationship. Though researchers such as Huntington posit

---

[225]The idea here is that coups, like most forms of political instability, are economically disruptive because they create environments of uncertainty, and that they move states away from democratic consolidation because of their undemocratic nature.

that greater professionalization of the military deters the onset of coups (because professionalized military forces are more likely to respect civilian control over the state), others argue that the opposite is true, known as *military centrality theory*.[226] They put forth that in situations where civilian politicians prove themselves incapable of governing, professionalized military forces will be more likely to intervene because they feel that they are better equipped to lead the country given their internal cohesion, discipline, and clear chain of command.[227] This may also be reinforced by citizen demands.[228] According to Samuel Finer, even the most poorly organized military forces are more tightly structured than civilian groups.[229] As a result, citizens will turn to the military as a solution to the problems created by inept civilian politicians.[230]

Despite the significant amount of theoretical discussion surrounding this topic, in general there have been few efforts to empirically assess the relationship between security institutional quality and coups. As Jonathan Powell writes, "though military professionalism or solider quality has widely been said to impact the military's willingness to attempt a coup, efforts to quantitatively explain this aspect are virtually nonexistent."[231] Powell points out that this is largely due to the difficulty of operationalizating the quality of security institutions.[232]

That being said, a handful of studies have emerged in recent years that have taken on this topic. Empirically, most of the evidence indicates that *professionalization deters coups*. Gabriel Leon, for one, finds that military coups are more likely when military funding is inadequate.[233] Using data from "World Military Expenditures and Arms Transfers" reports provided by the US Arms Control and Disarmament Agency, he finds that higher levels of military expenditures are associated with a lower coup risk. Paul Collier and Anke Hoeffler find a similar relationship.[234] They show that the relationship between military expenditures (as a percentage of GDP, using data from the Stockholm International Peace Research Institute) and the

---

[226]Huntington (1968). For military centrality theory see Kposowa and Jenkins (1993); McGowan and Johnson (1986); Maniruzzaman (1992).

[227]Perlmutter (1969).

[228]Nordlinger (1977); Nun (1967); Needler (1966: 616–26).

[229]Finer, Samuel Edward, *The Man on Horseback: The Role of the Military in Politics* (London, UK: Transaction Publishers, 1969).

[230]Perlmutter (1069: 369).

[231]Jonathan Powell, "Determinants of the Attempting and Outcome of Coups d'état," *Journal of Conflict Resolution* (2012): 6.

[232]Powell, 2012.

[233]Gabriel Leon, "Loyalty for Sale? Military Spending and Coups d'Etat" CWPE 1209 (February 2012).

[234]Paul Collier and Anke Hoeffler. "Military spending and the Risks of Coups d'etat," *Centre for the Study of African Economies, Department of Economics*, Oxford University (October 2007).

likelihood of coups is negative, but that this relationship only holds among countries at risk of coup in the first place, specifically low-income countries. Their argument is that in low-income countries governments are more likely to perform poorly economically. In such contexts, the overall coup risk is higher because, with greater civilian support for such an effort, the military has an easier time justifying an intervention. Governments can lower their coup risk, however, even in the face of poor economic performance, by buying off the military through greater military budget allocations.

Jonathan Powell also looks at this relationship.[235] He examines the impact of changes in military expenditures from one year to the next and military expenditures per soldier (both measured using data from the Correlates of War data set) on the likelihood of attempted coups. He finds that decreases in annual military expenditures increase the likelihood of coup attempts, while higher military expenditures per solider have the opposite effect. In other words, militaries that have larger financial endowments are less likely to stage coups. He argues that this occurs because additional resources give the military enough incentive to resist coup plots.

Thus many scholars have argued that militaries are more likely to stage coups when their *corporate interests are threatened*.[236] Eric Nordlinger argues that the "most important interventionist motive" is when attempts are made to limit its budget or threaten its status. When this happens, the military will feel compelled to intervene.[237] This was the case in Ghana. The 1972 coup staged by Colonel Ignatius Acheampong took place after the military budget had been reduced and fringe benefits had been removed.[238] This has also been the case of Thailand, Burma, Indonesia, and Cambodia. Military interventions took place because soldiers were unhappy with their salaries and equipment.[239] Soldiers in Kenya rebelled in 1982 when officers witnessed a decline in "ability or inclination of the government to provide equipment that worked, uniforms that fit, housing that was adequate, or food that was palatable – and pay that would enable the soldiers to live in reasonable comfort."[240]

These studies all indicate that when militaries receive sufficient budgets, they are less likely to stage a coup. Andrew Scobell points out that given this evidence, governments that need to make cuts to military budgets should consult with members of the military forces before carrying out this effort.[241] Scobell cites the failure to do so as a key cause of the 1987 military coup in Fiji.[242]

---

[235]Powell, "Determinants of the Attempting."
[236]Nordlinger (1977).
[237]Ibid., 57. See also Needler (1975: 70).
[238]Kposowa and Jenkins (1993: 122).
[239]Crouch (1985).
[240]Dianga (2002: 48–9).
[241]Scobell (1994: 187–201).
[242]Ibid.

There are a few exceptions to these findings, of course. Talukder Maniruzzaman, for example, looks at the impact of arms transfers on the likelihood of coups.[243] Arms transfers involve the receipt or purchase of military equipment. It could be argued that greater arms transfers are a sign of higher military budgets, one facet of professionalization. Maniruzzaman finds a direct link between arms transfers (as a percentage of the size of the state's economy) and coups: more arms transfers are associated with more coups. Though Maniruzzaman's study does not make this assertion, his findings could be seen as an implication that greater budget allotments to security institutions engender greater political instability via coups. We are cautious to interpret the results in this way, however. Most notably, the study excludes a number of potentially confounding factors, such as economic growth rates and level of development, both of which have been shown to contribute to coups.[244]

The basic message therefore appears to be that *greater budgetary allocations to the military decrease the likelihood of coups.*

A similar relationship appears to hold between military training and the onset of coups. Using the measure of training discussed earlier (the number of international US Professional Military Education attendees over a five-year span), Ruby and Gibler find that more extensive training is associated with fewer coups.[245] Specifically, the larger the number of foreign military officers in a country receiving this training, the lower the likelihood of coups in their home countries. This relationship holds, even in the midst of a multitude of control variables.

Last, a number of theoretical studies have posited that meritocratic promotions decrease coup risk.[246] The argument is that politicization of military promotions and demotions by civilian actors leads to disgruntled military forces and provides them with incentives to stage coups. For example Jean-Bédel Bokassa seized power in the Central African Republic in a coup in December of 1965 when it became clear that then-president David Dacko had been trying to demote him. Idi Amin staged a coup in 1971 against then-president Milton Obote when it became clear that he would be removed from his post of Commander in chief of the army.[247] In Thailand, Thaksin Shinawatra (2001–6) repeatedly interfered with the annual military promotions. He assigned key supporters and family members to important positions in order to consolidate his power against

---

[243]Maniruzzaman (1992).
[244]Londregan and Poole (1990); Gallego and Pitchik (2004). Though the study measures arms transfers as a percentage of Gross National Product per capita, this solely accounts for variations across countries in their level of economic development, but does not allow us to isolate the effects of this variable independently on the likelihood of coups.
[245]Ruby and Gibler (2010).
[246]Decalo (1976); Nordlinger (1977); Geddes (2003).
[247]Decalo (1976: 112).

civilian rivals.[248] He was ousted in a coup in 2006. Military promotion patterns in the Philippines under Marcos were also undermined by his desire to keep the military under his thumb. Marcos constantly rotated officers so that they never developed a power base. Nevertheless, efforts to promote and retain officers who were personally loyal to him eventually backfired as it led to resentment and discontent. A group of officers led the RAM movement that would eventually topple him in 1986.[249] Thus, though evidence from case studies points to the existence of this relationship, future studies could evaluate it cross-nationally.[250]

The existing evidence in the literature, therefore, indicates that *professionalization* (particularly in terms of greater budgetary allocations to the military) *lowers the risk of coups*. Future research, however, is clearly warranted in this area. Specifically, an examination of civilian accountability and how it factors into coup onset appears lacking. Doing so would improve our understanding of the ways in which the various features of security institutions interrelate to affect decisions on behalf of members of these institutions to intervene in politics.

Conflict

To date there are no studies that directly examine the effects of professionalized security institutions and conflict. Intuitively some scholars argue that when the security institutions have collapsed this is an opportunity for conflict, but this argument is somewhat circular.[251] A few studies, however, have looked at the effects of ethnically exclusive military recruitment patterns. In cases where the security institutions comprise a particular ethnic group but start to lose strength, this can provide an opening for conflict.[252] In other cases, when security institutions recruit along ethnic, sectarian, or regional lines, the apparatus may be more reluctant to protect a particular ethnic group or region and the absence of security for minority groups can lead to conflict.[253] Minority groups that feel unprotected by the national security forces may create guerrilla units to fill this void in security, such as has been the case in Lebanon and Colombia. In the Ivory Coast under the Laurent Gbagbo government, minority ethnic groups believed that he was

---

[248]Pathmanand (2008: 127).
[249]Kwok (2010: 95).
[250]Trinkunas (2002); Rustici and Sander (2012); and Lepingwell (1992). There have been no studies that have examined police professionalism and coup risk, but often times the responsibilities of the police and the military have become blurred. In fact the police have been involved in numerous coups in cases such as Ghana, Nigeria, and Sierra Leone (Hills 1996: 279).
[251]Zartman (1995); Musah (2002a).
[252]Goldstone et al. (2010: 190–208).
[253]Burton (1987).

filling the police and military units with those of his same ethnic group. The rebels in the northern and western regions claimed that they instigated a conflict in order to protect members of their own ethnic groups. Barry Posen states that ground forces with strong ethnic group solidarity will encourage fear from other ethnic groups, and may lead to violent conflict.[254] Another problem with militaries that are recruited along communal lines is that in the face of a civilian call for regime change, they are more likely to fight until the very end. This is certainly the case in Syria's ongoing conflict. The predominantly Alawite military has continued to fight against non-Alawite rebel forces. While other professionalized militaries in the Arab Spring such as Egypt and Tunisia stayed out of the fray, the communally recruited military in Syria has refused to back down.

Terrorism

A number of studies, primarily in the failed states literature, have posited that low-quality security institutions enable the proliferation of terrorist networks.[255] The argument is that low-quality security institutions do a poor job of securing the country's territory, allowing terrorist networks to emerge. Though some in the state failure literature challenge this claim, it has only been evaluated using broad measures of state failure, as opposed to more narrow assessments of security institutional quality.[256]

Despite the paucity of research that exists evaluating the relationship between security institutions and terrorism, a number of organizations have published handbooks dedicated to reforming security institutions, with an eye on preventing terrorist proliferation.[257] Policy makers have argued that terrorists flourish in states that are anarchic.[258] The US National Security Strategy argued that failed states . . . "become safe havens for terrorists."[259] They have also claimed that failed states were "breeding grounds for terrorism."[260] In addition, many governments regularly dedicate sizable portions of their counterterrorism budgets to providing military aid to states where terrorist havens exist or are at risk of emerging, the idea being

---

[254]Posen (1993). Kirwin (2006: 48–9).
[255]See, for example, Rotberg (2003).
[256]Hehir (2007); Patrick (2006a).
[257]See, for example, the Geneva Centre for Democratic Control of Armed Forces (DCAF) publication on parliamentary oversight of the security sector or the World Bank Institute's work on Parliaments for Peacebuilders, which deals with a similar subject.
[258]Rice (2003: 1–8).
[259]Wyler (2008: 1).
[260]Ibid., 1–27. Stephen Van Evera claimed that "al-Qaeda and other terror groups grow and thrive in failed states, using them as havens in which they can establish secure bases to mass-produce trained, motivated killers" (2006: 34). The Rand organization claims that "failed states" "breed terrorism" (Rabasa 2008: 1).

that greater military funding will help them combat terrorism by providing their security institutions with better equipment and training.[261] Yet these relationships are yet to be established.

Though states with stronger security institutions may be more effective in apprehending terrorist groups, in states with weak or absent security institutions, terrorists may find that they must deal with high levels of chaos and instability that make planning operations difficult. Like any resident, they can equally fall prey to extortion or other forms of violent crime. In his account on Somalia, Ken Menkhaus described it as a state with collapsed security institutions in which conditions were so chaotic and violent that even terrorist groups would find it difficult to operate.[262]

On the flip side, more important than the absence of order is the complicity of the government or de facto powers in supporting terrorist havens. States with strong security institutions can abet terrorist groups by providing financial, military, and operational support.

In the case of Afghanistan and its hosting of al-Qaeda, though the Taliban was an international pariah, there is no evidence that its security institutions were weak. It had an authoritarian grip on power and exercised almost complete control over its territory. Evidence of this strength was how rapidly it was able to eradicate 97 percent of the production of opium in 2000–1. Thus, it was not "state weakness" that attracted Osama bin Laden to Afghanistan but *state support*. Bin Laden also initially received support when he stayed in Sudan. He did not set up a base in the anarchic, lawless south, but in the controlled city of Khartoum (1991–6) where he enjoyed the protection of the National Islamic Front and the state. When his presence was no longer tolerated, he left. In this commonly cited case, it was not institutional weakness that caused the link between al-Qaeda and Sudan and Afghanistan but state support.

Thus, many previous assumptions about terrorism and state weakness do not hold up well when examined more closely. Clearly, improving our understanding of whether and how the quality of states' security institutions affects the proliferation of terrorist networks on their soil remains an important area for future research.

Crime

Though the causes of organized crime are multiple, organized crime has been adept at exploiting states with collapsed security institutions because there is more opportunity for them to exercise control. Nevertheless, there is

---

[261] As evidence of this, the US Department of Defense can allocate up to $200 million and the State Department up to $50 million to provide countries with security assistance as part of its counterterrorism efforts (Homeland Security News Wire 2012).
[262] Menkhaus (2004b).

no study that links low-quality security institutions directly with organized crime, with only anecdotal evidence from countries like Georgia. There is, however, some evidence that organized crime levels are highest in countries where the police are poorly trained.[263] Edgardo Buscaglia argues that the largest return for expenditures invested in criminal justice systems may lie in the training of specialized personnel. When countries create special *anti-organized crime units* and introduce more training, significant reductions in organized crime have been observed.[264] Studies have also shown that deterrence is higher with more convictions per crime committed.[265]

Moving forward

Few will deny the importance of security institutions to the functioning of the state. Tasked with protecting the state and its citizens, it is the duty of the state's security institutions to ensure that there is internal order and stability and that it is capable of defending itself against external threats. Without working security institutions, states are incapable of fulfilling their end of the bargain in the social contract to protect citizens. Security institutions are therefore vital to citizens' assessments of the state's legitimacy and performance.

In this chapter, we discussed the key purposes of security institutions. We reviewed the major features that distinguish high- versus low-quality security institutions, which include professionalization—specifically rigorous training requirements, a clear internal chain of command, merit-based promotions, and sufficient budgets—centralization, and monopolization of force and, finally, civilian accountability. In states with high-quality security institutions, the security apparatus is well-organized and cohesive and competent in combat. These institutions are also subject to civilian oversight, limiting their ability to intervene in the state's political affairs. In low-quality security institutions, by contrast, members are poorly trained, disgruntled, and rarely subject to monitoring. The state and its citizens are vulnerable to internal and external threats, and political interventions by the security apparatus are common.

To demonstrate our main points, we incorporated many examples and several case studies in the developing world. These studies help illustrate how the quality of security institutions can vary across states and what this means for states in practice.

---

[263]Buscaglia (2003: 12).

[264]Ibid., 10.

[265]Ibid. In many countries with an ineffective police force, victims lack confidence in state institutions and so citizens rarely report crimes (ibid., 10). In states where crime has become more entrenched, the state and the people may be less disposed to use whatever capacity they have to fight it.

We then turned to a discussion of the consequences of security institutional quality. The general consensus is that high-quality security institutions have implications for political stability. Specifically, professionalization of the military appears to be associated with a lower risk of coups. There are multiple avenues for future research in this area, however. Specifically, researchers need a wider variety of indicators of military professionalization, as well as proxies for civilian accountability. With such measures, researchers could expand the outcomes under consideration to include other important signs of political instability, like the proliferation of terrorist networks and outbreaks of civil war. This research agenda could also be expanded to include an analysis of the effects of high- (versus low-) quality law enforcement institutions, a subset of security institutions that largely escapes cross-national empirical evaluation in the literature.

Given the importance of encouraging political stability in the eyes of international organizations and state governments, improving our understanding of these relationships remains a critical endeavor.

CHAPTER SEVEN

Political institutions

Political institutions are the institutions of the state engaged in decision making, articulating policy, and the selection of public officials. Though there are a wide variety of political institutions, in this chapter we focus on the most basic: elections, legislatures, and political parties.

We note that political institutions house the government (i.e. the political leadership) but are not synonymous with it. Though the structure of political institutions can change with the inauguration of new governments, governments can come and go within the same institutional framework.

This chapter takes a different format than the prior three. Unlike other institutions of the state, there is no unique set of political institutions that uniformly leads to positive state performance. The same feature of a political institution that is associated with fewer coups, for example, may also be associated with more corruption. In addition, how the features of political institutions affect outcomes is often dependent on other components of the political institutional structure. As a result, whether a political institution is high or low in quality depends both on the particular outcome of interest as well as the larger political institutional context. We therefore do not identify a particular set of features of high-quality political institutions, as we did with the other institutions of the state.

Some may argue that high-quality political institutions are those that are democratic. While it is true that democratic political institutions lead to better outcomes in terms of the human rights enjoyed by citizens, states can fulfill their basic responsibilities in the social contract even if they do not always respect human rights (e.g. China).[1] Interestingly, democratic political institutions do not uniformly lead to better state performance (as we will discuss in this chapter) in every case.

---

[1] Poe and Tate (1994).

Political institutions also vary considerably by their degree of institutionalization. However, political institutions that are highly institutionalized do not always lead to optimal outcomes. Therefore, in this chapter we do not discuss high-quality or low-quality political institutions, but instead point out the variety of ways in which political institutions can affect key outcomes of interest.

The idea of how well political institutions are institutionalized was originally set forth in works by Samuel Huntington. For Huntington, political institutions take time to mature. Therefore many states in the developing world that received independence only in the 1950s and 1960s never had the opportunity "to incubate" their political institutions."[2] As mentioned in Chapter Two, Huntington argues that political institutions can be measured by the *coherence* of the organization and its procedures: Are the rules consistently applied? Are the procedures rational? Political institutions can also be measured by how *autonomous* they are from a particular person or noncivilian actors. What is the extent to which political organizations and procedures exist independently of certain individuals? Huntington adds that "political organizations and procedures which lack autonomy are . . . corrupt . . . they are easily penetrated by [outside] agents" and are more prone to coups.[3] Accordingly "coups occur where political institutions lack autonomy and coherence." Political institutions should also be *complex*. Again, institutions cannot be composed of one single person. The more people and procedures involved is an indication of a more complex institution. Adding to that, Huntington argues that "the simplest political system is that which depends on one individual."[4] Complexity is also important because it produces stability. Furthermore, institutions that are *adaptable* are also very long-lasting and stable. Institutions that are overly rigid cannot adapt to changes in society. The needs "of one age may be met by one set of institutions; the needs of the next by a different set."[5] In addition to the constant threat of coups, another effect of having weak political institutions is that they are prone to being taken over by personalist and charismatic leaders. For political institutions to be well institutionalized, leaders must be willing to give up some personal power.[6]

It's important to note that political institutions such as political parties and legislatures can be highly institutionalized in both democracies and authoritarian regimes. Even the methods of selecting or electing a leader can be institutionalized in authoritarian regimes.

Future studies, however, need to examine the effects of political institutionalization of basic political institutions on some of the key points of

---

[2]Huntington (1968: 422),
[3]Ibid., 408.
[4]Ibid., 400.
[5]Ibid.
[6]Ibid.

inquiry of the "failed state" literature, not on just how this may affect the quality of democracy.

In the following section, we discuss the basic political institutions, how they are often measured, and how they vary across states in practice in both democracies and autocracies. We then look at their impact on political stability and economic performance, the two focal points of this study. We close by pointing out the implications of this discussion for state-building efforts. We point out that because of the complex relationship between political institutions and state performance, reforms would be more likely to reap greater fruits when targeted toward other domains of the state.

Basic political institutions

Political institutions can take a variety of forms, ranging from federalism to electoral systems.[7] In this chapter, we examine three of the most basic political institutions: elections, legislatures, and political parties. It is important to note that though they differ in form significantly across countries, elections, legislatures, and political parties exist in most states today.[8] Though there are a handful of states that lack one or more of these political institutions, they are not the norm. We begin by defining what we mean by each of them and how these types of institutions can be measured.

Elections

Elections are formal, state-run events that determine the selection of political leaders. Elections differ across states along a number of lines, including who can vote in them, the types of positions that are up for grabs, their competitiveness, and the frequency with which they are held. In some states, elections are held on a regular basis, all citizens of a certain age

---

[7]Constitutions, for example, are a form of political institution (and one that has profound implications for how politics works in a state). We do not discuss constitutions here, however, because there is less cross-national research on constitutions than on elections, legislatures, and political parties (particularly for developing countries). As with the three basic institutions we discuss in this chapter, the type of constitution that works best for a state is highly context dependent. Constitutional design is an intensive process that requires significant attention to tailoring the framework used to the particular needs, demographic distribution, and cleavages of the society in question. There is no single blueprint that will elicit positive outcomes for all states.

[8]Research has shown that these political institutions are common even in autocratic contexts (see, for example, Geddes 2005 and Gandhi and Przeworski 2007). For this reason, we do not discuss in this chapter the literature on semi-competitive or electoral autocracies (Levitsky and Way 2002; Karl 1995; Diamond 1999; Schedler 2002). As Geddes (2005) has pointed out, most autocracies hold elections and this phenomenon is not something new.

can vote in them, and citizens' votes determine which individuals will hold major positions in government. In other states, voting is restricted to certain segments of the population, only a handful of positions are open for contestation, and the identity of those elected is largely predetermined. And in yet other states, elections are not held at all.

Elections receive significant attention in the literature because they are the key differentiating feature of political systems: democracy (to many) refers to states in which elections are "free and fair," whereas autocracy refers to states in which they are not.[9] In countries with free and fair elections, human rights are respected and coercion is absent during the electoral process.[10] There is equality and nondiscrimination in terms of who can vote and run for office and there are few hurdles in doing so. Voters and candidates are not harassed or intimidated and citizens' votes determine who is elected.[11] In democratizing countries or democratic countries, free and fair elections provide the simple benefit of ousting unpopular leaders from power or ushering in new leadership at regular intervals. Elections thus provide *accountability* to voters and give *legitimacy* to leaders that have been fairly voted into office.

In democracies, *electoral systems* and their effects have also been the focus of state building and conflict literature. Electoral systems are divided up into three main categories: proportional systems, which use some form of proportional representation where votes translate more literally into seats; majoritarian system, which are highly competitive where only the top vote getter(s) wins a seat; and mixed systems, which incorporate aspects of both of these systems. Proportional systems increase the opportunities while decreasing the threshold of electoral victory while majoritarian systems decrease the opportunities while increasing the threshold. Proportional systems have been highlighted as being more inclusive while majoritarian systems are lauded for possibly moderating extremism.

Institutionalized elections

Elections (or in authoritarian regimes, some method of selecting leaders) are well institutionalized when they are able to manage *succession of leadership*. Huntington writes that "the more often the organization has

---

[9]Przeworski et al. (2000).
[10]Goodwin-Gill (2006: 73).
[11]Though free and fair elections are usually considered one of the most basic requirements of democracy, assessing what constitutes a free and fair election is often difficult to do in practice. As Goodwin-Gill writes, "there is no coherent way to characterize free and fair elections apart from an exercise of judgment by one or other observer or participant" (2006: 73–4).

surmounted the problem of peaceful succession and replaced one set of leaders with another, the more highly institutionalized it is."[12]

Elections in authoritarian regimes

Authoritarian regimes hold elections because they help *maintain regime stability*.[13] Elections may help authoritarian regimes co-opt elites and larger groups within society.[14] Elections may also deter challenges to authoritarian regimes when the victories are large. Elections may signal to the opposition that competing is a lost cause.[15] High turnout and support for the incumbent may limit any potential opposition members' interest in defecting from the ruling party.[16] Elections can also divide and conquer the opposition, as they may resort to fighting against one another to be the successor to the incumbent regime.[17]

Elections also provide both the incumbent regime and the challengers important *information* about the support for the incumbent regime, and where its weaknesses in support lie. Singapore's People's Action Party (PAP) has routinely won all of the national elections since 1963. Nevertheless, though the PAP continues to dominate, the PAP can judge its performance by how much support goes to the opposition.[18] Elections at the local level can serve as important feedback mechanisms for the regime to understand what policies are working and what policies are not working. In China local elections are used as feedback mechanisms to inform the regime of what policies have been successful or not. Local elections can make citizens feel involved in the political process without serving as a threat to the regime. Andrew Nathan writes that the "Chinese participate at the local and work-unit levels in a variety of ways. These include voting, assisting candidates in local-level elections, and lobbying unit leaders. Participation is frequent, and activism is correlated with a sense of political efficacy."[19]

Legislatures

Legislatures are political bodies that deal with law making. Legislatures can differ quite a bit from one state to the next, including in their size,

---

[12]Huntington (1968: 14).
[13]Gandhi and Lust-Okar (2009: 406).
[14]Magaloni (2006); Boix and Svolik (2008: 1–35); Gandhi and Przeworski (2007: 1279–301).
[15]Geddes (2008: 5); Schedler (2006: 14).
[16]Geddes (2005); Gandhi and Lust-Okar (2009: 413).
[17]Lust-Okar (2005).
[18]Leong (2000: 436–55).
[19]Nathan (2003: 14).

de facto power vis-à-vis the executive, and whether members are appointed or elected. In some states, legislatures are solely tools of the executive, composed purely of political appointees who have little actual say in how laws are composed or determined. In other states, by contrast, members are directly elected by citizens, capable of sanctioning the executive, and serve as the driving force behind state legislation. Legislatures also differ in terms of the number of parties represented within them. In some states, multiple parties hold seats within the legislature, while in others only a single party (or no party) does. Legislatures are important because they serve as forums for political discussion, even if such discussion is severely restricted. Though some states do not have legislatures (most notably, a number of monarchic autocracies), today the vast majority do.

Institutionalized legislatures

M. Steven Fish identifies a detailed list of how to measure the strength and institutionalization of the legislature.[20] Some of these factors deal with *how powerful the legislature is vis-à-vis the executive*. Can the legislature remove the president or prime minister? Is the legislature immune to dissolution by the executive? Are the legislative members elected or appointed by the president? Is the legislature's approval necessary to confirm the appointment of individual ministers, declare war, or ratify treaties with foreign countries? In other words, in what ways can the legislative branch check the power of the executive?

Mexico's legislature used to be much more subservient to the president until the PRI lost control of the presidency in 2000 and the lower house in 1997. Though many of the legislatures in Latin America are still comparatively weak to the executive, their powers have increased. Kuwait is one of the few monarchies in the Gulf that makes use of a parliament. Though the parliament is not particularly powerful, it has challenged the ruling family at times. Like Kuwait, Jordan also has a parliament that has exercised a small degree of influence.[21]

Legislative branches in Central Asian republics are incredibly weak and are referred to as "pocket parliaments" because they operate in the pocket of the executive.[22] Instead the executives have extensive legislative powers and rule by decree. The presidents can dissolve the parliament at any time. The legislatures have no oversight over political appointments. The legislature is also composed of close supporters of the president.[23] The legislatures in Uzbekistan and Turkmenistan also have no power or influence

---

[20]Fish (2006).
[21]Herb (2004: 380).
[22]Starr (2006).
[23]Kubicek (1998: 32).

over internal affairs and are completely subservient to the leadership. In Turkmenistan, the legislative bodies, The Mejlis (Parliament) and Halk Maslahaty (People's Council), only rubber-stamp Saparmurat Niyazov's (1990–2006) decisions. The ministers do not have real power and they are frequently humiliated and sometimes fired by the president in live TV broadcasts.

Other factors deal with whether or not the legislature is given the opportunity to actually *legislate and make budgetary decisions*. The legislative branch in Singapore has played an important role in enacting policy. The legislature in Vietnam also has an elevated role in decision making and policy making. Different opinions are articulated.[24] In contrast, in the case of the Philippines under Ferdinand Marcos, during his "political normalization" program in the late 1970s, he set up a rubber-stamp legislature.[25] Most legislatures in Latin America rarely initiate legislation and the executive has considerable power to shape the legislative agenda.[26] The legislature in Venezuela under Hugo Chávez (1999–2013) played a relatively marginal role in policy making. In contrast, the legislatures in Chile, Uruguay, and Costa Rica do take initiative and often shape the agenda.

In Kazakhstan, Nursultan Nazarbaev has little esteem for the legislature remarking that they only engage in "meaningless debate."[27] In Kyrgyzstan, the legislature is allowed to debate the budget, but not allowed to make changes to it. Though the Kyrgyz government is also allowed more room to criticize and interact with the president in Kyrgyzstan (originally one of the more democratic countries in Central Asia), the legislature is still subsumed by the power of the president.

Another important factor is whether or not the legislature contains individuals who are *highly experienced in policy making*? Many countries such as Singapore and Taiwan have recruited politicians who have technocratic experience and expertise. They are able to use their expertise to help shape policy.[28] African legislatures are often manned by individuals who obtained their posts through patronage rather than merit.[29] Because of this, few are involved in policy making. There are some exceptions to this, however. In the case of Tanzania, the legislature has become increasingly more involved in policy making through the use of a committee system, which has encouraged specialization in specific areas of policy. The committee system has generated "more favorable conditions for parliament to act independently in the policy process."[30]

24Koh (2008: 672).
25Quimpo (2007).
26O'Toole (2007: 154).
27Starr (2006: 1).
28Tan (2009).
29Diamond and Plattner (2010).
30Wang (2005: 10).

Another important question is whether or not the legislature is *regularly in session*. In China, during the Mao Zedong years, "party congresses and National People's Congresses seldom met, and when they did it was rarely on schedule." Today China's legislature has become much more institutionalized with the National People's Congress meeting regularly. This compares with many legislatures in Africa. In many cases, African leaders have historically starved their countries' legislatures for cash.[31] Most "African legislatures with the exception of South Africa's National Assembly do not have the personnel needed to support a modern legislature."[32] Many African legislatures do not have enough rooms for legislative committees to regularly meet, which makes it difficult for them to be involved in policy making.[33]

A final factor examines whether or not the legislature has the *power to monitor the security institutions*. In China, the legislative institutions have the power to oversee the military. When the military was involved in numerous entrepreneurial activities (see Box 6.1 in Chapter Six), the parliament reviewed this and ultimately deemed that it was not beneficial to the military's professionalism.[34]

Legislatures in authoritarian regimes may not perform all or any of the functions mentioned by Fish, but their very existence still has a stabilizing effect on the regime. The next section explains why.

Legislatures in authoritarian regimes

There are several reasons why legislatures are also important in authoritarian regimes.[35] Even though legislatures in dictatorship are weak, they are nonetheless very important institutions used by dictatorships to entice opponents of the regime to cooperate and help maintain *regime stability*.

Legislatures can be an arena used by incumbent authoritarian regimes to maintain longevity. Legislatures assist in neutralizing threats from larger groups within society and help "solicit the cooperation of outsiders."[36] Though political parties may perform a similar function, sometimes parties are not enough, and legislatures provide more representation to prevent the possible overthrow of a dictator.[37] Prior to Tunisian's revolution, for

---

[31]Diamond and Plattner (2010: 38).
[32]Ibid., 39.
[33]Ibid., 41. Salaries may also pay a role in curbing corruption. Better pay is a step in professionalizing the legislature. Well-paid legislators are more likely to be impervious to the allure of executive patronage and more able to perform their duties. Higher salaries may attract better-qualified candidates who desire to strengthen institutions (Diamond and Plattner 2010: 41).
[34]Mani (2007: 591–611).
[35]Gandhi and Przeworski (2007).
[36]Ibid., 1270.
[37]Ibid., 1283.

unhappy Tunisian elites, the standard method of expressing dissent was informal and within the single-party framework working in the legislature.[38] Legislatures help dictators work out concessions and allow for demands to be revealed "without appearing as acts of resistance."[39] Legislatures are institutional settings where "compromises can be hammered out without undue public scrutiny, and where the resulting agreements can be dressed in a legalistic form and publicized as such."[40]

In addition to neutralizing threats from the opposition through representation, according to Jennifer Gandhi and Adam Przeworski, legislatures help dictators distribute spoils: "Partisan legislatures incorporate potential opposition forces, investing them with a stake in the ruler's survival. By broadening the basis of support for the ruler, these institutions lengthen his tenure."[41] Though it may seem costly for dictatorships to use legislatures to deal with potential opposition, the use of force may be more costly and more ineffective in imposing cooperation and to eliminating any threats of rebellion.[42] In the case of Jordan, King Hussein dealt with the Muslim Brotherhood by offering it "influence over education and social policies in exchange for cooperation with the regime."[43]

Legislatures can also oversee the executive in order to prevent exploitation by the executive, such as stacking the courts with biased judges who might serve as pawns to the executive. By doing so this promotes the integrity of the courts, which can in turn ensure the fairness and transparency of the rule of law.[44]

Though most of the Gulf monarchies lack official legislatures, consultative councils (which exist in Kuwait, Saudi Arabia, Oman, and Bahrain) have been useful to making the monarchies seem accessible to the people, reducing political alienation. These councils also provide the regime with valuable information about what policies should be followed, helping the monarchies anticipate, monitor, and address discontent before it gets out of hand.[45]

Political parties

Political parties are organizations that connect ordinary citizens to political actors. They help political actors secure and maintain positions of power by

---

[38]Angrist (1999: 738).
[39]Gandhi and Przeworski (2007: 1280).
[40]Ibid.
[41]Ibid.
[42]Ibid., 1281.
[43]Ibid., 1282.
[44]Levitsky and Cameron (2003: 5).
[45]Byman and Green (1999: 29).

providing a vehicle to mobilize supporters. Most political parties have an ideological platform that they advocate on behalf of, even if this platform is simply a reflection of the particular viewpoints of the political actor(s) they are designed to support. In this way, political parties play a role in the selection of leaders and the articulation of policies.

Political parties can take a variety of forms across states. Some are well-entrenched in society, functioning as massive organizational machines that have extensive local branches and ties to citizens and are ideologically coherent. Others are short-lived political entities that are personally controlled by a leader and only exist long enough to propel a particular candidate into office, before dissolving shortly afterward. The number and purpose of parties also differs across states. In some states, only one party is legally allowed to operate, and this party exists solely to elicit societal support for the particular government (or regime) in power. In other states, by contrast, there are multiple parties in existence, many of which oppose government policies and actively work to overturn them.

In this discussion, we do not consider political parties that are illegal or banned. We restrict our analysis to legal political parties because illegal or banned political parties fall outside of the state's constitutional or legal framework and therefore do not function as state institutions. Though many legal political parties are not government run or affiliated, they are still state institutions because they are part of the state's constitutional or legal framework. In general, there are many sources for measuring political institutions across states, far more than exist to measure administrative, judicial, or security institutions.[46]

We first focus on how party institutionalization is often measured and then illuminate the reasons why institutionalized parties are important in new democracies and non-democracies.

Institutionalized political parties

Political parties are important in consolidated democracies for a variety of reasons, primarily because they enhance the quality of representation. Political parties are also important in newly democratic and authoritarian regimes, particularly when they are well institutionalized, because they are a stabilizing factor. Huntington argues that a highly institutionalized political party is the one prerequisite for stability. He adds that "states with one such party are markedly more stable than states which lack such a party. States with no parties or many weak parties, are the least stable."[47]

---

[46]For measurements of political parties, for example, see Janda (1979) or Cheibub et al. (2010).
[47]Huntington (1968: 91).

Parties are institutionalized when they are autonomous, coherent, rooted in society, and have high levels of organization.[48]

Autonomy refers to how independent a political party is from external influence. In other words, parties need to be independent from other organizations, individuals, and military units that are outside the party. Autonomy from a powerful leader is particularly important when it comes to measuring party institutionalization. There are various ways of measuring this, including whether or not the party disintegrates when the leader dies or leaves the party?[49] It is also important to examine whether or not there is alteration in party leadership. Having no alteration in party leadership is an indication that power has been personalized in the hands of one individual to a degree where the party is a mere manifestation of a powerful person. The party's interests should not be subordinated to the personal preferences of the leader or even a small group of elites. Parties need to be independent and have their own values.[50]

Political parties in Africa have often served as tools of powerful leaders, with their most important function to dole out patronage. The same can be said of many parties in the Middle East. The Ba'ath parties in Syria and Iraq once institutionalized and programmatic eventually became tools of the Assad family and Saddam Hussein, respectively.[51] Political parties in the Islamic Republic of Iran are not autonomous from the religious hierarchy. The parties are heavily monitored by religious authorities and their platforms must be considered suitable.

Parties in Central Asia are built around personalities that utilize exclusive identities.[52] Because power is concentrated in the hands of one person, this makes it more difficult for parties to develop coherent programs and identities. In the case of Uzbekistan, the People's Democracy Power is only a rubber stamp to the power of leader Islam Karimov.[53]

Political parties in Latin American have also suffered from strong personalities overshadowing ideology. Parties have often been weakened by charismatic leaders who have incentives to prevent the strengthening of any organization that could challenge their power.[54] Parties in Venezuela were well institutionalized and disciplined until the late 1980s. Hugo Chávez's rise to power has done little to amend this problem as he made his disdain for political parties very clear.

Parties also need to maintain some semblance of *internal coherence*. The party needs to act as a unified organization, though still able to tolerate a

---

[48]See ibid.; Mainwaring and Torcal (2005: 1–40).
[49]Mainwaring and Torcal (2005).
[50]Huntington (1968: 12–24).
[51]Owen (1992: 140).
[52]Fairbanks (2001: 50).
[53]Ibid., 51.
[54]O'Donnell (1994).

degree of intra-party dissidence. If there is too much party defection and floor crossing, than the party lacks any ideological coherence. This makes it difficult for voters to use party identification as a shortcut to better understand the various programmatic differences between parties. Being coherent enables voters to keep parties accountable when they are elected in office. When parties are fragmented and appear and disappear with ease, they will be unable to provide voters with coherent platforms.

Parties also need to be *well rooted.* One way of measuring this is to ask how long the party has been established relative to when the country gained independence. How well is the party linked to civil society? How strong are the programmatic linkages to society? How attached are voters to the parties? In party systems where parties are well institutionalized, voters have strong linkages to the parties and vote for the same party most of the time. In societies where most voters are attached to one particular party this eliminates the number of apathetic voters who are essentially floating. Parties with strong roots provide more regular electoral competition and help diminish electoral volatility.[55] It is typical that in less developed countries the linkages between parties and voters are less ideological and programmatic.[56] Weaker programmatic linkages between voters and parties "are a key part of weaker party roots in society."[57] Though political parties are legal in Morocco and Jordan, the system is designed to encourage independent candidates, not strong political parties. Thus, the parties that exist are fractionalized and weak and do not have not roots in society.[58]

A final important aspect of party institutionalization is the *level of organization.* How well organized and financially strong is the party? Is the organizational apparatus present at all administrative levels and at a nationwide level? How often do party congresses meet? How strong is the membership? For example, in Tanzania, Tanganyika African National Union (TANU) was very well organized and had a large scope. TANU (currently called Chama cha Mapinduzi, or CCM) still is a large organization that has national support and ties to many different groups. It enjoys a "robust configuration of regime supporters" from all over the nation.[59] These are all important criteria for measuring the level of organization of the party, which is an indication of how well the party is able to represent and provide other important functions for society.[60]

---

[55]Mainwaring and Torcal (2005).
[56]Ibid., 17.
[57]Ibid.
[58]Herb (2003: 23).
[59]Smith (2005: 448).
[60]Basedau and Stroh (2008). In examining party institutionalization some correlations can be found that bear more exploration. Just looking at evidence from Africa, the countries that have parties assessed to be the most institutionalized are Tanzania, Botswana, and Ghana (Basedau and Stroh 2008). These countries are also the most stable. In Latin America, Chile and Uruguay have the most institutionalized parties. They also are considered to be

For example, India's Congress Party has been well institutionalized. Founded in 1885, the Congress Party has been cited as the reason why the first 15 years of independence for India produced stable and effective government.[61] This contrasts with political parties in Pakistan, which are generally controlled by personalist leaders or function as tools of the military. In contrast to India, Pakistan has accordingly suffered from greater levels of political instability.

Parties in new democracies

Parties are very important to *new democracies*.[62] New democracies are usually fragile, and prone to reverting back to authoritarianism. Democratic institutions are weak and are often unable to keep pace with the demands of the public and with the mobilization of new social forces. For new democracies, parties are particularly important. According to Huntington, parties are the main institutions that enable mass involvement in new democracies, particularly states that are undergoing modernization.[63]

Parties are important for new democracies for several reasons. First, they check the power and abuses of powerful politicians and help make them accountable for their actions. Parties make the government accountable in several ways, such as helping voters identify past performances, providing checks and balances on the executive, and diminishing the power of dominating personalities.[64] An organization that keeps leadership accountable may be important in preventing groups or individuals from taking power through extra-legal methods.

Strong parties also prevent the rise of anti-party candidates (or politicians who prefer to subordinate political parties to their own personal needs). In countries with weak parties, the voters are more likely to vote based on image, candidate characteristics, and personal connections to a politician rather than based on ideology. Thus, anti-party candidates are more common and more successful. In Peru in 1990, Fujimori created a makeshift party to help him win office. This success led to a slew of other anti-party politicians hoping to capitalize on the success of the anti-party movement.[65] These anti-party candidates were amateurs and lacked the ability to govern effectively. In Latin America, "the election of political

---

the most stable countries in the region (Mainwaring and Scully 1995). In Asia, Malaysia, Singapore, Taiwan, and Japan are also cited as the countries with the most institutionalized parties (Hicken and Kuhonta 2011). They are also considered to be very stable. Studies have measured the institutionalization of political parties outside these regions as well.
[61]Huntington (1968).
[62]Ibid.
[63]Ibid.
[64]Downs (1957).
[65]Levitsky and Cameron (2003).

outsiders has frequently resulted in ineffective, irresponsible, and in some cases undemocratic governments."[66] Because anti-party politicians are unrestrained by a party, this leads to erratic and disjointed policies, and more political instability.

Parties also help organize the legislative rules and procedures, the legislative committees, and the legislative agendas. In new democracies, where these norms and procedures have not been established, parties play a crucial role in establishing order and stability. Parties also discipline politicians within the legislature to prevent chaos and confusion. In Latin America, countries with weak parties are unable to legislate coherent policies and are prone to regime crisis.[67] In contrast, countries like Chile and Uruguay have strong party systems and have been less liable to crises of governability.[68]

Political parties in autocracies

Parties can also be important to autocracies both for maintaining regime stability and for improving the quality of party members. Parties, like elections, help maintain the stability of the regime in various ways. Parties can eliminate both the opportunity and the motive of potential rivals to overthrow a leader through violent methods.[69] Parties provide security and benefits for elites. Parties can help co-opt elites through power sharing, which may prevent defections. Parties serve as mechanisms to deliver spoils and privileges to their members making elites more likely to want to maintain the status quo, even amidst various factional disputes.[70] Parties offer individuals a means for career advancement and give elites access to wealth and status. This serves to stabilize expectations and lengthen time prospects.[71] Parties can also depose or weaken challengers. Parties can also disrupt communication and cooperation of potential adversaries. Parties can also "counterbalance the power of the military or particular factions within it."[72]

Parties are also useful for resolving elite disputes. Parties help manage elite conflict, and help hold elites together. Parties can arbitrate between elites and curb their ambitions for power. Parties process intra-elite disputes and provide "elites with guarantees that their interests would be served by supporting the incumbent even during times of crisis."[73] In the case of

---

[66]Ibid., 6.
[67]Ibid., 4.
[68]Mainwaring and Scully (1997).
[69]Magaloni (2008).
[70]Smith (2005: 449).
[71]Brownlee (2007: 60).
[72]Geddes (2005: 3).
[73]Gandhi and Przeworski (2007: 1292); see also Geddes (1999).

Malaysia, the United Malays National Organization (UMNO) serves as a safety valve, giving vent to factional rivalries in ways to mitigate those rivalries, enabling factions to unite against outsiders.[74]

Parties are also important in managing leadership succession. Managing the succession of leadership is one of the most unstable and violent periods for authoritarian regimes. Andrew Nathan claims that few authoritarian regimes have managed succession in an orderly and stable manner. More often than not, a crisis breaks out.[75] Parties help institutionalize the process of succession, which helps regimes survive the death of their leaders.[76] Parties often rely on rules to manage the succession process.

Leadership succession has been effectively managed in China. The rules for leadership succession in China have been clearly spelled out, with peaceful leadership turnover regularly taking place.[77] Because succession is managed strictly by the party, the military exercises no influence.[78] Succession in Singapore is also not decided upon arbitrarily. Procedures for succession are well institutionalized and former leaders are not able to handpick their successors.[79] The Socialist Party in Senegal helped manage the succession of leadership from Léopold Senghor to Abdou Diouf in 1980, helping him become the first African head of state to retire voluntarily.[80] TANU in Tanzania also helped manage succession at the end of Julius Nyerere's rule in 1985, ushering in another peaceful leadership transition.[81] In Mexico, under the PRI, term limits were used to keep leaders to a six-year term, known as the *sexenio*. The level of institutionalization of the PRI helps to "explain its durability."[82]

Parties may be able to check the abuses of corruption. In the case of China, the Communist Party has combated corruption by using the party to provide a greater degree of supervision and oversight over party behavior. Parties in autocracies may give elites less incentive to steal from the state as a "form of insurance against being ousted by irregular means."[83]

In the case of autocracies that allow opposition parties to exist, opposition parties can also check the abuses of corrupt leaderships. When parties are absent, however, this may enable corruption to continue. In Peru during the tenure of Alberto Fujimori (1992–2000), independent opposition politicians worked against each other in confronting the regime. None of these

---

[74]Case (1994: 930).
[75]Nathan (2003: 8).
[76]Smith (2005: 428).
[77]Nathan (2003).
[78]Ibid.
[79]Tan (2009: 22).
[80]Galvan (2001: 53).
[81]Smith (2005: 448).
[82]Ortiz (2000: 68).
[83]Wright (2008: 977).

politicians were able to check the abuses of the Fujimori government as they never coalesced to form a cohesive front.[84]

Parties can also help with recruitment, and ensure that potential office-holders are recruited based on merit instead of loyalty. Malaysia's Barisan Nasional coalition and the UMNO party (formed in 1957) have also ruled for more than five decades. The UMNO's longevity is due in part to smart recruitment. Barisan Nasional is an inclusive coalition formed by all of the main ethnic groups in multicultural Malaysia with representation of Malays, Chinese, and Indians. Thus, there is no ethnic group that is shut out of the coalition; power sharing also helps to maintain the status quo.[85] In Taiwan, the Kuomingtang party (KMT) also continued to improve its recruitment methods, recruiting and co-opting more and more native Taiwanese who could have served as potential opposition members. They also made sure to recruit those with high levels of education and more and more technocrats who would not just serve as rubber stamps to the interests of the higher leadership.[86] The same can be said of China. The Communist Party in China has concentrated on recruiting politicians with technical knowledge and educational background.[87]

BOX 7.1 The consequences of personalism in democracies

Though comparatively fewer studies have examined how political institutions impact state performance in democracies than in autocracies, there are a handful of studies that have taken up this topic. The bulk of these studies examine how *personalism* in democracies affects economic performance. Here, researchers capture personalism by looking to the electoral rules that are in place. Open-list balloting, the absence of vote pooling across the party, and the number of votes a voter can cast are all associated with greater personalism.[88]

Researchers have found that greater personalism in democracies incentivizes leaders to cultivate a personal vote, increasing their reliance on corruption as a source of campaign funding, as well as their need to pay off individual constituents through targeted spending.[89]

(Continued)

---

[84]Levitsky and Cameron (2003).
[85]Horowitz (1989: 18–35).
[86]Roy (2003: 115).
[87]Nathan (2003: 10).
[88]Carey and Shugart (1995); Wright (2010).
[89]Chang and Golden (2007: 115–37); Grossman and Helpman (2005: 1239–82); Hicken and Simmons (2008: 109–24).

BOX 7.1 *Continued*

Both corruption and targeted spending, in turn, decrease economic growth. As a result, personalism in democracies is associated with worse economic performance.

This relationship also carries over into the effectiveness with which democracies use foreign aid. The evidence indicates that aid is less likely to be used in ways that foster economic growth in personalist democracies than in non-personalist democracies, for the same reasons that this dynamic harms growth absent aid.[90]

As mentioned earlier in this chapter, we do not highlight personalism as a feature of low-quality political institutions in this study because the mechanism that underlies the relationship between personalism (as measured by features of the electoral system) and growth may not travel into autocratic environments, where it is yet to be tested (and where the same indicators of personalism may not be applicable).

Case study

Zimbabwe's spectacular economic decline has been accompanied by political institutional decline as well. Though the administrative and judicial institutions have eroded considerably, so have the political institutions, such as the ruling party. The Zimbabwe African National Union—Patriotic Front (ZANU-PF) emerged from independence as a well-institutionalized and organized political party.[91] It operated on Leninist organizational principles giving precedence to decisions taken by its Politburo and Central Committee over those of the cabinet led by the executive.[92] Its initial popularity was that it had served as a representative of the political interests of the African population. It also had extensive reach, and enjoyed grass roots support.

Robert Mugabe, ZANU's leader since the 1960s, transformed the party into his personal accessory. Other units such as the Politburo, the Central Committee, and the Cabinet have no say in making decisions. Mugabe eliminated and reintroduced the Senate at will and has the power to assign many posts in the Politburo and the cabinet, in addition to the 30 MPs he

---

[90]Wright (2010).
[91]In 1988 the Patriotic Front and the Zimbabwe National Union (ZANU) merged. ZANU was founded in 1963.
[92]Moore (2005: 133).

appoints after elections.[93] Mugabe also has made alliances outside of the party to bolster his support.[94]

Mugabe also carefully monitors party dynamics. He has played party members off one another, skillfully playing the younger generations against old guards to allow him to keep the upper hand.[95] He has brought people close to his power center, but then expelled them as they posed a threat.[96] Any other potential troublemakers are also eliminated.[97] He has also done nothing to prepare the party for succession. A new generation of leaders has not been given the leverage to take over the party. He has created a situation within ZANU-PF where he is "irreplaceable."[98]

ZANU-PF is also no longer guided by a strong socialist ideology. David Moore claims that there is a "complete absence of any ideological or substantive policy disputes within the party."[99] Free speech and open debate within the party are becoming increasingly rare. No one dares to challenge Mugabe and any opposition to his decisions within the party is suppressed.[100] The desires of the legislature and cabinet are also ignored.[101] Robert Rotberg writes that though the cabinet has been interested in pursuing vital economic reforms, they are simply unable to vote how they want—they fear the repercussions of their actions.[102] For example, a cabinet minister responsible for the economy had a clear response to the question of why reform had not taken place: "the boss won't let us."[103]

Key findings: The consequences of political institutions

Having defined what elections, legislatures, and political parties refer to and what their functions are, we now turn to a discussion of how they affect political outcomes, specifically political stability and economic performance, the two focal points of this study.

It is important to note that much of the existing literature on these political institutions focuses on their consequences for *democracy*. This is particularly true with respect to legislatures and political parties. Researchers

---

[93]Acemoglu and Robinson (2012: 370).
[94]Moore (2005: 133).
[95]Compagnon (2010: 37).
[96]Moore (2005: 133).
[97]Compagnon (2010: 9).
[98]Moore (2005: 133).
[99]Ibid., 124.
[100]Compagnon (2010: 44).
[101]Rotberg (2000: 56).
[102]Ibid., 56.
[103]Ibid.

interested in the consolidation of democracy have examined in depth the extent to which various features of legislatures and political parties are conducive to strengthening democracy.[104] They have identified a number of features of political institutions that make democratic consolidation more likely and refer to the process of reshaping these institutions to meet this goal as institutionalization. There is an abundant literature, for example, on how to institutionalize parties and party systems in ways that promote stable democracy.[105] Though democratic consolidation is an important topic in its own right (and one that is of high concern to many states and international organizations), it is not the focus of this study.

As noted throughout, we are interested in *state performance*, specifically the ability of states to meet the basic needs of their citizens through the maintenance of political stability and positive economic performance. Understanding how democracies are consolidated is a distinct task from understanding how to improve state performance. Many autocracies are fully capable of meeting the basic needs of their citizens, but a long way from democratization. China, for example, is very politically stable and one of the world's top economic performers. It is also very far from being a consolidated democracy. The features of political institutions that promote democratic consolidation do not necessarily overlap with those that are relevant to ensuring political stability and economic performance.[106] We therefore exclude from our analysis scholarship on how to promote or consolidate democracy and confine our focus in the discussion that follows to studies that examine how political institutions affect *state performance*.

This discussion will illuminate the ways in which elections, legislatures, and political parties positively affect state performance, as well as how they can detract from it. It will pay close attention to the particular features of these institutions that drive relationships of interest and how different political institutional contexts can alter them.

Before doing so, we should point out that much of the scholarship on elections, political parties, and legislatures and their consequences falls into two categories. The first group of studies compares how outcomes vary across states based on whether elections are free and fair. These studies essentially compare outcomes in democracies (which have free and fair elections) with those in autocracies (which do not). The second group of studies restricts the sample of states under consideration to either those with free and fair elections or those without them: these studies look at the

---

[104]See Fish (2006); Mainwaring and Torcal (2006);
[105]See Mainwaring and Torcal (2006); Mainwaring and Scully (1995).
[106]One might assert that consolidated democracies are politically stable, given that consolidation implies the absence of coups. Though this is true, consolidated democracies are not immune to other forms of political instability, including terrorist attacks and civil war.

impact of political institutions on outcomes in democracies or autocracies, exclusively.

In other words, aside from comparing how free and fair elections affect outcomes, few studies compare across the *full range* of the world's states how well other features of political institutions function. This is not surprising given that this distinction—whether elections are competitive or not—brings with it very different political institutional arrangements in states. In states where elections are free and fair (i.e. democracies), legislatures are always present (and their representatives are selected through elections) and at least two political parties compete for representation. Such states differ from one another not in terms of whether these institutions exist, but in terms of how they function, including the rules that underlie their electoral systems, the extent to which their legislatures hold executives accountable, and how institutionalized their party systems are. In states where elections are not free and fair (i.e. autocracies), by contrast, elections, legislatures, and political parties often exist, but not always. Such states differ from one another primarily in terms of whether these institutions operate in the first place and, if so, the extent to which they enable contestation (e.g. whether representatives are elected or appointed to the legislature, whether more than one party is allowed to contest positions in the legislature, etc.).

The use of free and fair elections clearly brings with it significant differences in the political institutional structures of states. This in turn can lead to differences in how these institutions interact to affect outcomes. For example, studies have indicated that in states with free and fair elections, greater transparency of the legislature increases public goods provisions, while in states with fraudulent elections it decreases them.[107] Because of this, it is often inadvisable to compare how political institutions affect outcomes across the full range of the world's states because doing so risks obscuring these interactive relationships.

The discussion that follows therefore divides each section on economic performance and political instability into two subsections. The first subsection examines how states with free and fair elections compare to those without them (i.e. looks at democracies versus autocracies), while the second section discusses how political institutions affect state performance in autocracies exclusively.

Economic performance

In this subsection, we look at how different features of a state's political institutions affect economic performance. We first examine the effects of free and fair elections and then turn to the impact of political institutions

---

[107]Malesky, Schuler and Tran (2012).

in countries that do not hold free and fair elections (i.e. autocracies) on economic performance. We argue that in *autocracies*, the existence of local elections, legislatures, and political parties leads to greater economic performance.

Free and fair elections

As discussed earlier, free and fair elections are the major distinguishing feature of democracies.[108] Therefore we are essentially first comparing how *democracies* compare with their autocratic counterparts in their economic performance.

There is a large body of literature illustrating that democracies elicit better human rights outcomes for citizens than autocracies.[109] Rates of state-sanctioned repression are simply far lower in democracies than in autocracies. The presence of free and fair elections, therefore, can bring about very real differences in the extent to which citizens are subjected to violence from the state. States can fulfill their responsibilities in the social contract with their citizens, however, even if they repress dissident behavior. The Chilean autocracy under Augusto Pinochet (1973–1989), for example, was brutally repressive toward citizens who challenged the regime, but by no means a failure in terms of state performance, given the Chilean economy's impressive growth during this period. Though it is clearly a finding of interest that democracies exhibit fewer human rights violations than autocracies, it is not necessarily relevant to economic performance.

We begin the discussion by examining public goods provisions. Public goods are important because, in general, they help economies grow.[110] There are a variety of avenues through which they do so, including facilitating trade and increasing human capital. Researchers have argued that democracies are more likely than autocracies to provide *public goods* because electoral accountability forces them to accede to citizen demands for them. The evidence supports this expectation. Some studies have found that autocratic governments are far less likely to provide public schooling, roads, safe water, and public sanitation than are democratic ones.[111] Similarly, Adam Przeworski and his colleagues (2000) find that democracies have higher life expectancy rates and lower infant mortality rates than autocracies.[112] Though these are not direct indicators of public goods, they do

---

[108]By free and fair elections we are referring to countries that have turnover in power of the executive.
[109]Davenport and Armstrong (2004).
[110]Knack and Keefer (1995).
[111]Deacon (2009).
[112]Przeworski et al. (2000).

imply their existence given that achieving both requires better healthcare provisions, particularly for the poor.

Though not directly related, there is also some evidence that the competitiveness of elections also affects levels of *public goods*. In India, for example, those states that have stiffer patterns of electoral competition are more likely to provide public goods.[113] The same relationship appears to hold even in autocracies, where elections are not free and fair. In Mexico under the autocratic rule of the PRI, though elections were not truly competitive, the ruling party did face electoral challenges from the opposition party. The evidence indicates that in areas where races were more competitive, there were more investments in public goods.[114] In both scenarios, the threat of electoral defeat appears to have incentivized incumbents to dedicate resources to public goods to bolster their chances of retaining their positions.

Democracies are also posited to be superior to autocracies at *reducing corruption*.[115] As mentioned elsewhere in this study, corruption is a deterrent to economic growth.[116] Democracies should exhibit lower rates of corruption because their officials are monitored through the process of elections. As Daniel Lederman et al. write: "Any institution or rule that provides a punishment mechanism for politicians, such as the loss of elections or the possibility of being forced out of office, can induce politicians to improve their behavior by aligning their own interests with those of their constituents. The more the system forces politicians to face the electorate, the higher are their incentives to stick to good governance."[117] The empirical record supports this expectation. Democracies have lower rates of corruption than do dictatorships.[118]

Given that democracies appear to be better public goods providers and experience lower rates of corruption, we would expect their economies to perform better than those in autocracies. In fact, understanding whether democracy or autocracy is preferable for growing a state's economy has been one of the major subjects of interest in the field of comparative politics. Theoretically, some have argued that democracies are better equipped to develop the state's economy because elections increase government accountability: governments will pursue growth-enhancing programs because otherwise their citizens will vote them out of office. But some have also argued that the opposite is true. Because democratic leaders are subject to elections, they are restricted in the types of policies that they can pursue.

---

[113]Chhibber and Nooruddin (2004).
[114]Magaloni et al. (2007).
[115]Linz and Stepan (1996); Rose-Ackerman (1999).
[116]Mo (2001).
[117]Lederman et al. (2005: 84).
[118]Ibid.

Growth-enhancing policies, though positive in the long term, may lead to negative consequences for citizens in the short term. Leaders in democratic systems may be incapable of enacting the tough reforms often required to improve a state's economic performance because they risk being voted out of office should they do so.

Empirically, the evidence indicates that, on average, neither political system has an advantage in this regard. In their extensive study on this issue, Przeworski and his colleagues find that average growth rates in democracies are the same as they are in autocracies, even when taking into account a host of potentially confounding factors (as well as the potential endogeneity of this relationship).[119] A different picture emerges, however, when we look at the variance of growth rates by political system type. Democracies exhibit less variation in their growth rates from one state to the next than do autocracies. Though on average democracies and autocracies have similar growth rates, the states with the highest growth rates *and* the lowest growth rates are autocracies. In other words, economic miracles—where growth rates are consistently very high from one year to the next—are more likely to occur in autocracies, as are economic disasters—where growth rates are consistently dismal from one year to the next. This finding indicates that democratic leaders, due to electoral accountability, face greater constraints on their behavior. The positive aspect of this is that they cannot completely destroy their economies like autocratic leaders can because voters will unseat them should they do so. But the negative aspect is that they also cannot dramatically reform their economies like autocratic leaders can, for the same reason. Regardless, at the average level, neither type of political system has the development advantage.

This result is perhaps surprising given that democracies have the edge over autocracies when it comes to public goods allocations and rates of corruption. Understanding why democracies are better public goods providers than are autocracies but do not experience higher average growth rates on account of this lies outside of the scope of this study. No clear message emerges from the research in this area. Citizens in democratic states may be more capable of pressuring their representatives to invest in public goods and to refrain from engaging in corruption, but such accountability also enables them to unseat those representatives who pursue politically popular but economically beneficial policy agendas. Despite the advantages of democracies in the areas of public goods and corruption, because democracies do not elicit higher growth rates than their autocratic compartments on average (and because autocracies, should they choose to, are capable of producing economic "miracles"), we simply cannot assert that free and fair elections are a guarantor of economic success.

---

[119]Przeworski et al. (2000).

Autocracies with partisan legislatures

In countries that do not hold free and fair elections, it is interesting to examine the relationships that exist between political institutions and economic performance. Overall, the evidence suggests that the existence of political institutions in autocracies is conducive to better performing economies. Specifically, researchers have shown that autocracies with partisan legislatures—as in, legislatures in which more than a single party is represented—have *higher growth rates* than other autocracies.[120] The argument is that autocrats use legislatures as a means of co-opting potential domestic opponents. In other words, they create legislatures and allow members of opposition parties to hold seats in them because doing so makes these groups more likely to support their rule.[121] Such cooperation between the leadership and outside groups in turn promotes economic growth. Rather than engaging in efforts to topple the leadership, for example, opposition groups instead seek political stability, making investment more likely.[122]

Autocracies with hegemonic parties

There is also some nominal evidence that autocracies that are run by strong political parties (such as China, Malaysia, Botswana, and Singapore) are able to attract more *foreign direct investment* due to the fact that they enjoy policy stability. In autocracies with hegemonic parties, power is shared by many elites within the party. Party elites often do not share the same preferences as the leader, and the preferences of the elite corps are heterogeneous. The diversity of policy preferences of dictatorships with strong single parties helps to generate alternative policy recommendations, but this also means that changes tend to be incremental and significant swings in policy are unlikely. For example in the case of Taiwan (prior to democratization), the ruling KMT's sessions were marked by furious debate over the direction of the country and which economic and foreign policies were most conducive to growth and stability. Because authoritarian regimes with hegemonic parties have a more predictable policy environment, they are

---

[120]Gandhi (2008); Wright's (2008a) study also lends support to this finding. He finds that states with binding legislatures (legislatures that are capable of constraining the behavior of the executive) have higher growth and investment rates than states with non-binding legislatures. Though binding legislatures are not synonymous with partisan legislatures, the existence of multiple parties in partisan legislatures does imply greater ability to challenge the executive.

[121]Gandhi (2008).

[122]Jensen (2008) finds that partisan legislatures do not reduce levels of political risk for multinational investors. The implication of their finding is that though partisan legislatures may increase economic growth, it is not by increasing levels of outside investment.

also more attractive to foreign investors, as there is less concern that policy could change dramatically on a whim.[123]

Autocracies with local elections

Regarding other economic outcomes, there is also some evidence indicating that elections in autocracies (even though they are not free and fair) increase the *provision of public goods*. Monica Martinez-Bravo et al., for example, find that among Chinese rural villages, those with elections had greater access to public goods than those without them.[124] We are hesitant to make too much of this finding because it is based solely on evidence from China, but it does suggest that even fraudulent elections can provide some level of accountability and government responsiveness to citizen demands.

BOX 7.2 Personalist dictatorships

Personalist dictatorships are regimes in which a single individual controls politics. In personalist dictatorships, one person "dominates the military, state apparatus, and ruling party (if one exists)."[125] Personalist dictators are often current or former members of the military; once in power, however, the military is completely subordinate to them. Neither a party nor the military has a role in policy making nor in the determination of the selection of successive leaders. Instead the dictator controls all policy decisions and the distribution of political posts.

Regimes are characterized as personalist when "the right to rule is ascribed to a person rather than an office" despite the official existence of a written constitution.[126] Because the personalist leader cannot create institutions without relinquishing power, no autonomous institutions exist independent of the leader.[127] Though the leader may ally with or create a political party, it is merely a tool of the leader. If a legislature exists, it merely acts as a rubber stamp for the leader's decisions. The judicial institutions are also rendered impotent, and stacked with pliable judges, if they operate at all. The administrative institutions are often (though not always) undermined. The bureaucracy's only purpose is to provide jobs to those loyal to him. All civil servants are dependent on his patronage for their appointments;

(Continued)

---

[123]Frantz and Ezrow (2011).
[124]Martinez-Bravo et al. (2010).
[125]Geddes (1999: 130).
[126]Bratton and van der Walle (1997: 62).
[127]Huntington (1968: 423).

BOX 7.2 Continued

there is no merit-based selection process. Moreover, to regulate and control potential challengers, there is a constant turnover in personnel. Finally, in order to coup proof (see Box 6.2 in Chapter Six) the regime, the security institutions are also deliberately weakened as well, by creating parallel armies, personal guards, and not providing the military with much training. Thus all of the institutions of the state are low functioning.

Personalist dictatorships also rarely—if ever—have institutional provisions for leadership turnover. Because of this, personalist leaders are frequently more paranoid about their political futures than their counterparts in other dictatorships. Lacking clearly defined rules for how long they will rule and who will succeed them when they retire, personalist dictators often live in constant fear that rivals are plotting to overtake them. In spite of their vast power and freedom, personalist dictators feel that they can trust no one. They have no means of ensuring that their subordinates are telling them the truth, as subordinates have few incentives to do so if it means displeasing the dictator.

Personalist dictators handpick a group of individuals to assist them in governing, which is often referred to as the *personalist clique*. These individuals are typically friends or family members of the leader. The balance of power between the leader and the clique is tilted significantly in the leader's favor; as such, personalist dictators face few checks on their power. Because of this, personalist dictators rule with extreme freedom. The result of ruling without constraints leads to eccentric and erratic policies.

Personalism in dictatorships is problematic for many reasons. Personalist dictatorships have underperformed economically, and in some cases they have plunged their countries into debt (see Chapter Four on predatory institutions). Transitions from personalist rule have also been particularly bloody, protracted, and chaotic. Moreover, rarely have personalist regimes left behind a well-functioning state. In almost all cases, none of the institutions function very well. Examples include Siad Barre of Somalia, Mobutu of Zaire and Idi Amin of Uganda, Saddam Hussein of Iraq, the Somozas of Nicaragua, and the Duvaliers of Haiti. Though personalist dictatorships appear to be stable, they leave behind a house of cards.

Political instability

In this section we focus on how different political institutions affect political instability focusing more specifically on conflict, coups, and terrorism. Broadly speaking, democracies and autocracies are considered to be more stable whereas partial democracies/anocracies (see Box 7.3) and/or democratizing countries are considered to be less stable. Thus whether states are democratic or autocratic is less important than how consolidated these systems are. This literature finds that states that are strongly autocratic or democratic do not experience political instability; rather it is those states that lie in the middle that do.[128]

BOX 7.3 Anocracies and civil war

The state failure literature posits that weak states, where power is yet to be consolidated, are especially prone to political instability. The argument is that states that are strongly democratic or autocratic have firm power structures in place that are less vulnerable to political maneuvering and conflict. States such as China (a consolidated autocracy) and the United Kingdom (a consolidated democracy) are posited to be less likely to experience political instability than states such as Madagascar (a weak autocracy) or Pakistan (a weak democracy). These weak states are often referred to in this literature as anocracies: states that are neither strong autocracies nor strong democracies, but fall in the middle of the autocratic–democratic spectrum. One of the major findings to emerge from this literature is that anocracies are more likely to experience civil war than other political systems.[129]

The bulk of the state failure literature measures these political systems using combined POLITY scores, which aggregate scores on individual POLITY components. States that have very high or very low combined POLITY scores are considered to be democratic or autocratic, respectively; states that fall in the middle are considered to be anocratic. Measuring political systems in this way, a strong tie appears between the type of political system and the likelihood of civil war: anocracies are far more likely to experience civil war than autocracies or democracies.

Recent research, however, seriously calls this finding into question.[130] When looking at the underlying components of the combined Polity scores, it is clear that certain components include a factional category, which captures whether political competition is "'intense, hostile, and frequently violent."[131] This means that states in the midst of civil war will be coded as experiencing extreme factionalism.[132] As a result, states are more likely to be coded as anocratic if they are experiencing civil war, virtually ensuring a

(*Continued*)

---

[128]See, for example, Bates (2005); Krueger and Laitin (2008); Eyerman (1998).
[129]For an in-depth discussion of this literature, see Vreeland (2008: 401–25).
[130]See ibid. for a rigorous analysis of this.
[131]Gurr et al. (1989: 12).
[132]Ibid.

BOX 7.3 *Continued*

relationship will emerge between anocratic political systems and civil war onset. As James Raymond Vreeland writes, "the finding is tautological: civil war is most likely where there is civil war."[133] Vreeland finds that once these components that measures factionalism are removed from combined Polity scores, the relationship between the type of political system and the likelihood of civil war disappears.

Much of the reason why studies in the failed states literature have revealed a relationship between weak (or anocratic) states and political instability is due to the misuse of combined Polity scores to capture the weakness of the state (see Chapter Two for more on this).

For *partial democracies*, just holding elections does not guarantee stability. In some states, elections may be free and fair but they may constitute a very dangerous period. For example, in Colombia though elections are often fair, 138 mayors and 569 members of parliament, deputies, and city council members and 174 public officials were murdered following their elections between 1989 and 1999.[134]

More specifically, there is a large pool of literature that has argued that *democratizing* countries are prone to instability and conflict, particularly ethnic conflict.[135] Alterations to political structures may cause more conflict because democratization may intensify ethnic group insecurity and this uncertainty may lead ethnic groups to act preemptively. The political institutions are also weaker and more vulnerable to being taken. Groups are also more likely to rebel in democratic systems because rebellions are easier to organize, whereas repression may be used in autocracies to prevent rebellion activity.[136]

In countries that have democratized and have regularly held elections, the literature specifies that *exclusionary institutions* are more problematic for stability, namely conflict. In countries that do not have free and fair elections (i.e. autocracies) the bulk of the evidence indicates that greater political institutionalization (as in the existence of elections, legislatures, and political parties) leads to greater political stability.

Regarding coups the literature is also mixed. Holding free and fair elections does not prevent coups as democracies may not be significantly less coup-prone. Within autocracies, the evidence shows that the presence of elections, parties, and legislatures does have an impact in coup deterrence.

---

[133]Vreeland (2008: 402).
[134]Manwaring (2002: 13).
[135]Snyder (2000); Young (2006).
[136]Davenport (1995).

The terrorism literature is also not optimistic about the role of free and fair elections in deterring acts of terrorism. Not only are democracies not better than authoritarian regimes at deterring acts of terrorism, but the bulk of the literature finds that democracies are even more prone to terrorism than autocracies. This finding is especially interesting given that much of the focus from policy makers in this field has been on "making the world safe for democracy."[137] Nevertheless, in authoritarian regimes some studies have shown that the presence of a partisan legislature may deter terrorism.

Conflict

As stated above, there is little relationship between democracies and autocracies in terms of their propensity for civil war—with scholars noting that "democracy is not a sufficient prerequisite to shield a society against violent threats."[138] Thus, whether or not a country holds free and fair elections does not have an impact on conflict. If this the case, what other factors may be important? We first explore in what ways specific political institutions impact conflict in countries with free and fair elections and then examine what impact legislatures and parties may have in authoritarian regimes.[139]

Electoral systems

Though holding elections may not have a huge impact on conflict, in countries that do hold free and fair elections, the electoral system does have an important effect. Studies have argued that systems that use proportional

---

[137]Bush (2006).
[138]Schneider and Wiesehomeier (2008: 194).
[139]More recently, scholars have weighed in on the debate on how government design may impact conflict, particularly ethnic conflict. Some scholarship has posited that parliamentary systems may be more threatening to minority groups who are not represented in the parliament. Ethnic minorities may feel more represented in presidential systems because the separation of powers allows for one branch to check the other, and thus there are "more points within the system to block unfavorable actions." Fearon and Laitin argue that presidential systems are less prone to war because theoretically in presidential systems the executive has more power to resist challenges from opposition forces. Studies that have tested these claims, however, have shown that the relationship between presidentialism and parliamentarism are not very significant. Clearly more work is needed to determine why one system may work better in different settings.federal and unitary systems have also been studied to better understand their impact on conflict. Scholars such as Arend Lijphart have argued that federalism can be a useful tool to manage and reduce ethnic strife. Groups are given more control over their own lives and this may dissipate conflict concerning who controls the central government. Federalism may also facilitate power sharing. Dawn Brancati offers evidence of this in the 1990s. She argues that "decentralized systems of government are less likely to experience inter-communal conflict and anti-regime rebellion than centralized systems of government." Other findings have shown that though federalism increases the propensity for low intensity conflicts, it decreases the propensity for high intensity conflicts.

representation rather than majoritarian systems have lower levels of conflict. In proportional systems, minority groups are more likely to have some form of representation in the legislature. Their members are more satisfied that their voices are being heard, preventing the chances for violence.[140] Plurality systems tend to amplify the power of the strongest parties, whereas proportional representation produces a more equal distribution of seats based on the votes received.[141] Proportional systems are often regarded as more inclusive, which may lessen the chances for conflict. Empirical studies have supported these claims with the results being very significant.[142]

Autocracies with hegemonic parties and partisan legislatures

In autocracies as well as democracies, the absence of political institutions are cited as an important factor that can cause conflict and make conflicts more enduring in countries that are ethnically diverse In states that lack legislatures and parties to effectively mediate the struggle between competing groups, this may alienate and anger different ethnic groups.[143] States without effective political parties and legislatures are unable to arbitrate between factions or provide credible commitments to different groups. In the absence of arbitration, groups have incentives to defect and use violent means to pursue their goals. Effective political institutions are needed to structure relations so that ethnic groups can live together harmoniously. Though most of the studies have focused on the role of parties, a partisan legislature may have a similarly stabilizing role in preventing and resolving conflict.

Parties help mediate and resolve conflicts between groups.[144] Parties frame policy alternatives and structure electoral choice in ways that promote peaceful political competition. Parties mediate by melding and broadening different interests. Parties mediate conflict when public policy has become too politicized and when demands have become irreconcilable. Parties can help shape political debate in ways that pacify highly charged issues. Seymour Martin Lipset and Stein Rokkan claim that in the past, parties have neutralized the "radicalizing effects of sudden industrialization."[145] Parties can also neutralize the polarizing effects of modernization for new democracies, particularly those beset by ethnic tensions by forcing compromise and conciliation.

---

[140]Lijphart (1977); Cohen (1997).
[141]Reynal-Querol (2002).
[142]Saideman et al. (2002: 110).
[143]Rothchild and Groth (1995: 74).
[144]Randall and Svåsand (2001).
[145]Lipset, and Rokkan (1967: 46).

Malaysia represents an important case of the role of parties in the easing of ethnic tensions. Ethnic tensions in Malaysia were so intense that it led to riots in 1969. Since then the UMNO has worked with the Malaysian Chinese Association and the Malaysian Indian Congress to compromise on a number of issues and form the dominant coalition known as Barisan Nasional (BN). In countries that have had a history of conflict on issues such as ethnicity and religion, parties can help frame these issues differently so that differences are dealt with through electoral competition rather than conflict.[146]

Tanzania provides another example of the role of parties in alleviating potential conflicts. Tanzania has more than 140 different ethnic groups, yet unlike other diverse countries in Africa that have devolved into conflict, power-sharing mechanisms within the ruling CCM party have been used to accommodate demands. In particular, religious diversity between Tanzania's powerful Christian and Muslim communities led to an alteration in power between Christian and Muslim leaders. Without the structure of the party to implement this informal power-sharing mechanism, tensions between the primary religious communities could have erupted into conflict.[147]

Parties also promote compromise.[148] Parties are often composed of different groups or factions that have joined together and have compromised on policy.[149] Parties enable compromise by increasing the commitment ability of politicians. Independent politicians may not be able to credibly commit to policies that do not coincide with their own preferences. Parties, however, allow politicians to convincingly commit to policies that they normally would not support in order to win a larger support base.[150]

Coups

With respect to the likelihood of coups some studies indicate that countries with free and fair elections (democracies) are less prone to coups than are autocracies. Staffan Lindberg and John F. Clark, for example, find using evidence from Africa that coups are more likely to occur in autocracies than democracies.[151] Other studies, however, find the opposite. Jonathan

---

[146]Horowitz (1989).
[147]Hydén (1999).
[148]Randall and Svåsand (2001).
[149]Levy (2004).
[150]Ibid.
[151]Lindberg and Clark (2008).

Powell, for one, finds that there is very little difference in the likelihood of a coup attempt in democracies versus autocracies.[152,153]

Within autocracies, the bulk of the literature on political institutions in autocracies focuses on their consequences for political instability, specifically their ability to reduce the likelihood of coups. The evidence overwhelmingly indicates that all three political institutions discussed here—elections, legislatures, and political parties—work to coup-proof autocracies. (And, indeed, governments allow these institutions to exist because they prolong their survival in office.)

Autocracies with elections

Regarding elections, one study has shown that autocracies that hold elections experience fewer coups than those that do not.[154] There is also evidence that autocratic elections prolong the duration of autocratic regimes by reducing the likelihood of coups.[155] Though regime stability is not synonymous with the absence of coups (in that autocratic regimes can and often do survive coups), the absence of coups bodes well for the survival of the regime.[156] The major argument behind the relationship between autocratic elections and coups is that elections provide autocratic incumbents with an opportunity to mobilize their supporters and demonstrate to potential challengers that attempts to unseat them are unlikely to be met with success.[157]

Autocracies with hegemonic parties

Similarly, political parties in autocracies (specifically those aligned with the government) also decrease the risk of coups. Political parties may be able to institutionalize succession of leadership. By doing so, political parties give their members a vested interest in the government's survival in power, making them less likely to support a coup.

Parties have the resources to mobilize mass demonstrations that *deter coups*. As Barbara Geddes writes, "it is easier for party workers to mobilize

---

[152]Powell (2012).

[153]Though Powell finds that states that are hybrids of autocracies and democracies (i.e. anocracies) are slightly more likely to experience coup attempts than are pure autocracies or democracies, such an assertion is problematic given that the classification of these hybrid systems is largely based on whether they experience political instability to begin with (see Vreeland 2008, for a discussion of this in the context of civil war).

[154]Cox (2009).

[155]Geddes (2005).

[156]Ezrow and Frantz (2011).

[157]Barbara Geddes (2005).

mass demonstrations to support the dictator than it would be for a group of previously unorganized individuals trying to rally the masses from scratch."[158] Such demonstrations can deter members of the military from staging a coup by signaling lack of popular support for such an endeavor. Hugo Chávez in Venezuela was saved from being overthrown with the help of his political party. Geddes argues that "support parties and organized 'movements' can create the infrastructure and cadre of organizers needed to mobilize huge demonstrations on short notice. Such demonstrations can of course be spontaneous, but the ones that save particular political leaders are almost always mobilized by [a] party . . . with a strong vested interest in the survival of the leader."[159]

As mentioned before, the absence of institutionalized parties has been a disservice to Pakistan's fledgling democracy. Its current party system is broken and parties are personality driven. Two of the main parties, the Pakistan People's Party (PPP) and the Pakistan Muslim League (PML-N), are instruments of two families, the Bhuttos and the Sharifs—both of whom have been accused of large-scale corruption. As a result, parties have been unable to provide accountability for poor leadership and the military has resorted to staging numerous coups.[160]

Autocracies with partisan legislatures

Partisan legislatures are also shown to reduce the likelihood of coups.[161] The argument underlying this relationship is that such legislatures, because they allow multiple political parties to have representation, incorporate potential opposition forces into the system, giving them something at stake in its survival. In other words, they broaden the support base of the autocratic government, making them less susceptible to coups.

Terrorism

Political institutions matter when it comes to terrorism. Since terrorism is a strategy aimed at impacting the government by targeting its citizens, terrorist incidents have occurred more frequently in democracies than autocracies. The bulk of the terrorist literature has focused on the importance of regime type, or whether or not countries are democratic or autocratic.

---

[158]Ibid., 4.
[159]Ibid., 12.
[160]Rizvi (1991: 1–2).
[161]Gandhi and Przeworski (2007); Boix and Svolik (2008).

Free and fair elections

Relationships emerge when we examine the impact of political institutions and terrorist activity. The majority of studies devoted to understanding the political conditions amenable to terrorist attacks indicates that *democracies* are more likely to be targets of terrorist attacks than are autocracies.[162] Authoritarian regimes generally have lower risks of terrorism.[163] Some of the more authoritarian states in the world do not have many recorded terrorist incidents, such as Belarus, Cuba, North Korea, Zimbabwe, Zambia, and Equatorial Guinea.[164] In contrast, democracies have had approximately four times as many incidents per capita as non-democratic regimes.[165] There are a number of theoretical arguments proposed to explain this. For one, terrorist groups are more likely to attack democracies because they are better able to coerce democratic leaders.[166] As terrorism is a strategy of signaling to the public vulnerabilities of the target regime, a democratic country targeted is more likely to heed to the public outcry of a terrorist group than an authoritarian regime. Suicide bombings, in particular, target mainly democracies because they can lead to a policy shift.[167] The 2004 Madrid bombings illustrate this case, as the incumbent pro-US regime was quickly ousted in the next election. Others argue that terrorism is more likely in a democracy because there is greater political competition in democracies.[168]

In addition to free and fair elections, democracies are often more permissive of freedom of movement and association. Because of this some scholars argue that terrorist activity may be more likely in democracies. These freedoms give terrorist groups opportunities to establish themselves in societies and plot actions against their own or foreign governments.[169] Though the particular reason why democracies are more likely to be targets of terrorist activities is up for debate, the relationship itself is fairly robust.

Autocracies with partisan legislatures

Though terrorism is a more infrequent occurrence in autocracies, there is also some indication that political institutions in autocracies bear the risk

---

[162]See Chenoweth (2010); Eubank and Weinberg (1994); Li (2005: 278–97); Li and Schaub (2004); Pape (2003).
[163]Lisanti (2010: 1–26); Abadie (2006).
[164]Hehir (2007).
[165]Blomberg and Hess (2008).
[166]Pape 2005b); (2003).
[167]Suicide attacks represent 3 percent of all attacks but half of all deaths according to a 1980–2001 study by Robert Pape (2005b).
[168]Chenoweth (2010).
[169]Ibid.

of being targets of terrorist activity. In particular, some studies have argued that autocracies with *partisan legislatures* are less likely to be victims of terrorism than are other forms of autocracy.[170] They argue that this occurs because legislative representation gives opposition groups an outlet for their discontents. As such, such groups are less likely to turn toward terrorist activity to express their positions.

Methodological issues

Identifying the "democraticness" or "autocraticness" of the system is a more in-depth endeavor than simply assessing whether it has free and fair elections, but regardless it is worth pointing out why doing so is often problematic. Many studies that examine the relationship between the strength of the political system type and political instability measure "strength" using data that use episodes of political instability to assess this. This almost guarantees that researchers will uncover a relationship between states that are weak (as in, neither strongly democratic nor autocratic) and political instability. For example, many researchers use combined polity scores to assess how consolidated the political system is. Yet the components that underlie combined polity scores often are direct measures of the presence of internal instability.[171] Because assessments of how democratic or autocratic a state is typically incorporate its record of political instability, it is often problematic for researchers to evaluate the relationship between consolidation of the political system and political instability.[172]

Thus, it is worth mentioning that a number of studies have looked not at how consolidated the political system is, but simply how new it is. The idea here is that states that are new democracies or autocracies will be more prone to political instability because contending groups may view the governments that rule them to be weaker and easier to topple. This "newness" of the political system does not face the same methodological issues as the strength of the political system does because researchers can capture it by simply looking at the number of years that a particular system has been in place (e.g. the number of years since the first free and fair or fraudulent election). The evidence appears to support the contention that new political systems are particularly vulnerable to political instability. Erica Frantz, for example, shows that all political systems (regardless of type) are more

---

[170]Aksoy et al. (2012).
[171]Other researchers use Freedom House political freedom scores to capture the "democraticness" or "autocraticness" of the system (see Abadie 2006). Yet this also brings with it problems, given that states that are vulnerable to political instability may be more likely to restrict political freedoms as a consequence.
[172]See Chapter Two in this book for a larger discussion of these measurement issues in the state failure literature.

likely to experience coups and civil wars during their first few years in power than later on in their lifetimes. Autocracies appear to be particularly prone to this: coups and civil wars occur at far higher rates when they are "newer."[173]

The message to emerge from this discussion of political system type and political instability is that whether states have free and fair elections or not does not appear to drive their experiences with all aspects of political instability. Democracies do not experience political instability at greater rates than their autocratic counterparts. What matters even more for political instability is not the type of political institution that a state adopts, but rather the *timing of its adoption* (which often affects the level of institutionalization) and that it chooses to adopt political institutions. States that have only recently become democratic (or autocratic) are far more vulnerable to political instability than states that have operated that way for some time. Though this message is not conducive to the provision of advice on building state political institutions, it does suggest that when states adopt new political institutions they will be more prone to episodes of instability.

Moving forward

Political institutions are some of the most fundamental institutions of the state. They play a major role in determining how leaders are selected and the processes through which policies are implemented. When assessing their impact, the evidence is mixed regarding the relationship between political institutions and state performance. Compared to autocracies, democratic systems appear to have some advantages, including greater public good allocations and lower rates of corruption; but they also have some disadvantages, including greater vulnerability to terrorist attacks. Thus, unlike with other institutional domains of the state, there is no set of features of political institutions that are desirable across all contexts.

There are two reasons for this. For one, features of political institutions have different implications for state performance depending on the other features of political institutions that are in effect. Political institutions often exhibit an interactive effect, shaping outcomes in different ways depending on the overall political institutional context. The second reason is that individual features of political institutions do not yield consistently positive or negative outcomes for state performance. As we show in this chapter, for example, free and fair elections are associated with states that experience lower rates of corruption, but they are also associated with states that are more prone to terrorist attacks. As a result, it is more difficult to identify

---

[173]Frantz (2012).

key features of high-quality political institutions, as we are able to do with other domains of the state. This is not to say that political institutions do not matter. Rather, our point is that when it comes to *economic perform-ance* and *political stability*, the consequences of political institutions for these outcomes is not clear-cut.

In spite of this, there are some lessons to be learned. The majority of the evidence on political institutions in *autocracies* suggests that the existence of elections, legislatures, and political parties work to reduce episodes of political instability. The same can be said when looking at economic per-formance. In autocracies, these institutions appear to uniformly improve state performance. Though these features may be a double-edged sword, in that they also help maintain the stability of authoritarian regimes, they also may better prepare countries that eventually end up democratizing for a more stable transition. Several scholars have claimed that countries that have more powerful parliaments compared to executives have been eventu-ally able to transition to democracy.[174]

Though democratization is usually a risky venture, democratizing autoc-racies that have had some experience with elections, political parties, and legislatures may be better able to withstand challenges to stability than their authoritarian counterparts that are poorly institutionalized. Mexico provides a good example of this. Years of elections won regularly by the PRI may have helped facilitate the transition to democracy in 2000, which took place in a relatively stable manner.

Nevertheless, state-building efforts would most likely bear greater fruit by concentrating on states' administrative, judicial, and security institu-tions. High-quality institutions in these three domains mean that citizens are provided with basic goods and services, access to justice, and security, all of which are key responsibilities of the state in the social contract. When these institutions are high in quality, states exhibit better economic per-formance and greater political stability. Though promoting high-quality institutions in these domains may require that governments reform their political institutions, the process of doing so would not be based on a set blueprint, but rather the particular social and political context of the state. Given that what constitutes high-quality political institutions is highly con-text dependent and variable, such an approach is the most pragmatic way of moving forward.

---

[174]Fish (2006); Starr (2006).

PART THREE

Warning signs and solutions

CHAPTER EIGHT

Warning sign: Corruption

Corruption may be the most pernicious effect of institutional decay. It is also the most obvious warning sign that the state is in peril. High levels of corruption often precede conflict and coups. Corruption and organized crime go hand in hand. Corruption is also a huge factor behind economic decline. For these reasons, we devote an entire chapter to institutional corruption.[1]

There are many different types of corruption that pervade state institutions. Corruption can take the form of civil servants, the police, and judges accepting bribes or false accounting. Corruption can involve a nontransparent process of decision making for job appointments and access to business contracts—a process that is entirely based on personal relationships rather than merit. Corruption can also entail the plundering of the state by the high-echelon leadership. Corruption can also involve the military using its coercive power to control key sectors of the economy, engage in illegal procurement kickbacks, or dominate the political process. Finally, in countries that hold elections, manipulating the results is another common form of corruption. In all of these cases, widespread corruption is a sign that the institutions are not functioning—and it is a clear sign that the capacity of the state is declining. We illustrate the different types of corruption that affect state institutions.

---

[1]We will be specifically looking at corruption that affects the state, not society. Societal corruption can exist but not necessarily be problematic for stability and economic performance. For example many businesses may make hiring decisions based on connections rather than merit, but this should not be deemed as a sign that the *state* is failing.

Administrative corruption

In what is sometimes referred to as a competitive-bribery state, low-level civil servants (nonelected officials) accepting bribes from ordinary citizens is commonplace.[2] This is otherwise known as *administrative corruption*. In its worst form, the expectation of constant bribes leads to administrative inaction and the refusal to provide vital services unless a bribe is paid. When bureaucrats assume that bribes are a systematic part of their remuneration, the entire output of the administrative institutions is in jeopardy.[3]

In a more benign version, basic services such as sanitation, water, and electricity are provided but more particular transactions require bribes. Corruption in Vietnam takes this form. Civil servants take a small margin or commission on the fixed charge for whatever they do. Unless this commission is an outrageously large sum, it is not considered corruption. This demonstrates the gap between formal institutions and informal cultures. Some cultures tolerate corruption to different degrees. In many cases, the officials do not acknowledge that bribery even constitutes a form of corruption. Russia's former minister of interior Vladmir Rushailo responded to accusations that 70 percent of Russia's civil servants were corrupt by saying that "you should not confuse corruption with bribe-taking."[4] In Mongolia, gifts are provided to civil servants to circumvent red tape.[5] Gift giving is also a source of corruption in Thailand and Cambodia.[6]

In particular, agencies that interact with the public such as immigration, internal revenue, customs, and licensing are more prone to corruption as they have more opportunities to ask for bribes.[7] During Ferdinand Marcos' rule in the Philippines, graft and corruption were widespread throughout all bureaucratic agencies, particularly in revenue collection, licensing, and customs. The more procedural complexity and ambiguity involving these agencies, the greater likelihood that illegal exchanges will take place. The tax system was so confusing and unclear in Indonesia under Suharto that it was impossible for an individual to assess one's tax rate. Taxes rates were thus "negotiable" by visiting a tax office in person. During this face-to-face consultation, a rate would be agreed to based on arbitrary criteria. In Indonesia, a job as a tax collector was one of the "surest roads to riches in the government bureaucracy."[8]

In addition to internal revenues services, customs agencies are also prone to corruption. Customs are responsible for allowing access to goods and

---

[2]Rose-Ackerman (1999: 124).
[3]Ulklah (2004: 433).
[4]Eigen (2002: 47).
[5]Quah (2006: 176).
[6]Ibid., 177.
[7]Ibid., 176.
[8]Robertson-Snape (1999: 594–5).

services (such as drugs) within a country, and because of this they have multiple opportunities to interact with those involved in the illicit economic activities.[9] In Lebanon, for example, customs officials reportedly refuse to process transactions unless bribes are forthcoming, and importers and exporters resort to bribes in order to avoid difficulties and expedite transactions.[10] In Indonesia, the whole economy was threatened by the "pervasiveness and extremism of corruption within the customs system which was seen to be one of the main causes of Indonesia's high-cost economy."[11] Just getting goods through customs inspections required "37 signatures" and unofficial fees.[12]

Licensing is another area ripe for corruption. In Ghana, the Ministry of Trade refused to issue import licenses without payment of a bribe between 5 and 10 percent of the value of the license requested.[13] In India, the License Raj was responsible for extracting bribes from businesses, making it difficult to start a business without using bribery. Civil servants got in the habit of causing delays until some kind of payment to them was made.

In Bangladesh, administrative corruption extends to other areas as well. In Bangladesh, payments were required to obtain an application form or a signature, to secure a copy of an approved sanction and to ensure proper services and billing from telephone, natural gas, electric power, and water employees.[14] In Dhaka, Bangladesh, a 1992 study found that 68.25 percent of respondents paid bribes to officials in order to receive services.[15] Studies in Indonesia found that it was necessary to pay a bribe when "registering the birth of a baby, or applying for a driving license or marriage certificate, or when obtaining a compulsory identity card."[16] In fact a 1998 study found that 78 percent of Indonesians felt that bribery was unavoidable when dealing with administrative offices.

BOX 8.1 Clientelism

Clientelism is a political system based on conditional loyalties and involving mutual benefits, in which individuals of unequal power are linked together through the exchange of favors. By favors we are referring to monetary compensation, jobs, loans, scholarships, or other forms of preferential

(*Continued*)

---

[9]Buscaglia (2003: 12).
[10]Gould (1980: 21).
[11]Robertson-Snape (1999: 595).
[12]Ibid.
[13]Gould and Amaro-Reves (1983: 8).
[14]Khan (2003: 398).
[15]Ibid., 398.
[16]Robertson-Snape (1999: 590).

BOX 8.1 *Continued*

treatment. This process is also often referred to as *patronage* or the distribution of government jobs or other favors to political allies irrespective of their qualifications. Rather than relying on rational-legitimate forms of governance based on the formation of sound policies, patron-clientelist systems sustain loyalty through the selective and particular distribution of favors to loyal clients. This differs from *pork barrel polices*, which have been commonplace in developed democracies.[17] With pork barrel legislation an entire geographic constituency may be the benefactor and the relationship between the legislator and the constituent is less personalized. With patronage, or patron-clientelism, the number of recipients is fewer and the relationship is much more individualized and particular.

Clientelism is often linked with countries that have weak administrative and political institutions. In these instances, regimes that have low levels of nationalism, poor economic performance and weak leaderships will rely on clientelistic practices in order to cultivate loyalties.[18] Without any legitimacy, leaders can build small winning coalitions based on steering benefits toward people of a similar ethnic group (when patron-clientelism takes place along ethnic lines it is referred to as prebendalism).[19]

Clientelistic practices have undermined state capacity in Latin America. Politicians use office as a source of particularized benefits for constituents. Programs that were supposed to resemble development projects actually delivered particularized benefits that went directly to partisan supporters. Supporters of a particular leader are more likely to receive land during land reform, small loans from the state banks, vouchers for free lunches or milk, scholarships, material to build houses, and so on.[20] Barbara Geddes writes that when Carlos Andrés Pérez, the former president of Venezuela, was campaigning in the countryside in 1985, he received over 1,000 personal requests in writing during a 4-day trip. In Brazil in 1992, under former president Fernando Collor, money that was supposed to go toward regional development went directly into the hands of deputies that were loyal to Collor.[21]

---

[17]Pork barrel funding involves the appropriation of public funds for geographically targeted projects that do not serve the interests of a large portion of the country's citizenry, often times circumventing funding procedures.
[18]Lemarchand (1972: 68–90).
[19]van de Walle (2000).
[20]Geddes (1994: 135).
[21]Ibid., 137.

Overcoming patron-clientelism can be very difficult because those involved in patron-clientelistic relationships feel that they are benefitting from the status quo. In spite of this perception, patron-clientelism fosters entrenched inequalities; most recipients of patronage are kept dependent on their patrons indefinitely.

Police corruption

Corruption can affect the security institutions as well. Law enforcement agencies can use their positions of power to exact bribes. In Bangladesh, the police have been cited as one of the most corrupt institutions in the country, with 90 percent reporting in 2003 study that it was impossible to obtain help from the police without offering a bribe. Another 68 percent claimed that police have propositioned them for bribes.[22] The police are involved in arbitrary arrests and because of this, many poor people simply avoid the police. The same can be said of the Indonesian police. The police may pull over cars to collect bribes for no apparent reason.[23] The same problems afflict the police in Africa. According to a 1998 National Integrity Survey, two-third of Ugandans had to pay a bribe to police.[24]

The police have been notoriously corrupt in Mexico as well. In Mexico a 2002 survey revealed that the average household spends 8 percent of their income on bribes to the police.[25] Worse than just accepting bribes, the police have been tempted to engage in crime. It is therefore not uncommon for the police to serve as fronts for criminal groups or to also extort criminal groups, in exchange for not arresting them. Poor salaries coupled by the enormous remuneration from the drug trade cause this problem to persist. Drug funds also help buy the police impunity.[26]

A survey of Mexico City demonstrated that 90 percent expressed no trust in the police.[27] A Mexican journalist echoed this survey, claiming that police commanders "have not realized what most citizens already know, that we are afraid to approach the police."[28] Thus police corruption fosters

---

[22]Ulklah (2004: 434).
[23]Robertson-Snape (1999: 590).
[24]United Nations Office for Drug Control and Crime Prevention (May 2000: 4).
[25]Reames (2003: 7).
[26]Davis (2006: 61–2).
[27]Reames (2003: 7).
[28]Davis (2006: 57).

low levels of trust in the state, making it difficult for the criminal justice system to function effectively.

In many states in Central Asia, the police have also been corrupted and are easily bought off. This has had serious implications for facilitating the drug trade and smuggling rings. Drugs, oil, gems, and guns are smuggled in easily into Central Asia from Afghanistan because police are paid to look the other way.[29] For example, from 1997 to 1998, Kyrgyzstan claimed that over 155 tons of oil was smuggled into the country.[30] Corruption within the security sector makes it difficult for the state to regulate what goods enter and leave the country.

Military corruption

One of the most common corrupt practices of the military involves illegitimate procurement practices.[31] An un-professionalized military has the power to procure equipment and defense supplies that are totally unnecessary in return for large kickbacks. In the case of Uganda, since the late 1990s the military has begun to buy more and more expensive and unnecessary equipment and military hardware in exchange for kickbacks and massive overpayments.[32] In 1998 the Ugandan government purchased four Mi-24 helicopters from the Republic of Belarus at an inflated price of US$12.3 million even though they were not airworthy. In return, a kickback of $800,000 was given to Major General Salim Saleh (also the brother of Ugandan President Yoweri Museveni).[33]

Military corruption persists because military budgets face limited scrutiny. Due to low levels of transparency little is known about the nature of the arms being procured, how much is being spent, the size of the kickbacks, and where the money from the kickbacks is being laundered.[34] Illegitimate procurement is facilitated to the extent that defense budgets are unaccountable and nontransparent to civilian actors. In the case of Uganda, though

---

[29]Thomas and Kiser (2002: 28).

[30]Ibid.

[31]The military can also engage in natural resource predation, such as the Nigerian military's role in operating the state-owned oil industry. In Angola, $1 billion a year in potential oil revenues is siphoned off by the military. Soldiers can also earn money by imposing taxes and levies arbitrarily. In Burundi, the military imposes taxes on farmers. In other countries in Africa, soldiers employ roadblocks to extract payments to supplement their salaries (see Willet 2009).

[32]Tangri and Mwenda (2003: 539).

[33]Willett (2009: 346).

[34]Ibid., 343.

illegal procurement practices went on for years, not a single leader has faced prosecution or punishment.[35]

Judicial corruption

The judicial institutions are also not immune to corruption. Judicial corruption "includes corrupt acts by judges, prosecutors, public defenders, court officials, and lawyers who are intimately involved in the operation of the judicial system."[36] Court users may pay bribes to employees of the courts in order to alter the legally determined treatment of files and discovery material. In other cases, court users may pay court employees to accelerate or delay a case by illegally altering the order in which the case is to be attended by the judge. There are also instances where court employees commit fraud and embezzle public property or private property in court custody. These cases of corruption are referred to as procedural and administrative irregularities.

Other types of judicial corruption are operational and have more serious repercussions. Judges may base their rulings not on evidence and legal considerations but based on bribes. This makes it difficult for the poor to get fair trials and skews outcomes in favor or those who have connections or wealth. For example, seeking justice is difficult for poor Indonesians since many judges sell rulings to the highest bidders.[37] Half of Ugandans have had to bribe court personnel.[38]

Additional types of operational corruption are part of grand corruption schemes where political and/or considerable economic interests are at stake. This type of corruption usually involves politically motivated court rulings or changes of venue. Judges stand to gain economically and career-wise as a result of their compliance. These cases involve substantive irregularities affecting judicial decision making where the politically and economically powerful are immune from punishment. Examples include irregular decision making that had allowed drug traffickers in Colombia to avoid punishment, or politically motivated decision making that ensures that powerful actors retain their authority. In the case of Russia, the judges do not have a commitment to the "rule of law, but to instructions" from politicians.[39] Operational types of corruption can be measured through the surveys of

---

[35]Tangri and Mwenda (2003: 539).
[36]US AID (2009: 8); see also Buscaglia (1997).
[37]Robertson-Snape (1999: 590).
[38]United Nations Office for Drug Control and Crime Prevention (2000: 4).
[39]Levin and Satarov (2000: 131).

judges, court employees, businesses, asking them to describe irregularities.[40] This type of corruption puts the rule of law in jeopardy.

Political corruption

In addition to other forms of corruption that affect the administrative, judicial, and security sectors, political corruption is just as pervasive and in some cases more damaging for stability and economic performance. Political corruption is defined as the abuse of *elected* office for personal gain.[41] This can involve using power of political office to dole out benefits to family members and friends. It can also entail embezzling and siphoning funds and assets for personal advancement. In extreme cases, political corruption reaches a stage known as kleptocracy, or sometime referred to as "rule by thieves."

In a kleptocracy, the primary beneficiary of corruption is the leader and his entourage. Kleptocracies occur where a single ruler exploits the resources of the state for personal gain and/or by accepting huge bribes and kickbacks in exchange for authorizing certain political decisions. The leader's main objective is personal enrichment and the political and economic system is structured to maximize the economic interests of the government elites.[42] Foreign aid is often embezzled. Resources extracted go directly into the leader's pockets. For example, Suharto in Indonesia and his family were worth more than $15 billion.[43] Malawi President Banda managed much of the country's commercial activity through family trusts.[44] After a decade in power, Liberia President Samuel Doe accumulated a fortune equivalent to half of Liberia's annual domestic income.[45] Sani Abacha (1993–8) of Nigeria stole $4 billion in less than five years by awarding contracts to front companies, accepting huge bribes, and stealing money directly from the treasury. Family members and friends were used to transfer the money abroad.[46]

Few leaders embody kleptocratic rule more than Mobutu of Zaire. Robert Rotberg writes: "What set Mobutu apart from other neo-patrimonial rulers was his unparalleled capacity to institutionalize kleptocracy at every level of the social pyramid and his unrivalled talent for transforming personal rule into a cult and political clientelism into cronyism. Stealing was

---

[40]Buscaglia (2001: 235).
[41]Kramer (1997: 17–21).
[42]Lundahl (1997: 39).
[43]Quah (2006: 178).
[44]Reno (2000b).
[45]Ibid.
[46]Goldsmith (2004: 91).

not so much a perversion of the ethos of public service as it was its raison d'etre."[47] Mobutu acquired over $8 billion by siphoning off Zaire's various resources that exceeded the recoded annual economic output of the country.[48] In the 1970s, 15–20 percent of the operating budget of the state went directly to Mobutu. In 1977 alone Mobutu's family took $71 million from the National Bank for personal use.[49]

President General Hussain Muhammad Ershad (1993–0) in Bangladesh used corruption to perpetuate his regime. He siphoned out huge amounts of state funds into his own pockets.[50] Ershad also received a fixed percentage on any business deal involving any amount of money.[51]

In Haiti under Jean-Claude Duvalier (1971–86), "checks of up to 6.8 million dollars were written out to members of the presidential family and other private citizens from the tobacco monopoly, the state lottery, the flour mill, the government gambling commission, the state owned car insurance company, the telecommunications and electricity companies, the cement factory."[52] Transparency International claimed that Duvalier stole the equivalent of 1.7–4.5 percent if Haiti's GDP for every year that he was in power.[53]

Kleptocracy has also occurred in Central Asia through rent-seeking activities of family owned firms. Even President Askar Akaev of Kyrgyzstan once considered to be relatively committed to democracy was eventually culpable of rampant corruption involving himself, his family, and his clan. Akaev's family amassed a large fortune from misusing foreign aid and rent seeking.[54] Other Central Asian presidents have benefited financially from taking power as well. In Tajikistan, Emomalii Rakhmonov also engaged in rent seeking, albeit on a smaller scale. Both Nursultan Nazarbaev in Kazakhstan and Islam Karimov of Uzbekistan benefited from large kickbacks from Russian oil and gas investors, respectively.[55] Saparmurat Niyazov of Turkmenistan reportedly gained a huge fortune from energy rents in offshore accounts that he directly pocketed.[56]

Business cannot thrive once a state becomes kleptocratic. Kleptocratic rulers may also gain wealth through stripping the business community of

---

[47]Rotberg (2003: 31).
[48]Reno (2000b).
[49]Leslie (1987: 72).
[50]Ulklah (2004).
[51]Khan (1998: 10).
[52]Lundahl (1997: 40).
[53]Rose-Ackermann (2007).
[54]Collins (2009: 267).
[55]Ibid.
[56]Ibid.

their assets. This discourages successful business practices and any sort of innovation.[57] As a result, legitimate businesses are driven underground and capital flees, often leading to staggering economic decline.[58]

BOX 8.2 Rent seeking

Rent seeking consists of actions by individuals and groups to alternate public policy and procedures in ways that generate more income for themselves.[59] Rent seeking differs from profit seeking, in that profit-seeking activities do provide some positive spillovers to the public. Rent seeking, by definition, provides no positive spillovers to the public.

Specifically a rent is known as a good whose supply remains constant irrespective of the price paid for the goods and whose price is completely determined by the demand of the good.[60] Economic rents are simply windfall gains that would be absent in competitive markets. When the government intervenes in markets, at times it can create "distortions" that can serve as a source of economic rents.[61] Rent seekers capture incomes, without producing output or making a productive contribution to society.

Rent seekers aim to profit from government power.[62] The state often exercises power in various areas such as allocating property rights, and providing regulations and subsidies, levying taxes, tariffs, and import quotas or by awarding contracts in public procurement.[63] In some cases, rent seekers *legally* lobby for measures to reduce competition so that they can sell their goods at much higher prices and earn monopoly profits. Rent seekers may try to persuade governments to provide them with higher returns than they could earn in the absence of government protection. Though this has deleterious effects on the economy, it is not illegal. Using illicit methods, rent seekers may *bribe* the state so that their inefficient company wins a key contract.[64] In other cases, the state wants to give preferential treatment to

(Continued)

---

[57]Lundahl (1997: 45).
[58]In Uganda under Idi Amin, the Asian community was deprived of $400 million in assets in 1972.
[59]Brinkerhoff and Goldsmith (2002: 13). For some early definitions of rent seeking see Buchanan, Tollison, and Tullock (1980).
[60]Lambsdorff (2002: 123).
[61]Brinkerhoff and Goldsmith (2002: 13).
[62]Rowley et al. (1988: 10).
[63]Though rent seeking is often illegal, it can also be a legal activity.
[64]Note that illegal rent seeking is a type of corruption.

BOX 8.2 *Continued*

key support groups by using rent-seeking tactics as a means of *patronage*.[65] Often those who benefit are family members of those in power or important cronies that offer support for the regime.

Rent seeking, both legal and illegal, distorts economic incentives and deflects the productive energy of society's most able members. Rent seekers benefit from preferential treatment by gaining political support, which may impede competitors from entering the market.[66] Potential competition must deal with regulations and laws that favor the monopoly. Expenses paid for preferential treatment do not add to welfare; they are simply wasteful.[67] With rent seeking, a share of income is earned in a nonproductive manner.[68] Rent seeking generates social waste rather than surplus.[69]

Institutions serve as obstacles for illegal forms of rent seeking. High functioning administrative institutions can monitor illicit activity better. They also have more motivation to make sure that transactions that take place are transparent and are in the best interest of the state. High functioning judicial institutions are also important as they can punish illegal rent-seeking activity, in accordance with following the rule of law. Institutions can impact the prevalence of legal forms of rent seeking as well. Pius Fischer writes that "institutions determine the profitability of rent-seeking relative to profit-seeking activities."[70] Fischer adds that "the more the rules in a society determine that income can be earned only by making a productive contribution the more a society will prosper."[71]

Systems that have few institutional restraints to check insiders when they use their contacts to pursue self-serving government policies suffer from economic underperformance.[72] This has affected many states in the developing world. Indonesia under Suharto is a case in point. In Indonesia those who were connected were granted a monopoly and served as the sole importer of a particular product. For example, Panca Holding was the only enterprise that could import plastics. This artificially inflated the price of plastic and directly benefited Suharto's cousin and sons who headed

(Continued)

---

[65]Lambsdorff (2002: 101).
[66]Ibid.
[67]Ibid., 102.
[68]Fischer (2006: 2).
[69]Michael A. Brooks and Ben J. Heudra, "An Exploration of Rent Seeking," *Economic Record* 65, no. 1 (2007): 32.
[70]Fischer (2006: 7).
[71]Ibid., 2.
[72]Brinkerhoff and Goldsmith (2002: 13). In Egypt, rent-seeking elites have inflated the costs of important public goods (see Box 6.1, Chapter Six, on military entrepreneurship).

BOX 8.2 Continued

the company.[73] One notable crony of Suharto named Bob Hasan built an empire around controlling a monopoly on the wood industry. The price for wood exports, the number of wood exports, and which shipping and insurance companies would be used was determined by Hasan's connections to Suharto. Hasan's timber company benefited greatly from this relationship, while any other company was unable to compete.[74] The prevalence of these types of activities meant that in Indonesia, it was not always the most efficient company that received access to a monopoly; just the most politically connected one. Therefore, efficiency under Suharto was sidelined in favor of maintaining a robust elite support group.

Rent seeking can also have a disastrous effect on the economy, when it takes place in the banking industry. In Bangladesh under General Ershad, rent-seeking practices were common in the banking industry. Banks were doled out to dishonest businessmen who were connected to Ershad. As a result, defaulting on loans was commonplace. By the time that Ershad left power in late 1990s, the amount of defaulted loans stood at US$2 billion.[75]

Electoral fraud is another type of political corruption that has less destructive effects on the economy than kleptocracy, but nonetheless erodes the legitimacy of democracy and fosters voter apathy. Electoral fraud constitutes some form of illegal interference during elections. Elections can be interfered with primarily through vote buying, ballot stuffing, and vote miscounting. With vote buying, voters are simply paid to vote in favor of a particular candidate or party, with little regard for their true interests and beliefs. Politics in this instance is merely an economic transaction. With ballot stuffing, the voters usually do not play any role in the process and the ballot results are manipulated by creating phantom voters. In other cases voters are given the chance to vote multiple times. Ballots of opposition candidates can also be destroyed. When votes are miscounted, the true results are hidden, and the announced result is manufactured to appear legitimate.[76] If votes have been stuffed or miscounted, and results are disputed, corrupt regimes can rely on positioning pliable individuals to "electoral commissions," which then oversee the results. This type of corruption is commonplace in many developing countries. In Bangladesh

---

[73]Robertson-Snape (1999: 594).
[74]Ibid., 596.
[75]Ulklah (2004: 434).
[76]Lehoucq (2003: 233–56).

under General Ershad, his regime was known for "destroying the credibility of the electoral system."[77] He used the Electoral Commission in Bangladesh to serve his own personal interests, and members of the Commission were appointed by him directly.[78]

Nepotism and cronyism are forms of corruption that also undermine the efficiency of the state. Nepotism is the bestowal of patronage (jobs, economic opportunities, favors) by reason of familial relationship rather than due to merit. Cronyism encompasses the same concept except that benefits are passed along to friends and loyal lackeys. Nepotism and cronyism often go hand in hand with kleptocracies, but nepotism and cronyism are more encompassing concepts than stealing from the state. It entails granting all types of political favors to family members and friends.

In many developing countries the key sectors of the economy are controlled by family members of the ruler. The economy of Kazakhstan is controlled by President Nazarbaev and his relatives. His daughter controls the media while another daughter controls the construction industry, water, and gas. A son-in-law has controlled the oil monopoly and a former son-in-law controlled parts of the food industry (sugar and alcohol and taxation.[79] In Kyrgyzstan, Akayev's wife's clan controlled the ministries responsible for gold mining. In Indonesia, the Suharto family held major interests in all the important sectors of the economy including "roads, car manufacturing and telecommunications."[80] By the end of Rafael Trujillo's (1930–61) regime in the Dominican Republic, the fortune of the Trujillo family was equal to about 100 percent of its GDP at current prices and the family "controlled almost 80% of the country's industrial production."[81] In the Philippines under Marcos, 10 percent of all ministerial budgets went to the First Lady's personal projects.[82]

Family members can benefit directly from laws that undermine competitors. In the case of the Philippines under Marcos, one of his in-laws Herminio Disini benefited from a 1975 presidential decree that imposed a 100 percent tax on tobacco filler for all companies other than Diseni's Philippines Tobacco Corporation. His firm was the only firm that faced a 10 percent tax. The IMF-sponsored tariff reduction program was undermined because family run corporations were exempted through presidential decrees.[83]

---

[77]Khan (1998: 10).
[78]Ibid.
[79]Franke et al. (2009: 114).
[80]Robertson-Snape (1999: 595).
[81]Acemoglu et al. (2004: 162–92).
[82]Ellison (2005: 117); Montes (1988).
[83]Aquino (1997: 5).

Nepotism can extend beyond running the economy.[84] Trujillo also made sure family members held important government posts. His brother held the presidency and other family members held two senatorial posts, six major diplomatic assignments, the positions of commander in chief of the armed forces, undersecretary of defense, chief of staff of the air force, inspector general of the army, inspector of embassies, just to name a few. As many as 153 relatives were employed by the government.[85]

Under Trujillo loyalty trumped competence. Trujillo appointed Jacinto Bienvenido Peynado as vice president "due to his loyalty and the fact that he preferred leisure to power."[86] Similarly, General Jose Estrella's loyalty was said to be "of a kind not often encountered except among four-legged animals.[87] It also helped to be related to Trujillo. Though most of his family members embarrassed him, he chose to make his son a colonel at the age of four and a brigadier general at the age of nine.[88]

Ershad's government was primarily based on the selective patronage distribution to a favored few cronies. Friends and cronies of Ershad received enormous sums of money and access to business deals though they had no understanding of business ethics or norms. Friends that had criminal records became millionaires.[89] Cronies of Ershad in Bangladesh became prominent in politics as members of parliament and the cabinet and eventually some of them became leaders of different chambers and other bodies.[90]

Both excessive cronyism and nepotism can impact the functioning of the economy when undeserving individuals are given opportunities that they would otherwise never be presented with. Deserving individuals may be precluded from being involved in key positions of the state and from gaining access to contracts. In other cases, successful entrepreneurs are undermined to bolster the business of family members of the leader. Nepotism and cronyism may not only impact economic growth but can lead to poor policy decisions in other areas as well.

State capture

In a *captured state*, all areas of government have been taken over, bought off, and are penetrated by organized crime. Thus, there is a de facto

---

[84]For example in Kyrgyzstan, the head of the security forces was an individual whose sole credentials was that he was related to the president.
[85]Acemoglu et al. (2004: 173).
[86]Crassweller (1966: 167).
[87]Ibid., 185.
[88]Hartlyn (1998).
[89]Khan (1998: 10).
[90]Ibid.

takeover of political, administrative, judicial, and security institutions for criminal activity.[91] State capture is an entirely different beast than pervasive low-level corruption. State capture subverts and replaces the legitimate and transparent channels of politics. All decisions made are biased. World Bank scholars have coined the term "state capture" to define the illicit provision of private gains to public officials via informal, nontransparent, and highly preferential channels of access.

In a captured state, crime often first inserts itself in the political institutions and uses this power and insider knowledge to achieve their aims in a more subtle way to weaken the administrative, judicial, and security institutions from within.[92] Thus, a captured state goes beyond just accepting bribes or allowing crime to occur. The police, the customs agents, the courts, and more specifically the ministries that deal with financial and economic matters are all captured by criminal groups; the state is not only filled with criminals but it also perpetuates crime.[93]

There are huge costs on citizens because funds are diverted from public goods that could be going toward safety, social services, and infrastructure. Moreover, corruption decreases the chances of attaining investment and entrepreneurship. Furthermore, when officials cannot be trusted this leads to low levels of public trust. A 1998 survey in Russia reveals that 80 percent of Russians polled believed that "criminal structures" exercise "significant influence" in Russia. In another survey, 51 percent affirm the proposition that "real power in Russia belongs to criminal structures and the mafia"

In the case of Mexico, counter-narcotics units have often been co-opted by drug cartels. Some heads of state at the highest levels have been implicated for collusion with the drug industry.[94] Non-state actors in Thailand, Laos, and Vietnam have also captured parts of the state to help facilitate the cultivation of opium and the heroin trade.[95] In some countries in Africa government officials have linked up with or directly run smuggling rings. In Liberia and Sierra Leone, both governments were easily penetrated by criminal elements involved in the smuggling of diamonds.[96]

Afghanistan also represents a state that has been captured. The bureaucracy, judges, the politicians, and the military are not functioning autonomously. They are captured by other powerful groups, such as warlords, that do not have a vested interest in any state-building project. Corruption is so pervasive that it is difficult to point the finger at who is at fault. In particular, the Afghan Ministry of Interior has been singled out as entirely

---

[91]Klitgaard (1988: 75).
[92]Cornell (2006: 40).
[93]Karklins (2002: 28).
[94]Cornell (2005b).
[95]Goodhand (2008).
[96]Reno (2000b).

ineffective, poorly led, and corrupt. Funds for the budget have been unaccountable. Finance Minister Ashraf Ghani estimated that 10–30 percent of the salaries were being stolen before the intended beneficiaries received them.[97] Firing incompetent individuals is near impossible due to political connections and bribes.[98]

Tajikistan has also been prey to state capture. The police and high- and low-level government officials have been involved in organized crime. In Tajikistan, low-paid government officials in law enforcement are bribed to look the other way as smugglers take a shipment through. More importantly, high-level government officials have also been involved in the trafficking of drugs and have been accused of being narco-barons. Warlords from the civil war have also been absorbed into the government, and maintain close ties with trafficking. After the war ended, the United Tajik Opposition (UTO), one of the groups involved in the civil war, took a 30 percent share in the government, though they continued to engage in drug trafficking.[99] Many drug traffickers are key members of the government. In May 2000, Tajikistan's ambassador to Kazakhstan was seized with 63 kg of heroin in his car.[100] As a result of state capture, levels of public trust are extremely low.

Georgia has been one of the few countries to reverse state capture. After Georgia had achieved independence, it was one of the consistently lowest ranked countries on the corruption perceptions index. A 1998 World Bank study of Georgia found that the prices of "high rent" public positions were "well known" among public officials and the general public, suggesting that corruption is "deeply institutionalized."[101]

For many years after achieving independence, Georgia did not display the will or the capacity to deal with organized crime. The de facto South Ossetian government, a disputed region within Georgian territory, developed a huge illegal free trade zone, where all kinds of legal and illegal merchandise were sold. Georgia allowed organized criminal groups to base themselves in the Pankisi Gorge region bordering Chechnya. Drug smuggling, abductions, and other forms of crime ensued. None of this activity would have been possible without the complete cooperation and participation of Georgian law enforcement structures.[102] Evidence later emerged of high-level government collusion with organized crime. Many of President Shevardnadze's cabinet were credibly alleged to be directly

---

[97]Giustozzi (2004: 12).
[98]Ibid.
[99]Markowitz (2012).
[100]Cornell (2005b: 581).
[101]Kaufman et al. (1998: 7).
[102]Fairbanks (2001: 50).

involved in organized crime.[103] Criminal groups had totally infiltrated the state structures.

When Mikheil Saakashvili (2004–13) came to power, he inherited one of the most corrupt regimes in the world. His two main priorities were to reunify Georgia with its breakaway regions of Abkhazia and South Ossetia and eradicate corruption and crime. He believed that the former could not happen without completing the latter. As he saw it, the separatist territories were connected to the illegal economy and organized crime. South Ossetia survived on smuggling and this greased the corruption and crime inside Georgia. Saakashvili moved against the corrupt police force to transform it into a professionalized one.[104]

He also implemented measures to increase the costs of smuggling by cutting off the Ergneti market and targeting roads leading into Georgia. He then went after organized crime by making it illegal to be a member of an organized crime network. Georgia has become more inhospitable for organized crime. Georgian law enforcement was trained and paid better. The police no longer allowed the illegal free trade zone to take place in South Ossetia.[105]

Georgia also reformed the administrative institutions. During the height of its instability, the state was unable to even collect taxes or pay state workers.[106] Reform programs were introduced that utilized a merit-based hiring process to replace the process of the previous regime of hiring close family members or friends into the civil service.[107] Saakashvili reasoned that attacking all types of graft would reinvigorate the private and public sectors and could serve as a source to draw revenues to bolster the fiscal strength of the state.[108]

Why does corruption persist?

There are multiple different reasons why corruption may afflict the various state institutions. One of the commonly cited causes of *administrative corruption* is low pay for civil servants. Think tanks, scholars, and international organizations (World Bank, IMF) have argued that civil servants who maintain their lives on low wages may be forced to ask for bribes in order to survive. This is known as "survival corruption."[109] In Ghana, in

---

[103]Kukhianidze (2009: 215–34).
[104]Ibid.
[105]Ibid.
[106]Fairbanks (2001: 51).
[107]The university admission system was reformed.
[108]George (2009: 135–54).
[109]Quah (2008: 242). Scholars such as Rose-Ackerman (1999), and Cokgezen (2004) have focused on this.

the 1960s and 1970s, salary levels for civil servants were so low in Ghana that many public sector employees could not afford a balanced diet, even if they spent their entire income on food.[110]

In the case of Vietnam, the low salary of civil servants is considered to be a reason for high levels of administrative corruption. In Mexico, meanwhile, middle-level bureaucrats are expected to live a certain type of lifestyle, which is impossible based on their incomes. Civil servants supplement their income with bribes and kickbacks from clients.[111]

Underpaid civil servants may illegally spend a substantial amount of office time on money-earning activities, thus detracting from their appointed duties and diminishing productivity. This situation may be exacerbated in some cases by the bureaucrat's lack of job security in the absence of unions, protection, and guarantees of future income.[112]

In other cases, officials may occupy bureaucratic positions to acquire personal wealth and status rather than to perform public service.[113] Some offices in administrative institutions can be lucrative for civil servants and are treated as a type of income generating property. In particular, institutions that interface frequently with the public provide opportunities for graft. For example in some developing countries government officials have to provide large sums of money to buy the offices they seek to occupy.[114] In Pakistan lucrative positions, such as customs posts, are often auctioned off to the highest bidders.[115]

In Zaire under Mobutu (1965–97), civil servants were encouraged to ask for bribes. Mobutu declared that in Zaire "everything is for sale . . . anything can be bought in our country. And in this flow, he who holds the slightest cover of public authority uses it illegally to acquire money, goods, prestige or to avoid obligations."[116]

Much of the reason why administrative corruption persists is the lack of punishment for transgressions. Thus countries with ineffective judicial institutions (either because they are not independent, not well funded, or poorly run) lack any means of deterring corruption. For example, there is almost no punishment for corrupt officials in India. Corruption in India persists due to "the ease with which corrupt officials are able to get away without punishment [that is] commensurate with their offence."[117] In Bangladesh, civil servants involved

[110]Gould and Amaro-Reves (1983: 28).
[111]Ibid.
[112]Ibid.
[113]Bratton and Walle (1994).
[114]Lenski and Lenski, (1987: 193).
[115]Islam (1989: 281).
[116]Dowden (1994).
[117]Quah (2008: 244).

in corruption do not lost their jobs, and are not required to return ill-gotten wealth.[118]

In contrast, both Singapore and Hong Kong have enacted legislation to give extensive powers to anticorruption commissions. In both states, the government severely punishes corrupt individuals "regardless of their status or position. Graft is perceived as a high-risk, low-reward activity."[119] A comparison of prosecution rates in Hong Kong and the Philippines demonstrated that a "civil servant committing a corrupt offense in Hong Kong was 35 times more likely to be detected and punished than his counterpart in the Philippines."[120] Since 1986, China established the Ministry of Supervision to curb corruption in the civil service.[121] Though civil society and the media generally has a critical role in curbing corruption, independent commissions have been established in authoritarian regimes and have achieved some success is diminishing graft.[122]

Some scholars have argued that too many rules and regulations can lead to the rule of law always being circumvented and present more opportunities for administrative staff to collect bribes. Many of the economies in Central Asia suffer from excessive restrictions. Repressive regulations in the private sector have led to widespread bribes by government officials.[123] More than 60 percent of firms in Central Asia claimed corruption made it hard to do business.[124] The long list of confusing rules and regulations makes it easier for civil servants to demand bribes from businesses. The World Bank estimates that one-third of the small-business profits in Uzbekistan go to bribes. It can also take 16 procedures to get a license to do business, which can take 152 days.[125] This deters the incentives to invest in Central Asia and also deters the impetus to engage in entrepreneurial activity.

Many countries in Latin America are unable to enforce rules and contracts because there are too many rules.[126] Though the state demands that mountains of paperwork are filled out, it is unable to enforce this paperwork.[127] States such as Peru have a tremendous amount of bureaucratic red tape to start a business, but weak enforcement of the laws. A study found that it required 289 days of full-time work, with bribe payments being

---

[118]Khan (2003: 398).
[119]Quah (2006: 177).
[120]Ibid.
[121]Ibid.
[122]Eigen (1996: 162).
[123]Franke et al. (2009: 112).
[124]World Bank (2012: 70).
[125]Ibid., 76.
[126]Fernández-Kelly and Shefner (2005: 35).
[127]Ibid., 28.

asked for on ten occasions.[128] In Ukraine, a study revealed that 64 percent of firms admitted to paying bribes to overcome red tape.[129] The excessive regulatory burden has made it difficult for the licit economy to flourish, and provides more incentives for the growth of the informal economy.[130]

BOX 8.3 Shadow economy

The shadow economy refers to the economic activities that are conducted *outside state regulated frameworks* and are not audited by the state institutions. Though actors involved in the shadow economy may rely on some state networks to draw their resources, they mainly override the purpose of the state and skirt the laws. The goods and services that form the output are legal and have the potential to be sold as intermediate goods and services to other producers or final users; the production and distribution of these goods, however, involve some illegality. The key activities of the shadow economy include the drug trade, cross border smuggling, extraction of natural resources, smuggling of high value commodities, and aid manipulation. Countries in the developing world have sizable shadow economies, with large levels of goods being taken illegally. For example, two-third of cocoa in Ghana was taken illegally. Another 15 percent of gold and diamonds in Ghana are also mined illegally.[131]

The shadow economy consists of a wide range of actors such as those involved in the transport sector, businessmen, drug traffickers, and downstream actors such as truck drivers, poppy farmers—all of whom

(Continued)

---

[128]Blackburn et al. (2008: 4).

[129]Ibid.

[130]Anwaruddin (2004: 299–311).

[131]Bulĭř (2002: 413–39). The shadow economy can be measured by examining the gap between the expenditure measure of the GDP and the income measure of the GDP (31). Another measure to look at is the decline in participation of the labor force in the official economy. A decreasing official rate of participation can be seen as an indicator of an increase in the activities in the shadow economy (IMF Working Paper, 2000). Recent estimates show that the average size of the shadow economy over 1989–93 as a percentage of GDP is 39 percent for developing countries and 12 percent for OECD countries. From 1997 to 8 the average labor force employed in the shadow economy was 50.1 percent in developing countries compared to 17.3 percent in the OECD countries. In countries like Nigeria and Egypt, the shadow economy from 1990 to 1993 consisted of 68–76 percent of their GDP. In Kyrgyzstan, according to the UN, the unofficial economy is 53 percent of the GDP (for more on this see Emran and Stiglitz 2005: 600).

BOX 8.3 *Continued*

are interested in making a profit by circumventing the state. Rulers may also engage in shadow economic activities, much of which may be used to help sustain patronage-based networks. For example, leaders in Sierra Leone benefited from clandestine diamond smuggling, which gave leaders easy access to money and added incentives to perpetuate the shadow economy.[132]

When administrative and judicial institutions (such as the rule of law) are weak, inefficient, inept, and corrupt, the shadow economy flourishes. Studies have shown that the relationship between the share of the unofficial economy and the strength of the rule of law is strong. Countries with more corruption have higher shares of the unofficial economy."[133] Using data for 69 countries, Eric Friedman et al. find evidence that "greater corruption, and a weaker legal environment are all associated with a larger unofficial economy . . ."[134] They conclude that ". . . poor institutions and a large unofficial economy go hand in hand."[135] The shadow economy is also facilitated by weak enforcement of laws and regulations. A low probability of being caught makes illicit activity more attractive. It is also provoked by heavy administrative burdens for entrepreneurs but weak enforcement.

As this chapter acknowledges, excessive rules and regulations can also lead to the emergence of a shadow economy. In this case, the business community faces too many regulations with weak enforcement and chooses to operate outside the official legal constraints. By doing so, important revenues from business are not collected.

Sometimes hiding in the shadows is essential for businesses. In Iraq under Saddam Hussein, starting a new business required an application to the Ministry of Trade that might take a year to complete. Worse, applications also attracted the attention of other parts of the government, like the secret police. Applicants were typically investigated to determine whether they had any relatives who belonged to opposition groups, who had deserted or avoided service in the army, or who had belonged to the regional militia in the restive Kurdish part of the country. A relative of the wrong person would be unable to start a business. Worse yet they could be arrested. This deterred people from registering their businesses.[136] When businesses went underground, government inspectors may have come by, but paying a bribe avoided further action.

(Continued)

---

[132]Bøås et al. (2001: 708); see also Reno (2000b: 43–68).
[133]Friedman et al. (2000: 460).
[134]Ibid.
[135]Ibid.
[136]Looney (2005: 561–80).

> ## BOX 8.3 *Continued*
>
> The shadow economy has mostly negative effects on overall economic growth and development. Power and wealth become more concentrated because only those with wealth and connections are able to run their business effectively. Inflation worsens because transaction costs are higher. Patron-client relationships also dominate because survival is dependent on favors. Furthermore, though the emergence of the shadow economy is predicated on the weakness of administrative institutions, the shadow economy, in turn, also further weakens these institutions. It becomes harder for the state to collect revenues to provide a public good to its citizens, such as providing support for industry, loans, infrastructure, and information. In Africa, the informal sector contributes to half of the GDP and employment.[137] This means that half of the GDP is un-taxable.
>
> The shadow economy is a clear sign that the administrative and judicial institutions are not functioning properly, and that the state has low levels of legitimacy.

Corruption levels are also lower in states that have higher functioning criminal justice systems.[138] In many cases corruption infiltrates judicial institutions. Judges can be easily bought off. Decisions are for sale. Even if a given country's judicial system is not entirely corrupt, "laws may be widely flouted with near impunity." Most countries have laws prohibiting bribery, yet their effect is often minimal if punishments are not enacted. Countries that have been effective in minimizing corruption have used monitoring and punishment to give the impression that corruption is a high-risk and low-reward activity.[139] In this regard, it is important to have an independent judiciary that is insulated from influence from the executive and legislative branches. It is also important to improve the pay and working conditions for the judiciary and to improve the language used in written laws to make them more lucid.[140]

Corruption within the courts is also more prevalent when the internal organizational roles are concentrated in the hands of a few decision makers within the court.[141] Too much power concentrated in the hands of the few facilitates opportunities for judges to commit graft. This is especially true if there is little internal oversight of the judicial institutions or

---

[137]Sindzingre (2006).
[138]Buscaglia (2003: 16).
[139]Eigen (1996: 161).
[140]Rose-Ackerman (1999).
[141]Moore and Buscaglia (1999: 8–9).

mechanisms in place to maintain accountability for their behavior. Judicial corruption is also more common if the procedures for the courts are not transparent and are too complex and numerous.[142] When it is unclear what the rules are, judges have more leeway to act arbitrarily. Too many rules and procedures can lead to greater inconsistencies in term of how the law is applied.

As Chapter Seven argued, *democracies* that provide accountability and transparency can also help curb corruption.[143] As support for this argument, there appears to be a correlation between high corruption levels and authoritarianism. Not one country rated in the bottom ten on the corruption perceptions index is a consolidated democracy.[144] In democracies (assuming that civil liberties are guaranteed), countries with an active press are able to publicize the offences of corrupt politicians. A vibrant civil society can also monitor transgressions of its politicians.[145] Moreover, if countries use free and fair elections, the citizens are then able to punish corrupt officials to prevent them from incurring more violations. Finally, countries with stronger legislative and judicial institutions may be better at keeping the executive branch accountable. Because of this, democratic countries may be especially more equipped at curbing kleptocratic behavior.[146]

Moreover, studies have shown that countries that have overly strong executive branches are more prone to political corruption than others.[147] The level of power of the chief executive vis-à-vis other institutions, such as the legislature, judicial branch, and political parties, affects corruption levels because there are few checks on the executive to prevent the abuse of power. The absence of horizontal accountability enables leaders to steal from the state with impunity.

For example, in Nicaragua the constitutional rules allow for the presidency to enjoy a considerable concentration of power. When Arnoldo Alemán came to power in 1997 he made changes to the constitution that concentrated power even further in the hands of the executive.[148] Though corruption took place under the Sandinista regime (1979–90) and under Violeta Chamorro's regime (1990–7), the extent of corruption that took place during the Alemán years was significant. Transparency International

---

[142]Ibid.
[143]Robertson-Snape (1999).
[144]Just holding elections does not eliminate corruption. For example, Lebanon is one of the more democratic countries in the Middle East and yet it scores as one of the worst in the region when it comes to corruption.
[145]Quah (2006).
[146]World Bank (1997).
[147]Hochstetler (2006).
[148]Anderson (2006: 143).

had estimated that Alemán had looted over $100 million dollars in the five years that he was in power.[149]

Effects of corruption

Corruption has numerous negative repercussions on a state's economic and political development. For this reason, rising corruption levels should be taken seriously. Corruption is one of the most obvious symptoms of *institutional decay.*

Paolo Mauro from the IMF was one of the first to quantify the economic impact of *administrative corruption.*[150] He argued that corruption (in the form of civil servants taking bribes for business licenses) creates huge inefficiencies because it acts as an additional tax on business. Instead of a centralized mechanism for collection of set fees, there are innumerable "consumers of graft" that must be dealt with.[151] In Russia, to invest in a company a foreigner must bribe every agency involved in foreign investment, such as the finance ministry, the central bank, the state property bureau, and so on.[152]

Corruption also undermines the implementation of policies because individuals are not hired based on their professional qualifications. Thus, administrators may have fewer incentives to train their subordinates. When civil servants go untrained, it is impossible to delegate authority, which is necessary in order to implement policies. This coupled with incompetent personnel lowers productivity levels and efficiency.[153]

With high levels of corruption, professionally competent and honest civil servants are undermined. Innovation and reform is punished. This may lead to emigration of the skilled and educated workforce, also known as a brain drain. In 1960 Haiti, all of the nurses who graduated that year left the country.[154] In notoriously corrupt Equatorial Guinea under Macias Nguema, by the time he was killed in 1979 it was estimated that not a single university graduate remained in the country, constituting the largest proportion of any nation to ever go into exile![155]

Judicial corruption also has a profound impact on economy. Corruption within the judiciary denotes that there is little certainty that contracts

---

[149]"Nicaragua Profile" (2012).
[150]Mauro (1995: 681–712).
[151]Drury et al. (2006: 122).
[152]Ibid.
[153]Gould and Amaro-Reves (1983).
[154]Lundahl (1997: 44).
[155]Ibid., 45.

will be honored without the use of bribes. This creates fewer incentives for investment and international trade, and leads to capital flight, which has long-term effects on economic growth rates.[156] Because judicial corruption is so high in Russia, entrepreneurs are obliged to purchase unlawful services from state officials.[157] It's been estimated that Russia loses up to $10 billion a year in potential investment because of "corruption, inadequate accounting procedures, weaknesses in its legal system and a lack of reliable financial information."[158]

In the case of the Philippines, the Ombudsman's Office estimated in 1997 that the government lost "$48 billion to corruption over the previous twenty years, a figure that outstripped the country's $40.6 billion foreign debt."[159] A UN Development Program report found that corruption was causing Bangladesh to lose hundreds of millions of dollars in lost unrealized investment and income.[160]

Political corruption in the form of nepotism, cronyism, and patron-clientelism also leads to falls in public spending on human capital and falls in productivity because it biases the composition of government expenditures and dissipates resources that could be used on productive activity.[161] Corruption distorts public expenditures from sectors such as health care and education. Resources are diverted to benefit well-connected individuals and politicians.[162] Labor may also be drawn away from productive activities.[163] In the case of Lebanon, some of the billions of investment that were to go to reconstruction (such as in improving welfare, public housing, and public transport) after its civil war were instead wasted away on corrupt activities. The rebuilding of Beirut was riddled with problems. The estimated cost of rebuilding Beirut was $5 billion, but the actual cost amounted to $50 billion. Public resources were wasted on bribes to facilitate construction.[164] Contracts for rebuilding were given exclusively to cronies and clients of Prime Minister Rafik Hariri (1992–8, 2000–4).

Political corruption also leads to inefficiency because gains made through corruption are unlikely to be transferred to the investment sector—but is more likely used for conspicuous consumption to support a domestic constituency (such as patron-clientelism) or transferred to foreign bank

---

[156]Dreher and Herzfeld (2005).
[157]Levin and Satarov (2000: 131).
[158]Eigen (2002: 48).
[159]Quimpo (2009: 339).
[160]Mustafa (1997).
[161]Drury et al. (2006: 123).
[162]Tanzi and Davoodi (1997: 1–23).
[163]Gould and Amaro-Reves (1983: 28).
[164]Hoeckel (2011: 7).

accounts (such as kleptocracy). These types of transfers are referred to as a capital leakage from the domestic economy.[165]

Political corruption (in the form of rent-seeking) can also generate allocative inefficiencies when it comes to procurement of state contracts because the least efficient or qualified contractor is often the beneficiary of government contracts.[166] Corruption distorts competition by denying public access to the competitive marketplace. Corruption may induce wrong decisions, which lead to the wrong projects, the wrong prices, the wrong contractors, and substandard delivery.[167] In Ghana there has been little concern about which contractor is the most qualified. What is most important is the amount of kickback received.

Accepting kickbacks is also commonplace among the security institutions. In the security sector, an un-professionalized military can abuse its power by engaging in corrupt procurement practices in exchange for lucrative kickbacks. Examples abound of kickbacks being taken on contracts for endeavors that are completely unnecessary. In the case of Nigeria, the military government "placed a cement order that amounted to 2/3 of the estimated needs of all of Africa and which cost 2 billion dollars or 25% of all Nigeria's oil revenues in 1975."[168] Billions of dollars that could have been invested in the economy was spent on useless items for the sole purpose of padding the pockets of key members of the military.

Corruption within the *security institutions* and customs agencies also raises transaction costs. Though Kazakhstan is committed to free trade, local businessmen estimate that getting a truckload of produce from Kyrgyzstan across Kazakhstan and into Russia would cost several thousand dollars in bribes. In Turkmenistan, Uzbekistan, and Kyrgyzstan small traders are stopped over a dozen times to pay bribes to the police, border guards, and customs agents.[169] It is no wonder that positions in the Customs Agencies are highly coveted, and in the case of Afghanistan are purchased for large sums of money. An International Crisis Group Report in Kyrgyzstan states that posts in the Ministry of Internal Affairs are bought and sold for between US $100 and $50,000 depending on the rank of the position, due to how easily these payments can be reimbursed with bribes.[170]

In Kyrgyzstan, like many other states in Central Asia, the police are notoriously corrupt, and this has had a negative effect on legitimate businesses. A report by the International Crisis Group assessed that corruption

---

[165]Gould and Amaro-Reves (1983: 28).
[166]Ibid.
[167]Pope (1996: 23).
[168]Lundahl (1997: 40).
[169]Collins (2009: 268).
[170]Cokgezen (2004: 91–2).

in the Kyrgyz Police was "rampant and systemic." Non-state actors have successfully bribed the police, and have been given almost free reign to traffic drugs. At the same time, for legitimate businesses, getting across the borders can be a costly experience. Checkpoints are numerous and costly.[171]

Overall, corruption generates an atmosphere of resentment and frustration. Corruption may foster contempt for public servants, which erodes the capacity to collect revenues.[172] Corruption adds transactions costs and excludes those who cannot pay.[173] Corruption may also lead to the avoidance of having to interact with the state.

Corruption also undermines democracy because it bypasses the processes of representation, debate, and choice.[174] Corruption delegitimizes regimes and leads to more disillusionment with leadership.[175] This disillusionment then perpetuates a culture of corruption that is hard to abolish.

World Bank studies also linked corruption to violence and instability. Corruption can create wide frustration, social unrest and disorder.[176] Governments may be compelled to resort to force in order to maintain order.[177] The World Bank also claims that high levels of corruption have been cited as a reason for military coups.[178]

---

[171]Burnashev (2007: 65–70).
[172]Pope (1996: 23).
[173]Ibid.
[174]Thompson (1993).
[175]Eigen (2002).
[176]Rose-Ackerman (1996: 1–4).
[177]Gould and Amaro-Reves (1983: 28).
[178]Rose-Ackerman (1996: 1–4).

CHAPTER NINE

State building, foreign aid, and interventions

Up until this point, this study has focused on the institutional landscapes of countries in the developing world and their impact on state performance. The major goal of this effort is to gain insights into how states can create or reform their institutions in ways that promote political stability and positive economic performance. We refer to this process as state building, the focal point of this chapter.

Though state building can be taken on by a state's government, it is usually spearheaded by outsiders, typically members of the policy and development communities. In some cases, state governments work closely with the international community to build and reform their institutions, while in other cases the international community entirely drives the process. This can occur either because the state's government has proven itself incapable of fixing the state's problems or because it is absent altogether (as may happen, for example, following serious episodes of political instability and/or regime transitions). In this discussion, we operate under the assumption that state-building efforts are being driven by outsiders working in conjunction with state governments, given the frequency with which the empirical reality fits this pattern.

There are a variety of ways in which state building is carried out. In some cases, an international organization assists the state with training personnel and provides advice on how to structure state institutions. In other cases, a development agency offers financial assistance to the state, under the conditions that it be devoted to developing particular state institutions. And in yet other cases, states are offered what are essentially blank checks, with the idea that additional investment in the state will jumpstart its economy and bolster its security. Not only does the form of state building vary widely from case to case, but so does its scope, both in terms of the financial costs and the number of organizations and actors involved. In this chapter, we offer some background on state building, before turning to an in-depth discussion of our approach to state building and how it addresses contemporary challenges in this field. Because international interventions are often precursors to state-building efforts, we devote the latter part of this chapter to this topic. Here, we discuss what interventions refer to and the controversies that surround them, offering examples of intervention successes and failures to illustrate these points. We close by offering suggestions for moving forward, emphasizing the importance of early action and using more rigorous measurements of institutional quality rather than waiting until institutional collapse has taken place.

Background

Up until the end of the Cold War, the issue of how to build and reform states was not a major topic of discussion. A state's internal problems were seen as the responsibility of the state, due to state sovereignty. By the 1990s, however, several factors led to a wave of political instability and economic decline in the developing world. For one, many developing countries had borrowed money from international financial institutions, such as the International Monetary Fund, to jumpstart their development. These loans, however, came with conditions, most notably that governments pursue neoliberal economic reforms. As a result, many governments in developing countries were forced to cut their budgets dramatically. In addition, during the Cold War, the United States and the USSR (as part of their Cold War strategies) gave financial assistance to many governments in the developing world to bolster their security apparatuses. When the Cold War came to a close, however, the aid stopped flowing, putting a major strain on many governments' financial resources. Both of these factors led to political upheaval in a number of developing countries, as citizens reacted to their governments' large reductions in spending. The end of the Cold War also led to the breakup of the USSR and newfound independence for a number of regions formerly under its control. These new states, however, were poorly equipped to handle the challenges that came with self-rule. Internal clashes erupted in many countries shortly after independence. As evidence of this, the number of intra-state conflicts in the post-World War II era reached an all-time high in the years following the Cold War.[1]

---

[1]Human Security Centre (2006: 22).

In line with these developments, the concept of state failure started to gain steam in the international community.[2] With the emergence of state failure, came its logical counterpart, *state building*. Because state failure was viewed as a threat to international security, as well as a source of human suffering, the international community moved quickly to formulate prescriptions for building and reforming states, a subject to which we now turn.

The challenges of state building

In our conceptualization, state building refers to *the process of building and reforming state institutions in ways that foster political stability and positive economic performance*. As stated before, this process is usually undertaken by outside actors, working in conjunction with state governments.

To date, state-building efforts have been the subject of heated criticism, so much so that some question whether it is even possible for outsiders to improve state institutions. The argument is that these efforts are unsuccessful more often than not, occasionally creating larger problems than existed in the first place.[3] Though it is difficult to quantify precisely how many state-building projects have "succeeded" or "failed," the overall consensus appears to be that successes are rare. As Christopher Coyne writes, while "the failure of endogenous institutions in countries with weak and failed states may indeed be significant, the failures generated by foreign governments may be even greater."[4] Eva Bertram seconds this, asserting that "there are grave limits to the ability of any international force to 'build' sustainable local institutions."[5]

Though it is true that existing state-building efforts undertaken by outsiders have been far from perfect at the aggregate, it is also true that many of these efforts have been flawed in their approach. In this section we advocate an approach to state building that entails three elements: (1) conceptual clarity, (2) empirical grounding, and (3) realistic expectations. Woven throughout our discussion of this approach is a review of contemporary challenges in the field of state building.

Conceptual clarity

In the literature and in practice, state building is typically viewed as the solution to state failure. Most definitions of state building, in other words,

---

[2]See Chapter Two in this book for a more in-depth discussion of the emergence of the concept of state failure.
[3]Pei (2003: 52). Pei, for example, calculates that only 26 percent of US-led reconstruction efforts have been successful.
[4]Coyne (2006: 345).
[5]Bertram (1995: 412).

center on the idea of state building as a process of strengthening weak or failing states. They usually incorporate one or more of the following objectives: establishing internal security, ensuring the rule of law, installing a legitimate government, and providing basic social services.[6] The particular objectives emphasized vary based on how state failure is conceptualized, which (as discussed in Chapter Two) differs widely from one organization or researcher to the next. Those who see state failure as the state's inability to provide security for its citizens will assert that the provision of security is the goal of state building. Those who see it as encompassing more than this, however, will expand the list of goals to include other things, like infrastructure development or the expansion of political rights.

In other words, because the definition of state failure is highly malleable, so are definitions of state building, as currently conceptualized. Existing approaches to state building often diverge in their assessments of what state building means and what its specific objectives are as a result. They can be (and often are) molded to suit the particular agendas of the organizations or governments promoting them.

Because of this, we promote a more concrete and focused definition of state building, in line with our emphasis throughout this study on state institutions (as opposed to the ambiguous concept of state failure) as a critical component of state performance. We argue that articulating with greater precision the variables and outcomes that we are interested in, paves the way for greater focus in the execution of state-building efforts.

For this reason, not only do we advocate emphasizing state institutions as the focal point of state-building efforts, but we also disaggregate these institutions into four domains: administrative, judicial, security, and political. Being specific about the particular element of the state's institutional apparatus that efforts should target allows resources to be allocated in a more efficient manner.

In addition, it is essential to be clear about what attributes of the state's institutions are desirable for improving state performance. As discussed above, most approaches to state building seek to strengthen state institutions (occasionally referred to as increasing institutional capacity), with particular focus on building democratic institutions. It is often difficult to know, however, whether institutional strength correlates with positive state performance because what institutional strength refers to in practice is often poorly defined. What does it mean to have a "strong" state institution? To curtail this problem, we instead focus on the quality of state institutions as opposed to their strength and define in unambiguous terms the particular features of state institutions that make them high versus low in quality.

---

[6]USAID (2005: 1–20).

It is also important to be clear about what the objectives are of state building. What outcomes are we striving toward? We argue that the goal of state building is to improve state performance, which encompasses political stability and economic performance. Both of these outcomes are easily measurable, such that it is possible to assess whether states are improving their performance or not in an objective and clear-cut fashion. By promoting a clear objective (political stability and economic performance), it is also less likely for state-building efforts to be molded to suit the particular political objectives of the groups mounting them.

Greater conceptual clarity is therefore desirable because it enables us to disentangle the particular features of state institutions that bear on state performance. This, in turn, paves the way for the provision of more precise policy guidance regarding where state-building resources should be targeted, making state-building efforts more focused and efficient.

Empirical grounding

Our approach to state building also emphasizes empirical grounding. Without some awareness of the empirical relationship between institutions and outcomes, as well as the efficacy of existing state-building efforts, state building is unlikely to elicit successes. Empirical grounding is important because individuals respond to incentives, the structures of which may not be initially obvious to observers. The current policy-oriented work on state building has no discussion of incentives, however.[7] As a result, financial, technical, and training assistance are often allocated blindly, under the assumption that greater resources will improve state performance.[8] This is problematic because theories regarding what should work may not always work in practice (due to the fact that how incentives will structure behavior is not always easy to anticipate). Basing our assessments on what the empirical record tells us, instead, improves the likelihood that resources will be used efficiently and state-building efforts will be met with success.

This is particularly true with respect to identifying the features of the state's institutions that state-building efforts should target. Currently, most state-building projects seek to "strengthen" state institutions. Besides the fact that this is a conceptually vague endeavor, as mentioned above, it may also be empirically shaky. For example, many international organizations dedicate resources toward strengthening the security sector, the idea being that "stronger" institutions are "better" institutions. Though it is possible that a strong security sector will enable the state to provide better security for its citizens, it is also possible that a strong security sector could destabilize

---

[7]Krasner (2011a: 70).
[8]Ibid.

the state by staging a coup and taking over the state's government. Without some sort of empirical assessment of how strong security institutions bear on state performance, it is impossible to know with any certainty whether strengthening them will lead to positive or negative outcomes. In other words, theorizing about what should improve state performance is one thing, but efforts are far more likely to be successful if they are based on methodologically sound evidence that has worked in practice. For this reason, throughout this study not only have we presented the major features of high-quality state institutions (rather than merely strong), but we have also identified the particular ways in which they have been shown to affect state performance. In our discussions, we have been quick to point out features of state institutions that have not exhibited an impact on state performance and where research is currently lacking.

It is also important for empirics to guide our assessments of how to build and reform state institutions. Simply assuming that a state-building strategy works, without evaluating whether or not it has worked in similar contexts, can lead to wasted resources. As mentioned earlier, this is largely because incentives matter, yet how they are structured and how individuals will respond to them is not always clear to the observer. Empirical research can help to alleviate this problem by providing an assessment of how various strategies affect patterns of behavior.

Democracy promotion is one such area where policy makers have especially ignored some of the empirical realities. Though European and American policy makers differed in terms of which approach worked best (soft versus hard, respectively), both sides viewed democracy promotion as an integral part of their foreign policy agendas.[9] Policy makers have reasoned that no state-building strategy is complete without democracy—and foreign powers have been quick to push for the implementation of elections.

More recently, scholars have been critical of democracy promotion programs, arguing instead for a sequential process.[10] Scholars have reasoned that policy makers should hold off on promoting democracy because democratizing can be a particularly violent and destabilizing process. For example, Edward Mansfield and Jack Snyder argue that promoting democracy leads to conflict. Amy Chua echoes this, and claims that the simultaneous promotion of democracy and market reform, leads to anti-market backlashes as well as ethnic conflict. This wider body of skeptical thought about democracy promotion is referred to as *democratic sequentialism*. Sequentialists argue that pursuing democratic change too quickly may lead to volatility and unpredictability.[11] Moreover, as Chapter Seven illustrated,

---

[9]Kopstein (2006: 85–98).
[10]Carothers (2007: 5–10); Chua (2004).
[11]Carothers (2007).

holding elections does not guarantee that the state will be more effective. This does not mean that democracy is without its merits, rather that creating effective institutions is not just about holding elections. As Barnett Rubin writes in the case of Afghanistan, "electing officials to preside over a non-functional pseudo-state that can provide neither security nor services does not constitute a success."[12]

Before introducing democratic institutions, sequentialists have highlighted the importance of developing strong security institutions to maintain order and stability. As they see it, decision makers should give priority to establishing professionalized military forces.[13] As the subsequent section on *intervention* will highlight, after a decade long civil war in Sierra Leone left the country devastated, the United Kingdom in 2000 sent in a peacekeeping force, and went on to train 8,500 members of the new Sierra Leone army. The United Kingdom spent about $120 million on the project, and by 2002 it was deemed a success. Michael Chege argues that considering the billions of dollars in Western government and multilateral development aid that had gone to waste over the years—mostly going toward the promotion of free and fair elections as a peacemaking tool— it's important to note "the highly positive impact of a small amount of carefully targeted aid."[14]

Premature democratization is a well-known problem, but building security institutions without building the rule of law needed to restrain them can lead to a repetition of the same problems.[15] The $120 million that the United Kingdom spent on Sierra Leone also went toward improving the judicial institutions in order to help establish the rule of law, which may explain why Sierra Leone has remained stable. Thus, programs that can help make the judicial institutions effective are particularly important.

In addition to building effective judicial institutions, priority should also be placed on building effective and transparent systems of public administration. Civil servants should be trained in the importance of merit selection procedures and inculcating a bureaucratic ethic.[16] Programs may want to start with providing training of specific basic tasks such as the tracking, monitoring, and storage of documents and records.[17] State-building efforts may be more effective if goals are specific, with a focus on areas of institutional reform that have worked well in the past.

Some of the most successful cases of state building have illustrated that working with existing administrative institutions is preferable to rebuilding administrative institutions entirely from scratch. Often purging the existing

---

[12]Rubin (2006: 181).
[13]Chege (2002).
[14]Ibid., 156.
[15]Fukuyama (2005: 84–8).
[16]Wesley (2008: 377–9).
[17]Ibid.

bureaucracy completely is not a good way to build local capacity. Even in state-building efforts in Germany and Japan, much of the bureaucracy remained intact.[18] The failure of US state-building efforts in Iraq in 2003–4 to utilize the existing Ba'ath administration has been highlighted by both scholars and policy makers alike as a critical mistake.[19] Though it may have not been necessary to keep the entire administration intact, dismantling it completely proved to be counterproductive.[20]

Extending this point, state building has often undermined domestic actors and led to long-run dependence because local actors have not been involved enough in the process.[21] Scholars have argued that domestic actors should play a bigger role in the process so that the institutions will be considered more legitimate to locals. Past cases have illustrated that if domestic actors are more involved in their state-building projects, they will have a greater incentive to make the project work. As former US treasury secretary Larry Summers stated, "no one ever washes a rented car."[22]

The strategy of providing foreign aid perhaps exemplifies the problem of ignoring empirical realities. Allocating foreign aid to a state is one of the most basic ways in which state building is executed. Yet proponents of this strategy have often paid little attention to incentive structures (or fundamentally misunderstood them) and to the specific needs of recipient countries. Moreover, supporters of foreign aid have tended to hail NGOs (often tasked with administering foreign aid) as beyond reproach. Yet donors need to keep the agencies they work with accountable as well. Foreign aid also needs to be used to help recipient countries gain specific skills, not serve as a means to fund the creation of parallel institutions to be exclusively run by NGOs. Because of the prominence of foreign aid as a state-building strategy and the controversy that surrounds it, we devote the following subsection to this topic.

Foreign aid

Foreign aid involves the distribution of financial resources from international actors to the state. The extent to which the provision of aid comes with strings attached varies greatly from one context to the next. Foreign aid can come from another state (or states), international and/or regional organizations, and international development agencies. For most, the

---

[18]Fukuyama (2005: 87).
[19]Diamond (2004: 34–56).
[20]Fukuyama (2005: 87).
[21]Diamond (2004).
[22]Quoted from Fukuyama (2005: 87).

objective of foreign aid is to improve economic performance, but others have also viewed aid as a tool to promote political stability as well as democratization.[23]

The major proponent of foreign aid is Jeffrey Sachs.[24] Sachs argues that massive increases in foreign aid are needed to lift the world's poorest countries out of poverty. The argument is that these countries are in the midst of a poverty trap. Governments cannot provide services to citizens because they lack revenues, yet they lack revenues because citizens are too impoverished to pay taxes. To break out of the poverty trap, high levels of foreign assistance are required, far greater than are currently being allocated.

Though Sachs is aware that some governments are more likely to use foreign aid in more productive ways than others, he argues that the "biggest problem today is not that poorly governed countries get too much help, but that well-governed countries get far too little."[25] For example, developed countries have promised to give about 0.7 percent of their national income to foreign aid. Yet the total amount of foreign aid donated amounts to much less than that, averaging around 0.3 percent of national income. The total amount of foreign aid given each year, in the last five years has hovered around $120 billion, with only approximately $25 billion of that aid going to the world's poorest countries.[26]

Sachs notes that aid works best when it is part of an overall market-driven growth strategy. Many World Bank programs have rarely constituted a growth strategy. Aid should be more selective and only go to countries taking strong measures to promote market-based, export-led growth. Sachs also argues that aid should be limited in duration to remind governments that it does not constitute a substitute for exports or long-term growth. Sachs advocates a pre-announced sliding scale of aid that is more generous at the start, and declines later. Sachs also argues that part of the assistance should come in the form of canceling debt to give states a fresh start. Debt cancellation should be a phased process with conditions for reform. Further, many of the aid programs should be in support of implementing public goods such as investing in infrastructure for land-locked countries to ensure that they have efficient access to ports. More aid to regional peacekeeping operations would also be effective. Additionally, Sachs argues that science and technology in the health and agricultural industries is also important.[27]

Critics of Sachs have charged that the aid industry is a big business that has reaped few positive results. Development agencies employ thousands

---

[23]We base some of the discussion from Stephen Krasner's review of the foreign aid literature (2011b). Krasner (2011b: 123–49).
[24]Sachs (2005).
[25]Ibid., 269.
[26]OECD, 2012
[27]Sachs (1996: 19–21).

of officials and there are millions of firms and NGOs that manage the aid industry. Yet many aid-recipient countries have made limited progress, and instead have become aid dependent.[28] *Aid dependence* is known as a condition where the transfers of aid make no contribution to the achievement of self-sustaining development.[29] There are several arguments for why foreign aid can be counterproductive.

Critics of Sachs are quick to point out that his optimism regarding the potential for high levels of foreign aid to jumpstart states' economic development ignores the role of individual incentives. According to Dambisa Moyo, millions are poorer today because of aid: "misery and poverty have not ended but have increased. Aid has been, and continues to be, an unmitigated political, economic, and humanitarian disaster for most parts of the developing world."[30] The argument here is that aid undermines the development of high-quality state institutions because it skews incentives, creating an environment in which governments are responsive to donors rather than their own citizens. Budgets may also become more volatile because they are dependent upon the mood and interests of external donors. This is worsened by the lack of coordination between donors.[31] In Moyo's perspective, all foreign aid needs to be withdrawn if states in the developing world are going to grow their economies.

States may also use the aid to *delay real policy reform*. Receiving foreign aid relieves states of pressure to make any changes that are necessary for development. Aid also reduces the incentives to cooperate and to make sacrifices. Elites have little incentive to make the right changes. Some scholars also argue that aid creates a *moral hazard* in that government officials feel that they have an insurance policy (through their access to aid) that allows them to engage in risky behavior. When the government staff faces no internal sanctions for the aid that they receive, they are free to spend the aid in any way they please rather than invest in the state. A collective-action problem may also result in that it is in the interests of all actors today to continue to reap the benefits they receive from giving and receiving aid, even though this aid will create problems for future governments, known as a *tragedy of the commons*.[32]

For example, states that receive aid may be less inclined to use available sources of tax revenues. In Sub-Saharan Africa, 71 percent of the countries receiving more than 10 percent of GDP in aid in 1995 were also in the group of countries judged in an IMF study to have lower than expected tax effort.[33] William Easterly claims that higher aid levels are associated with

---

[28]Brett (2006: 1–25).
[29]Brautigam and Knack (2004).
[30]Moyo (2009: xix).
[31]Sindzingre (2007: 615–32).
[32]Easterly (2002: 1692).
[33]Brautigam and Knack (2004: 264).

larger declines in the quality of governance and in tax revenues as a share of GDP.[34] He argues that the process of bargaining over revenues and taxation may be critical for the development of accountability. When revenues come from aid and not from taxes raised from citizens and businesses, there is little reason for the government to be accountable. When the flow of revenue is not affected by government efficiency, there is also little incentive to improve state capacity. Easterly claims that private investment may also cease. Thus, many years of receiving aid has made states less inclined to be proactive.[35]

Some scholars argue that foreign aid makes little difference when going to states whose leaders have no intention of improving state capacity and performance.[36] This aid may serve only to assist incumbents and marginalize opponents.[37] States may prefer to distribute the aid as patronage to their support groups without investing it and improving capacity and effectiveness. In other cases, it may create instability as individuals dedicate their efforts toward trying to control the government and get their hands on a piece of the "aid pie" as opposed to economically productive activities. In the worst-case scenario, aid may be siphoned off and go directly into the hands of the leadership (see Chapter Eight). In the case of Nicaragua under the Somoza regime, after a devastating earthquake had taken place in Managua in 1972, the Somoza government appealed for international aid. Later it was discovered that the regime stockpiled most of the aid in their own private bank accounts.[38] Thus, aid has been dispersed to countries regardless of whether or not their commitment to development was strong.[39]

There is also much criticism of the donor community pertaining to how they select donor countries, and implement and monitor aid programs. The first issue is that recipient countries are often selected according to geopolitical criteria and a host of political and economic motives related to the *donor countries* rather than their needs and levels of poverty. For example, aid may assist in job creation for the donor countries, but not necessarily for the recipient. Moreover, many foreign technical assistants repatriate their income to their country of origin rather than back into the economy of the recipient.[40]

---

[34]Easterly (2002).
[35]Ibid.
[36]Brett (2006); Patrick (2006: 1–31).
[37]Brett (2006).
[38]"1972: Earthquake wreaks devastation in Nicaragua," BBC, December 23, 1972, http://news.bbc.co.uk/onthisday/hi/dates/stories/december/23/newsid_2540000/2540045.stm.
[39]Tangri and Mwenda (2006: 101–24).
[40]Sindzingre (2007).

Donors have also often been unaware of how institutions function in specific countries and in what ways they need to be improved. Scholars have argued that there is a need for a more tailored approach rather than a one-size-fits-all approach.[41] There is need for more understanding of the needs of the specific recipient countries and the best ways to build up their capacity. It is often difficult to understand the needs of the recipient country when those involved do not know the local language. People who are involved in the training process should know the language of the people that they are training.[42]

In other cases, there are issues with donors failing to keep aid agencies accountable for their programs. Donors have been satisfied when aid is given to an agency, not when a program is actually implemented. There are often no accounts of expenditures by the numerous agencies. For example in Afghanistan, the Afghan Donor Assistance Database tracks the number of deposits or disbursements by donors of funds into these accounts instead of tracking the implementation of these programs. Sometimes these funds just remain in these accounts.

Opponents of foreign aid also argue that there are negative effects bringing in Non-Governmental Organizations (NGOs) or foreign staff to assist in aid projects. NGOs may import tons of equipment and consumer goods for their staff without paying import duties or local income taxes for the staff. NGOs can also increase the prices for capable staff and pull the best staff from the private and productive sectors. NGOs may divert competent staff away from the government. This may weaken institutions further and lower morale. NGOs put pressures on the local economies due to their presence as well. For example, in the case of Afghanistan, the salary scales of the non-Afghan agencies are very high, luring the most capable Afghan nationals into the service of international organizations. Comparatively lower state salaries become that much more unappealing.[43] Additionally, the influx of cash from NGOs puts pressure on housing prices and basic commodities, which causes the cost of living to go up. Much of the costs of delivering the aid are very high since possibly as much as 60 cents for every dollar goes toward overheads.[44]

Some NGOs are more interested in convincing their donors that they are doing something than they are committed to being effective. This can make many aid projects wasteful and unproductive. "Conditions" are often

---

[41]Fritz and Menocal (2007: 545).
[42]One of the issues of training the Afghan police has been the problem of finding individuals who have expertise in security matters who also speak the local Afghan languages. The reliance on translators who are not familiar with basic security terms has made it difficult for instructors to communicate effectively with Afghan police recruits.
[43]Rubin (2006: 182).
[44]François and Sud (2006: 152).

not imposed, because there are imperatives of international financial and donor institutions that are more focused on just getting "money out of the door" rather than focusing on whether or not that money is being used effectively.[45]

Another problem is that most donor funds go directly to NGOs, which bypasses the government and local populations' involvement in providing services. Instead of local capacity building, parallel institutions are created to supplant the government. As a result, the recipient government is unable to make its own decisions about what services should be provided and how to track expenditures.[46] Monika François and Inder Sud argue that governments need to have more authority over their budgets and be kept accountable. The government gains little experience providing a public good, a critical function to making the state appear more legitimate in the eyes of the public. François and Sud argue that capacity building can only take place by doing, not from being sidelined.[47] As they see it though learning technical skills is a time consuming endeavor for the recipient country, it is a necessary one. Otherwise, any growth that takes place is often due to the expenditure and technical skills of the NGOs and not due to any endogenous growth that can be sustainable once the reduction in expenditure winds down.[48]

Though many scholars have been critical of foreign aid and how it has been administered, foreign aid has played a positive role in the case of East Asia. Aid can often serve as a positive stimulus to economic growth, by helping to build administrative capacity. But several things are worth mentioning. First, in the case of Asia local technocrats were used, who happened to have coinciding interests with donors, such as the United States. Alliances were built toward key reforms, including land reform and pursing an export led growth strategy.[49] Thus much of the impetus for success came from within and the large volumes of aid that were given were used effectively.

More recently, Vietnam has been the darling of the donor community for achieving low inflation and unemployment levels, reducing poverty, and experiencing growth rates of 7 percent a year. Vietnam's leadership has been particularly focused on the tasks of economic growth and building administrative capacity. Manufacturing, information technology, and high-tech industries form the fastest growing part of the national economy. Poorer areas have received investment, and education and healthcare have been subsidized. Intellectual property rights are protected, which has enabled Vietnam to become a member of the WTO in 2007. Though Vietnam's

---

[45]Milliken and Krause (2002: 769).
[46]François and Sud (2006: 152).
[47]Ibid., 153.
[48]Ibid., 155.
[49]Haggard (1990).

state exercises strong administrative guidance in the economy, it has one of the most open economies in Asia.

However, for every Vietnam, there are countries like the Ivory Coast that have wasted donor aid and have been mired in debt. The Ivory Coast in 1997 received 1,276 times more per capita aid net flow than India in 1997, yet India's growth rates have consistently been much higher, coming in at 7.8 percent compared to Ivory Coast's—5.8 percent.[50] Much of the drive for economic growth in India has been internally driven. But perhaps more importantly, India has had more institutional development. Countries that already have some institutional capacity are better able to reap the benefits of foreign aid, as are countries that have internal forces eager to make aid effective. We now turn to several case studies of aid failure and success to help illuminate the discussion.

Aid failure

Afghanistan is a case commonly cited as country where foreign aid has not materialized into effective state institutions, and instead has led to *aid dependence*. International donors have been hesitant to give funding directly to the Afghan government. Rather than distributing the money to be placed under the control of a political authority that can be held accountable, most donor countries and agencies have maintained separate accounts that are accountable to their own political authorities and subject to their own procedures. Donors deliver their aid through their own agencies or through the use of domestic NGOs. The Afghan Minister of Finance (Ashraf Ghani) claimed in 2004 that of the $4.9 billion spent on public expenditure, only $1.4 billion was channeled through the government budget.[51] In the 2005 budget less than 30 percent of all expenditures was channeled through the Afghan government's own budget, leaving most of the budget outside the government's control.[52]

What has resulted is a dual public sector, which undermines the ability of the state to develop its own fiscal capacity, accumulate capital, learn how to manage the economy, and be accountable to its citizens.[53] As Barnett Rubin sees it, Afghanistan will be unable to provide any services if it does not focus on local capacity building of the Afghan administrative institutions particularly in the areas of fiscal and monetary management. Gaining

---

[50]Easterly (2002: 1692).
[51]Rubin (2006: 182).
[52]Ibid.
[53]Ibid., 179.

control over its own budget will help the Afghan government learn how to coordinate and mobilize resources, and will also force the government to be more accountable to the public.[54]

This is especially problematic for Afghanistan's hopes of running its own security sector.

Currently Afghanistan is unable to sustain its security forces on its own. The Afghan National Army (ANA) costs about $1 billion a year to maintain.[55] This means that Afghanistan will need to quintuple the size of its legal economy in order to pay for these costs.[56] Because of this, Rubin argues that state-building efforts in Afghanistan need to focus on improving the capacity of the state to collect customs revenues.[57] But the incentives to do so have been undermined by the way that foreign aid is distributed.

Joint funds that have worked have been the Afghanistan Reconstruction Trust Fund (ARTF), administered by the World Bank, and the Law and Order Trust Fund for Afghanistan (LOTFA). Donors deposit un-earmarked contributions into these funds, but they are given a voice in how the funds are managed. Moreover, the Afghan government must provide clear documentation for how these funds are spent. These types of funds increase responsibility and build capacity.

Aid success

Ghana is reportedly one of the cases where foreign aid has made a positive impact, but it is important to note that this aid was coupled with market-based reforms. Ghana received a windfall of aid after 1987 when it agreed to embark on an Economic Recovery Program (ERP). The ERP demanded that Ghana open up its economy and curtail the amount of subsidies it provided its industries. Due to the heavy involvement and eagerness of the Ghanaian government during the reform process, the international donor community was especially interested in helping Ghana make its reforms a success. The amount of foreign aid almost tripled within a decade, from a low of $303 million in 1980 to a high of over $800 million in 1991. Much of the aid went to the social sectors in healthcare, education, and infrastructure, such as supporting water and sanitation programs. About 12 percent of the aid came in the form of technical cooperation.[58]

---

[54]Ibid., 181.
[55]Ibid.
[56]Ibid.
[57]Ibid.
[58]Carlsson et al. (1997: 72).

The aid was directed at helping the government reduce its expenditures. Balance of payment support allowed imports to fill the shelves, which people viewed as a sign of better things to come. Later on foreign aid supplemented all of the weak export earnings to pay for imports and softened the impact of any negative shifts in the terms of trade that may have been caused by liberalizing the economy.[59] As a result of the foreign aid, coupled with a market-based approach, within ten years Ghana saw stable economic growth rates, inflation fell from 36 to 10 percent, gross national savings increased from 3 to 11.6 percent and gross national investment rose from 3.7 percent in 1983 to 16 percent by 1990.[60] The World Bank clearly noted that in the absence of foreign aid, the advances from the reform program in Ghana would not have been possible.[61]

Aid reform

Measures were taken to make aid more effective in 2005 with the signing of the Paris Declaration of Aid Effectiveness. This agreement was signed by 61 bilateral and multilateral donors and 56 aid-recipient countries (with 14 civil society organizations acting as observers). The Declaration aimed to give the donor recipients more ownership in the development agenda and to align the priorities of donors with recipients. The Declaration also aimed to harmonize actions among multiple donors and reform the administrative institutions of the recipient countries with a focus on delivering health, education, and water and sanitation services. More than $4 billion of aid was spent on "improving government administration" in 2005, according to the OECD's aid database.[62]

Though reforms have taken place, the scholarly debate on the virtues of foreign aid showcases the many challenges of state building. At present, the international community appears to have taken the side of Sachs, in that aid allocation remains high (though not from Sachs' point of view). The expectation continues to be that aid will elicit positive outcomes, most notably economic growth. As these examples illustrate, the area of foreign aid exemplifies a strategy of state building that operates in virtual isolation of empirical grounding. For reasons such as this, we argue that state building should be driven by what the empirical pattern of behavior indicates, rather than what any particular theory might anticipate. The empirical

---

[59]Ibid., 83.
[60]Ibid., 82.
[61]Ibid.
[62]Fritz and Menocal (2007: 544).

record should guide not only the particular features of state institutions that state-building efforts seek to build or reform, but also the strategies they use to do so.[63]

More recently scholars have noted that aid can produce results in cases where states are committed to making the right changes and are involved in a reform process. Aid also works best when recipients and donors share the same goals, have excellent communication, and aid staff are well trained and understand the conditions in which they are working. Furthermore, aid is more effective when *conditions* are imposed that focus on achieving good governance and the rule of law.[64] When aid is conditioned with specific policy reforms, it may have the best chance of being effective. Moreover, going beyond promising aid in return for changes in policy, aid works best when it is targeting institutional reform.[65] Though this is often difficult to do in practice, it is important that the international community becomes more aware that blank checks do not ensure positive economic performance.

Realistic expectations

In addition to having conceptual clarity and using empirical grounding to direct the state-building process, our approach to state building stresses the need for realistic expectations about what state-building efforts will accomplish. We highlight three areas where this is particularly true.

The first area is the *time frame* under which we expect to see improvements in state performance. The process of building and reforming state institutions in ways that are conducive to political stability and positive economic performance is simply very slow. According to Marina Ottaway, it is reasonable to expect peace-building efforts to take at least five years; state-building efforts should take even longer.[66] State building is a long-term process that requires ample time to reap results; it is also most effective when undertaken slowly.[67] As Guillermo O'Donnell writes, "the emergence, strengthening, and legitimation of . . . institutions take time, during which a complex process of position learning occurs."[68] The problem is that those engaged in state building tend to emphasize quick results.[69] It is important

---

[63]According to Paul Collier, on average aid has a small, but positive, impact on growth. Indeed, the evidence on aid effectiveness is largely mixed. Aid can, in some circumstances, spur growth, but it by no means assures it. Collier (2007: 110–12). See also Burnside and Dollar (2000: 847–68); Easterly (2009).
[64]Rotbert (2004).
[65]Chege (2002: 151).
[66]Ottaway (2002).
[67]Fritz and Menocal (2007).
[68]O'Donnell (1994: 68).
[69]Wesley (2008: 377).

that we maintain realistic expectations about the duration of time required for state-building efforts to make an impact on state performance. The second area where realistic expectations are needed is the *size of the results* we expect to see. Attaining the ideal set of state institutions may not always be feasible. The same is true regarding state performance: political stability and strong economic performance may not be attainable in all states. Rather than seeking perfection, we should seek out conditions that are superior to the status quo. According to Stephen D. Krasner, many states that are the targets of state-building efforts have state institutions that are in the shambles. Such states are unlikely to reach the "ideal" point of high-quality state institutions. As a result, they are apt to experience episodes of political instability and economic decline from time to time, and we should not view this as a failure of state building. Krasner argues: "Specification of some intermediate condition, better than civil strife but short of a fully functioning modern polity, would make state building efforts more tractable and coherent."[70] He writes that a reasonable goal may be to impose some institutional changes or reforms in a state that are durable enough to lead to a level of order in the country that was absent prior. In other words, it is important to have practical expectations about the size of the results that state-building efforts will engender.

The state-building efforts in Kosovo illustrate this point. Spending on the intervention in Kosovo was 25 times more per capita than it was in Afghanistan.[71] Nevertheless, it is still considered to be an "unfinished state" with limited sovereignty, low levels of economic development", and few achievements in establishing the rule of law. However, it is important to note that great improvements have taken place in Kosovo. Though Kosovo is still a work in process, it is relatively peaceful and stable.

The third area where expectations need to be altered is the *return to full state sovereignty*. Though state sovereignty is a concept that is widely respected and honored in the international community, the states that are most in need of assistance in building and reforming their institutions require "substantial external involvement in domestic governance, involvement that frequently requires violations of . . . sovereignty."[72] Many state-building programs, however, explicitly include the return to full state sovereignty as a key objective. For example, the 2009 United States Government Integrated Civilian-Military Campaign Plan for Support of Afghanistan asserts that its goal is to "build the capacity needed to provide Afghanistan with a stable future," such that the government of Afghanistan has "full responsibility for its own security and administration as the international

---

[70]Krasner (2011a: 70).
[71]"Nation-Building: The Inescapable Responsibility of the World's Only Superpower" (2003).
[72]Krasner (2011a: 71).

community continues to offer economic assistance, training, and other non-combat support for the continued development of the country."[73] According to Krasner, this type of objective is problematic.[74] A full return to state sovereignty may not be feasible, or even desirable, for some states where external assistance in the functioning of state institutions may be required indefinitely. Rather than viewing external actors engaged in such efforts as violators of sovereignty (an appellation that can cause anxiety for both host countries and the international community), Paul Collier argues that we should see them as "independent service providers," groups that are contracted by the state's government to assist its institutions in their operations.[75] Because a return to full sovereignty is a goal that is often unrealistic, we should exclude it as an objective of state building.

To summarize this discussion, in our approach to state building we advocate maintaining realistic expectations, particularly in three areas: time frames, outcomes, and return to sovereignty. In addition to realistic expectations, we also emphasize the importance of conceptual clarity and empirical grounding, especially with directing foreign aid. Taken together, these factors address many of the current challenges in the area of state building and pave the way for more effective state-building efforts in the years to come.

BOX 9.1 Territorial restructuring

Some scholars form part of a revivalist school of scholars who argue against the idea of nation-states. This school argues that not every state has to be a nation-state and that states should be *territorially restructured*. Robert Jackson refers to these weak states that automatically gained statehood at independence as *quasi-states*. For Jackson, continuing to support the legitimacy of quasi-states perpetuates both underdevelopment and domestic and personal insecurity because it blocks the formation of jurisdictions that might be less arbitrary, more legitimate, and more cohesive.[76]

Jeffrey Herbst challenges the international community's commitment to the state system.[77] Herbst argues that in Africa in particular, the idea of the sovereign state has not worked well. He argues that Africa should be

(Continued)

---

[73]Krasner (2011b).
[74]Ibid.
[75]Collier (2009: 217) from Krasner (2011a).
[76]Jackson (1990: 91).
[77]Herbst (1996: 120–144.

BOX 9.1 *Continued*

studied regionally without examining the boundaries of the country. States should be redrawn by looking at where a cohesive group or region exercises control. For example, Somaliland exercises control over its territory and provides numerous administrative functions to its people but is not considered sovereign by the international community because it exists within Somalia, a collapsed state. Some states should be consolidated (or absorbed by stronger neighbors), some should be partitioned, and others should be decertified. Herbst claims that secessionist movements should be given the chance to run their governments effectively if they have satisfied some stringent criteria. Herbst believes that supporting de facto governments is a much better alternative to forcing secessionist governments to remain as underground operators, forced to resort to crime. He argues that this would be an innovative solution. He writes that the "very magnitude of the problems affecting millions of people . . . suggest[s] that the current emphasis on resuscitating states that have never demonstrated the capacity to be viable is a mistake."[78]

Herbst is creative, but many of these suggestions may be very unlikely. Partitions have rarely happened. Rarely has the international community allowed the splitting of countries or the changing of borders. Some secessionist movements have gained independence such as Eritrea from Ethiopia in 1991, and Southern Sudan from Sudan in 2011. Rarely has international law allowed for the reconfiguration of borders, since it prefers to defend the status quo. Scholars have noted that states have a "legal personality that outlives any one regime or government."[79] It is therefore very difficult to legally terminate their status.

Interventions

We close this chapter by switching gears and discussing international interventions. Though some in the literature view international interventions as a form of state building, we see them as *distinct*. Interventions, in our view, are a tool that can be used—in addition to or independently of state building—to address the internal struggles of states. They are particularly challenging endeavors, which are often the subject of significant criticism.

---

[78]Ibid., 144.
[79]Dunlap (2004: 470).

Though an analysis of how to improve the success rates of interventions falls outside the scope of this study, we include interventions in this chapter because they often occur in tandem with or prior to extensive state-building projects.

Intervention involves the physical involvement of international actors in ensuring the security of a state (it can involve more than just security, but provision of security is typically the central component). It entails the placement of security (and other) personnel from outside of the state within the state's borders. Interventions can be driven by another state, an alliance of states, or international and/or regional organizations with security forces, such as the United Nations. They can occur either through force or with the state's compliance. Interventions include both peace-making efforts (intervening during an ongoing episode of political instability) and peace-building efforts (intervening in a post-conflict setting).

Interventions are controversial because they entail an infringement on state sovereignty, even in cases where they are executed with the tacit approval of the state. Part of the problem is that there is little consensus in the international community regarding whether there are limits to state sovereignty and if so, what they are. Some argue that states have a responsibility to act in ways that meet the approval of the international community, while others view state sovereignty as sacrosanct under all conditions. Defining the terms under which state sovereignty should be respected is very difficult. For example, does the international community have a responsibility to intervene when civil wars become particularly brutal, as is occurring in Syria today? Or is establishing security up to the Syrian state to resolve? The same questions can be asked of humanitarian crises. Should the international community intervene when large numbers of citizens are dying from famine due to the state's inability to fulfill its basic duties, as has occurred in Ethiopia on numerous occasions? Or should this be left to the state?

At present, there are no internationally agreed upon conditions under which interventions should be permissible, nor are there guidelines for how they should be executed. In the United Nations, for example, decisions to intervene are determined by the Security Council. This raises concerns that the process is too arbitrary, prompting many to question why interventions are agreed to in one situation, but not the next. The lack of set conditions and guidelines also elicits criticism that decisions to intervene by the UN are driven by political concerns, as opposed to the intensity of the political instability and/or economic decline.

Beyond the controversy that surrounds interventions, the question remains: Are they effective tools for increasing state performance? Though there is no set of criteria to determine whether interventions are successful, the consensus position appears to be that interventions have failed more often than they have succeeded.[80] The main reason cited for this is that it takes too long for decisions to intervene to be reached. According to Marina Ottaway, interventions are more likely to be effective the *earlier* they occur, the idea being that prevention is often easier than finding a cure. By the time the international community (or other actors) has agreed to intervene, it is often too late.[81]

For this reason, many argue that the international community needs to pay closer attention to red flags (such as spiraling corruption, as argued in Chapter Eight). Once red flags appear that a state is on the verge of serious political instability and/or economic decline, the decision-making process should begin regarding whether to intervene. Instead, too often interventions occur after states' internal turmoil has already escalated beyond repair.

This is often easier said than done, of course. It is difficult to derive agreed-upon red flags. In addition, these red flags may exist in a number of states, but only intensify in severity in some. Whether to intervene is not a black and white decision even when red flags have been established. And it is not an easy decision to make given that interventions are extremely costly.

Beyond the delayed timing of interventions, other reasons cited for their failure include insufficient funding and inattention to local environments in their execution. Interventions are often poorly funded, leading to situations in which far too few security personnel (and other resources) are devoted to the effort. This can make it impossible for security personnel to effectively provide order, ensuring the intervention's failure. In addition, interventions are, in many cases, hastily planned, such that inadequate attention is paid to the particular dynamics of the state in question. The interveners should also have a clear understanding of their objectives and choose the most appropriate strategy.[82] Without an understanding of the objectives of the mission, this can contribute to the intervention's failure as the appropriate strategy for ensuring security often varies greatly depending on the context.

There are also issues for interveners of what role local people have in making the intervention a success. Generally, studies have shown that relying on warlords has been ineffective while ignoring other local groups is also equally problematic.[83] Local groups that do not have a vested interest in the intervention are more likely to view the intervention as illegitimate, which may dampen the chances for its success.

---

[80]Foley (2008).
[81]Ottaway (2002: 1001–23).
[82]Foley (2008).
[83]Williams (2001: 140); Gizelis and Kosek (2005: 377).

BOX 9.2 Civil society

Civil society consists of associations, clubs, guilds, syndicates, federations, unions, parties, and groups, which serve as an intermediary between the state and the citizen and work to advance their interests.[84] Although civil society is distinct from both the state and society, it "constantly interacts with both."[85]

Civil society constitutes a form of *social capital*. Social capital refers to high levels of trust among the members of a society that make collective action possible.[86] Civil society organizations socialize their participants to the norms of reciprocity, help generate trust, and facilitate patterns of communication.[87] Civil society networks and links can cut across social cleavages and foster more cooperation. Civil society links are distinct from patron-client ties because civil society links are horizontal whereas patron-client links are vertical and hierarchical and often based on shared ethnic ties.[88]

Civil society is an important component to state building. Civil society helps provide the state institutions with information and feedback that is necessary for it to function most effectively. Civil society can also help the state coordinate action. The challenge is that "a functioning state is important for civil society to flourish."[89] When state institutions decay, citizens no longer work with institutions but rather try to subvert them. For this reason, the donor community has focused on supporting civil society, in the hope that this will facilitate larger state-building projects.

The final comment is that for interventions to be successful there also must be some commitment from the interveners. Giving up quickly sends a bad message. Demonstrating a credible commitment to seeing the intervention through is equally important.[90]

The following brief case studies illustrate these points. The first is from Sierra Leone, which is widely viewed to be an example of an intervention success; the second is from Somalia, which is widely viewed to be an example of an intervention failure.

---

[84]Hutchful (1995–6: 56).
[85]Ibid.
[86]Pye (1999: 764).
[87]Foley and Edwards (1996: 2).
[88]Ibid.
[89]Ghani et al. (2009: 2).
[90]Holmes (1998).

Intervention success

One of the more successful interventions was the case of Sierra Leone. Sierra Leone had been ravaged by a decade of war and chaos, which began in 1991. By early 2002 Sierra Leone was a completely different place. Over 45,000 rebels and militias demobilized and weapons were surrendered and symbolically destroyed.

The British government played a major role in this process, as 1,300 British troops were deployed in May of 2000 and another 650 personnel were deployed in October and November. The British along with a "beleaguered" UN force provided support in many different areas including support for the Truth and Reconciliation Commission, various civic associations, military and police training, and economic and social aid.[91] The mission went beyond peace-keeping but also included state-building efforts in tandem with securing the country. The British mission was lauded for several key reasons. First, the British moved quickly in their decision. Second, the use of mercenaries was not condoned. Third, the British did not pull out after some casualties were incurred. It remained more committed to seeing the mission through. Finally, the UK operations aided the UNAMSIL mission (17,500 in total) in Sierra Leone and received "overwhelming support" within the UN Security Council.[92] For all of these reasons, the UK intervention in Sierra Leone is considered to be one of the few cases of modest success in intervention.[93]

Intervention failure

The intervention in Somalia is a commonly cited failure of the perils of intervention. The initial mission in Somalia, known as the United Nations Operation Mission in Somalia (UNOSOM I), began in April 1992 until its duties were taken over by the US led mission United Task Force (UNITAF) in December 1992, which later became UNOSOM II in March 1993. The prime objective of the UNOSOM I mission was to provide food for starving Somalis. The objective of UNOSOM II was to continue to provide food and aid by creating an environment that was secure enough to do so. The problem according to some policy analysts was that the United States did not understand that its objective was going beyond humanitarianism.

---

[91]Williams (2001: 140).
[92]Ibid., 163.
[93]Ibid.

The objective of the mission was interpreted liberally and escalated into attempting to disarm the factions that were loyal to Mohamed Farah Aideed, one of the warlords involved in the conflict. This meant that the US and UN forces went from being a neutral dispatcher of food to taking a clear side in the conflict.[94] Thus, it was "humanitarianism mixed with militarism."[95] Because the objectives were clearly going beyond providing humanitarian aid, more resources and a more comprehensive plan were needed.

The objective of disarmament led to the Battle of Mogadishu on October 3 and 4, 1993. In the process 17 US soldiers were killed and their bodies dragged through the streets.[96] These images were broadcast all over the world. Public outcry at home led President Bill Clinton to scale back troops considerably. Overall, the mission was considered a huge failure. The intervention in Somalia not only failed to bring an end to the conflict, but some argue that it even produced greater levels of violence, by exacerbating divisions among local factions.

The intervention in Somalia was considered a failure for several reasons. First, Somalia was at a very advanced stage of state collapse, in that none of the formal institutions were working. Somalia was often described as a situation of "anarchy."[97] This made it very difficult to know whom to work with. Many scholars now claim that intervention in Somalia should have come years before. Relief should have been delivered much earlier but Somalia fell through the cracks of the international system. Somalia had already been afflicted by a famine as early as 1990.[98] The US decision to airlift food into Somalia was very delayed.[99] By the time President George Bush Sr. made the decision to intervene, 80 percent of the relief goods were being looted and famine was claiming more than 1,000 people a day.[100]

There were also missed opportunities to act even after the famine had been in full swing. As early as March 1992, a ceasefire had been declared that was not exploited. During the ceasefire, the UN could have trained the local militia in Somalia to offset the power of the warlords.[101] The other missed opportunity was that $68 million that the UN had earmarked for Somalia was left unused since it lacked a signature from the nonexistent government in Mogadishu.[102]

---

[94]Gros (1996: 467).
[95]Ibid.
[96]Ibid., 466.
[97]Ibid., 467.
[98]Clark (1992: 112).
[99]Ibid., 116.
[100]Ibid.
[101]Ibid., 117.
[102]Ibid., 116.

Another issue was that locals were involved very little in the peace-building efforts. As a result, they never developed a vested interest in the success of the intervention.[103] Locals instead were suspicious of the involvement of foreigners. Local knowledge was also not used to the full extent. Early local participation increases likelihood of creating sustainable institutions that have some chance of eventually surviving an exit by the outside powers.[104]

The other issue in Somalia was that weapons and ammunition were everywhere, which made the objective of disarmament very difficult. Decision makers misconstrued the problems that they faced. The United States failed to view the operation strategically and provide resources to complete the mission. The United States was simply not prepared. Marina Ottaway and Stefan Mair concur that the intervener must have adequate strength, especially in the beginning, in order to ensure that the intervention is a success.[105]

Finally, the political will of the interveners was very low in Somalia. The commitment of the UN to tackle the problems in Somalia early on was very weak. After Siad Barre had left the country in January 1991, instead of introducing a peacekeeping force, the UN staff relocated to Nairobi. US political will to commit to the effort was low, as evidenced by the relatively quick exit of the bulk of US troops. This view is consistent with advice from policy makers of interventions. The intervener must demonstrate staying power.[106]

As this discussion makes clear, interventions are particularly challenging endeavors that are usually only sought out when state institutions are in total disarray and state performance, as a result, is abysmal. They are often resorted to in the worst-case scenario. We do not broach the subject of how to improve the efficacy of international interventions, however, because it lies outside the scope of this study. Interventions, in our view, are but one of many tools that the international community has at its disposal to improve the domestic conditions of states.

BOX 9.3 Should Somaliland be made into a state?

While Somalia is often considered the poster child for the "collapsed state," scholars are in disagreement about the fate of Somaliland. Somaliland, which is located in North-Western Somalia and borders Ethiopia and Djibouti, has remained relatively stable. Somaliland declared itself independent from the rest of Somalia in May 1991. Somalilanders argue that

(Continued)

---

[103]Gizelis and Kosek (2005: 377).
[104]Fukuyama (2005).
[105]Ottaway and Mair (2004).
[106]Holmes (1998: 115–26).

BOX 9.3 *Continued*

this was not a declaration of succession but rather constituted dissolution of its union with the rest of Somalia.[107]

Somaliland maintains high levels of security, and retains a functioning police and military (50 percent of the state's budget goes to the security sector).[108] Political structures have been erected that are considered to be legitimate in the eyes of its inhabitants.[109] It made a transition from a clan-based representative system to a multiparty democracy. It continues to hold presidential and legislative elections and has managed to deal with a disputed presidential election without violence and the peaceful succession of one leader to the next.[110] Administrative institutions have been built up, with the national budget deriving from customs revenues and landing fees. A public school system has been established.

All of these accomplishments have led some observers to call for the recognition of Somaliland. This viewpoint argues that Somaliland has established peace, stability, some nominally effective administrative institutions, and democracy, whereas the Transitional National Government in Mogadishu has established none of these things.

Critics of Somaliland secession argue, however, that granting Somaliland secession would have far-reaching consequences across much of Africa and that secession should only be allowed with a national referendum in support of it. Others charge that the accomplishments in Somaliland have been over-exaggerated. There are still internal and political divisions between the ruling government and the opposition. The media is somewhat repressed and government critics have been jailed. The Sool and Sanaag groups that straddle Somaliland and the region to the south of Somaliland, known as Puntland, support a united Somalia instead of an independent Somaliland. Moreover, the Somaliland administrative institutions are still plagued by corruption.[111]

Nevertheless, in spite of these criticisms, no one would argue that Somaliland is not head and shoulders more stable and secure than the rest of Somalia. Somaliland is more committed to the rule of law. This commitment to the rule of law has served as a "deterrent to would-be criminals, warlords, and politicians tempted to exploit clan tensions from violating the basic rules of the game."[112] The achievements of Somaliland are all the more impressive given that it has received only modest levels of foreign aid. This may indicate that the success of state building is not always dependent on foreign aid.[113]

---

[107]Menkhaus (2006/7: 81).
[108]Walls (2009: 372).
[109]Ibid., 373.
[110]Menkhaus (2006/7: 91).
[111]Ibid., 92.
[112]Ibid., 93.
[113]Ibid.

Moving forward

State building is a costly endeavor. Each year, governments and organizations around the world allocate $120 billion dollars toward state-building efforts.[114] This money is used in a variety of ways, including bolstering the coffers of state governments, offering them training and supplies, and dedicating external personnel to guide and direct the effort. Despite the vast resources that are allocated annually to state building, many view the process as a waste, arguing that external actors have proven incapable of building and reforming state institutions in ways that improve state performance. Some even argue that state-building efforts have only made things worse for many countries in the developing world.

In this study, we remain optimistic about the potential for state-building efforts to bear fruit. We advocate, however, a different approach to state building to fulfill this task. Our approach emphasizes: (1) conceptual clarity (articulating with greater specificity the desired objectives and results of state-building efforts), (2) empirical grounding (basing the direction and execution of state-building projects on empirical evidence), and (3) realistic expectations (altering the goals of what we expect state-building efforts to accomplish so that they are more pragmatic). This approach addresses some of the contemporary challenges in the execution of state building, with the ultimate intention of increasing their efficacy.

Early action

Our final comment on state building and intervention is to reemphasize the importance of early action. Scholars have noted that early action is imperative to help prevent states from collapsing. Once a state has collapsed it becomes nearly impossible to rebuild it.[115] Much of the literature on "state failure" has focused on looking at indicators of collapse such as the number of refugees, decreasing GDP per capita, increasing crime rates, rising conflict, and high rates of infant mortality. However, the problem is that by the time these indicators appear, "state collapse" may have already taken place. Therefore it is important to offer assistance to states that are in the process of institutional decay rather than in full on "failure."

Before turning to what the warning signs might be, it is important to mention that state building is often a matter of will, regarding the recipient country.[116] Providing assistance to states facing "institutional decay" is

---

[114]OECD (2012).
[115]Zartman (1995).
[116]Patrick (2006).

impossible if the state in question is not open to making changes. In these cases, the most the international community can do is avoid humanitarian crises by acting early to provide critical items such as food and medical supplies when a need emerges. Large volumes of foreign aid without any attention to progress, as the previous section commented, will go to waste.

Certain regimes may be reluctant to enact reforms that they fear may be destabilizing to their grip on power. However, as previous chapters have emphasized, reforming the political institutions may not be as important as reforming the administrative, security, and judicial institutions. It may also be important for the donor community to provide incentives to encourage states to take steps to improve these nonpolitical institutions *before* they are no longer functioning. This case of Ghana may serve as an illustration. Authoritarian leader Jerry Rawlings rose to power in Ghana by staging a coup in 1981. Because the country was experiencing economic turmoil, he agreed to work with the IMF to enact a series of economic reforms in 1983. Though the main impetus behind the reforms was to liberalize the economy, much of the reforms also focused on improving the administrative institutions. For example, higher salaries for the ministries responsible for the collection of taxes and overseeing customs resulted in improvements in performance. After salaries were raised to be on par with the banking sector and financial incentives were given for high performance, tax and customs revenues almost doubled as a share of GDP.[117]

Though the previous section highlighted the arguments against giving foreign aid, when the recipient country is motivated to reform, the role of the international community can be instrumental in helping realize key reforms. Thus, any state that is eager to enact constructive reforms should be given attention by the donor community, not just those that may be politically strategic to donor countries.[118] Donors need to be aware of where conditions are ripe for developmental states. These types of states are likely to use aid effectively. Donors need to support these "emerging local visions of development."[119]

But making an impact is difficult if the institutions have decayed so much that they are barely functioning. For this reason it is important to act early to help states with low functioning institutions before they collapse. Previous chapters have highlighted important criteria for how to evaluate the quality of institutions. We argue that policy makers should use clear criteria to measure state institutions (and not rely on indicators of "failure"

---

[117]Goldsmith (1999: 545).
[118]Though there were many cases of instability around the world, Kosovo was considered to be a priority. Its proximity to Western Europe made intervention a "necessity" as there were worries that violence and instability could spill-over into neighboring states in Europe.
[119]Fritz and Menocal (2007: 549).

such as large flows of refugees, famine, conflict, and dire poverty) and be prepared to assist states that are *willing* to make improvements to their existing institutions, using strategies that have worked in the past while still taking into account the particular realities of the country in question. If one is looking for a precise warning sign, however (as Chapters Eight emphasized), the biggest red flags are rising levels of *corruption*. This often precedes coups, conflict, and economic decline. Moreover, it enables organized crime to be pervasive.

In sum, the previous chapters highlighted the major insights from the institutionalist literature, synthesizing the particular features of state institutions that have been empirically shown to improve state performance. Though more studies are needed to focus on the effects of specific reforms, we advocate that state-building efforts focus on building and reforming state institutions in line with these suggestions.

Conclusion

About half of the world's people (or more than three billion individuals) live below the poverty line.[1] The vast majority of these individuals reside in the developing world, where per capita incomes are simply far lower, on average, than those in the developed world. Though some developing countries are quickly catching up, such as China, India, and Brazil, many, particularly in Sub-Saharan Africa, have proven incapable of growing their economies, a virtual necessary condition for average incomes to rise. For citizens of these countries, persistent poverty translates into lower life expectancy and literacy rates, as well as higher infant mortality rates. Poverty, in other words, has very tangible negative consequences for those who experience it.

The same is true for political instability. Though the number of civil wars has declined markedly since the end of the Cold War, the incidence of civil war still remains a major problem for many.[2] For those who experience it, economic opportunities plummet, assets are destroyed, and, perhaps most importantly, the lives of loved ones are lost. Other violent manifestations of political instability, like coups and terrorist attacks, bring with them similar pernicious costs for citizens.

For these reasons (and many more), improving economic performance and reducing political instability remain important tasks for state governments in much of the developing world, as well as for members of the international policy and development communities concerned with these issues. To date, the state failure framework has been the predominant approach used to address these tasks, where the set of states that have proven to be the most

---

[1] This is computed in 2005, when poverty was defined as earning less than $2.50 a day (World Development Indicators, 2008).

[2] Around a dozen of the world's countries have been engaged in civil war in any given year since 2000 (The Peace Research Institute Oslo, www.prio.no/, accessed November 24, 2012).

challenged are labeled as "failed," "failing," or "weak." This framework has virtually dominated discussions in the international community, eliciting a vast body of literature dedicated to identifying failed states, examining their causes and consequences, and developing strategies to "strengthen" them.

In this study, we have argued that the state failure framework, though well intentioned, is conceptually vague. As a result, it has served as a poor tool for improving state performance in those parts of the world that need this most. We discussed the central problems with this framework in depth in Chapter One and advocate instead an approach that centers on state institutions. We posit that the tie between state institutions, on the one hand, and state performance (defined here as political stability and economic performance), on the other, is what fundamentally underlies much of our interest in state failure. Understanding this relationship is of great importance, but remains severely limited by the emphasis on state failure. Restricting our focus from the state to state institutions narrows the line of inquiry in ways that increase our analytical leverage.

In Chapter Two, we define what we mean by state institutions and disaggregate them into four categories: administrative, judicial, security, and political. We do so because these four types of state institutions encapsulate the vast majority of the domains of the state, providing us with valuable insights into how the state's institutions as a whole are functioning. We argue that state institutions can be assessed based on whether they are high or low in quality. High-quality state institutions are those that improve state performance; low-quality state institutions, by contrast, are those that worsen it.

In Chapter Three we highlight the challenges that many developing nations face in constructing and maintaining effective institutions. We also provide an overview of the literature on the causes of state failure. Using early scholarly work on state failure, we examine the effects of both macro-historical and micro-situational causes. More specifically, the chapter explains the effects of colonialism, the Cold War, neoliberal policies, and globalization. We also provide a summary of the situational causes such as the environment, resources, and demographic issues.

In Chapters Four through Seven, we identify the particular features of each type of state institution that make them high (versus low) quality. We base this discussion primarily on insights gleaned from the institutionalist literatures devoted to each type. The goal of pointing out these features is to provide guidance regarding what, in an ideal scenario, state institutions should look like.

Because it is possible that these features, though emphasized in the literature as important to state performance, do not affect it in practice, we also summarize in these chapters what has been established about these relationships empirically. In most cases, few studies have been carried out taking up these issues. The lack of evidence does not necessarily mean that a particular feature does not affect state performance, but rather that additional research is necessary to establish this. The major purpose of this endeavor is to provide insights into how to more efficiently engage in state building, which we define as the process of building and reforming state institutions in ways that are conducive to political stability and positive state performance. We advocate sculpting state institutions in line with the features identified, but argue that those that have been empirically shown to be associated with improved state performance should be prioritized. In addition, greater resources need to be dedicated to research, examining how more of these features affect key outcomes of interest.

Here, we briefly summarize what the key features of high-quality institutions are for each domain, as well as the major findings pertaining to each regarding their effect on state performance.

In Chapter Four, we discuss administrative institutions. We assess the key features of high-quality administrative institutions:

1 *Meritocratic recruitment and promotion*: civil servants are hired and promoted based on their competence and the needs of the state (as opposed to their political or elite ties).

2 *Salary competitiveness*: civil servants are paid sufficiently to deter their propensity to engage in corrupt behavior.

3 *Autonomy*: civil servants have career stability, lifelong tenure, and special laws that cover the terms of their employment.

A number of empirical studies have examined how these features affect economic performance (to our knowledge, there are no studies that directly examine the impact on political stability). They find that both meritocratic recruitment and promotion and autonomy decrease levels of corruption; there is not enough evidence yet, that salary competitiveness does. The evidence also indicates that high-quality administrative institutions (as a whole) increase levels of economic growth. State-building efforts, therefore, that target the administrative sector should emphasize these three features, particularly meritocratic recruitment and promotion and autonomy.

In Chapter Five, we examine judicial institutions and highlight the following as key features:

1 *Independence*: the government and other sectors of society do not affect how cases are decided; instead, judgments are made based on well-qualified judges' understanding of the law. Budget allocations are not politicized and officials are protected from political retaliations for their decisions.

2 *Integrity and accountability*: ethical standards of conduct for judicial officials exist and are enforced.

3 *Transparency and efficiency*: sophisticated case management systems are in place that ensure standards are adhered to in the assignment of cases to judges and other officials, allocation of

financial resources, and logic underlying judicial decisions, and that the judicial process is swift and minimizes costs.

4 *Equal access*: the judicial system is equally accessible and available to any citizen regardless of their income or geographic location.

Very few empirical studies have looked at the relationship between judicial institutional quality and key outcomes of interest, with the focus instead being on the rule of law, property rights enforcement, and governance. This is problematic, however, because though these concepts are closely related to judicial institutional quality, they are broader and do not lend themselves as well to the provision of state-building advice. Though the general expectation is that high-quality judicial institutions lead to better economic performance and lower levels of organized crime, greater research is needed to establish this.

Chapter Six looks at security institutions and identifies two key features of high-quality security institutions, which are:

1 *Professionalization*: rigorous training requirements exist, promotions are based on merit, and budgets are sufficiently allocated. This lowers the likelihood of corruption, disincentivizes political interference, increases performance in combat, and ensures effective law enforcement.

2 *Centralized military command structure*: the centralized military should have a monopoly over the legitimate use of force, and should therefore be the best-trained, best-equipped, and best-paid military unit in the country. It should not compete with parallel armies, which can divert valuable resources elsewhere. The creation of parallel armies severely undermines the legitimacy and effectiveness of the central armed forces. There should also be a clear internal chain of command.

3 *Civilian accountability*: the security sector answers to the state's political institutions, reducing the likelihood of rogue behavior and protecting the boundary between the security and political spheres.

States characterized by both of these features have high-quality security institutions, while those that have only one or neither of them have low-quality security institutions. A number of empirical studies have examined the relationship between security institutional quality and political instability, primarily how professionalization affects the likelihood of coups. The consensus finding is that greater professionalization, specifically higher military budgets, lowers the incidence of coups. There is also some evidence that greater military training (another aspect of professionalization) does the same. Future research is needed, however, to better understand how (if at all) civilian accountability factors in. The central message to emerge here is that state-building efforts targeting the security sector should work toward professionalizing the state's security institutions, particularly increasing the size of military budgets and providing greater military training.

It is worth mentioning that significant state-building resources are currently dedicated every year to reforming the security sector in a number of developing countries with the goal of reducing the proliferation of terrorist networks. No studies, to our knowledge, however, have directly examined whether security institutional quality affects terrorism. In our view, those funding such efforts should reevaluate whether doing so represents the most efficient use of their resources given the absence of an empirical basis to guide them.

Chapter Seven, which looks at political institutions, breaks from the prior three, in that we do not promote any features as characteristic of high-quality political institutions. We assess that political institutions vary from other institutional domains in that there are no features that uniformly elicit a positive impact on state performance. The relationship between political institutions and state performance is highly context dependent; it also varies based on the particular element of state performance that is of interest. Though there are institutional structures that are conducive to *democratization*, there is no concrete evidence that they improve *state performance* in consistent ways.

Because of this, we argue that rather than promoting a particular set of political institutions as universally desirable, state-building efforts would perhaps be more effective if they focused on urging governments to pursue high-quality institutions in other domains. Governments would most likely be required to reform their political institutions to be able to fulfill this task, but the process of doing so would vary from one state to the next based on the particular social and political context in which they are operating. This would enable political institutions to take shape in states in ways that are appropriate for the local environment in question, while ensuring high-quality state institutions in other key domains.

An additional benefit of this strategy is that external pressures for states to pursue political reforms tend to be very politically sensitive, as they are often viewed as infringements on state sovereignty. Focusing on reforms in the administrative, judicial, and military sectors are less likely to stir such controversies, while still reaping large rewards in terms of the political stability and economic performance enjoyed by the state.

One of the major messages that comes out of Chapters Four through Seven is that future research is needed that examines how the particular features of state institutions affect political stability and economic performance. Though we know how some parts of the state's institutional structure impact state performance, there is far more that we do not know.

The greatest impediment by far to filling this void is the lack of adequate data capturing institutional quality. More resources are needed to fund research efforts that take up this task.

Chapter Eight focused on one of the main signs of institutional decay: corruption. Here we delineate between the different types of corruption; what causes different types of corruption; and how different types of corruption, in turn, affect performance. We highlight why corruption is such a significant omen of state decline. Throughout we provided in-depth examples of how corruption manifests itself in developing countries and demonstrate its harmful effects. Through case studies we demonstrate that strengthening institutions can reap valuable rewards in reducing corruption.

This leads us to the issue of state building, which we take up in Chapter Nine. Though the international community devotes sizable resources every year to trying to "strengthen" states in the developing world, many view this process as a waste, so much so that some argue that external actors are incapable of building and reforming state institutions in ways that better state performance and that these efforts should be dropped altogether. We are less pessimistic about the potential for state-building efforts to bear fruit. We argue, however, that a different approach to state building is needed. The approach we advocate emphasizes the need for greater conceptual clarity, more empirical grounding, the use of realistic expectations in current and future state-building efforts, and early action when states are willing to enact meaningful reforms to their institutions. It addresses some of the major challenges the process of state building has encountered to date, with an eye toward improving its effectiveness and value.

We close by emphasizing that the relationship between state institutions and state performance is complex. It is simply not an easy task to disentangle how institutional landscapes interact to shape key outcomes of interest. Before we can embark on the process of state building, however, it is imperative that we have some understanding of this relationship. Hopefully, this study offered some clarity in this regard, identifying the things we do know with respect to how state institutions affect political stability and economic performance, as well as the things we do not. We remain optimistic about this endeavor. Though the task that lies ahead remains sizable, it is not beyond reach.

BIBLIOGRAPHY

Abadie, Alberto. "Poverty, Political Freedom, and the Roots of Terrorism." *American Economic Review* 96, no. 2 (2006): 159–77.

Abdukadirov, Sherzod. "The Failure of Presidentialism in Central Asia." *Asian Journal of Political Science* 17, no. 3 (2009): 285–98.

Acemoglu, Daron and James Robinson. *Why Nations Fail: The Origins of Power, Prosperity, and Poverty.* London, UK: Crown Business, 2012.

Acemoglu, Daron, Simon Johnson, and James Robinson. "The Colonial Origins of Comparative Development: An Empirical Investigation." *American Economic Review* 91 (2001): 1369–401.

—. "Institutions as the Fundamental Cause of Long-Run Growth." *NBER Working Paper* 10481. National Bureau of Economic Research, Cambridge, Mass (2004): 1–111.

Acemoglu, Daron, Davide Ticchi, and Andrea Vindigni. "A Theory of Military Dictatorships." *National Bureau of Economic Research* 13915 (April 2008): 1–63.

Acemoglu, Daron, Thierry Verdier, and James Robinson. "Kleptocracy and Divide and Rule: A Model of Personal Rule." *Journal of European Economic Association* 2, no. 2–3 (April–May 2004): 162–92.

Acquaah-Gaisie, Gerald. "Combating Third World Corruption" (2008): 1–15, www.buseco.monash.edu.au/mgt/research/governance/pdf-downloads/g-acquaah-wshop.pdf.

Adepoju, Aderanti. "Issues and Recent Trends in International Migration in Sub-Saharan Africa." *International Social Science Journal* 52, no. 165 (December 2002): 383–94.

Afoaku, Osita G. "The Politics of Democratic Transition in Congo (Zaire): Implications of the Kabila Revolution." *Journal of Conflict Studies* 19, no. 2 (1999).

Aguirre, Mariano. "Failed States or Weak Democracies? The State in Latin America." *Open Democracy* (January 17, 2006): 1–6.

Agyeman-Duah, Baffour. "Military Coups, Regime Change, and Interstate Conflicts in West Africa." *Armed Forces & Society* 16, no. 4 (1990): 547–70.

Aksoy, Deniz, David B. Carter, and Joseph Wright. "Terrorism in Dictatorships." *Journal of Politics* 74, no. 3 (July 2012): 810–26.

Alagappa, Muthiah and Takashi Inoguchi. *International Security Management and the United Nations.* Tokyo, Japan: United Nations University Press, 1999.

Alao, Charles. "The Problem of the Failed State in Africa." In *International Security Management and the United Nations.* Edited by Muthiah Alagappa and Takashi Inoguchi. Tokyo: United Nations University Press, 1999, 83–102.

Albrecht, Holger and Oliver Schlumberger. "Waiting for Godot": Regime Change without Democratization in the Middle East." *International Political Science Review* 25, no. 4 (2004): 371–92.

Alcaraz, Jesus Puente and Luis Felipe Linares Lopez. "A General View of the Institutional State of Decentralization in Guatemala." In *Decentralization and Democratic Governance in Latin America*. Edited by Joseph S. Tulchin and Andrew Selee. Woodrow Wilson Center Report on the Americas #12. Washington, DC: Woodrow Wilson International Center for Scholars.

Alchian, Armen. "Property Rights." *The Concise Encyclopedia of Economics*, Library of Economics and Liberty, 2008, www.econlib.org/library/Enc/PropertyRights.html.

Ali, Leila, El Sayed Yassin, and Monte Palmer. "Apathy, Values, Incentives and Development: The Case of the Egyptian Bureaucracy." *Middle East Journal* 39, no. 3 (Summer 1985): 341–61.

Allen, Chris. "Understanding African Politics." *Review of African Political Economy* 65 (1995): 301–20.

—. "Warfare, Endemic Violence and State Collapse in Africa." *Review of African Political Economy* 26, no. 81 (1999): 367–84.

Alter, Peter. *Nationalism*. London, UK: Edward Arnold, 1989.

Amsden, Alice H. *Asia's Next Giant: South Korea and Late Industrialization*. Oxford, UK: Oxford University Press, 1989.

Anderson, James and Cheryl Gray. "Anticorruption in Transition 3: Who Is Succeeding and Why?" Washington, DC: The World Bank, 2006.

Anderson, Leslie. "The Authoritarian Executive? Horizontal and Vertical Accountability in Nicaragua." *Latin American Politics & Society* 48, no. 2 (Summer 2006): 141–69.

Anderson, Lisa. "Political Decay in the Arab World." Paper Delivered Eighteenth Annual Joseph (Buddy) Strelitz Lecture (December 8, 1999).

Andreski, Stanislav. "On the Peaceful Disposition of Military Dictatorships." *Journal of Strategic Studies* 3, no. 3 (1980): 3–10.

Angrist, Michele Penner. "The Expression of Political Dissent in the Middle East: Turkish Democratization and Authoritarian Continuity in Tunisia." *Comparative Studies in Society and History* 41, no. 4 (1999): 730–57.

Annan, Kofi. "In Larger Freedom: Towards Development, Security and Human Rights for All. Report of the Secretary General." UN document, A/59. New York: United Nations, 2005, 1–62.

Antunes, Antonio R. and Tiago V. de V. Cavalcanti. "Start Up Costs, Limited Enforcement, and the Hidden Economy." *European Economic Review* 51 (2007): 203–24.

Anwaruddin, Awang. "Improving Public Service Delivery through Bureaucracy Reform." *JURNAL Ilmu Administrasi* 1, no. 4 (2004): 299–311.

Aponte, David. "The Tonton Macoutes: The Central Nervous System of Haiti's Reign of Terror." *Council on Hemispheric Affairs* (March 11, 2010).

Aquino, Belinda. Politics *of Plunder: The Philippines under Marcos*. Manila, Philippines: University of the Philippines Press, 1997.

Arifianto, Alexander. "Corruption in Indonesia: Causes, History, Impacts, and Possible Cures." (2001): 1–26, www.academia.edu/1337711/Corruption_in_Indonesia_Causes_History_Impacts_and_Possible_Cures.

Arkoubi, Khadija al- and Willy McCourt. "The Politics of HRM: Waiting for Godot in the Moroccan Civil Service." *The International Journal of Human Resource Management* 15 (2004): 979.

Armstrong, Andre and Barnett R. Rubin. "Conference Summary: Policy Approaches to Regional Conflict Formations." New York: Center on International Cooperation, New York University, November 2002.

Arrellano-Gault, David. "Civil Service Reform: Challenges and Future Prospects for Mexican Democracy." In *Handbook of Administrative Reform, An International Perspective*. Edited by Jerri Killian. Boca Raton, FL: CRC Press, 2008, 233–45.

Atran, Scott. "Genesis of Suicide Terrorism." *Science* 299 (2003): 1534–9.

—. "Mishandling Suicide Terrorism." *The Washington Quarterly* 27, no. 3 (2004): 65–90.

Aufrecht, Steven E. and Li Siu Bun. "Reform with Chinese Characteristics: The Context of Chinese Civil Service Reform." *Public Administration Review* 55, no. 2 (March–April 1995): 175–82.

Ayoob, Mohammed. "State-Making, State-Breaking and State Failure: Explaining the Roots of 'Third World' Insecurity." In *Between Development and Destruction*. Edited by Luc van de Goor, Kumar Rupesinghe, and Paul Sciarone. London, UK: Palgrave, 1996, 67–86.

—. *The Third World Security Predicament: State-Making, Regional Conflict and theInternational System*. Boulder, CO: Lynne Rienner, 1995.

Azam, Jean-Paul. "The Political Geography of Redistribution." In *The Political Economy of Economic Growth in Africa, 1960–2000, Vol. 1*. Edited by B. J. Ndulu, S. A. O'Connell, R. Bates, P. Collier, and C. C. Soludo. Cambridge, UK: Cambridge University Press, 2007, 225–48.

Azarya, Victor and Naomi Chazan. "Disengagement from the State in Africa: Reflections on the Experience of Ghana and Guinea." *Comparative Studies in Society and History* 29, no. 1 (January 1987): 106–31.

Bach, Daniel. "The African Neo-patrimonial State as a Global Prototype." *Heidelberg Papers in South Asian and Comparative Politics, Working Paper* 59 (February 2011): 33–41.

Baeza, Tito. "Accountability and Transparency in Mexico: The Case of the Federal Institute of Access to Public Information, the Ministry of Foreign Affairs and Promexico." Lee Kuan Yew School of Public Policy, 1–22.

Baghat, Gawdat. "Education in the Gulf Monarchies: Retrospect and Prospect." *International Review of Education* 45, no. 2 (1999): 127–36.

Baines, John M. "U.S. Military Assistance to Latin America: An Assessment." *Journal of Inter-American Studies and World Affairs* 14, no. 4, Special Issue: Military and Reform Governments in Latin America (November 1972): 469–87.

Baker, Bruce. "Living with Non-State Policing in South Africa: The Issues and Dilemmas." *Journal of Modern African Studies* 40, no. 1 (March 2002): 29–53.

Bakke, Kristin and Erik Wibbels. "Diversity, Disparity, and Civil Conflict in Federal States." *World Politics* 59, no. 1 (October 2006): 1–50.

Baldor, Lolita. "More Military Aid to Africa as Terrorism Increases." *The Seattle Times* (August 2, 2012).

Ball, Nicole and Michael Brzoska. "Voice and Accountability in the Security Sector." BICC Paper 21 (2002).

Barany, Zoltan. "The Role of the Military." *Journal of Democracy* 22, no. 4 (2011): 24–35.

Barbero, Jesus Martin. "The City: Between Fear and the Media." In *Citizens of Fear: Urban Violence in Latin America*. Edited by Susana Rotker. Piscataway, NJ: Rutgers State University Press, 2002, 25–36.

Barfield, Thomas. "Afghanistan Is Not the Balkans: Ethnicity and Its Political Consequences from a Central Eurasian Perspective." Publication of the Central Eurasian Studies Society 4, no. 1 (2005): 1–76.

Barro, Robert J. "Rule of Law, Democracy, and Economic Performance." *2000 Index of Economic Freedom* (2000): 31–51.

Basedau, Matthias and Alexander Stroh. "Measuring Party Institutionalization in Developing Countries: A New Research Instrument Applied to 28 African Political Parties." Giga Working Paper Series No. 9, GIGA German Institute of Global and Area Studies, 2008.

Bates, Robert. "Political Insecurity and State Failure in Contemporary Africa." *Center for International Development Working Paper* 115 (January 2005): 1–54.

—. *Political Instability Task Force Report: Phase IV Findings*, 2003.

—. *Prosperity and Violence: The Political Economy of Development*. New York, NY: Norton Publisher, 2001.

—. "State Failure." *Annual Review of Political Science* 11 (June 2008a): 1–12.

—. *When Things Fell Apart: State Failure in Late-Century Africa*. Cambridge, UK: Cambridge University Press, 2008b.

Bayart, J. *The State in Africa: The Politics of the Belly*. London, UK: Longman, 1993.

Bayuni, Endy. "In Indonesia, Social Media Checks the Military." *Foreign Policy* (May 11, 2012).

Beblawi, Hazem and Giacomo Luciani. *The Rentier State: Nation, State and Integration in the Arab World*. London, UK: Croom Helm, 1987.

Becker, G. S. and G. J. Stigler. "Law Enforcement, Malfeasance, and the Compensation of Enforcers." *Journal of Legal Studies* 2 (1974): 1–19.

Bejarano, Ana Maria and Eduardo Pizarro. *The Crisis of Democracy in Colombia: From Restricted Democracy to Besieged Democracy*. Unpublished manuscript, 2001.

Bellin, Eva. "The Robustness of Authoritarianism in the Middle East: Exceptionalism in Comparative Perspective." *Comparative Politics* 36, no. 2 (January 2004): 139–57.

Bendix, Richard. *Nation-Building & Citizenship: Studies of Our Changing Social Order*. New Brunswick, NJ: Transaction Publishers, 1996.

Bergman, Marcelo. "Crime and Citizen Security in Latin America: The Challenges for New Scholarship." *Latin American Research Review* 41, no. 2 (June 2006): 213–27.

Berkman, Heather. "The Politicization of the Judicial System of Honduras and the Proliferation of Las Maras." *Journal of International Policy Studies* (2005): 1–15.

Berkowitz, David and Karen Clay. "The Effect of Judicial Independence on Courts: Evidence from the American States." *Journal of Legal Studies* 35 (June 2006): 399–440.

Berrebi, Claude. "Evidence about the Link between Education, Poverty and Terrorism mong Palestinians." Mimeo. Princeton, NJ: Princeton University, 2003.

Bertram, Eva. "Reinventing Governments: The Promise and Perils of United Nations Peace Building." *Journal of Conflict Resolution* 39, no. 3 (1995): 387–418.

Besley, Timothy. "Property Rights and Investment Incentives: Theory and Evidence from Ghana." *Journal of Political Economy* 103, no. 5 (October 1995): 903–37.

Bhatia, Michael and Mark Sedra. *Afghanistan, Arms and Conflict: Armed Groups, Disarmament and Security in a Post-War Society*. London, UK: Routledge, 2008.

Bhattarai. Keshab. "Political Economy of Conflict, Cooperation and Economic Growth: Nepalese Dilemma," May 2005, http://pdfsb.com/readonline/625646 42657731305758642b4148316855513d3d-4254509.

Bibes, Patricia. "Transnational Organized Crime and Terrorism Colombia, a Case Study." *Journal of Contemporary Criminal Justice* 17, no. 3 (2001): 243–58.

Bielasiak, Jack. "Substance and Process in the Development of Party Systems in East Central Europe." *Communist and Post-Communist Studies* 30, no. 1 (1997): 23–44.

Bienen, Henry, *The Military and Modernization*. New Brunswick, NJ: Transaction Books, 2008.

Bienen, Henry and Jeffrey Herbst. "The Relationship between Political and Economic Reform in Africa." *Comparative Politics* 29, no. 1 (October 1996): 23–42.

Bilgin, Pinar and Adam David Morton. "Historicising Representations of 'Failed States': Beyond the Cold War Annexation of the Social Sciences?" *Third World Quarterly* 23, no. 1 (2002): 55–80.

—. "From 'Rogue' to 'Failed' States? The Fallacy of Short-termism." *Politics* 24, no. 3 (September 2004): 169–80.

Binder, Alberto. *Justicia Penal y Estado de Derecho*. Buenos Aires, Argentina: Ad Hoc, 1993.

Black, Craig R. "Deterring Libya: The Strategic Culture of Muammar Qaddafi." *The Counter-Proliferation Papers*. Future Warfare Series No. 8, USAF Counter-proliferation Center, Air War College (2000): 1–30.

Blackburn, Keith, Niloy Bosey, and Salvatore Capasso. "Living with Corruption: Threshold Effects in Red Tape and Rent Seeking." DES (Department of Economic Studies), University of Naples "Parthenope," Italy Working Papers, 2008.

Blair, Tony. "A Battle for Global Values." *Foreign Affairs* 86, no. 1 (January–February 2007): 79–90.

Blaydes, Lisa. "Authoritarian Elections and Elite Management: Theory and Evidence from Egypt." *Princeton University Conference on Dictatorships*, 2008.

Blochlinger, Karen. "Primus Inter Pares: Is the Singapore Judiciary First among Equals?" *Pacific Rim Law & Policy Journal* 9 (2000): 591–618.

Blomberg, B. and G. D. Hess. "From (no) Butter to Guns? Understanding the Economic Role in Transnational Terrorism." In *Terrorism, Economic Development, and Political Openness*. Edited by P. Keefer and N. Loyaza. New York, NY: Cambridge University Press, 2008, 83–115.

Bluhm, Richard and Adam Szirmai. "Institutions, Inequality and Growth: A Review of Theory and Evidence on the Institutional Determinants of Growth and Inequality." Innocenti Working Paper 2011–02, Florence, UNICEF Innocenti Research Centre (May 2001): 1–65.

Bøås, Morten. "African Conflicts and Conflicts Drivers: Uganda, Congo and the Mano River." *Nordic Africa Institute Lecture Series on African Security* (2008): 1–12.

—."Liberia and Sierra Leone—Dead Ringers? The Logic of Neo-patrimonial Rule." *Third World Quarterly* 22, no. 5 (2001): 697–723.

Bøås, Morten and Kathleen M.. "'Failed States' and 'State Failure': Threats or Opportunities?" *Globalization* 4, no. 4 (December 2007): 475–85.

—. "Insecurity and Development: The Rhetoric of the 'Failed States.' *The European Journal of Development Research* 17, no. 3 (September 2005): 385–95.

Bøås, Morten, Kathleen M. Jennings, and Timothy M. Shaw. "Dealing with Conflicts and Emergency Situations." In *Doing Development Research*. Edited by Vandana Desai and Rob Potter. Thousand Oaks, CA: Sage Publications, 2006, 70–8.

Boege, Volker, Anne Brown, Kevin Clements, and Anna Nolan. "On Hybrid Political Orders and Emerging States: State Formation in the Context of 'Fragility.'" Berghof Research Center for Constructive Conflict Management (October 2008): 1–21.

—. "On Hybrid Political Orders and Emerging States: What are Failing-States in the Global South or Research and Politics in the West?" Research Center for Constructive Conflict Management (April 2009): 15–31.

Bogaards, Matthijs. "How to Classify Hybrid Regimes? Defective Democracy and Electoral Authoritarianism." *Democratization* 16, no. 2 (2009): 399–423.

Boix, Carles and Milan Svolik. "The Foundations of Limited Authoritarian Government: Institutions and Power-Sharing in Dictatorships" (April 2008): 1–35.

Bonturi, Marcos. "The Brazilian Pension System: Recent Reforms and Challenges Ahead." *OECD Economics Department Working Papers* 340 (August 2002): 1–36.

Boone, Catherine. "Electoral Populism where Property Rights Are Weak: Land Politics in Contemporary Sub-Saharan Africa." *Comparative Politics* 41, no. 2 (January 2009): 183–201.

Börzel, Tanja A. and Yasemin Pamuk. "Pathologies of Europeanisation: Fighting Corruption in the Southern Caucasus."*West European Politics* 35, no. 1 (2012): 79–97.

Botero, Juan Carlos and Ponce, Alejandro. "Measuring the Rule of Law." The World Justice Project Working Paper Series 1 (November 30, 2011): 1–120, http://dx.doi.org/10.2139/ssrn.1966257.

Botero, Juan Carlos, Rafael La Porta, Florencio López-de-Silanes, Andrei Shleifer, and Alexander Volokh. "Judicial Reform." *The World Bank Research Observer* 18, no. 1 (2003): 61–88.

Boulden, Jane. *Dealing with Conflict in Africa: The United Nations and Regional Organizations.* New York, NY: Palgrave, 2004.

Bourne, Michael. *Arming Conflict: The Proliferation of Small Arms.* New York, NY: Palgrave Macmillan, 2007.

—. "Netwar Geopolitics: Security, Failed States and Illicit Flows." *British Journal of Politics and International Relations* (2011): 1–24.

Boutwell, Jeffrey and Michael T. Klare, eds. *Light Weapons and Civil Conflict: Controlling the Tools of Violence.* Lanham, MD: Rowman and Littlefield, 1999.

Bradley, P., D. Charbonneau, and S. Campbell. "Measuring Military Professionalism." 45th Annual Conference of the International Military Testing Association, Pensacola, Florida 3–6 (November 2003): 760–6.

Braibant, Ralph. "Public Bureaucracy and Judiciary in Pakistan." In *Bureaucracy and Political Development.* Edited by Joseph Palombra. Princeton, NJ: Princeton University Press, 1963.

Brancati, Dawn. "Decentralization: Fuelling the Fire or Dampening the Flames of Ethnic Conflict." *International Organization* 60 (Summer 2006): 651–85.

Bratt, Duane. "Rebuilding Fractured Societies." *Security Dialogue* 28, no. 2 (1997): 173–6.

Bratton, Michael. "Beyond the State: Civil Society and Associational life in Africa." *World Politics* 41, no. 3 (April 1989): 407–30.

—. "Second Elections in Africa." *Journal of Democracy* 9, no. 3 (1998): 51–66.

Bratton, Michael and Eric C. C. Chang. "State Building and Democratization in Sub-Saharan Africa: Forwards, Backwards or Together?" *Comparative Political Studies* 39, no. 9 (November 2006): 1059–83.

Bratton, Michael and Mwangi S. Kimenyi. "Voting in Kenya: Putting Ethnicity in Perspective." *University of Connecticut Department of Economics Working Paper Series* (March 2008): 1–24.

Bratton, Michael and Nicolas van de Walle. *Democratic Experiments in Africa: Regime Transitions in Comparative Perspective.* Cambridge, UK: Cambridge University Press, 1997.

—. "Neo-patrimonial Regimes and Political Transitions in Africa." *World Politics* 44, no. 4 (July 1994): 453–89.

Brautigam, Deborah A. and Stephen Knack. "Foreign Aid, Institutions and Governance in Sub-Saharan Africa." *Economic Development and Cultural Change* 52, no. 2 (January 2004): 255–85.

Brett, E. A. "Aid Dependence, Conditionality, and Poverty Focussed Development Building Pro-Poor Organisational Systems." Development Studies Institute, London School of Economics (2010): 1–10.

— "State Failure and Success in Uganda and Zimbabwe: The Logic of Political Decay and Reconstruction in Africa." *Crisis States Programme Working Paper Series* 1, no. 78 (February 2006): 1–25.

Brinkerhoff, Derick W. and Jennifer M. Brinkerhoff. "Governance Reforms and Failed States: Challenges and Implications." *International Review of Administrative Sciences* 68, no. 4 (2002): 511–31.

Brinkerhoff, Derick W. and Arthur A. Goldsmith. "Clientelism, Patrimonialism and Democratic Governance: An Overview and Framework for Assessment and Programming." *U.S. Agency for International Development Office of Democracy and Governance under Strategic Policy and Institutional Reform* (December 2002): 1–50.

Brinkerhoff, Derick W. and Ronald W. Johnson. "Decentralized Local Governance in Fragile States: Learning from Iraq." *International Review of Administrative Sciences* 75 (2009): 585–607.

Brooks, Michael A. and Ben J. Heudra. "An Exploration of Rent Seeking." *Economic Record* 65, no. 1 (2007): 32–50.

Brooks, Risa. *Political-Military Relations and the Stability of Arab Regimes.* Adelphi Paper 324. New York: Oxford University Press, 1998.

Brooks, Risa and Elizabeth Stanley, eds. *Creating Military Power: The Sources of Military Effectiveness.* Stanford, CA: Stanford University Press, 2007.

Brown, Nathan J. *The Rule of Law in the Arab World: Courts in Egypt and the Gulf.* Cambridge, UK: Cambridge University Press, 1997.

—. "Why Won't Saudi Arabia Write Down Its Laws?" *Foreign Policy* (January 23, 2012).

Brownlee, Jason. *Authoritarianism in an Age of Democratization.* Cambridge, UK: Cambridge University Press, 2007.

—. "The Decline of Pluralism in Mubarak's Egypt." *Journal of Democracy* 13, no. 4 (2002): 6–14.

Brunetti, Aymo, Gregory Kisunko, and Beatrice Weder. "Credibility of Rules and Economic Growth: Evidence from a Worldwide Survey of the Private Sector." *The World Bank Economic Review* 12, no. 3 (1998): 353–84.

Brym, Robert J. and Vladmir Gimpelson. "The Size, Composition and Dynamics of the Russian State Bureaucracy in the 1990s." *Slavic Review* 63, no. 1 (Spring 2004): 90–112.

Brzoska, Michael. *Development Donors and the Concept of Security Sector Reform.* Geneva: Geneva Centre for the Democratic Control of Armed Forces, 2003.

—. "Introduction: Criteria for Evaluating Post-conflict Reconstruction and Security Sector Reform in Peace Support Operations." *International Peacekeeping* 13, no. 1 (2006): 1–13.

Buchanan, James M., Robert D. Tollison, and Gordon Tullock. *Toward a Theory of the Rent-Seeking Society.* College Station, TX: Texas A & M University Press, 1980.

Buchanan Smith, Margaret, and Susanna Davies. *Famine Early Warning and Response: The Missing Link.* London, UK: Intermediate Technology Publications, 1995.

Buira, Ariel. *Challenges to the World Bank and IMF: Developing Country Perspectives.* London, UK: Anthem Press, 2003.

Bulíř, Aleš. "Can Price Incentive to Smuggle Explain the Contraction of the Cocoa Supply in Ghana?" *Journal of African Economies* 11, no. 3 (2002): 413–39.

Bulmer-Thomas, Valerie. *The Economic History of Latin America since Independence.* Cambridge, UK: Cambridge University Press, 2003.

Burgis, Michelle L. "Judicial Reform and the Possibility of Democratic Rule in Jordan: A Policy Perspective on Judicial Independence." *Arab Law Quarterly* 21 (2007): 135–169.

Burgoon, Brian. "On Welfare and Terror: Social Welfare Policies and Political Economic Roots of Terrorism." *Journal of Conflict Resolution* 50, no. 2 (April 2006): 176–203.

Burnashev, Rustam. "Terrorist Routes in Central Asia: Trafficking Drugs, Humans, and Weapons." *Connections* 6 (2007): 65–70.

Burnside, Craig and David Dollar. "Aid, Policies, and Growth." *American Economic Review* 90, no. 4 (2000): 847–68.

Bush, George W. "President Bush Delivers State of the Union Address." Washington, DC, White House, January 31, 2006, www.whitehouse.gov/news/releases/2006/01/20060131–10.html.

Burton, John. *Resolving Deep Rooted Conflict: A Handbook*. Lanham, MD: University Press of America, 1987.

Buscaglia, Edgardo. "An Analysis of Judicial Corruption and Its Causes: An Objective Governance-Based Approach." *International Review of Law and Economics* 21 (2001): 233–49.

—. "Controlling Organized Crime and Corruption in the Public Sector." *Forum on Crime and Society* 3 (2003): 3–34.

—. "An Economic Analysis of Corrupt Practices within the Judiciary in Latin America." In *Essays in Law and Economics V*. Edited by Claus Ott and Georg Von Waggenheim. Amsterdam, Netherlands: Kluwer Press, 1997.

—. "Obstacles to Judicial Reform in Latin America." In *Justice Delayed: Judicial Reform in Latin America*. Edited by Edmundo Jarquin and Fernando Carrillo. Washington, DC: Inter-American Development Bank, 1998.

—. "The Paradox of Expected Punishment: Legal and Economic Factors Determining Success and Failure in the Fight against Organized Crime." *Review of Law & Economics* 4, no. 1 (2008): 290–317.

Buscaglia, Edgardo and Maria Dakolias. "An Analysis of the Causes of Corruption in the Judiciary." Technical Papers, Legal Department, Washington, DC, The World Bank, 1999.

—. "A Quantitative Analysis of the Judicial Sector: The Cases of Argentina and Ecuador." World Bank Technical Paper No 353, Washington, DC, World Bank, 1996.

Buscaglia Edgardo and Jan van Dijk. "Controlling Organized Crime and Corruption in the Public Sector." *Forum on Crime and Society* 3, no. 1–2 (December 2003): 1–32.

Buscaglia, Edgardo, Maria Dakolias, and William E. Ratliff. *Judicial Reform in Latin America: A Framework for National Development*. No. 65. Stanford, CA: Hoover Inst. Press, 1995.

Byman, Daniel. "Passive Sponsors of Terrorism." *Survival* 47, no. 4 (Winter 2005): 117–44.

Byman, Daniel L. and Jerrold D. Green. "The Enigma of Political Stability in the Persian Gulf Monarchies." *Middle East Review of International Affairs* 3, no. 3 (1999): 20–37.

Caldeira, Teresa. "Crime and Individual Rights: Reframing the Question of Violence in Latin America." In *Constructing Democracy: Human Rights,*

Citizenship, and Society in Latin America. Edited by Elisabeth Jelin and Eric Hershberg. Boulder, CO: Westview Press, 1996.

Call, Charles. "The Fallacy of the 'Failed State.'" *Third World Quarterly* 29, no. 8 (2008): 1491–507.

Cammack, Paul. "The Resurgence of Populism in Latin America." *Bulletin of Latin American Research* 19, no. 2 (April 2000).

Carey, John M. and Matthew Soberg Shugart. "Incentives to Cultivate a Personal Vote: A Rank Ordering of Electoral Formulas." *Electoral Studies* 14, no. 4 (1995): 417–39.

Carlan, Philip E. and John A. Lewis. "Dissecting Police Professionalism: A Comparison of Predictors within Five Professionalism Subsets." *Police Quarterly* 12, no. 4 (2009a): 370–87.

—. "Professionalism in Policing: Assessing the Professionalization Movement." *Professional Issues in Criminal Justice* 4, no. 1 (2009b): 39–58.

Carlsson, Jerker, Gloria Somolekae, and Nicolas Van de Walle. *Foreign Aid in Africa: Learning from Country Experiences.* Stockholm, Sweden: Nordic Africa Institute, 1997.

Carment, David. "Assessing State Failure: Implications for Theory and Policy." *Third World Quarterly* 24, no. 3 (2003): 407–27.

Carment, David and Patrick James. "Third Party States in Ethnic Conflict: Identifying the Domestic Determinants of Intervention." In *Ethnic Conflict and International Politics: Explaining Diffusion and Escalation.* Edited by Steven E. Lobell and Phillip Mauceri. Basington, UK: Palgrave Macmillan, 2004, 11–34.

Carothers, Thomas. "The Rule of Law Revival." *Foreign Affairs* 77 (1998): 95.

—. "The 'Sequencing' Fallacy." *Journal of Democracy* 18, no. 1 (2007): 12–27.

Case, William. "The UMNO Party Election in Malaysia: One for the Money." *Asian Survey* 34, no. 10 (1994): 916–30.

Castañeda, J. G. *Utopia Unarmed: The Latin American Left after the Cold War.* New York, NY: Vintage, 1993.

Castells, Manuel and Alejandro Portes. "World Underneath: The Origins, Dynamics, and Effects of the Informal Economy." In *The Informal Economy: Studies in Advanced and Less Developed Countries.* Edited by Alejandro Portes et al. Baltimore, MD: Johns Hopkins Press, 1989, 11–37.

Centeno, Miguel Angel. *Blood and Debt. War and the Nation-State in Latin America.* University Park, PA: The Pennsylvania State University Press, 2002.

Chabal, P. and J.-P. Daloz. *Africa Works: Disorder as Political Instrument.* Bloomington, IN: Indiana University Press; London: James Currey, 1999.

Chai, Sun-Ki. "An Organizational Economics Theory of Anti-government Violence." *Comparative Politics* 26, no. 1 (October 1993): 99–110.

Chamberlain, Heath B. "On the Search for Civil Society in China." *Modern China* 19, no. 2 (April 1993): 199–215.

Champion, Daryl. "The Kingdom of Saudi Arabia: Elements of Instability within Stability" *MERIA* 3, no. 4 (December 1999).

Chandler, Andrea M. *Shocking Mother Russia: Democratization, Social Rights and Pension Reform in Russia, 1990–2001.* Toronto, Canada: University of Toronto Press, 2004.

Chandler, David. *Empire in Denial.* London, UK: Pluto, 2006.

Chang, Eric C. C. and Miriam Golden. "Electoral Systems, District Magnitude, and Corruption." *British Journal of Political Science* 37 (2007): 115–37.

Chang, Ha-Joon. "Understanding the Relationship between Institutions and Economic Development. Some Key Theoretical Issues." *Revista de Economía Institucional* 8, no. 14 (2006): 125–36.

Chari, P. R. "Civil-Military Relations in India." *Armed Forces & Society* 4, no. 1 (1977): 3–28.

Chaudhry, Shahid Amjad, Gary James Reid, and Waleed Haider Malik. *Civil Service Reform in Latin America and the Caribbean: Proceedings of a Conference*. No. 259. Washington, DC: World Bank, 1994.

Chaudry, K. A. "Economic Liberalization and the Lineages of the Rentier State." *Comparative Politics* 27 (1994): 1–24.

Chauvet, Lisa and Paul Collier. "What Are the Preconditions for Turnarounds in Failing States?" Center for the Study of African Economies, University of Oxford (January 2007): 1–19.

Chauvet, Lisa, Paul Collier, and Anke Hoeffler. "The Cost of Failing States and the Limits to Sovereignty." In *Fragile States: Causes, Costs and Responses*. Edited by Wim Naude, Amelia U. Santos Paulino, and Mark McGillvray. Oxford, UK: Oxford University Press, 2007, 91–110.

Chazan, Naomi. *Irredentism and International Politics.*Boulder, CO: Lynne Rienner, 1991.

Chege, Michael. "Sierra Leone: The State that Came Back from the Dead." *The Washington Quarterly* 25, no. 3 (Summer 2002): 147–60.

Cheibub, José Antonio, Jennifer Gandhi, and James Raymond Vreeland. "Democracy and Dictatorship Revisited." *Public Choice* 143, no. 1 (2010): 67–101.

Chemin, Matthieu. "The Impact of the Judiciary on Entrepreneurship: Evaluation of Pakistan's Access to Justice Programme." *Journal of Public Economics* 93 (2009) 114–25.

Cheng, Li and Lynn White. "The Sixteenth Central Committee of the Chinese Communist Party: Hu Gets What?" *Asian Survey* 43, no. 4 (2003): 553–97.

Chenoweth, Erica. "Democratic Competition and Terrorist Activity." *Journal of Politics* 72, no. 1 (2010): 16–30.

Chesterman, Simon. *You, the People: The United Nations, Transitional Administration, and State-Building*. Oxford, UK: Oxford University Press, 2004.

Chesterman, Simon, Michael Ignatieff, and Ramesh Chandra Thakur, eds. *Making States Work. State Failure and the Crisis of Governance*. Tokyo, Japan: United Nations University Press, 2005.

Cheung, Anthony B. "The Politics of Administrative Reforms in Asia: Paradigms and Legacies, Paths and Diversities." *Governance: An International Journal of Policy, Administration, and Institutions* 18, no. 2 (April 2005): 257–82.

Chevigny, Paul. *Edge of the Knife: Police Violence in the Americas*. New York, NY: New York University Press, 1995.

Chhibber, Pradeep and Irfan Nooruddin. "Do Party Systems Count? The Number of Parties and Government Performance in the Indian States." *Comparative Political Studies* 37, no. 2 (2004): 152–87.

Cho, Wonhyuk and Greg Porumbescu. "Weberian Bureaucracy and Performance of Civil Service: Cross-County Analysis." Seoul National University, 2011, 1–24, www.kapa21.or.kr/data/data_download.php?did=5072.

Chong, Alberto and Cesar Calderon. "Causality and Feedback between Institutional Measures and Economic Growth." *Economics and Politics* 12, no. 1 (2000): 69–81.

Chou, Yuan K. and Hayat Khan. "Explaining Africa's Growth Tragedy: A Theoretical Model of Dictatorship and Kleptocracy." *University of Melbourne Department of Economics Research Paper* 922 (November 2004): 1–40.

Chu, Yun-han, Chih-cheng Lo, and Ramon H. Myers, eds. *The New Chinese Leadership: Challenges and Opportunities after the 16th Party Congress.* Cambridge, UK: Cambridge University Press, 2004.

Chua, Amy. *A World on Fire: How Exporting Free Markets and Democracy Breeds Ethnic Hatred and Global Instability.* New York, NY: Anchor Books, 2004.

Clapham, Christopher. *Africa and the International System: The Politics of State Survival.* Cambridge, UK: Cambridge University Press, 2002a.

—. "The Challenge to the State in a Globalized World." *Development and Change* 33, no. 5 (2002b): 775–95.

Claessens, Stijn and Luc Laeven. "Financial Development, Property Rights, and Growth." *The Journal of Finance* 58, no. 6 (December 2003): 2401–36.

Clark, Jeffrey. "Debacle in Somalia." *Foreign Affairs* (1992): 109–23.

Cleveland, William L. *A History of the Modern Middle East.* Boulder, CO: Westview Press, 1994.

Clunan, Ann and Harold Trinkunas. *Ungoverned Spaces: Alternatives to State Authority in an Era of Softened Sovereignty.* Stanford, CA: Stanford University Press, 2010.

Coatsworth, John. "Inequality, Institutions and Economic Growth in Latin America." *Journal of Latin American Studies* 40 (2008): 545–69.

Coelho, Marco Antônio. "From Pickpocket to Bank Robber." *Estudos Avançados* 21, no. 61 (2007): 71–5.

Cohen, Frank S. "Proportional versus Majoritarian Ethnic Conflict Management in Democracies." *Comparative Political Studies* 30, no. 5 (1997): 607–30.

Cokgezen, Murat. "Corruption in Kyrgyzstan: The Facts, Causes and Consequences." *Central Asian Survey* 23, no. 1 (2004): 79–94.

Collier, Paul. *Bottom Billion: Why the Poorest Countries Are Failing and What Can Be Done about It.* Oxford, UK: Oxford University Press, 2007.

—. *Breaking the Conflict Trap: Civil War and Development Policy.* Oxford, UK: Oxford University Press, 2003.

—. "Economic Causes of Civil Conflict and Their Implications for Policy," April 2006, http://users.ox.ac.uk/~econpco/research/pdfs/EconomicCausesofCivilCo nflict-ImplicationsforPolicy.pdf.

—. *Wars, Guns and Votes: Democracy in Dangerous Places.* New York, NY: HarperCollins, 2009.

Collier, Paul and Jan Willem Gunning. "The Microeconomics of African Growth, 1950–2000." *A Thematic Paper* (1999a): 1–35.

—. "Why Has Africa Grown Slowly?" *The Journal of Economic Perspectives* 13, no. 3 (Summer, 1999b): 3–22.

Collier, Paul and Anke Hoeffler. "On Economic Causes of Civil War." *Oxford Economic Papers* 50, no. 4 (1998): 563–73.

—. "Grand Extortion: Coup Risk and the Military as a Protection Racket." Open Access publications from University of Oxford, April 2006, 1–32.

—. "Greed and Grievance in Civil War." *Oxford Economic Papers* 56 (2004): 563–95.

—. "Military Spending and the Risks of Coups d'Etat." Centre for the Study of African Economies, Department of Economics. Oxford, UK: Oxford University, October 2007, 1–32.

Collins, Kathleen. "Clans, Pacts, and Politics in Central Asia." *Journal of Democracy* 13, no. 3 (2002): 137–52.

—. "Economic and Security Regionalism among Patrimonial Authoritarian Regimes: The Case of Central Asia." *Europe-Asia Studies* 61, no. 2 (2009): 249–81.

Common, Richard. "Administrative Change in the Gulf: Modernization in Bahrain and Oman." *International Review of Administrative Sciences* 74, no. 2 (2008): 177–93.

Compagnon, Daniel. "Political Decay in Somalia: From Personal Rule to Warlordism." *Refugee* 12, no. 5 (November–December 1992): 8–13.

—. *A Predictable Tragedy: Robert Mugabe and the Collapse of Zimbabwe.* Philadelphia, PA: University of Pennsylvania Press, 2010.

Concha-Eastman, Alberto. "Urban Violence in Latin America and the Caribbean: Dimensions, Explanations, Actions." *Citizens of Fear: Urban Violence in Latin America.* Edited by Susana Rotker. Rutgers State University Press, 2002, 37–54.

Cooley, John K. *Unholy Wars: Afghanistan, America and International Terrorism.* London, UK: Pluto Press, 1999.

Corden, W. Max."Booming Sector and Dutch Disease Economics: Survey and Consolidation." *Oxford Economic Papers* 36 (1984): 359–80.

Cordesman, Anthony H. *Saudi Arabia: National Security in a Troubled Region.* Washington, DC: Praeger Publishers, 2009.

Cordesman, Anthony H. and Khalid R. Al-Rodhan. *Gulf Military Forces in an Era of Asymmetric Wars.* Westport, CT: Greenwood International, 2006.

Cornell, Svante. "The Interaction of Narcotics and Conflict." *Journal of Peace Research* 42, no. 6 (2005a): 751–60.

—. "Narcotics, Radicalism, and Armed Conflict in Central Asia: The Islamic Movement of Uzbekistan." *Terrorism and Political Violence* 17 (2005b): 577–97.

—. "The Narcotics Threat in Greater Central Asia: From Crime-Terror Nexus to State Infiltration?" *China and Eurasia Forum Quarterly* 4, no. 1 (2006): 37–67.

Corrales, Javier and Michael Penfold. "Venezuela: Crowding out the Opposition." *Journal of Democracy* 18, no. 2 (April 2007): 99–113.

Court, Julius, Göran Hydén, and Ken Mease. "Governance Performance: The Aggregate Picture." *World Governance Survey Discussion Paper* 3, United Nations University, November 2002, 1–29.

—. "The Judiciary and Governance in 16 Developing Countries." *World Governance Survey Discussion Paper* 9, United Nations University, May 2003, 1–28.

Court, Julius, P. Kristen, and B. Weder. "Bureaucratic Structure and Performance: New Evidence from Africa." United Nations University Working Paper. Tokyo, Japan: UN University 1999.

Cox, Gary. "Authoritarian Elections and Leadership Succession, 1975–2004." Paper presented at the American Political Science Association 2009 Toronto Meeting Paper, August 2009.

Coyne, Christopher J. "Reconstructing Weak and Failed States: Foreign Intervention and the Nirvana Fallacy." *Foreign Policy Analysis* 2, no. 4 (2006): 343–60.

Crabtree, John. "Populisms Old and New: The Peruvian Case." *Bulletin of Latin American Research* 19 (2000):163–76.

Crassweller, Robert D. *Trujillo: The Life and Times of a Caribbean Dictator.* London, UK: Macmillan Press, 1966.

Crespo, Jose Antonio. "Party Competition in Mexico: Evolution and Prospects." In *Dilemmas of Political Change in Mexico.* Edited by Kevin Middlebrook. London: University of London, in cooperation with University of California– San Diego, 2004, 57–81.

"Crisis, Fragile and Failed States: Definitions Used by the CSRC," Crisis States Workshop, London, March 2006, 1.

Crocker, Chester A., Fen Osler, and Pamela Aall. *Leashing the Dogs of War: Conflict Management in a Divided World.* Washington, DC: United States Institute of Peace, 2007.

Crouch, Harold. *Military Civilian Relations in Southeast Asia.* Oxford, UK: Oxford University Press, 1985.

Cunha, Derek Da. "Sociological Aspects of the Singapore Armed Forces." *Armed Forces & Society* 25, no. 3 (1999): 459–75.

Dahlström, Carl, Victor LaPuente, and Jan Teorell. "Bureaucracy, Politics and Corruption." APSA 2009 Toronto Meeting Paper, http://ssrn.com/abstract=1450742.

—. "Dimensions of Bureaucracy: A Cross-National Dataset on the Structure and Behavior of Public Administration." University of Gothenburg Working Paper, June 2010, 1–59.

—. "The Merit of Meritocratization: Politics, Bureaucracy, and the Institutional Deterrents of Corruption." *Political Research Quarterly* 20, no. 10 (2011): 1–13.

Danopoulos, Constantine P. and Konstantinos S. Skandalis. "The Military and Its Role in Albania's Democratization." *Armed Forces & Society* 37, no. 3 (July 2011): 399–417.

Das, Gurcharan. "The India Model." *Foreign Affairs* (July/August 2006): 1–6.

Davenport, Christian."Multi-Dimensional Threat Perception and State Repression: An Inquiry into Why States Apply Negative Sanctions." *American Journal of Political Science* 39, no. 3 (1995): 683–713.

Davenport, Christian and David A. Armstrong. "Democracy and the Violation of Human Rights: A Statistical Analysis from 1976 to 1996." *American Journal of Political Science* 48, no. 3 (2004): 538–54.

Davies, Victor A. B. "Alluvial Diamonds: A New Resource Curse Theory." University of Oxford, February 2009, 1–15.

Davis, Diane E. "Irregular Armed Forces, Shifting Patterns of Commitment, and Fragmented Sovereignty in the Developing World." *Theory and Society* 39 (2010): 397–413.

—. "Undermining the Rule of Law: Democratization and the Dark Side of Police Reform in Mexico." *Latin American Politics and Society* 48, no. 1 (2006): 61–2.

Davis, Michael L. "Time and Punishment: An Intertemporal Model of Crime." *The Journal of Political Economy* (1988): 383–90.

Davis, Peita. "Filling the Void: Hizbullah's State Building in Lebanon," 2007, http://ses.library.usyd.edu.au/bitstream/2123/2163/1/Peita%20Davis.pdf.

Deacon, Robert T. "Public Good Provision under Dictatorship and Democracy." *Public Choice* 139, no. 1 (2009): 241–62.

Debiel, Tobias. "Violent Conflict and State Fragility in Sub-Saharan AfricaTrends, Causes and Policy Options." Presentation at the Scribani Conference "Africa and Europe: Cooperation in a Globalized World," September 6–8, 2006, 1–14.

Decalo, Samuel. "African Personalist Dictatorships." *Journal of Modern African Studies* 23, no. 2 (1985): 209–37.

—. *Coups and Army Rule in Africa: Studies in Military Style.* New Haven, CT: Yale University Press, 1976.

—. "Military Coups and Military Regimes in Africa." *Journal of Modern African Studies* 11, no. 1 (March 1973): 105–27.

—. "Modalities of Civil-Military Stability in Africa." *The Journal of Modern African Studies* 27, no. 4 (December 1989): 547–78.

De la Torre, Luis V. "Drug Trafficking and Police Corruption: A Comparison of Colombia and Mexico." PhD dissertation, Naval Postgraduate School, 2008.

Demombynes, Gabriel and Berk Őzler. "Crime and Local Inequality in South Africa." *Journal of Development Economics* 76 (2005): 265–92.

Dempsey, Thomas. "Counterterrorism in African Failed States: Challenges and Potential Solutions." *Strategic Studies Institute Publications* (April 2006): 1–44.

De Nevers, Renee. "Democratization and Ethnic Conflict." *Survival* 35, no. 2 (1993): 31–48.

De Soto, Hernando. *The Mystery of Capital: Why Capitalism Triumphs in the West and Fails Everywhere Else.* New York, NY: Basic Books, 2000.

Deyo, Frederic C. *The Political Economy of the New Asian Industrialism.* Ithica, NY: Cornell University Press, 1987.

Deutsch, Karl W. and William J. Foltz. *Nation-Building.* New York: Atherton Press, 1963.

Devisch, Rene. "Colonial State Building in the Congo and Its Dismantling." *Journal of Legal Pluralism* 42 (1998): 221–44.

De Waal, Alex. "Class and Power in a Stateless Somalia," Discussion Paper, August 1996.

Diamond, Larry. *Developing Democracy: Toward Consolidation.* Baltimore, MD: Johns Hopkins University Press, 1999.

—."Is Pakistan the (Reverse) Wave of the Future?" *Journal of Democracy* 11, no. 3 (July 2000): 91–106

—. "Promoting Democracy in Post-Conflict and Failed States: Lessons and Challenges." Prepared for the National Policy Forum on Terrorism, Security and America's Purpose, Washington, DC, September 6–7, 2005, 1–29.

—. "What Went Wrong in Iraq." *Foreign Affairs* (2004): 34–56.

Diamond, Larry and Richard Gunther, eds. *Political Parties and Democracy.* Baltimore, MD: Johns Hopkins University Press, 2001.

Diamond, Larry and Leonardo Morlino. "The Quality of Democracy: An Overview." *Journal of Democracy* 15, no. 4 (2004): 20–31.

Diamond, Larry and Marc F. Plattner, eds. *Democratization in Africa: Progress and Retreat.* Baltimore, MD: Johns Hopkins University Press, 2010.

—. "Introduction." In *Civil-Military Relations and Democracy.* Edited by Larry Diamond and Marc F. Plattner. Baltimore, MD: The Johns Hopkins University Press, 1996, xxvii–xxxiv.

Dianga, J. W. *Kenya, 1982: The Attempted Coup.* London, UK: Penn Press, 2002.

Dickson, Bruce. *Democratization in China and Taiwan.* Oxford, UK: Oxford University Press, 1997.

Dietrich, Chris. "The Commercialization of Military Deployment in Africa." *African Security Review* 9, no. 1 (July 2000): 3–17.

Di John, Jonathan. "'Failed States' in Sub-Saharan Africa: A Review of the Literature." *School of Oriental and African Studies.* ARI (May 2011): 1–10.

Dissel, Amanda and Stephen Ellis. "Reform and Stasis: Transformation in South African Prisons." Center for the Study of Violence and Reconciliation, July 2002, 1–16.

Domingo, Pilar. "Judicial Independence and Judicial Reform in Latin America." In *The Self-Restraining State: Power and Accountability in New Democracies.* Edited by Andreas Schedler. Boulder, CO: Lynne Rienner, 1999, 151–76.

Doornbos, Martin. *Global Forces and State Restructuring. Dynamics of State Formation and Collapse.* Basingstoke, UK: Palgrave, 2006.

—. "State Collapse and Fresh Starts: Some Critical Reflections." *Development and Change* 33, no. 5 (2002): 797–815.

Doornbos, Martin, Susan Woodward, and Silvia Roque, eds. "Failing States or Failed States? The Role of Development Models: Collected Works." *Madrid FRIDE Working Paper* 19 (2006): 1–38.

Dorff, Robert H. "Addressing the Challenges of Failed States." Paper presented at the Failed States Conference, Florence, Italy, April 2000a.

—. "Democratization and Failed States: The Challenge of Ungovernability." *Parameters* 26, no. 2 (Summer 1996): 17–31.

—. "Failed States after 9/11: What Did We Know and What Have We Learned?" 6, no. 1 (February 2005): 20–34.

—. "Responding to the Failed State: Strategic Triage." In *Beyond Declaring Victory and Coming Home: The Challenges of Peace and Stability Operations.* Edited by Max G. Manwaring and Anthony James Joes. Westport, CT: Praeger, 2000b, 225–45.

Dornbusch, Rudiger and Sebastian Edwards. "The Macro-Economic Populism." *Journal of Development Economics* 32, no. 2 (April 1990): 247–77.

Dougherty, Beth K. "Right-sizing International Criminal Justice: The Hybrid Experiment at the Special Court for Sierra Leone." *International Affairs* 80, no. 2 (2004): 311–28.

Dowden, Richard. "Mobutu Puts His Country on the Market." *The Independent* (March 16, 1994).

Downs, Anthony. "An Economic Theory of Democracy." New York: Harper and Row, 1957, 260–76.

Dreher, Axel and Thomas Herzfeld. "The Economic Costs of Corruption: A Survey and New Evidence," June 2005, 1–33, http://papers.ssrn.com/sol3/papers.cfm?abstract_id=734184.

Dreher, Alex, Christos Kotsogiannis, and Steve McCorriston. "How Do Institutions Affect Corruption and the Shadow Economy? *International Tax and Public Finance* 16, no. 6 (2009): 773–96.

Dreher, Axel and Friedrich Schneider. "Corruption and the Shadow Economy: An Empirical Analysis." *IZA Discussion Paper Series* 1936 (January 2006): 1–39.

Driscoll, Jesse. "Inside the Leviathan: Coup Proofing after State Failure." *Stanford University Working Paper* (October 18, 2008): 1–56.

Drury, A. Cooper, Jonathan Krieckhaus, and Michael Lusztig. "Corruption, Democracy, and Economic Growth." *International Political Science Review* 27, no. 2 (2006): 121–36.

Duffield, Mark. *Development, Security and Unending War.* London, UK: Polity, 2007.

——. *Global Governance and the New Wars: The Merging of Development and Security.* London, UK: Zed Books, 2001.

——. "Post-Modern Conflict: Warlords, Post-Adjustment States andPrivate Protection." *Civil Wars* 1 (Spring 1998): 65–102.

Dung, Liu Tien. "Judicial Independence in Transitional Countries." *United Nations Development Programme Oslo Governance Centre* (January 2003): 1–44.

Dunlap, Ben N. "State Failure and the Use of Force in the Age of Global Terror." *Boston College International and Comparative Law Review* 27, no. 2 (May 1, 2004): 453–75.

Du Plessis, Anton and Antionette Louw. "Crime and Crime Prevention in South Africa: 10 Years After." *Institute for Security Studies, Crime and Justice Program* (April 2005): 427–46.

Dwivedi, O. P., R. B. Jain, and B. D. Dua. "Imperial Legacy, Bureaucracy, and Administrative Changes: India 1947–1987." *Public Administration and Development* 9 (1989): 253–69.

Džihić, Vedran and Helmut Kramer. "Kosovo after Independence: Is the EU's EULEX Mission Delivering on Its Promises?"*International Policy Analysis* (July 2009).

Easter, Gerald M. "Preference for Presidentialism: Post-communist Regime Change in Russia and the NIS." *World Politics* 49, no. 2 (January 1997): 184–211.

Easterly, William. "Can Foreign Aid Buy Growth?" *The Journal of Economic Perspectives* 17, no. 3 (August 1, 2003): 23–48.

——. "Can the West Save Africa?" *Journal of Economic Literature* 47, no. 2 (2009): 373–447.

—. "How Did Heavily Indebted Poor Countries Become Heavily Indebted? Reviewing Two Decades of Debt Relief." *World Development* 30, no. 10 (2002): 1677–96.

Easterly, William and Laura Freschi, "Top Five Reasons Why Failed State Is a Failed Concept." *Aid Watch* (January 13, 2010).

Easterly, William and Ross Levine. "Tropics, Germs, and Crops: How Endowments Influence Economic Development." *Journal of Monetary Economics* 50 (2003): 3–39.

Echebarría, Koldo and Juan Carlos Cortdzar. "Public Administration and Public Employment Reform in Latin America." In *The State of State Reform*. Edited by Eduardo Lora. Stanford, CA: Stanford University Press, 2006, 123–56.

Egorov, Georgy and Konstantin Sonin. "Dictators and Their Viziers: Endogenizing the Loyalty Competence Trade-off." *Journal of Economic Association* 9, no. 5 (October 2011): 903–30.

Ehteshami, Anoushiravan. "Reform from Above: The Politics of Participation in the Oil Monarchies." *International Affairs* 79, no. 1 (January 2003): 53–75.

Eigen, Peter. "Corruption in a Globalized World." *SAIS Review* 22, no. 1 (Winter–Spring 2002): 45–59.

—. "Field Reports: Combating Corruption around the World." *Journal of Democracy* 7, no. 1 (1996): 158–68.

Eisenstadt, Schmuel. *Traditional Patrimonialism and Modern Neo-patrimonialism*. Thousand Oaks, CA: Sage Publications, 1973.

Eker, Varda. "On the Origins of Corruption: Irregular Incentives in Nigeria." *Journal of Modern African Studies* 19, no. 1 (1981): 173–82.

Ellis, S. *The Making of Anarchy*. New York, NY: New York University Press, 1999.

Ellison, Katherine. *Imelda: Steel Butterfly of the Philippines*. New York, NY: MacGraw Hill, 2005.

Ellner, Steve. "The Contrasting Variants of the Populism of Hugo Chávez and Alberto Fujimori." *Journal of Latin American Studies* 35, no. 1 (February 2003): 139–62.

Elmi, Afyare Abdi and Abdullahi Barise. "The Somali Conflict: Root Causes, Obstacles, and Peace-Building Strategies." *African Security Review* 15, no.1 (2006): 32–54.

Emran, M. Shahe and Joseph Stiglitz. "On Selective Indirect Tax Reform in Developing Countries." *Journal of Public Economics* 89 (2005): 599– 623.

Emrich-Bakenova, Saule. "Trajectory of Civil Service Development in Kazakhstan: Nexus of Politics and Administration," 2009, www.academia.edu/2547643/Trajectory_of_Civil_Service_Development_in_Kazakhstan_Nexus_of_Politics_and_AdministrationEnders, Walter and Todd Sandler. "Is Transnational Terrorism Becoming More Threatening?: A Time Series Investigation." *Journal of Conflict Resolution* (June 2000): 307–32.

Engel, Ulf and Gero Erdmann. "Neo-patrimonialism Reconsidered: Critical Review and Elaboration of an Elusive Concept." *Commonwealth and Comparative Politics* 45, no. 1 (2007): 95–119.

Engerman, Stanley and Ken Sokoloff. "Factor Endowments, Inequality, and Paths of Development among New World Economies." *NBER Working Paper* #9259 (2002): 1–55.

Englebert, Pierre. *State Legitimacy and Development in Africa.* Boulder, CO: Lynne Rienner, 2002.

Englebert, Pierre and James Ron. "Primary Commodities and War: Congo-Brazzaville's Ambivalent Resource Curse." *Comparative Politics* (2004): 61–81.

Englebert, Pierre and Denis M. Tull. "Post-Conflict Reconstruction in Africa: Flawed Ideas about Failed States." *International Security* 32, no. 4 (Spring 2008): 106–39.

Erdmann, Gero and Ulf Engel. "Neopatrimonialism Revisited—Beyond a Catch-All Concept." *German Institute of Global and Area Studies Working Paper* 16 (February 2006): 1–29.

Esty, Daniel C., Jack A. Goldstone, Ted Robert Gurr, Barbara Harff, Marc Levy, Geoffrey D. Dabelko, Pamela T. Surko, and Alan N. Unger. "State Failure Task Force Report: Phase II Findings," July 31, 1998.

Esty, Daniel C. et al. "The State Failure Project: Early Warning Research for U.S. Foreign Policy Planning." Paper on the Failed States website, Purdue University, West Lafayette, February 25–27, 1998.

Eubank, William and Leonard Weinberg. "Does Democracy Encourage Terrorism?" *Terrorism and Political Violence* 6, no. 4 (1994): 417–43.

Evans, Peter B. *Embedded Autonomy: State and Industrial Transformation.* Princeton, NJ: Princeton University Press, 1995.

—. "Predatory, Developmental, and other Apparatuses: A Comparative Political Economy Perspective on the Third World State." *Sociological Forum* 4, no. 4 (1989): 561–87.

—. "The State as Problem and Solution: Predation, Embedded Autonomy and Structural Change." In *Politics of Economic Development.* Edited by Stephan Haggard and Robert R. Kaufman. Princeton, NJ: Princeton University Press, 1992, 139–81.

—. "Transferable Lessons? Reexamining the Institutional Prerequisites of East Asian Economic Policies." *Journal of Development Studies* 34, no. 6 (1998): 66–86.

Evans, Peter and James Rauch. "Bureaucracy and Growth: A Cross-National Analysis of the Effects of 'Weberian' State Structures on Economic Growth." *American Sociological Review* 64, no. 5 (1999): 748–65.

Eyerman, Joe. "Terrorism and Democratic States: Soft Targets or Accessible Systems." *International Interactions* 24, no. 2 (1998): 151–70.

Ezrow, Natasha and Erica Frantz. "State Institutions and the Survival of Dictatorships." *Journal of International Affairs* 65, no. 1 (Fall/Winter 2011): 1–14.

Fair, C. Christine. "Militant Recruitment in Pakistan: A New Look at the Militancy-Madrasah Connection." *Asia Policy* 4, no. 1 (2007): 107–34.

Fairbanks, Charles. "Disillusionment in the Caucasus and Central Asia." *Journal of Democracy* 12, no. 4 (October 2001): 49–56.

Fajnzylber, Pablo, Daniel Lederman, and Norman Loayza. *Determinants of Crime Rates in Latin America and the Rest of the World: An Empirical Assessment.* Washington, DC: World Bank Publications, 1998.

—. "Inequality and Violent Crime." *Journal of Law and Economics* 65 (April 2002a): 1–40.

—. "What Causes Violent Crime?" *European Economic Review* 46 (2002b): 1323–57.

"Fall of Idi Amin." *Economic and Political Weekly* 14, no. 21 (May 26, 1979): 907–10.

Fandy, Mamoun. *Saudi Arabia and the Politics of Dissent*. Basington, UK: Palgrave Macmillan, 2001.

Farazmand, Ali. *Bureaucracy and Administration*. Boca Raton, FL: CRC Press, 2009,

Fatton, Jr., Robert. "Africa in the Age of Democratization: The Civic Limitations of Civil Society." *African Studies Review* 38, no. 2 (September 1995): 67–99.

FDFA Working Group 2007. "Fragile Statehood—Current Situation and Guidelines for Switzerland's Involvement." Working Group of the Federal Department of Foreign Affairs (FDFA), Politorbis, Zeitschrift zur Aussenpolitik, 42, 45–53.

Fearon, James D. "Iraq's Civil War." *Foreign Affairs* 86, no. 2 (March/April 2007): 2–8.

—. "Why Do Some Civil Wars Last So Much Longer Than Others?" *Journal of Peace Research* 41, no. 3 (2004): 275–301.

Fearon, James D. and David D. Laitin. "Ethnicity, Insurgency and Civil War." *American Political Science Review* 97, no. 1 (February 2003): 75–90.

—. "Neo-trusteeship and the Problem of Weak States." *International Security* 28, no. 4 (Spring 2004): 5–43.

Feaver, Peter D. "The Civil-Military Problematique: Huntington, Janowitz, and the Question of Civilian Control." *Armed Forces & Society* 23, no. 2 (1996): 149–78.

Feder, Gershon and David Feeny. "Land Tenure and Property Rights: Theory and Implications for Development Policy." *World Bank Economic Review* 5, no. 1 (1991): 135–53.

Felbab-Brown, Vanda. *The Violent Drug Market in Mexico and Lessons from Colombia*. Washington, DC: Brookings Institution, 2009.

Feld, Lars P. and Stefan Voigt. "Economic Growth and Judicial Independence: Cross-Country Evidence Using a New Set of Indicators." *European Journal of Political Economy* 19, no. 3 (2003): 497–527.

Feld, Maury D. "Middle-Class Society and the Rise of Military Professionalism: The Dutch Army 1589–1609." *Armed Forces & Society* 1, no. 4 (1975): 419–42.

Ferguson, James. *Papa Doc, Baby Doc: Haiti and the Duvaliers*. New York, NY: Blackwell, 1988.

Fernández-Kelly, Patricia and Jon Shefner. *Out of the Shadows: Political Action and the Informal Economy in Latin America*. University Park, PA: Penn State University Press, 2005.

Fields, Frank E. and Jack J. Jensen. "Military Professionalism in Post-communist Hungary and Poland: An Analysis and Assessment." *European Security* 7, no. 1 (1998): 117–55.

Findlay, Ronald. "The New Political Economy: Its Explanatory Power in LDCs." *Economics and Politics* 2, no. 2 (July 1990): 193–221.

Finer, Samuel Edward. *The Man on Horseback: The Role of the Military in Politics*. London, UK: Transaction Publishers, 1969.

Fischer, Pius. *Rent Seeking, Institutional Reforms in Africa: Theory and Empirical Evidence for Tanzania.* New York, NY: Springer, 2006.

Fish, M. Steven. "Post-communist Subversion: Social Science and Democratization in East Europe and Eurasia." *Slavic Review* 58, no. 4, Special Issue: Ten Years after 1989: What Have We Learned? (Winter 1999): 794–823.

—. "Stronger Legislatures, Stronger Democracies." *Journal of Democracy* 17, no. 1 (January 2006): 6–20.

Fitch, John Samuel. *The Armed Forces and Democracy in Latin America.* Baltimore, MD: Johns Hopkins University Press, 1998.

—. "Military Professionalism, National Security and Democracy: Lessons from the Latin American Experience." *Pacific Focus* 4, no. 2 (Fall 1989): 99–147.

Foley, Conor. *The Thin Blue Line: How Humanitarianism Went to War.* London, UK: Verso, 2008.

Foley, Mike and Bob Edwards. "The Paradox of Civil Society." *Journal of Democracy* 7, no. 3 (1996): 38–52.

Foweraker, Joe. "Institutional Design, Party Systems and Governability-Differentiating the Presidential Regimes of Latin America." *British Journal of Political Science* 28, no. 4 (October 1998): 651–76.

Fox, John G. "Approaching Humanitarian Intervention Strategically: The Case of Somalia." *SAIS Review* 21, no. 1 (2001): 147–58.

François, Monika and Inder Sud. "Promoting Stability and Development in Fragile and Failed States." *Development Policy Review* 24, no. 2 (2006): 141–60.

Franke, Anja, Andrea Gawrich, and Gurban Alakbarov. "Kazakhstan and Azerbaijan as Post-Soviet Rentier States: Resource Incomes and Autocracy as a Double 'Curse' in Post-Soviet Regimes." *Europe-Asia Studies* 61, no. 1 (2009): 109–40.

Frankel, Jeffrey A. and David Romer. "Does Trade Cause Growth?" *American Economic Review* 89 (June 1999): 379–99.

Frantz, Erica and Natasha M. Ezrow. *The Politics of Dictatorship: Institutions and Outcomes in Authoritarian Regimes.* Boulder, CO: Lynne Rienner, 2011.

—. "'Yes Men' and the Likelihood of Foreign Policy Mistakes Across Dictatorships." APSA 2009 Toronto Meeting Paper, 2009, http://papers.ssrn.com/sol3/papers.cfm?abstract_id=1450542.

Freedman, Amy L. "The Effect of Government Policy and Institutions on Chinese Overseas Acculturation: The Case of Malaysia." *Modern Asian Studies* 35 (2001): 411–40.

Friedman, Eric, Simon Johnson, Daniel Kaufmann, and Pablo Zoido-Lobaton. "Dodging the Grabbing Hand: The Determinants of Unofficial Activity in 69 Countries." *Journal of Public Economics* 76 (2000): 459–93.

Fritz, Verena and Alina Rocha Menocal. "Developmental States in the New Millennium: Concepts and Challenges for a New Aid Agenda." *Development Policy Review* 25, no. 5 (2007): 531–52.

Fukuyama, Francis. "Social Capital, Civil Society and Development." *Third World Quarterly* 22, no. 1 (2001): 7–20.

Fukuyama, Francis. "Stateness' First." *Journal of Democracy* 16, no. 1 (2005): 84–8.

Fund for Peace. Failed States Index. Washington, DC: The Fund for Peace, 2006, www.fundforpeace.org/programs/fsi/fsindex.php.

Funke, Nikki and Hussein Solomon. "The Shadow State in Africa: A Discussion." *Development Policy Management Forum Occasional Paper* 5 (2002): 1–20.

Gagnon, Jr., V. P. P. "Ethnic Nationalist and International Conflict: The Case of Serbia." *International Security* 19, no. 3 (Winter 1994–5): 130–66.

Gallego, Maria and Carolyn Pitchik. "An Economic Theory of Leadership Turnover." *Journal of Public Economics* 88 (2004): 2361–82.

Galvan, Dennis Charles. "Political Turnover and Social Change in Senegal." *Journal of Democracy* 12, no. 3 (2001): 51–62.

Gaman-Golutvina, Oxana. "The Changing Role of the State and State Bureaucracy in the Context of Public Administration Reforms: Russian and Foreign Experience." *Journal of Communist Studies and Transition Politics* 24, no. 1 (2008): 37–53.

Gandhi, Jennifer. "Dictatorial Institutions and Their Impact on Economic Growth." *European Journal of Sociology* 49, no. 1 (April 2008): 3–30.

Gandhi, Jennifer and Ellen Lust-Okar. "Elections under Authoritarianism." *Annual Review of Political Science* 12 (June 2009): 403–22.

Gandhi, Jennifer and Adam Przeworski. "Authoritarian Institutions and the Survival of Autocrats." *Comparative Political Studies* 40, no. 11 (November 2007): 1279–301.

Ganguly, Sumit. "Explaining the Kashmir Insurgency: Political Mobilization and Institutional Decay." *International Security* 21, no. 2 (Autumn 1996): 76–107.

Gause III, F. Gregory. *Saudi Arabia in the New Middle East.* New York, NY: Council on Foreign Relations Press, 2011.

Gaviria, A. "Increasing Returns and the Evolution of Violence Crime: The Case of Colombia." Discussion Paper 98–14 (May 1998).

Gawrick, Andrea, Inna Melnykovska, and Rainer Schweickert, "More than Oil and Geography: Neo-patrimonialism as an Explanation of Bad Governance and Autocratic Stability in Central Asia." Working Paper Series 1 (September 2011): 1–32

Geddes, Barbara. "Building 'State' Autonomy in Brazil, 1930–1964." *Comparative Politics* 22, no. 2 (1990): 217–35.

—. *Paradigms and Sandcastles: Theory Building in Research Design in Comparative Politics.* Ann Arbor, MI: University of Michigan Press, 2003.

—. "Party Creation as an Autocratic Survival Strategy." Paper presented at Conference on Dictators, Princeton University, April 2008.

—. *Politician's Dilemma: Building State Capacity in Latin America.* Berkeley, CA: University of California Press, 1994.

—. "What Do We Know about Democratization Twenty Years Later?" *Annual Review of Political Science* 2 (June 1999): 115–44.

—. "Why Parties and Elections in Authoritarian Regimes?" Paper presented at the American Political Science Association, Washington, DC, September 2005.

Gellner, Ernest. *Nations and Nationalism.* Ithica, NY: Cornell University Press, 1983.

George, Julie A. "The Dangers of Reform: State Building and National Minorities in Georgia." *Central Asian Survey* 28, no. 2 (2009): 135–54.

Gerschenkron, Alexander. *Economic Backwardness in Historical Perspective.* Cambridge, MA: Belknap, 1962.

Gertzel, Cherry. "Uganda after Amin: The Continuing Search for Leadership and Control." *African Affairs* 79, no. 317 (October 1980): 461–89.

Ghadyan, Ahmed A. al-. "The Judiciary in Saudi Arabia." *Arab Law Quarterly* (1998): 235–251.

Ghani, Ashraf, Michael Carnahan, and Clare Lockhart. "Closing the Sovereignty Gap: An Approach to State-Building." *Overseas Development Institute Working Paper* 253 (September 2005): 1–20.

—. *Fixing Failed States: A Framework for Rebuilding a Fractured World.* Oxford, UK: Oxford University Press, 2009.

Ghoshal, Baladas. "The Military and Politics: A Review Article of *Military-Civilian Relations in South-East Asia* by Zakaria Haji Ahmad and Harold Crouch; *The Political Dilemmas of Military Regimes* by Christopher Clapham and George Philip." *Contemporary Southeast Asia* 8, no. 2 (September 1986): 160–9.

Gibbs, David N. "Realpolitik and Humanitarian Intervention: The Case of Somalia." *International Politics* 37, no. 1 (2000): 41–56.

Giddens, Anthony. *The Nation State and Violence, Volume Two of A Contemporary Critique of Historical Materialism.* Berkeley, CA: University of California Press, 1987.

Gingerich, Daniel W. "Abandoning Bureaucracy with Adjectives: The Gap between Bureaucratic Reputation and Bureaucratic Reality in South America," 2009, 1–64, www.learningace.com/doc/755638/60bd92621e01fd6775073e61b 7440dbf/gingerichdaniel.

Giustozzi, Antonio. "'Good' State vs. 'Bad' Warlords? A Critique of State-Building Strategies in Afghanistan." Crisis States Programme working paper series no. 1, Development Research Center, Development Studies Institute, 2004, 1–19.

—. "Military Reform in Afghanistan. Confronting Afghanistan's Security Dilemma: Reforming the Security Sector." *Brief* 28 (2003a): 23–31.

—. "Respectable Warlords: The Challenge of State Building in Post Taleban Afghanistan." *Crisis Research Center Working Paper* 33 (September 2003b): 1–22.

Gizelis, Theodora-Ismene and Kristin E. Kosek. "Why Humanitarian Interventions Succeed or Fail The Role of Local Participation." *Cooperation and Conflict* 40, no. 4 (2005): 363–83.

Gleason, Gregory. "Corruption, Decolonization and Development in Central Asia." *European Journal on Criminal Policy and Research* 3, no. 2 (1995): 38–47.

Gleditsch, Nils, Havard Strand, Mikael Eriksson, Margareta Sollenberg, and Peter Wallensteen. "Armed Conflict 1946– 2001: A New Dataset." *Journal of Peace Research* 39, no. 5 (2002): 615–37.

Goes, Eva and Reinoud Leenders. "Promoting Democracy and Human Rights in Lebanon and Syria." In *Crescent of Crisis: US-European Strategy for the Greater Middle East.* Edited by Ivo Daalder, Nicole Gnesotto, and Philip Gordon. Washington, DC: The Brookings Institution, 2006, 94.

Golder, Matt and Leonard Wantchekon. "Africa: Dictatorial and Democratic Electoral Systems since 1946." *Handbook of Electoral System Design* (2004): 401–18.

Goldsmith, Andrew. "Policing Weak States: Citizen Safety and State Responsibility." *Policing and Society: An International Journal of Research and Policy* 13, no. 1 (2002): 2–21.

Goldsmith, Arthur A. "Africa's Overgrown State Reconsidered: Bureaucracy and Economic Growth." *World Politics* 51 (1999): 520–46.

—. "Democracy, Property Rights and Economic Growth." *Journal of Development Studies* 32, no. 2 (1995): 157–74.

—. "Donors, Dictators and Democrats in Africa" *The Journal of Modern African Studies* 39, no. 3 (2001): 411–36.

—. "Predatory versus Developmental Rule in Africa." *Democratization* 11, no. 3 (2004): 88–110.

Goldstone, Jack. "Pathways to State Failure." *Conflict Management and Peace Science* 25 (2008): 285–96.

Goldstone, Jack, Robert Bates, David Epstein, Ted R. Gurr, Michael B. Lustik, Monty G. Marshall, Jay Ulfelder, and Mark Woodward."A Global Model for Forecasting Political Instability." *American Journal of Political Science* 54, no. 1 (2010): 190–208.

Goldstone, Jack et al. *State Failure Task Force Project, Phase III Report.* McLean, VA: SAIC, 2003.

Goodhand, Jonathan. "Corrupting or Consolidating the Peace? The Drugs Economy and Post-conflict Peace-Building in Afghanistan." *International Peacekeeping* 15, no. 3 (June 2008): 405–23.

—. "From War Economy to Peace Economy? Reconstruction and State Building in Afghanistan." *Journal of International Affairs* 58, no. 1 (Fall 2004): 155–74.

Goodman, Louis Wolf, Johanna Mendelson Forman, and Juan Rial Roade. *The Military and Democracy: The Future of Civil-Military Relations in Latin America.* New York: Free Press, 1990.

Goodwin-Gill, Guy S. *Free and Fair Elections.* Geneva: Inter-Parliamentary Union, 2006.

Gootenberg, Paul. "Paying for Caudillos: Emergency Finance in Peru, 1820–1845." In *Liberals, Politics and Power: State Formation in Nineteenth Century Latin America.* Edited by Vincent Peloso and Barbara A. Tenenbaum. Georgia: University of Georgia Press, 1996, 134–65.

Gordon, Ruth. "Saving Failed States: Sometimes a Neo-Colonialist Notion." *American U.J. International Law& Policy* 12, no. 6 (1997): 908–74.

Gould. David J. *Bureaucratic Corruption and Underdevelopment in the Third World: The Case of Zaire.* New York, NY: Pergamon Press, 1980.

Gould, David and Jose A. Amaro-Reves. "The Effects of Corruption on Administrative Performance: Illustrations from Developing Countries." *World Bank Staff Working Papers* 580, no. 7 (1983): 1–48.

Goyer, K. C. "Prison Privatization in South Africa: Issues, Challenges and Opportunities." *Institute for Security Studies* (2011): 1–54.

Grant, Thomas. "Partition of Failed States: Impediments and Impulses." *Indiana Journal of Global Legal Studies* 11, no. 2 (Summer 2004): 51–82.

Gray, David and Kristina LaTour, "Terrorist Black Holes: Global Regions Shrouded in Lawlessness." *Global Security Studies* 1, no. 3 (Fall 2010): 154–63.

Grindle, Merilee. *Challenging the State: Crisis and Innovation in Latin America and Africa.* Cambridge, UK: Cambridge University Press, 1996.

Gros, Jean-Germain. "Review—Haiti: The Political Economy and Sociology of Decay and Renewal." *Latin American Research Review* 35, no. 3 (2000): 211–26.

—. "Toward a Taxonomy of Failed States in the New World Order: Decaying Somalia, Liberia, Rwanda and Haiti." *Third World Quarterly* 17, no. 3 (1996): 455–72.

Grossman, Gene and Elhanan Helpman. "A Protectionist Bias in Majoritarian Politics." *Quarterly Journal of Economics* 120 (2005): 1239–82.

Grossman, Herschel I. "A General Equilibrium Model of Insurrections." *American Economic Review* 81 (1991): 912–21.

Grossman, Herschel I. and S. J. Noh. "Proprietary Public Finance and Economic Welfare." *Journal of Public Economics* 53 (1994): 187–204.

Grzymala-Busse, Anna and Pauline Jones Luong. "Re-conceptualizing the State: Lessons from Post Communism." *Politics & Society* 30, no. 4 (December 2002a): 529–54.

—. "The Ignored Transition: Post-Communist State Development." Weatherhead Center for International Affairs, Harvard University (March 2002b): 1–47.

Guha, Ranajit. *Dominance without Hegemony: History and Power in Colonial India.* Cambridge, UK; Cambridge, MA: Harvard University Press, 1997.

Gunaratna, Rohan. *Inside Al Qaeda.* New York, NY: Berkeley Books, 2002.

Gurr, Ted Robert. "Peoples against States: Ethno-Political Conflict and the Changing World System." *International Studies Quarterly* 38 (1994): 347–77.

—. "Sources of Rebellion in Western Societies: Some Quantitative Evidence." *The Annals of American Academy of Political and Social Science* 391 (September 1970): 128–44.

Gurr, Ted Robert, Keith Jaggers, and Will H. Moore. *Polity II: Political Structures and Regime Change, 1800 –1986, Study No. 9263.* Ann Arbor, MI: Inter-University Consortium for Political and Social Research, 1989.

Gurr, Ted Robert, Monty G. Marshall, and Barbara Harff. "State Failure Task Force Report: Phase III Findings." *Center for International Development and Conflict Management* (August 4, 2003): 1–234.

Gylfason, Thorvaldur. "Exports, Inflation, and Growth." *World Development* 27 (June 1999): 1031–57.

—. "Natural Resources, Education, and Economic Development." *European Economic Review* 45, no. 4 (2001): 847–59.

Gylfason, Thorvaldur and Gylfi Zoega, "Natural Resources and Economic Growth: The Role of Investment." *Central Bank of Chile WorkingPaper* 142 (February 2002): 1–52.

Gylfason, Thorvaldur, Tryggvi Thor Herbertsson, and Gylfi Zoega. "A Mixed Blessing: Natural Resources and Economic Growth." *Macroeconomic Dynamics* 3 (June 1999): 204–25.

Haber, Stephen. *How Latin American Fell Behind: Essays on the Economic Histories of Brazil and Mexico, 1800–1914.* Stanford, CA: Stanford University Press, 1997.

Haber, Stephen and Victor Menaldo. "Do Natural Resources Fuel Authoritarianism? A Reappraisal of the Resource Curse." *American Political Science Research* 105, no. 1 (February 2011): 1–26.

Hack, Karl. *Colonial Armies in Southeast Asia.* Vol. 33. London, UK: Routledge, 2006.

Hadenius, Axel and Jan Teorell. "Authoritarian Regimes: Stability, Change and Pathways to Democracy, 1972–2003." Working Paper 331 (November 2006): 1–39.

Haggard, Stephan. *Pathways from the Periphery: The Politics of Growth in the Newly Industrialising Countries.* Ithaca, NY: Cornell University Press, 1990.

—. "The Philippines: Picking up after Marcos." *The Promise of Privatization.* Edited by Raymond Vernon. New York, NY: NY Council for Foreign Relations, 1988.

Haggard, Stephan and Robert R. Kaufman. *Politics of Economic Adjustment.* Princeton, NJ: Princeton University Press, 1992.

Hagmann, Tobias and Markus Hoehne. "Failures of the State Failure Debate: Evidence from the Somali Territories." *Journal of International Development* 21 (2009): 42–57.

Halebsky, S. and R. L. Harris (eds). *Capital, Power, and Inequality in Latin America.* Boulder, CO: Westview Press, 1995.

Hall, R. H. "Professionalization and Bureaucratization." *American Sociological Review* 33 (1968): 92–104.

Hameiri, Shahar. "Failed States or a Failed Paradigm? State Capacity and the Limits of Institutionalism." *Journal of International Relations and Development* 10 (2007): 122–49.

Hamilton, Clive. "Can the Rest of Asia Emulate the NICs?" *Third World Quarterly* 9, no 4 (1987): 1225–56.

Hammergren, Linn A. "Corporatism in Latin American Politics: A Re-examination of the Unique Tradition." *Comparative Politics* 9 (July 1977): 443–61.

Hänggi, Heiner. "Making Sense of Security Sector Governance." *Challenges of Security Sector Governance* (2003): 17–18.

Hannan, U. and Besada, H. "Dimensions of State Fragility: A Review of the Social Science Literature." *Working Paper* 33 (November 2007): 1–59

Hanson, Mark. "Organizational Bureaucracy in Latin America and the Legacy of Spanish Colonialism." *Journal of Inter-American Studies and World Affairs* 16, no. 2 (1974): 199–219.

Haq, Ikramul. *Pakistan: Drug-Trap to Debt-Trap.* Lahore, Pakistan: Lahore Publications, 2003.

Haque, M. Shamsul. "Governance and Bureaucracy in Singapore: Contemporary Reforms and Implications." *International Political Science Review* 25, no 2 (2004): 227–40.

Harb, Imad. "The Egyptian Military in Politics: Disengagement or Accommodation?" *The Middle East Journal* (2003): 269–90.

Harbeson, John W., Naomi Chazan, and Donald Rothschild. *Civil Society and the State in Africa.* Boulder, CO: Lynne Rienner Publishers, 1996.

Hardin, Russell. "The Crippled Epistemology of Extremism." In *Political Extremism and Rationality.* Edited by Albert Breton, Gianluigi Galeotti,

Pierre Salmon, and Ronald Wintrobe. Cambridge, UK: Cambridge University Press, 2002.

Harries-Jenkins, Gwyn. "The Concept of Military Professionalism." *Defense Analysis* 6, no. 2 (1990): 117–30.

Harrison, David. *The Sociology of Modernization and Development*. New York, NY: Routledge, 1988.

Harrison, Lawrence E. *Underdevelopment Is a State of Mind*. Lanham, MA: Madison Books, 2000, 1985.

Hastings, Justin V. "Geographies of State Failure and Sophistication in Maritime Piracy Hijackings." *Political Geography* 28 (2009): 213–23.

Hartlyn, Jonathan. *The Struggle for Democratic Politics in the Dominican Republic*. Chapel Hill, NC: University of North Carolina Press, 1998.

Hawkins, Robert and Kate Semerad. *Conflict Prevention and U.S. Foreign Assistance: A Framework Q4 for the 21st Century*. Oakland, CA: Institute for Contemporary Studies, 2001.

Haynie, Stacia. "Structure and Context of Judicial Institutions in Democratizing Countries." Prepared for Presentation at the World Democratization Conference, February 2000, 1–39.

Hehir, Aidan. "The Myth of the Failed State and the War on Terror: A Challenge to the Conventional Wisdom." *Journal of Intervention and Statebuilding* 1, no. 3 (2007): 307–32.

Helling, Dominik. "Anatomy of a 'Political Chameleon': Re-examining Fluid Shapes and Solid Constants of Nationalism and Nation-Building." CSRC Discussion Paper 17. London: Crisis States Research Centre, 2009.

Helman, Gerald and Steven R. Ratner. "Saving Failed States." *Foreign Policy* 89 (Winter 1992–3): 3–20.

Helmke, Gretchen and Frances Rosenbluth. "Regimes and the Rule of Law: Judicial Independence in Comparative Perspective." *Annual Review Political Science* 12 (2009): 345–66.

Hensel, P. and P. F. Diehl. "Testing Propositions about Shatterbelts, 1945–1976." *Political Geography* 13, no. 1 (1994): 33–51.

Herb, Michael. *All in the Family: Absolutism, Revolution, and Democracy in the Middle Eastern Monarchies*. Albany, NY: SUNY Press, 1999.

—. "No Representation without Taxation? Rents, Development and Democracy." *Comparative Politics* 37, no. 3 (2005): 297–316.

—. "Princes and Parliaments in the Arab World." *The Middle East Journal* 58, no. 3 (2004): 367–84.

—. "Taxation and Representation." *Studies in Comparative International Development* (SCID) 38, no. 3 (2003): 3–31.

Herbst, Jeffrey. "Let them Fail: State Failure in Theory and Practice—Implications for Policy." In *When States Fail: Causes and Consequences*. Edited by Robert Rotberg. Princeton, NJ: Princeton University Press, 2004, 302–18.

—. "Responding to State Failure in Africa." *International Security* 21, no. 3 (1996): 120–144.

—. *States and Power in Africa: Comparative Lessons in Authority and Control*. Princeton, NJ: Princeton University Press, 2000.

Herspring, Dale. "Vladimir Putin and Military Reform in Russia." *European Security* 14, no. 1 (March 2005): 137–55.

Hesse, Brian. "Introduction: The Myth of 'Somalia.'" *Journal of Contemporary African Studies* 28, no. 3 (July 2010): 247–59.

Hewko, John. "Foreign Direct Investment in Transitional Economies: Does the Rule of Law Matter." *East European Constitutional Review* 11 (2002): 71.

Hicken, Allen and Erik Martinez Kuhonta. "Shadows from the Past: Party System Institutionalization in Asia." *Comparative Political Studies* 44, no. 5 (2011): 572–97.

Hicken, Allen and Joel Simmons. "The Personal Vote and the Efficacy of Education Spending." *American Journal of Political Science* 52 (2008): 109–24.

Hill, Michael and Kwen Fee Lian. *Politics of Nation-Building and Citizenship in Singapore.* London, UK: Routledge, 1995.

Hills, Alice. "Towards a Critique of Policing and National Development in Africa." *The Journal of Modern African Studies* 34, no. 2 (June 1996): 271–91.

Hinnebusch, Raymond. "Authoritarian Persistence, Democratization Theory and the Middle East: An Overview and Critique." *Democratization* 13, no. 3 (2006): 373–95.

Hironaka, Ann. *Never Ending Wars.* Cambridge, MA: Harvard University Press, 2005.

Hittle, J. D. *The Military Staff: Its History and Development.* Harrisburg, PA: The Stackpole Company, 1961.

Hobbes, Thomas. *The Leviathan.* New York: EP Dutton, 1947.

Hochstetler, Kathryn. "Rethinking Presidentialism: Challenges and Presidential Falls in South America." *Comparative Politics* (2006): 401–18.

Hoeckel, Kathrin. *Beyond Beirut: Why Reconstruction in Lebanon Did Not Contribute to State-Making and Stability.* Crisis States Research Centre no. 4 (2011): 1–19.

Hodgson, Geoffrey M. "What Are Institutions?" *Journal of Economic Issues* 60, no. 1 (March 2006): 1–25.

Hoff, Karla and Joseph Stiglitz. "The Creation of the Rule of Law and the Legitimacy of Property Rights: The Political and Economic Consequences of a Corrupt Privatization." *National Bureau of Economic Research Working Paper* 11772 (November 2005): 1–51.

Hollyer, James and Leonard Wantchekon. "Corruption in Autocracies." (May 2011): 1–44, https://files.nyu.edu/jrh343/public/Draft3b.pdf.

Holm, Hans-Henrik. "The Responsibility that Will Not Go Away: Weak States in the International System." Paper presented at the Failed States Conference, Purdue University, West Lafayette, February 25–27, 1998.

Holmes, Karl C. "The Lessons of Somalia: Who Learned What, from Whom, and for What Purpose?" *Northeast African Studies* 5, no. 1 (1998): 115–26.

Holsti, Kalevi J. "Political Causes of Humanitarian Emergencies." In *War, Hunger and Displacement: The Origins of Humanitarian Emergencies.* Vol. 1. Edited by Wayne Nafziger, Frances Stewart, and Raimo Väyrynen. Oxford, UK: Oxford University Press, 2000.

Holzer, Thomas. "Theory of Regimes and Failed States Theory: A Common Issue or Talking Across Purposes?" 2011, www.psa.ac.uk/journals/pdf/5/2011/1142_634.pdf.

Homeland Security News Wire. "US to Help Libya Create an Elite Anti-Terror Force" (October 17, 2012).

Horowitz, Donald L. *Ethnic Groups in Conflict*. Berkeley, CA: University of California Press, 1985.

—. "Incentives and Behaviour in the Ethnic Politics of Sri Lanka and Malaysia." *Third World Quarterly* 11, no. 4 (October 1989): 18–35.

Hosmer, Stephen, *Why Was the Iraqi Resistance to the Coalition Invasion So Weak?* Santa Monica, CA: RAND, 2007.

Howe, Herbert. *Ambiguous Order: Military Forces in African States*. Boulder, CO: Lynne Rienner, 2001.

Hoyt, Katherine. "Parties and Pacts in Contemporary Nicaragua." Paper prepared for delivery at the 2001 Meeting of the Latin American Studies Association, Washington, DC, September 6–8, 2001: 1–34.

Hoyt, Timothy. "Military Force." In *Attacking Terrorism*. Edited by A. K. Cronin and J. Ludes. Washington, DC: Georgetown University Press, 2004, 162–85.

Hudson, Rex A. *The Sociology and Psychology of Terrorism: Who Becomes a Terrorist and Why?* Washington, DC: Federal Research Division, Library of Congress, 1999.

—. "Terrorist and Organized Crime Groups in the Tri-Border Area (TBA) of South America." Report prepared by the Federal Research Division, Library of Congress, December 2010, 1–87.

Huliaras, Asteris. "Qadhafi's Comeback: Libya and Sub-Saharan Africa in the 1990s." *African Affairs* 100 (2001): 5–25.

Human Security Centre. "Human Security Report 2005: War and Peace in the 21st Century." Oxford, UK: University Press, 2006.

Humphreys, Macartan. "Economics and Violent Conflict." Harvard University, February 2003, 1–31, www.preventconflict.org/portal/economics/.

Hunter, Wendy. *Eroding Military Influence in Brazil: Politicians against Soldiers*. Chapel Hill, NC: University of North Carolina Press, 1997.

Huntington, Samuel. "The Modest Meaning of Democracy." In *Democracy in the Americas: Stopping the Pendulum*. Edited by Robert A Pastor. New York, NY: Holmes and Meier, 1989.

—. "Political Development and Political Decay." *World Politics* 17, no. 3 (April 1965): 386–430.

—. *Political Order in Changing Societies*. New Haven, CT: Yale University Press, 1968.

—. *The Solider and the State: The Theory and Politics of Civil-Military Relations*. Cambridge, MA: Harvard University Press, 1957.

—. *The Third Wave: Democratization in the Late 20th Century*. Norman, OK: University of Oklahoma Press, 1991.

Huria, Sonali. "Failing and Failed States: The Global Discourse." IPCS Issue Brief 75 (July 2008): 1–4.

Hutchcroft, Paul D. "Oligarchs and Cronies in the Philippine State: The Politics of Patrimonial Plunder." *World Politics: A Quarterly Journal of International Relations* 43, no. 3 (April 1991): 414–50.

Hutchful, Eboe. "Civil Society Debate in Africa: The Africa Prospect." *International Journal* 51 (1995–6): 54–77.

Hydén, Göran. "Top-Down Democratization in Tanzania." *Journal of Democracy* 10, no. 4 (1999): 142–55.

Hydén, Göran, Julius Court, and Ken Mease. "The Bureaucracy and Governance in 16 Developing Countries." *World Governance Survey Discussion Paper* 7 (July 2003): 1–27.

—. *Making Sense of Governance: Empirical Evidence from Sixteen Developing Countries.* Boulder, CO: Lynne Rienner Publishers, 2004.

IADB. *Economic and Social Progress Report: Development beyond Economics.* Baltimore, MD: John Hopkins University Press, 2000, 13.

Ignatieff, Michael. "Intervention and State Failure." *Dissent* 49, no. 1 (Winter 2002): 114–23.

Ikpe, Ukana B. "Patrimonialism and Military Regimes." *African Journal of Political Science* 5, no. 1 (2000): 146–62.

"Inactive Workers, Inactive Congress." *The Economist* (June 5, 1997).

Inside Defense.com. "DOD, State Propose Multimillion-Dollar Counterterrorism Aid for Libya." (November 12, 2012).

"International Country Risk Guide Methodology." *Political Risk Services Guide* (2012): 1–17.

Iqbal, Zaryab and Harvey Starr. "Bad Neighbors: Failed States and Their Consequences." *Conflict Management and Peace Science* 25, no. 4 (2008): 315–31.

Isham, Jonathan, Michael Woolcock, Lant Pritchett, and Gwen Busby. "The Varieties of Resource Experience: Natural Resource Export Structures and the Political Economy of Economic Growth." *The World Bank Economic Review* 19, no. 2 (September 28, 2005): 141–74.

Ishiyama, John. "Neo-patrimonialism and the Prospects for Democratization in Central Asia." In *Power and Change in Central Asia.* Edited by Sally Cummings. London, UK: Routledge, 2002, 42–58.

Iskandar, Adnan. *The Civil Service of Lebanon.* New York, NY: UMI Dissertation Services; A Bell & Howell Company, 1997.

Islam, Nasir. "Colonial Legacy, Administrative Reform and Politics: Pakistan 1947–1987." *Public Administration and Development* 9 (1989): 271–85.

Jabbra. Joseph G. *Bureaucracy and Development in the Arab World.* Vol. 5. Leiden, Netherlands: Brill, 1989.

Jackson, Richard, "The State and Terrorist Sanctuaries: A Critical Analysis." Paper prepared for the British International Studies Association (BISA) Annual Conference, December 18–20, 2006, University of Cork, Ireland, 1–18.

Jackson, Robert H. "Quasi-states, Dual Regimes, and Neoclassical Theory: International Jurisprudence and the Third World." *International Organization* 41 (1987): 519–49.

—. *Quasi States: Sovereignty, International Relations and the Third World.* Cambridge, UK: Cambridge University Press, 1990.

Jackson, Robert H. and Carl G. Rosberg. *Personal Rule in Black Africa: Prince, Autocrat, Prophet, Tyrant.* Berkeley, CA: University of California Press, 1982.

Jacoby, Lowell. "Current Projected National Security Threats to the United States." Senate Select Committee on Intelligence, February 24, 2004, 1–23.

Janda, Kenneth. *Comparative Political Parties Data, 1950–1962*. Compiled by Kenneth Janda, Northwestern University. Ann Arbor, MI: Inter-university Consortium for Political and Social Research, 1979.

Janowitz, Morris. *Military Institutions and Coercion in the Developing Nations: The Military in the Political Development of New Nations*. Chicago, IL: University of Chicago Press, 1988.

Jappelli, Tullio, M. Pagano, and M. Bianco. "An Analysis of Judicial Corruption and Its Causes: An Objective Governance-Based Approach." *International Review of Law and Economics* 21, no. 2 (2005): 233–49.

Jarbou, Ayoub M. al-. "Judicial Independence: Case Study of Saudi Arabia." *Arab Law Quarterly* 19, no. 1/4 (2004): 5–54.

Jenkins, J. Craig and Augustine J. Kposowa. "Explaining Military Coups D'Etat: Black Africa, 1957–1984." *American Sociological Review* 55, no. 6 (December 1990): 861–85.

Jensen, Nathan. "Political Risk, Democratic Institutions, and Foreign Direct Investment." *Journal of Politics* 70, no. 4 (2008): 1040–52.

Johnson, Chalmers. *MITI and the Japanese Miracle: The Growth of Industrial Policy 1925–1975*. Stanford, CA: Stanford University Press, 1982.

—. "Political Institutions and Economic Performance: The Government-Business Relationship in Japan, South Korea, and Taiwan." In *The Political Economy of the New Asian Industrialism*. Edited by Federic C. Deyo. Ithaca, NY: Cornell University Press, 1987.

Johnson, Paul. "Colonialism's Back—And Not a Moment too Soon." *New York Times Magazine* April 18, 1993: 22, 43.

Joireman, Sandra F. "Colonization and the Rule of Law: Comparing the Effectiveness of Common Law and Civil Law Countries." *Constitutional Political Economy* 15, no. 4 (2004): 315–38.

—. "Inherited Legal Systems and Effective Rule of Law: Africa and the Colonial Legacy." *Journal of Modern African Studies* 39, no. 4 (2001): 571–96.

Jones, Mark P. "The Role of Parties and Party Systems in the Policymaking Process." Paper prepared for Inter-American Development Bank Workshop on State Reform, Public Policies and Policymaking Processes, February 28–March 2, Washington, DC, 2005.

Jones, Seth G. "The Rise of Afghanistan's Insurgency: State Failure and Jihad." *International Security* 32, no. 4 (Spring 2008): 7–40.

Joseph, Gilbert M. and Daniela Spenser. *In from the Cold: Latin America's New Encounter with the Cold War*. Durham, NC: Duke University Press Books, 2007.

Jowitt, Ken. "Soviet Neo-traditionalism: The Political Corruption of a Leninist regime." *Europe-Asia Studies* 35, no. 3 (1983): 275–97.

Jreisat, Jamil E. "Bureaucracy and Reform in the Arab World." In *Bureaucracy and Administration*. Edited by Ali Farazmand. Boca Raton, FL: CRC Press, 2009, 583–97.

Kabutaulaka, Tarcisius Tara. "'Failed State' and the War on Terror: Intervention in Solomon Islands." *Analysis from the East-West Center* 72 (March 2004): 1–8.

Kachkeev, Maksat. "Judicial Independence in Kyrgyzstan and Kazakhstan: A Legislative Overview." *Judicial Independence in Transition* (2012): 1255–75.

Kaersvang, Dana. "Equality Courts in South Africa: Legal Access for the Poor." *The Journal of the International Institute* 15, no. 2 (Spring 2008): 4–9.

Kally, Jackie. "Swaziland Election Dossier 2003." Electoral Institute of Southern Africa, 2004.

Kalyvas, Stathis. *The Logic of Violence in Civil War*. Cambridge, UK: Cambridge University Press, 2006.

—. "The Paradox of Terrorism in Civil War." *Journal of Ethics* 8, no. 1 (2004): 97–138.

Kang, David Chan-oong. *Crony Capitalism: Corruption and Development in South Korea and the Philippines*. Cambridge, UK: Cambridge University Press, 2002.

Kaplan, Robert D. "The Coming Anarchy." *The Atlantic Monthly* (February 1994): 44–76.

Kaplan, Seth D. *Fixing Fragile States: A New Paradigm for Development*. London, UK: Praeger Security International, 2008.

—. "Rethinking State-Building in a Failed State." *Washington Quarterly* 33, no. 1 (January 2010): 81–97.

Karklins, Rasma. "Typology of Post-Communist Corruption." *Problems of Post Communism* 49, no. 4 (2002): 22–32.

Karl, Terry Lynn. "The Hybrid Regimes of Central America." *Journal of Democracy* 6, no. 3 (1995): 72–86.

—. *Paradox of Plenty: Oil Booms and Petro States*. Berkeley, CA: University of California Press, 1997.

Kasfir, Nelson. "Domestic Anarchy, Security Dilemmas, and Violent Predation: Causes of Failure." In *When States Fail: Causes and Consequences*. Edited by Robert Rotberg. Princeton, NJ: Princeton University Press, 2004, 53–76.

Kasozi, Abdu Basajabaka Kawalya, Nakanyike Musisi, and James Mukooza Sejjengo. *The Social Origins of Violence in Uganda, 1964–1985*. Montreal, Canada: McGill/Queen's Press, 1994.

Katz, Mark N. "Breaking the Yemen Al-Qaeda Connection." *Current History* 102 (2003): 40–3.

Kaufmann, Daniel, Aart Kraay, and Massimo Mastruzzi. "Governance Matters VII: Aggregate and Individual Governance Indicators 1996–2008." Policy Research Working Paper 4978, World Bank Development Research Group Macroeconomics and Growth Team, June 2009, 1–105.

Kaufmann, D., A. Kray, and P. Zoido-Lobaton, "Governance Matters I." Policy Research Working Paper, WPS 2196, Washington, DC, World Bank, 1998.

Kaufman, D. et al. "Fighting Systemic Corruption: Foundations for Institutional Reforms." World Bank Governance Team, 1998, 1–10.

Keefer, Phillip and Steven Knack. "Polarization, Politics and Property Rights: Links between Inequality and Growth." *Public Choice* 111 (2002): 127–54.

Keefer, Philip and Norman Loayza. *Terrorism, Economic Development and Political Openness*. Cambridge, UK: Cambridge University Press, 2008.

Kelman, Herbert C. "The Role of National Identity in Conflict Resolution: Experiences from Israeli-Palestinian Problem Solving Workshops." In *Social Identity, Inter-group Conflict and Conflict Reduction*. Edited by Richard D. Ashmore, Lee Jussim, and David Wilder. Oxford, UK: Oxford University Press, 2001.

Keohane, Robert. *Humanitarian Intervention: Ethical, Legal, and Political Dilemmas.* Cambridge, UK: Cambridge University Press, 2003, 276–77.

Khadka. Narayan. "Nepal's Stagnant Economy: The Panchayat Legacy." *Asian Survey* 31, no. 8 (August 1991): 694–711.

Khairan, bin Mohd. "The Influence of Islam in the Military; Comparative Study of Malaysia, Indonesia and Pakistan." Naval Post-graduate School of Monterey, 2004.

Khaled, Mortuza. "Aspects of Colonialism in Asia: A Comparative Study of the Japanese in Korea (1910–1945) and the British in India (1757–1947)." In *Embracing the Other: The Interaction of Korean and Foreign Cultures: Proceedings of the 1st World Congress of Korean Studies, I.* Songnam, Republic of Korea: The Academy of Korean Studies, 2002.

Khalilzad, Zalmay. "The Politics of Ethnicity in Southwest Asia: Political Development or Political Decay?" *Political Science Quarterly* 99, no. 4 (Winter 1984–5): 657–79.

Khan, Mohammad Mohabbat. "Political and Administrative Corruption: Concepts, Comparative Experiences and Bangladesh Case." *Transparency International* (1998): 1–20.

—."State of Governance in Bangladesh." *The Round Table* 92, no. 370 (2003): 391–405.

Kiiza, Julius. "Institutions and Economic Performance in Africa: A Comparative Analysis of Mauritius, Botswana and Uganda." Research Paper, UNU-WIDER, United Nations University 73 (2006): 1–23.

Kilcullen, David J. "Countering Global Insurgency." *Journal of Strategic Studies* 28, no. 4 (2005): 597–617.

King, Gary, Robert Keohane, and Sidney Verba. *Designing Social Inquiry: Scientific Inference in Qualitative Research.* Princeton, NJ: Princeton University Press, 1994.

Kirwin, Matthew. "The Security Dilemma and Conflict in Côte d'Ivoire." *Nordic Journal of African Studies* 15, no. 1 (2006): 42–52.

Klare, Michael. "The International Trade in Light Weapons: What Have We Learned?" In *Light Weapons and Civil Conflict: Controlling the Tools of Violence.* Edited by Jeffrey Boutwell and Michael Klare. New York, NY: Rowman and Littlefield Publishers, 1999.

—. *Resource Wars: The New Landscape of Global Conflict.* New York, NY: Henry Holt, 2001.

Klitgaard, Robert. *Controlling Corruption.* Berkeley, CA: University of California Press, 1988.

Knack, Stephen and Philip Keefer. "Institutions and Economic Performance: Cross-Country Tests Using Alternative Institutional Measures." *Economics and Politics* 7, no. 3 (1995): 207–28.

Knight, Malcolm, Norman Loayza, and Delano Villaneuva. "The Peace Dividend: Military Spending and Economic Growth." *IMF Staff Papers* 43 (March 1996): 1–37.

Knoester, Matthew. "War in Colombia." *Social Justice* 25, no. 72 (1998): 85–109.

Knight, M., N. Loayza, and D. Villanueva. "The Peace Dividend: Military Spending Cuts and Economic Growth." *IMF Staff Papers* 43, no. 1 (1996): 1–37.

Kocher, Matthew Adam. "State Capacity as a Conceptual Variable." *Yale Journal of International Affairs* 5 (2010): 137.

Koh, David. "Leadership Changes at the 10th Congress of the Vietnamese Communist Party." *Asian Survey* 68, no. 4 (July/August 2008): 650–72.

Kohnert, Dirk. "Togo: Thorny Transition and Misguided Aid at the Roots of Economic Misery." Institute of African Affairs, MPRA Paper 9060 (October 2007): 1–37.

Kolhatkar, Sonali. "In Afghanistan, U.S. Replaces One Terrorist State with Another." *Foreign Policy in Focus* (October 3, 2003).

Kolsto, Pal. "The Sustainability and Future of Unrecognized Quasi-States." *Journal of Peace Research* 43, no. 6 (2006): 723–40.

Koonings, Kees and Dirk Kruijt. *Armed Actors: Organized Violence and State Failure in Latin America*. London, UK: Zed Books, 2004.

Kopstein, Jeffrey. "The Transatlantic Divide over Democracy Promotion." *Washington Quarterly* 29, no. 2 (2006): 85–98.

Kposowa, Augustine J. and J. Craig Jenkins. "The Structural Sources of Military Coups in Post-colonial Africa, 1957–1984." *American Journal of Sociology* (1993): 126–63.

Kramer, J. J. "Political Corruption in Post-Communist Russia: The Case for Democratization." In 17th World Congress of International Political Science Association (IPSA) held in Seoul, Korea on August, 1997, 17–21.

Kramer, Katherine. "Legal Controls on Small Arms and Light Weapons in Southeast Asia." *Small Arms Survey Occasional Paper* 3 (July 2001): 1–38.

Krasner, Stephen D. "International Support for State-Building: Flawed Consensus." *Prism* 2, no. 3 (June 2011a): 65–74.

—. "Review Article: Foreign Aid: Competing Paradigms." *Journal of Intervention and State-Building* 5, no. 2 (2011b): 123–49.

—. "Shared Sovereignty: New Institutions for Collapsed and Failing States." *International Security* 29, no. 2 (Fall 2004): 85–120.

Kraxberger, Brennan M. "Failed States: Temporary Obstacles to Democratic Diffusion or Fundamental Holes in the World Political Map?" *Third World Quarterly* 28, no. 6 (2007): 1055–71.

Krueger, Alan B. and David D. Laitin. "Kto Kogo?: A Cross-Country Study of the Origins and Targets of Terrorism." In *Terrorism, Economic Development, and Political Openness*. Edited by Philip Keefer and Norman Loayza. Cambridge, UK: Cambridge University Press, 2008, 148–73.

Krueger, Alan and Jitka Maleckova. "Education, Poverty, and Terrorism: Is There a Causal Connection?" *Journal of Economic Perspectives* 17, no. 4 (Fall 2003): 119–44.

Kruijt, Dirk and Kees Koonings. "Introduction: Violence and Fear in Latin America." In *Societies of Fear: The Legacy of Civil War, Violence and Terror in Latin America*. Edited by Kees Koonings and Dirk Kruijt. London, UK: Zed Books, 1999.

Kubicek, Paul. "Authoritarianism in Central Asia: Curse or Cure?" *Third World Quarterly* 19, 1 (1998): 29–43.

Kukhianidze, Alexandre. "Corruption and Organized Crime in Georgia before and after the 'Rose Revolution.'" *Central Asian Survey* 28, no. 2 (2009): 215–34.

Kuran, Timur. "Why the Middle East Is Economically Underdeveloped: Historical Mechanisms of Institutional Stagnation." *The Journal of Economic Perspectives* 18, no. 3 (2004): 71–90.

Kwok, Jia-Chuan. "Explaining Civil Military Relations in Southeast Asia." Master's Dissertation, Massachusett's Institute of Technology, September 2010.

LaFree, G. and N. Morris (2004) "Corruption as a Global Social Problem." In *Handbook of Social Problems: A Comparative International Perspective.* Edited by G. Ritzer. Thousand Oaks, CA: Sage, 600–18.

Lake, Anthony. "Confronting Backlash States." *Foreign Affairs* 73, no. 2 (March/April 1994): 45–55.

Lambsdorff, Johan Graf. "Corruption and Rent-Seeking." *Public Choice* 113 (2002): 97–125.

Langford, Tonya. "Things Fall Apart: State Failure and the Politics of Intervention." *International Studies Review* 1, no. 1 (Spring 1999): 59–79.

Laqueur, Walter. *The New Terrorism: Fanaticism and the Arms of Mass Destruction.* Oxford, UK: Oxford University Press, 1999.

—. *No End to War: Terrorism in the Twenty-First Century.* New York, NY: Continuum, 2003.

Larrain, Jorge. "Modernity and Identity: Cultural Change in Latin America. In *Latin American Transformed: Globalization and Modernity.* Edited by Robert N. Gwynne and Cristobal Kay. London, UK: Arnold, 1999, 182–202.

Le Billon, Philippe. "Angola's Political Economy of War: The Role of Oil and Diamonds 1975–2000." *African Affairs* 100, no. 398 (2001): 55–80.

Le Billon, Philippe and Eric Nicholls. "Ending 'Resource Wars': Revenue Sharing, Economic Sanction or Military Intervention?" *International Peacekeeping* 13, no. 5 (2007): 613–32.

Leblang, David A. "Property Rights, Democracy and Economic Growth." *Political Research Quarterly* 49, no. 1 (March 1996): 5–26.

Lederman, Daniel, Norman V. Loayza, and Rodrigo R. Soares. "Accountability and Corruption: Political Institutions Matter." *Economics & Politics* 17, no. 1 (2005): 1–35.

Lee, Terence. "Military Cohesion and Regime Maintenance: Explaining the Role of the Military in 1989 China and 1998 Indonesia." *Armed Forces & Society* 32, no. 1 (October 2005): 80–104.

Leeson, Peter T. "Better off Stateless: Somalia before and after Government Collapse." *Journal of Comparative Economics* 35, no. 4 (2007).

Lefebvre, Jeffrey A. *Arms for the Horn: US security policy in Ethiopia and Somalia, 1953–1991.* Pittsburgh, PA: University of Pittsburgh Press, 1992.

Leftwich, Adrian. *States of Development: On the Primacy of Politics in Development.* London, UK: Polity, 2000.

—. "What Are institutions?" *IPPG Briefing* 1 (2006): 1–4.

Legum, Colin. "Behind the Clown's Mask." *Transition* 75 (1997): 250–8.

Lehoucq, Fabrice. "Electoral Fraud: Causes, Types, and Consequences." *Annual Review of Political Science* 6, no. 1 (2003): 233–56.

Lemarchand, René. *African Kingships in Perspective.* London, UK: Routledge, 1977.

—. "Patters of State Collapse and Reconstruction in Central Africa: Reflections on the Crisis in the Great Lakes Region." *Africa Spectrum* 32, no. 2 (1997): 173–93.

—. "Political Clientelism and Ethnicity in Tropical Africa: Competing Solidarities in Nation-Building." *The American Political Science Review* (1972): 68–90.

——. "Uncivil States and Civil Societies: How Illusion Became Reality." *Journal of Modern African Studies* 30 (June 1992): 187.

Lenski, Gerhald E. and Jean Lenski. *Human Societies: An Introduction to Sociology.* New York, NY: McGraw Hill, 1987.

Leon, Gabriel. "Loyalty for Sale? Military Spending and Coups d' Etat." *CWPE* 1209 (February 2012): 1–49.

Leong, Ho Khai. "Citizen Participation and Policy Making in Singapore: Conditions and Predicaments." *Asian Survey* 40, no. 3 (May–June 2000): 436–55.

Lepingwell, John W. R. "Soviet Civil-Military Relations and the August Coup." *World Politics* 44, no. 4 (1992): 539–72.

Leslie, Winsome J. *The World Bank and Structural Transformation in Developing Countries: The Case of Zaire.* Boulder, CO: Lynne Rienner Publishers, 1987.

—. *Zaire: Continuity and Political Change in an Oppressive State.* Boulder, CO: Westview Press, 1993.

Leveau, Rémy. "Morocco at the Crossroads." *Mediterranean Politics* 2, no. 2 (1997): 95–113.

Levi, Margaret. *Of Rule and Revenue.* Berkeley, CA: University of California Press, 1988.

Levin, Mark and Georgy Satarov. "Corruption and Institutions in Russia." *European Journal of Political Economy* 16, no. 1 (2000): 113–32.

Levitsky, Steven and Maxwell A. Cameron. "Democracy without Parties? Political Parties and Regime Change in Fujimori's Peru." *Latin American Politics and Society* 45, no. 3 (2003): 1–33.

Levitsky, Steven, and Lucan Way. "The Rise of Competitive Authoritarianism." *Journal of Democracy* 13, no. 2 (2002): 51–65.

Levy, Gilat. "A Model of Political Parties." *Journal of Economic Theory* 115, no. 2 (2004): 250–77.

Lewis, David. The *Temptations of Tyranny in Central Asia.* New York, NY: Columbia University Press, 2008.

Li, David. "Changing Incentives of the Chinese Bureaucracy." *American Economic Review: Papers and Proceedings* 88 (1998): 393–7.

Li, Quan. "Does Democracy Promote or Reduce Transnational Terrorist Incidents?" *Journal of Conflict Resolution* 49, no. 2 (2005): 278–97.

Li, Quan and Drew Schaub. "Economic Globalization and Transnational Terrorist Incidents: A Pooled Time Series Analysis." *Journal of Conflict Resolution* 48, no. 2 (2004): 230–58.

Li, Shuhe and Peng Lian. "Decentralization and Coordination: China's Credible Commitment to Preserve the Market under Authoritarianism." *China Economic Review* 10, no. 2 (1999): 161–90.

Liddle, R. William. "Soeharto's Indonesia: Personal Rule and Political Institutions." *Pacific Affairs* 58, no. 1 (Spring 1985): 68–90.

Lijphart, Arend. *Democracy in Plural Societies: A Comparative Exploration.*
New Haven, CT: Yale University Press, 1977.
—. *Patterns of Democracy: Government Forms and Performance in Thirty-Six Countries.* New Haven, CT: Yale University Press, 1999.
Lindberg, Staffan I. and John F. Clark. "Does Democratization Reduce the Risk of Military Interventions in Politics in Africa?" *Democratisation* 15, no. 1 (2008): 86–105.
Linz, Juan J. "The Perils of Presidentialism." *Journal of Democracy* 1, no. 1 (Winter 1990): 51–69.
—. "Presidential or Parliamentary Democracy: Does It Make a Difference?" In *The Crisis of Presidential Democracy: The Latin American Evidence.* Edited by Juan J. Linz and Arturo Valenzuela. Baltimore, MD: The Johns Hopkins University Press, 1994, 3–37.
—. "Some Thoughts on the Victory and Future of Democracy." In *Democratization: The State of Art.* Edited by Dirk Berg-Schlosser. Ridgebrook, MI: Barbara Budrich Publishers, 2007, 133–53.
Linz, Juan J. and Alfred Stepan. *Problems of Democratic Consolidation.* Baltimore, MD: Johns Hopkins University Press, 1996.
Lisanti, Dominic. "Do Failed States Really Breed Terrorists?: An Examination of Terrorism in Sub-Saharan Africa—Comparing Statistical Approaches with a Fuzzy Set Qualitative Comparative Analysis." Paper Prepared for the CAPERS Workshop at NYU, May 14, 2010, 1–26.
Lipschutz, Ronnie and Beverly Crawford. "Economic Globalization and the 'New' Ethnic Strife: What Is to Be Done?" Policy Paper 25, Institute on Global Conflict and Cooperation, University of California, Berkeley, 1996, 1–23.
Lipset, Seymour Martin. "The Indispensability of Political Parties." *Journal of Democracy* 11 (January 2000): 48–55.
—. "Some Social Requisites of Democracy: Economic Development and Political Legitimacy." *American Political Science Review* 53, no. 1 (March 1959): 69–105.
Lipset, Seymour Martin and Stein Rokkan. *Party Systems and Voter Alignments: Cross-National Perspectives.* New York, NY: Free Press, 1967.
Liwanga, Roger-Claude. "Judicial Independence in the Democratic Republic of Congo: Myth or Reality?" *Journal of African Law* 56, no. 2 (October 2012): 194–214.
Llorente, Maria V. "Demilitarization in Times of War? Police Reform in Colombia." In *Public Security and Police Reform in the Americas.* Edited by Lucía Dammert and John Bailey. Pittsburgh, KS: University of Pittsburgh Press, 2005, 111–31.
Locke, John. *Two Treatises of Government.* Cambridge, UK: Cambridge University Press, 1991.
Logan, Justin and Christopher Preble. "Failed States and Flawed Logic: The Case against a Standing Nation-Building Office." *Policy Analysis* 560 (January 11, 2006): 1–32.
Londregan, John B. and Keith T. Poole. "Poverty, the Coup Trap, and the Seizure of Executive Power." *World Politics* 42, no. 2 (1990): 151–83.
Looney, Robert. "Iraq's Shadow Economy." *Rivista Internazionale di Scienze Economiche e Commerciali* (2005): 561–80.

Lowenthal, Abraham F. "Review: Armies and Politics in Latin America." *World Politics* 27, no. 1 (October 1974): 107–30.

Lubin, Doe. "Economic Development of Francophone Africa: A Comparison with the Republic of Korea." *International Social Science Journal* 151 (1997): 105–21.

Luckman, R. "A Comparative Typology of Civil-Military Relations." *Government and Opposition* 6 (1971): 5–35.

Lundahl, Mats. "Inside the Predatory State: The Rationale, Methods, and Economic Consequences of Kleptocratic Regimes." *Nordic Journal of Political Economy* 24 (1997): 31–50.

Luong, Pauline Jones. *Institutional Change and Political Continuity in Post Soviet Central Asia: Power, Perceptions and Pacts.* Cambridge, MA: Cambridge University Press, 2002.

—. *The Transformation of Central Asia: States and Societies from Soviet Rule to Independence.* Ithica, NY: Cornell University Press, 2004.

Luong, Pauline Jones and Erika Weinthal. "New Friends, New Fears in Central Asia." *Foreign Affairs* (March/April 2002): 61–70.

Lust-Okar, Ellen. "Divided They Rule: The Management and Manipulation of Political Opposition." *Comparative Politics* (2004): 159–79.

—. "Elections under Authoritarianism: Preliminary Lessons from Jordan." *Democratization* 13, no. 3 (June 2006): 456–71.

—. *Structuring Conflict in the Arab World: Incumbents, Opponents, and Institutions.* Cambridge, UK: Cambridge University Press, 2005.

Lust-Okar, Ellen and Amaney Ahmad Jamal. "Rulers and Rules Reassessing the Influence of Regime Type on Electoral Law Formation." *Comparative Political Studies* 35, no. 3 (2002): 337–66.

Luttwak, Edward N. *Coup D'Etat: A Practical Handbook.* London, UK: Penguin, 1968.

Lynch, Dov. "Separatist States and Post-Soviet Conflicts." *International Affairs* 78, no. 4 (2002): 831–48.

MacDonald, Brian. *Military Spending in Developing Countries.* Montreal, Canada: McGill Queen University Press, 1997.

Mackinlay, John. "Defining Warlords." *International Peacekeeping* 7, no. 1 (2000): 48–62.

Magaloni, Beatriz. "The Comparative Logic of Autocratic Survival." Paper presented W. Glenn Campbell and Rita Ricardo-Campbell National Fellow and the Susan Louis Dyer Peace Fellow at the Hoover Institution, 2006–7, 1–42.

—. "Credible Power-Sharing and the Longevity of Authoritarian Rule." *Comparative Political Studies* 20, no. 10 (April/May 2008): 715–41.

—. *Voting for Autocracy: Hegemonic Party Survival and Its Demise in Mexico.* Cambridge, UK: Cambridge University Press, 2006.

Magaloni, Beatriz, Alberto Diaz-Cayeros, and Federico Estévez. "Clientelism and Portfolio Diversification: A Model of Electoral Investment with Applications to Mexico." In *Patrons, Clients, and Policies: Patterns of Democratic Accountability and Political Competition.* Edited by Herbert Kitschelt and Steven Wilkinson. Cambridge, UK: Cambridge University Press, 2007, 182–205.

Maguii, Moreno Torres and Michael Anderson. "Fragile States: Defining Difficult Environments for Poverty Reduction." Poverty Reduction in Difficult Environments Team Working Paper 1, August 2004, 1–34.

Mahdavy, H. "The Patterns and Problems of Economic Development in Rentier States: The Case of Iran." In *Studies in Economic History of the Middle East*. Edited by M. A. Cook. New York: Oxford University Press, 1970, 428–67.

Mahoney, J. T. "A Resource-Based Theory of Sustainable Rents." *Journal of Management* 27 (2001): 651–60.

Mainwaring, Scott P. "Party Systems in the Third Wave." *Journal of Democracy* 9, no. 3 (1998): 67–81.

—. *Rethinking Party Systems in the Third Wave of Democratization: The Case of Brazil*. Stanford, CA: Stanford University Press, 1999.

Mainwaring, Scott, and Timothy Scully, eds. *Building Democratic Institutions: Party Systems in Latin America*. Stanford, CA: Stanford University Press, 1995.

—. "Building Democratic Institutions: Party Systems in Latin America." *Electoral Studies* 16, no. 1 (1997): 131.

Mainwaring, Scott and Matthew S. Shugart. "Juan Linz, Presidentialism, and Democracy: A Critical Appraisal." *Comparative Politics* 29, no. 4 (July 1997): 449–71.

Mainwaring, Scott P. and Mariano Torcal. "Party System Institutionalization and Party System Theory after the Third Wave of Democratization." In *Handbook of Party Politics*. Edited by Richard S. Katz and William J. Crotty. Thousand Oaks, CA: Sage Publications, 2006.

Mair, Stefan. "The New World of Privatized Violence." *Challenges of Globalization: New Trends in International Politics and Society* (2005): 1–12.

Mallaby, Sebastian. "The Reluctant Imperialist: Terrorism, Failed States and the Case for American Empire." *Foreign Affairs* 81, no. 2 (March/April 2002).

Mallat, Chibli. "The Lebanese Legal System." *The Lebanon Report* 2 (1997): 29–36.

Mallett, Richard, "Beyond Failed States and Ungoverned Spaces: Hybrid Political Orders in the Post-Conflict Landscape." *eSharpe* no. 15 (2010): 65–91.

Mangu, André Mbata B. "Separation of Powers, Independence of the Judiciary, and Good Governance in African Union Member States." Paper for the Annual Meeting of the African Network of Constitutional Lawyers, Cape Town, South Africa, August 2009.

Mani, Kristina. "Militaries in Business: State-Making and Entrepreneurship in the Developing World." *Armed Forces and Society* 33, no. 4 (July 2007): 591–611.

—. "Military Entrepreneurs: Patterns in Latin America." *Latin American Politics and Society* 53, no. 3 (Fall 2011): 25–55.

Maniruzzaman, Talukder. "Arms Transfers, Military Coups, and Military Rule in Developing States." *Journal of Conflict Resolution* 36, no. 4 (1992): 733–55.

Mann, Michael. "The Autonomous Power of the State: Its Origins, Mechanisms and Results." *European Journal of Sociology* 25, no. 2 (November 1984): 185–213.

—. *The Sources of Social Power, Volume II*. Cambridge, UK: Cambridge University Press, 1993.

Mansfield, Edward and Jack Snyder. "The 'Sequencing' Fallacy." *Journal of Democracy* 18, no. 3 (2007a): 5–10.

—. "Turbulent Transitions: Why Emerging Democracies Go to War in the Twenty-First Century." In *Leashing the Dogs of War: Conflict Management in a Divided World*. Edited by Chester A Crocker. United States Institute of Peace Press, 2007b.

Manwaring, Max. "Non-state Actors in Colombia: Threat and Response." *Strategic Studies Institute* (May 2002): 1–37.

Marcouiller, Douglas and Leslie Young. "The Black Hole of Graft: The Predatory State and the Informal Economy." *American Economic Review* 85, no. 3 (1995): 630–46.

Markowitz, Lawrence P. "Tajikistan: Authoritarian Reaction in a Post-war State." *Democratization* 19, no. 1 (2012): 98–119.

Marshall, Monty G. and Keith Jaggers. "Polity IV Project: Political Regime Characteristics and Transitions, 1800–2002." Dataset Users' Manual, Integrated Network for Societal Conflict Research (INSCR), Program Center for International Development and Conflict Management (CIDCM), University of Maryland, September 2002, 1–87.

Marshall, Monty G., Ted Robert Gurr, and Barbara Harff. *Political Instability Task Force Problem Set Codebook*, April 2009, http://globalpolicy.gmu.edu/p olitical-instability-task-force-home/pitf-problem-set-codebook/

Martinez-Bravo, Monica, Gerard Padró i Miquel, Nancy Qian, and Yang Yao. "Accountability in an Authoritarian Regime: The Impact of Local Electoral Reforms in Rural China." *NBER Working Paper* (August 2, 2010): 1–60.

Masoud, Tarek. "The Road to (and from) Liberation Square." *Journal of Democracy* 22, no. 3 (2011): 20–34.

Matsumoto, Mitsutoyo. "Political Democratization and KMT Party–Owned Enterprises in Taiwan." *The Developing Economies* 40, no. 3 (2002): 359–380.

Matti, Stephanie A. "The Democratic Republic of the Congo? Corruption, Patronage, and Competitive Authoritarianism in the DRC." *Africa Today* 56, no. 4 (2010): 42–61.

Mauro, Paolo. "Corruption and Growth." *Quarterly Journal of Economics* 110 (1995): 681–712.

—. "The Effects of Corruption on Growth, Investment, and Government Expenditure: A Cross-country Analysis." *Corruption and the Global Economy* 83 (1997).

Mayall, James. "The Legacy of Colonialism." In *Making States Work: State Failure and the Crisis of Governance*. Edited by Simon Chesterman, Michael Ignatieff, and Ramesh Thakir. New York, NY: United Nations University Press, 36–58.

Mazrui, Ali. "Decaying Parts of Africa Need Benign Colonization. *International Herald Tribune* (August 4, 1994): 6.

McGowan, Pat and Thomas H. Johnson. "Sixty Coups in Thirty Years–Further Evidence Regarding African Military Coups d'État." *The Journal of Modern African Studies* 24, no. 3 (1986): 539–46.

Mcloughlin, Claire. "Topic Guide on Fragile States." Governance and Social Development Resource Center GSDRC, University of Birmingham, 2012, 1–88.

Medici, André. "The Political Economy of Reform in Brazil's Civil Servant Pension Scheme." Program on the Global Demography of Aging Working Paper Series 5, September 2004, 1–25.

Meissner, Hannes. "Informal Politics in Azerbaijan: Corruption and Rent Seeking Patterns." *Caucasus Analytical Digest* 24 (February 11, 2011): 6–9.

Menkhaus, Ken. "African Diasporas, Diasporas in Africa and Terrorist Threats." *Center for Security Studies* 80 (2009): 83–116.

—. "Analysis Vicious Circles and the Security Development Nexus in Somalia Conflict," *Security & Development* 4, no. 2 (August 2004a): 149–165.

—. "The Crisis in Somalia: Tragedy in Five Acts." *African Affairs* 106, no. 204 (2007a): 357–90.

—. "Governance without Government in Somalia Spoilers, State Building, and the Politics of Coping." *International Security* 31, no. 3 (Winter 2006/07): 74–106.

—. "Political Islam in Somalia." *Middle East Policy* 9, no. 1 (March 2002): 109–23.

—. "Quasi States, Nation Building, and Terrorist Safe Havens." *Journal of Conflict Studies* 23, no. 2 (Fall 2003a): 7–23.

—. "Somalia: State Collapse and the Threat of Terrorism." *Adelphi Paper* 364 (2004b).

—. "State Collapse in Somalia: Second Thoughts." Review of African Political Economy. *The Horn of Conflict* 30, no. 97 (September 2003b): 405–22.

—. "Terrorist Activities in Ungoverned Spaces: Evidence and Observations from the Horn of Africa." Paper prepared for the "Southern Africa and International Terrorism" workshop, January 25–27, 2007b, South Africa, 1–19.

Menon, Rajan. "In the Shadow of the Bear: Security in Post-Soviet Central Asia." *International Security* 20, no. 1 (Summer 1995): 149–81.

Mercer, Pamela. "Growing Coffee Is Losing Its Savor for Colombians." *New York Times* (January 9, 1996): 4.

Meredith, Martin. *The State of Africa: A History of the Continent since Independence*. London, UK: Free Press, 2005.

Merryman, John H. *The Civil Law Tradition*. Stanford, CA: Stanford University Press, 1985.

Messick, Richard E. "Judicial Reform and Economic Development: A Survey of the Issues." *The World Bank Research Observer* 14, no. 1 (1999): 117–36.

Mezey, Michael. "The Functions of Legislatures in the Third World." *Legislative Studies Quarterly* 8, no. 4 (November 1983): 511–50.

Mickolus, Edward F. and Susan L. Simmons. *Terrorism, 1996–2001: A Chronology, Vols. 1–2*. Westport, CT: Greenwood, 2002

Migdal, Joel. *Strong Societies and Weak States: State-Society Relations and State Capabilities in the Third World*. Princeton, NJ: Princeton University Press, 1988.

Miller, Andrew P. "Afghanistan, the Future of Al Qaeda in Failed States." *Pi Sigma Alpha Undergraduate Journal of Politics* 6, no. 2 (Fall 2004): 64–94.

Milliken, Jennifer. *State Failure, Collapse and Reconstruction.* Oxford, UK: Wiley-Blackwell Press, 2003.

Milliken, Jennifer and Keith Krause. "State Failure, State Collapse, and State Reconstruction: Concepts, Lessons and Strategies." *Development and Change* 33, no. 5 (2002): 753–74.

Mills, Greg. "Africa's New Strategic Significance." *Washington Quarterly* 27, no. 4 (Autumn 2004): 157–69.

Mitchell, Katharyne. "Transnational Neo-liberalism, and the Rise of the Shadow State." *Economy and Society* 30, no. 2 (2001): 165–89.

Mkandawire, Thandika. "Thinking about Developmental States in Africa." *Cambridge Journal of Economics* 25, no. 3 (2001): 289–314.

Mo, Pak Jung. "Corruption and Economic Growth." *Journal of Comparative Economics* 29 (2001): 66–79.

Mohtadi, Hamid and Terry Roe. "Democracy Rent Seeking, Public Spending and Growth." *Journal of Public Economics* (May 2001): 1–26.

Montes, Manuel F. "The Business Sector and Development Policy." In *National Development Policies and the Business Sector in the Philippines.* Edited by Aachiro Ishii et al. Tokyo, Japan: Institute of Developing Economies, 1988, 23–75.

Moore, David. "'When I Am a Century Old': Why Robert Mugabe Won't Go." *Legacies of Power: Leadership Change and Former Presidents in African Politics.* Edited by Roger Southall and Henning Melber. Cape Town and Uppsala: HSRC Press and Nordic Africa Institute, 2005, 120–50.

Moore, Michael. "A Natural Law Theory of Interpretation." *Southern California Law Review* 58 (1985): 277–398.

—. "'Revenues, State Formation, and the Quality of Governance in Developing Countries." *International Political Science Review* 25, no. 3 (2004): 297–319.

Moore, Mick. "Death without Taxes: Democracy, State Capacity and Aid Dependence in the Fourth World." In *Towards a Democratic Developmental State.* Edited by G. White and M. Robinson. Oxford, UK: Oxford University Press, 1997.

Moore, Stephen and Edgardo Buscaglia. *Judicial Corruption in Developing Countries: Its Causes and Economic Consequences,* 88. Stanford, CA: Hoover Institute Press, 1999.

Moran, John P. "Praetorians or Professionals? Democratization and Military Intervention in Communist and post-Communist Russia." *Journal of Communist Studies and Transition Politics* 15, no. 2 (1999): 41–68.

Moss, Todd, Gunilla Pettersson, and Nicolas van de Walle. "An Aid-Institutions Paradox? A Review Essay on Aid Dependency and State Building in Sub-Saharan Africa." Center for Global Development, Working Paper 74, January 2006, 1–28.

Moustafa, Tamir. "Law versus the State: The Judicialization of Politics in Egypt." *Law & Social Inquiry* 28, no. 4 (2003): 883–930.

Moya Pons, Frank. *The Dominican Republic: A National History.* Princeton, NJ: Princeton, 1995.

Moyo, Dambisa. *Dead Aid: Why Aid Is Not Working and How There Is a Better Way for Africa.* New York, NY: Farrar, Straus and Giroux, 2009.

Mullerson, Rein. "Precedents in the Mountains: On the Parallels and Uniqueness of the Cases of Kosovo, South Ossetia and Abkhazia." *Chinese Journal of International Law* 8, no. 1 (2009): 2–25.

Munkler, Herfried. *The New Wars.* Cambridge, UK: Polity Press, 2005.

Murphy, Kevin M., Andrei Shleifer, and Robert W. Vishny. "Why Is Rent-Seeking So Costly to Growth?" *The American Economic Review* 83, no. 2 (May 1993): 409–14.

Murphy, William P. "Military Patrimonialism and Child Soldier Clientelism in the Liberian and Sierra Leonean Civil Wars." *African Studies Review* 46, no. 2 (September 2003): 61–87.

Murray, Tonita. "Police-Building in Afghanistan: A Case Study of Civil Security Reform." *International Peacekeeping* 14, no. 1 (2007): 108–26.

Musah, Abdel-Fatau. "Privatization of Security and Arms Proliferation in Africa." *Development and Change* 33, no. 5 (2002a): 911–33.

—. "Small Arms: A Time Bomb under West Africa's Democratization Process." *The Brown Journal of World Affairs* 9, no. 1 (Spring 2002b): 239–49.

Mustafa, S. "Corruption Costs Millions, says UNDP." *Financial Express* (July 31, 1997).

Mutalib, Hussin. "Illiberal Democracy and the Future of Opposition in Singapore." *Third World Quality* 21, no. 2 (2000): 313–42.

Mutua, Makau. "Justice under Siege: The Rule of Law and Judicial Subservience in Kenya." *Human Rights Quarterly* 23, no. 1 (2001): 96–118.

Nasuti, Peter. "The Determinants of Anti-Corruption Reform in the Republic of Georgia," 2011, 1–4, www.irex.org/sites/default/files/NASUTI%20 Research%20Summary.pdf.

Nathan, Andrew. "Authoritarian Resilience: China's changing of the Guard." *Journal of Democracy* 14, no. 1 (January 2003): 6–17.

"Nation-Building: The Inescapable Responsibility of the World's Only Superpower." *Rand Review* (Summer 2003), www.rand.org/publications/randreview/issues/summer2003/nation3.html.

Nee, Victor V., Sonja Opper, and Sonia M. L. Wong. "Politicized Capitalism: The Developmental State and the Firm in China," January 7, 2004, 1–53, www.economyandsociety.org/publications/NeeOpperWong07JAN05.pdf.

Needler, Martin C. "Military Motivations in the Seizure of Power." *Latin American Research Review* 10, no. 3 (1975): 63–79.

—. "Political Development and Military Intervention in Latin America." *The American Political Science Review* 60, no. 3 (1966): 616–26.

Newberg, Paula R. *Judging the State: Courts and Constitutional Politics in Pakistan.* Cambridge, UK: Cambridge University Press, 2002.

Newburn, Tim. *Understanding and Preventing Police Corruption: Lessons from the Literature.* Edited by Barry Webb. Home Office, Policing and Reducing Crime Unit, Research, Development and Statstics Directorate, 1999.

Newman, Edward. "Weak States, State Failure, and Terrorism." *Terrorism and Political Violence* 19, no. 4 (2007): 463–88.

"Nicaragua Profile," BBC News, accessed October 25, 2012, www.bbc.co.uk/news/world-latin-america-19909695.

Nonneman, Gerd. "Political Reform in the Gulf Monarchies: From Liberalization to Democratization? A Comparative Perspective." *Durham Middle East Papers* 80, Sir William Luce Publication Series 6 (June 2006): 1–37.

Nordlinger, Eric A. "Soldiers in Mufti: The Impact of Military Rule on Economic and Social Change in non-Western States." *America Political Science Review* 64 (December 1970): 1131–48.

—. *Soldiers in Politics: Military Coups and Governments.* Englewood Cliffs, NJ: Prentice Hall, 1977.

Noriega, Roger. "Venezuela under Chávez: The Path toward Dictatorship." *American Enterprise Institute for Public Policy Research* 3 (2006): 1–9.

North, Douglas. "Economic Performance through Time." *American Economic Review* 84, no. 3 (June 1994): 359–67.

—. *Institutions, Institutional Change and Economic Performance.* Cambridge, UK: Cambridge University Press, 1990.

—. *Structure and Change in Economic History.* New York, NY: WW Norton, 1981.

North, Douglas C. and Robert Paul Thomas. "An Economic Theory of Growth of the Western World." *The Economic History Review* 23, no. 1 (1970): 1–17.

—. *The Rise of the Western World, A New Economic History.* Cambridge, UK: Cambridge University Press, 1973.

North, Douglas C., William Summerhill, and Barry R. Weingast. "Order, Disorder and Economic Change: Latin America vs. North America." In *Governing for Prosperity.* Edited by Bruce Bueno de Mesquita and Hilton Roots. New Haven, CT: Yale University Press, 2000, 17–58.

Norton, Augustus. *Civil Society in the Middle East Volume 1.* Leiden, Netherlands: EJ Brill, 1995.

Nourzhanov, Kirill. "Saviours of the Nation or Robber Barons? Warlord Politics in Tajikistan." *Central Asian Survey* 24, no. 2 (2005): 109–30.

Nun, José. *The Middle Class Military Coup.* Oxford, UK: Oxford University Press, 1967.

Nzongola-Ntanlaja, G. *The Congo from Leopold to Kabila.* London, UK: Zed Books, 2002.

O'Donnell, Guillermo. "Delegative Democracy." *Journal of Democracy* 5, no. 1 (January 1994): 55–69.

—. *Modernization and Bureaucratic-Authoritarianism.* Berkeley, CA: Institute for International Studies, 1973.

—. "On the State, Democratization and Come Conceptual Problems: A Latin American View with Glances at Some Post-communist Countries." *Working Paper* #192 (1993): 1–26.

—. "Poverty and Inequality in Latin America: Some Political Reflections." The Helen Kellog Institute for International Studies Working Paper 225 (July 1996): 1–26.

—. "The Quality of Democracy: Why the Rule of Law Matters." *Journal of Democracy* 15, no. 4 (October 2004): 32–46.

—. "Reflections on Contemporary South American Democracies." *Journal of Latin American Studies* 33 (2001): 599–609.

O'Donnell, Guillermo, Jorge Vargas Cullel, and Osvaldo Miguel Iazzetta. *The Quality of Democracy: Theory and Applications*. Helen Kellogg Institute for International Studies, 2004.

O'Dwyer, Conor. *Runaway State-Building: Patronage Politics and Democratic Development*. Baltimore, MD: Johns Hopkins University Press, 2006.

OECD. 2012, www.oecd.org/investment/aidstatistics/developmentaidrosein2009-andmostdonorswillmeet2010aidtargets.htm

Office of the High Commissioner for Human Rights in Cooperation (OHCHRC) with the International Bar Association. "Independence and Impartiality of Judges, Prosecutors and Lawyers." In *Human Rights in the Administration of Justice: A Manual on Human Rights for Judges, Prosecutors and Lawyers, United Nations Professional Training Series* 9 (2003): 113–58.

Olken, Benjamin A. and Rohini Pande. "Corruption in Developing Countries." NBER Working Paper no. 17398 (August 2011): 1–48.

Öniş, Ziya. "Review: The Logic of the Developmental State." *Comparative Politics* 24, no. 1 (October 1991): 109–26.

Ortiz, Reynaldo Yunuen Ortega. "Comparing Types of Transitions: Spain and Mexico." *Democratization* 7, no. 3 (2000): 65–92.

Oszlak, Oscar. "The Historical Formation of the State in Latin America: Some Theoretical and Methodological Guidelines for Its Study." *Latin American Research Review* 16, no. 2 (1981): 3–32.

Ottaway, Marina. "Rebuilding State Institutions in Collapsed States." *Development and Change* 33, no. 5 (2002): 1001–23.

Ottaway, Marina and Stefan Mair. "States at Risk and Failed States: Putting Security First." Policy Outlook, *Carnegie Endowment for International Peace* (September 2004): 1–10.

O'Toole, Gavin. *Politics in Latin America*. Harlow, UK: Pearson, 2007.

Owen, Roger. *State, Power and Politics in the Making of the Modern Middle East*. New York, NY: Routledge, 1992.

Painter, Martin. "Sequencing Civil Service Pay Reforms in Vietnam: Transition or Leapfrog? *Governance* 19, no. 2 (April 2006): 325–47.

Palacios, Marco and Frank Safford. *Colombia: Fragmented Land, Divided Society*. New York, NY: Oxford University Press, 2002.

Palmer, Monte, Ali Leila, and El Sayyid Yassim. *The Egyptian Bureaucracy*. Syracuse, NY: Syracuse University Press, 1988.

Panizza, Francisco. "Populism and the Mirror of Democracy." Paper prepared for the panel on Populism and Democratic Politics of the 53rd Annual Conference of the Political Studies Association "Democracy and Diversity," April 15–17, 2003, the University of Leicester, 1–50.

—. "A Reform without Losers: The Symbolic Economy of Civil Service Reform in Uruguay, 1995–96." *Latin American Politics and Society* 46, no. 3 (2004): 1–28.

Panizza, Francisco and George Philip. "Second Generation Reform in Latin America: Reforming the Public Sector in Uruguay and Mexico." *Journal of Latin American Studies* 37, no. 4 (2005): 667–91.

Pape, Robert. "Blowing Up an Assumption." *New York Times* (May 18, 2005a).

—. *Dying to Win: The Logic Suicide Terrorism*, New York, NY: Random House, 2005b.

—. "The Strategic Logic of Suicide Terrorism." *American Political Science Review* 97, no. 3 (August 2003): 1–19.

Paris, Roland. *At War's End: Building Peace after Civil Conflict.* Cambridge, UK: Cambridge University Press. 2004.

"Parliamentary Oversight of the Security Sector." ECOWAS Parliament-DCAF Guide for West African Parliamentarians, September 29, 2010, 1–344.

Pathmanand, Ukrist. "A Different Coup d'état?" *Journal of Contemporary Asia* 38, no. 1 (2008): 124–42.

Patrick, Stewart. "The Brutal Truth." *Foreign Policy* (July/August 2011a).

—. "Failed States and Global Security: Empirical Questions and Policy Dilemmas." *International Studies Review* 9 (2007): 644–62.

—. *Weak Links: Fragile States, Global Threats and International Security.* Oxford, UK: Oxford University Press, 2011b.

—. "Weak States and Global Threats: Fact or Fiction." *Washington Quarterly* 29, no. 2 (Spring 2006a): 27–53.

—. "Weak States and Global Threats: Assessing Evidence of 'Spillovers.'" *Center for Global Development Working Paper* 73 (January 2006b): 1–31.

Payne, J. Mark, Daniel Zovatto G., Fernando Carrillo Floréz, and Andrés Allamand Zavala. "La Política Importa. Democracia y Desarrollo en América Latina. Banco Interamericano de Desarrollo e Instituto Internacional para la Democracia y la Asistencia Electoral," Washington, DC, 2003.

Peake, Gordon and Kaysie Studdard Brown. "Police Building: The International Deployment Group in the Solomon Islands." *International Peacekeeping* 12, no. 4 (2005): 520–32.

Pegg, Scott. *International Society and the De facto State.* Aldershot, UK: Ashgate, 1998.

Pei, Minxin. "Lessons from the Past." *Foreign Policy* 137 (2003): 52–5.

Peerenboom, Randall. *China's Long March toward Rule of Law.* Cambridge, UK: Cambridge University Press, 2002.

Perito, Robert M. "Afghanistan's Police—The Weak Link in Security Sector Reform." USIP Special Report, United States Institute of Peace, Washington, DC, 2009, 79.

Perlmutter, Amos. *Egypt, The Praetorian State.* New Brunswick, NJ: Transaction Books, 1974.

—. "The Praetorian State and the Praetorian Army: Toward a Taxonomy of Civil-Military Relations in Developing Polities." *Comparative Politics* 1, no. 3 (April 1969): 382–404.

Pfaff, William. "A New Colonialism? Europe Must Go Back into Africa." *Foreign Affairs* 74, 1 (1995): 6.

Pfaller, Alfred and Marika Lerch. *Challenges of Globalization: New Trends in International Politics and Society.* New Brunswick, NJ: Transaction Publishers, 2005.

Piazza, James A. "Draining the Swamp: Democracy Promotion, State Failure, and Terrorism in 19 Middle Eastern Countries." *Studies in Conflict & Terrorism* 30, no. 6 (2007): 521–39.

—. "Incubators of Terror: Do Failed and Failing States Promote Transnational Terrorism?" *International Studies Quarterly* 52 (2008): 469–88.

Pilster, Ulrich and Tobias Bohmelt. "Coup-Proofing and Military Effectiveness in Interstate Wars, 1967–99." *Conflict Management and Peace Science* 28, no. 4 (2011): 1–20.

Pion-Berlin, David. "Military Autonomy and Emerging Democracies in South America." *Comparative Politics* 25, no. 1 (1992): 83–102.

—. "The Armed Forces and Politics: Gains and Snares in Recent Scholarship." *Latin American Research Review* (1995): 147–62.

Pirseyedi, Bobi. *The Small Arms Problem in Central Asia: Features and Implications.* United Nations Institute for Disarmament Research, 2000.

Plott, Charles. "The Application of Laboratory Experimental Methods to Public Choice." In *Collective Decision Making: Applications from Public Choice Theory.* Edited by C. S. Russell. Baltimore, MD: Johns Hopkins University Press, 1979, 137–60.

Pollack, Kenneth. *Arabs at War: Military Effectiveness, 1948–1991.* Lincoln, NE: University of Nebraska Press, 2002.

Pope, Jeremy. "National Integrity Programs." Partnership for Governance Conference, Copenhagen, Denmark, May 31, 1996, 23–6.

Popescu, Nicu. "Outsourcing De Facto Statehood: Russia and the Secessionist Entities in Georgia and Moldova." *Policy Perspectives* (June 2006): 1–15.

Posen, Barry. "The Security Dilemma and Ethnic Conflict." *Survival* 5 (1993): 27–47.

Pound, Roscoe. "The Causes of Popular Dissatisfaction with the Administration of Justice." *American Law Review* 40 (1906): 729–49.

Powell, Benjamin, Ryan Ford, and Alex Nowrasten. "Somalia after State Collapse: Chaos or Improvement?" *Independent Institute Working Paper* 64 (November 30, 2006): 1–30.

Powell, Jonathan. "Determinants of the Attempting and Outcome of Coups d'état." *Journal of Conflict Resolution* (2012): 1–24.

Prah, Kwesi Kwaa. "African Wars and Ethnic Conflicts Rebuilding Failed States." *Human Development Report Occasional Paper* 10 (2004): 1–29.

Prempeh, H. Kwasi. "Marbury in Africa: Judicial Review and the Challenge of Constitutionalism in Contemporary Africa." *Tulane Law Review* 80, no. 4 (2006).

Prillaman, William C. *The Judiciary and Democratic Decay in Latin American: Declining Confidence in the Rule of Law.* Westport, CT: Greenwood Publishing, 2000.

"Property Rights." 2012 Index of Economic Freedom, www.heritage.org/index/ property-rights.

Przeworski, Adam, Michael E. Alvarez, Jose Antonio Cheibub, and Fernando Limongi. *Democracy and Development: Political Institutions and Well Being in the World, 1950–1990.* Cambridge, UK: Cambridge University Press, 2000.

Pugh, Michael and Waheguru Pal Singh Sidu. *The United Nations and Regional Security: Europe and Beyond.* Boulder, CO: Lynne Rienner, 2003.

Pugh, Michael Charles, Neil Cooper, and Jonathan Goodhand. *War Economies in a Regional Context: Challenges of Transformation.* Boulder, CO: Lynne Rienner Publishers, 2004.

Putnam, Robert D. "Bowling Alone: America's Declining Social Capital." *Journal of Democracy* 6, no. 1 (1995): 1–13.

—. *Making Democracy Work: Civic Traditions in Modern Italy* (Princeton: Princeton University Press, 1993.

—. "Social Capital: Measurements and Consequences" *Canadian Journal of Policy Research* (2001): 1–32.

Putzel, James. "Research in Latin America." Crisis States Research Programme Working Paper 4 (April 2001): 1–16.

Pye, Lucian W. "Civility, Social Capital, and Civil Society: Three Powerful Concepts for Explaining Asia." *Journal of Interdisciplinary History* 29, no. 4 (1999): 763–82.

Quah, Jon S. T. "Curbing Asian Corruption: An Impossible Dream?" *Current History* 105, no. 690 (April 2006): 176–9.

—. "Curbing Corruption in India: An Impossible Dream?" *Current History* (April 2008): 240–59.

Quandt, William B. *Algerian Military Development: The Professionalization of a Guerrilla Army.* Santa Monica, CA: Rand Corporation, 1972.

Quimpo, Nathan Gilbert. "The Philippines: Political Parties and Corruption." *Southeast Asian Affairs* (2007): 277–94.

—. "The Philippines: Predatory Regime, Growing Authoritarian Features." *Pacific Review* 22, no. 3 (July 2009): 335–53.

Quinlivan, James T. "Coup Proofing: Its Practice and Consequences in the Middle East." *International Security* 24, no. 2 (Fall 1999): 131–65.

Rabasa, Angel. "Ungoverned Territories." *Rand Organization* (February 14, 2008): 1–15.

Raemakers, Timothy. "Collapse or Order? Questioning State Collapse in Africa." Working Paper 1, May 2005, 1–10.

Rahman, A. T. R. "Legal and Administrative Measures against Bureaucratic Corruption in Asia." In *Bureaucratic Corruption in Asia: Causes, Consequences, and Controls.* Edited by Carino Ledivina V. Carino and Maria Concepcion P. Alfiler. Quezon City, Phillipines: NMC Press, 1986, 109–62.

Rajan, Raghuram G. "Failed States, Vicious Cycles, and a Proposal." Center for Global Development, Working Paper 243, March 2011, 1–14.

Randall, Vicky and Lars Svåsand. "Political Parties and Democratic Consolidation in Africa." Paper for ECPR Joint Sessions of Workshops, Workshop on Parties, Party Systems and Democratic Consolidation in the Third World, Grenoble, France, April 6–11, 2001, 1–27.

Rauch, James and Peter B. Evans. "Bureaucratic Structure and Bureaucratic Performance in Less Developed Countries." *Journal of Public Economics* 75 (2000): 49–71.

Ravenhill, F. J. "Military Rule in Uganda: The Politics of Survival." *African Studies Review* 17, no. 1 (April 1974): 229–60.

Reames, Benjamin. "Police Forces in Mexico: A Profile." USMEX Working Paper Series, 2003, www.escholarship.org/uc/item/1sq4g254.

"Rebuilding Failed States, from Chaos, Order: What Can the World Do about State Failure? Surprisingly, Quite A Lot." *The Economist* (March 3, 2005).

Reilly, David A. "The Growing Importance of the Failing State: Sovereignty, Security and the Return to Power Politics." *Journal of Conflict Studies* 26, no. 1 (Summer 2004): 1–14.

—. "The Two-Level Game of Failing States: Internal and External Sources of State Failure." *The Journal of Conflict Studies* (2008): 17–32.

Reinert, Eric. The Economics of Failed, Failing, and Fragile States: Productive Structure as the Missing Link." Working Papers in Technology Governance and Economic Dynamics 18, January 2009, 1–38.

Reisman, Lainie. "Breaking the Vicious Cycle: Responding to Central American Youth Gang Violence." *SAIS Review* 26, no. 2 (Summer–Fall 2006): 147–52.

Reiter Dan and Allan C. Stam III. "Democracy, War Initiation, and Victory." *American Political Science Review* 92 (June 1998): 259–77.

Renner, Michael. *Small Arms, Big Impact: The Next Challenge of Disarmament.* Darby, PA: Diane Publishing, 1997.

Reno, William. "Arms Trafficking and the Local Political Economy of Conflict." In *Security, in Reconstruction and Reconciliation: When the Wars End.* Edited by Muna Ndulo. London, UK: Routledge, 2007, 13–25.

—. *Corruption and State Politics in Sierra Leone.* New York, NY: Cambridge University Press, 1995a.

—. "The Politics of Insurgency in Collapsing States." *Development and Change* 33, no. 5 (November 2002): 837–58.

—. "The Real War Economy of Angola." In *Angola's War Economy: The Role of Oil Diamonds.* Edited by Jakkie Cilliers and Christian Dietrich. Pretoria: Institute for Security Studies, 2000a, 219–35.

—. "Reinvention of an African Patrimonial State: Charles Taylor's Liberia." *Third World Quarterly* 16, no. 1 (1995b): 109–20.

—. "Shadow States and the Political Economy of Civil Wars." In *Greed and Grievance: Economic Agendas and Civil Wars.* Edited by M. Berdal and D. Malone. Boulder, CO: Lynne Rienner, 2000b, 43–68.

—. *Warlord Politics in African States.* Boulder, CO: Lynne Rienner Publishers, 1998.

Reynal-Querol, Marta. "Ethnicity, Political Systems, and Civil Wars." *Journal of Conflict Resolution* 46, no. 1 (2002): 29–54.

Rhodes, R. A. W., Sarah A. Binder, and Bert A. Rockman (eds). *The Oxford Handbook of Political Institutions*, Oxford, UK: Oxford University Press, 2006.

Rice, Susan E. "The New National Security Strategy Focus on Failed States." The Brookings Institution, Policy Brief 116, February 2003, 1–8.

Rice, Susan E. and Stewart Patrick. "Index of State Weakness in the Developing World." Brookings Global and Economic Development, 2008, 1–47.

Richani, Nazih. "The Political Economy of Violence: The War-System in Colombia." *Journal of Inter-American Studies and World Affairs* 39, no. 2 (April 1997): 37–81.

Riedel, Bruce. "Al Qaeda Strikes Back." *Foreign Affairs* (2007): 24–40.

—. "Pakistan and Terror: The Eye of the Storm." *The Annals of the American Academy of Political and Social Science* 618, no. 1 (2008): 31–45.

Riker, William H. "Implications from the Disequilibrium of Majority Rule for the Study of Institutions." *The American Political Science Review* (1982): 432–37.

Rizvi, Hasan-Askari. "The Military and Politics in Pakistan." *Journal of Asian and African Studies* 26, no. 1–2 (1991): 1–2.

Roberts, Kenneth M. "Neo-liberalism and the Transformation of Populism in Latin America: The Peruvian Case." *World Politics* 48, no. 1 (October 1995): 82–116.

—. "Populism and Democracy in Latin America." Paper presented at the Challenges to Democracy Conference, Carter Center, Washington, DC, 2000, 1–32, http://cartercenter.org/documents/nondatabase/roberts.pdf.

—. "Social Inequalities without Class Cleavages in Latin America's Neo-Liberal Era." *Studies in Comparative International Development* 36, no. 4 (2002): 3–33.

Robertson-Snape, Fiona. "Corruption, Collusion and Nepotism in Indonesia." *Third World Quarterly* 20, no. 3 (1999): 589–602.

Robinson, Adam. *Bin Laden: Behind the Mask of the Terrorist.* New York: Arcade Publishing, 2002.

Robinson, James, Ragnar Torvik, and Theirry Verdier. "Political Foundations of the Resource Curse." *Journal of Development Economics* 79 (2006): 447–68.

Rodgers, Dennis. "Old Wine in New Bottles or New Wine in Old Bottles? Conceptualizing Violence and Governmentality in Contemporary Latin America." *Crisis States Research Center Discussion Paper* 6 (November 2004): 1–22.

Rodrik, Dani. "Getting Institutions Right." Working paper, April 2004, 1–13, www.wcfia.harvard.edu/sites/default/files/807__ifo-institutions%20article%20_April%202004_.pdf.

—. "Growth Strategies." In *Handbook of Economic Growth* Vol. 1A. Edited by Philippe Aghion and Steven N. Durlauf. Amsterdam, Netherlands: Elsevier, 2005, 967–1014.

—. "Institutions for High Quality Growth: What They Are and How to Acquire Them." National Bureau of Economic Research Working Paper Series 7540 (February 2000): 1–50.

—. *One Economics, Many Recipes: Globalization, Institutions, and Economic Growth.* Princeton, NJ: Princeton University Press, 2008.

—. "Where Did All the Growth Go? External Shocks, Social Conflict, and Growth Collapses." *Journal of Economic Growth* 4, no. 4 (1999): 385–412.

Rose, Richard and Don Chull Shin. "Democratization Backwards: The Problem of Third-Wave Democracies." *British Journal of Political Science* 31 (2001): 331–54.

Rose-Ackermann, Susan. *Corruption and Development.* Washington DC: The World Bank Annual Bank Conference on Development Economics, 1997.

—. *Corruption and Government: Causes, Consequences, and Reform.* Cambridge, UK: Cambridge University Press, 1999.

—. "Judicial Independence and Corruption." In *Transparency International, Global Corruption Report.* Cambridge, UK: Cambridge University Press, 2007, 15–24.

—. "The Political Economy of Corruption—Causes and Consequences." Washington, DC: World Bank, 1996, 1–4.

Rosh, Robert. "Ethnic Cleavages as a Component of Global Military Expenditures." *Journal of Peace Research* 33 (1989): 21–30.

Ross, Michael. "Does Oil Hinder Democracy?" *World Politics* 53, no. 3 (April 2001): 325–61.

—. "Oil, Drugs and Diamonds: How Do Natural Resources Vary in Their Impact on Civil War?: The Varying Role of Natural Resources in Civil War." In *The Political Economy of Armed Conflict: Beyond Greed and Grievance*. Edited by Karen Ballentine and Jake Sherman. Boulder, CO: Lynne Rienner, 2003, 47–70.

—. "What Do We Know about Natural Resources and Civil War?" *Journal of Peace Research* 41, no. 3 (2004): 337–56.

Rosser, Andrew. "The Political Economy of the Resource Curse: A Literature Survey." IDS Working Paper Series 268. Brighton: Institute of Development Studies at the University of Sussex, 2006, 1–36.

Rostow, Walt. "The Stages of Economic Growth." *Economic History Review* 12, no. 2 (August 1959): 1–16.

Rotberg, Robert. "Africa's Mess, Mugabe's Mayhem." *Foreign Affairs* 79 (2000): 47–61.

—. "The New Nature of Nation-State Failure." *Washington Quarterly* (Summer 2002): 85–96.

—. *State Failure and State Weakness in a Time of Terror*. Washington, DC: Brookings Institute Press, 2003.

—. *When States Fail: Causes and Consequences*. Princeton, NJ: Princeton University Press, 2004.

Rothchild, Donald and Alexander J. Groth. "Pathological Dimensions of Domestic and International Ethnicity." *Political Science Quarterly* 110, no. 1 (1995): 69–82.

Rouquié, Alain. *The Military and the State in Latin America*. Berkeley, CA: University of California Press, 1989.

Rowe, Edward Thomas. "Aid and Coups d'Etat: Aspects of the Impact of American Military Assistance Programs in the Less Developed Countries." *International Studies Quarterly* 18, no. 2 (June 1974): 239–55.

Rowley, Charles K., Robert D. Tollison, and Gordon Tullock, eds. *The Political Economy of Rent Seeking*. Vol. 1. Boston, MA: Klewer Publishers, 1988.

Roy, Denny. *Taiwan: A Political History*. Ithica, NY: Cornell University Press, 2003.

Rubin, Barry. *Armed Forces in the Middle East: Politics and Strategy*. London, UK: Routledge, 2001.

Rubin, Barnett. "Peace Building and State-Building in Afghanistan: Constructing Sovereignty for Whose Security?" *Third World Quarterly* 27, no. 1 (2006): 175–85.

—. *Post-Soviet Political Order: Conflict and State Building*. London, UK: Routledge, 1998.

—. "Saving Afghanistan." *Foreign Affairs* 86, no. 1 (January–February 2007): 57–78.

Rubin, Barnett and Andrea Armstrong. "Regional Issues in the Reconstruction of Afghanistan." *World Policy Journal* (Spring 2003): 31–40.

Ruby, Tomislav Z. and Douglas Gibler. "US Professional Military Education and Democratization Abroad." *European Journal of International Relations* 16, no. 3 (2010): 339–64.

Rudoni, Dorothy, Ralph Baker, and Fred A. Meyer Jr. "Police Professionalism: Emerging Trends." *Policy Studies Journal* 7 (1978): 454–60.

Rueschemeyer, Dieter and Theda Skocpol. *Bringing the State Back In.* Cambridge, UK: Cambridge University Press, 1985.

Rugege, Sam. "Judicial Independence in Rwanda." *Pacific McGeorge Global Business & Development Law Journal* 19 (2006): 411.

Rupiya, Martin. "A Survey of Civil-Military Relations in the SADC Sub-Region." Civil Military Relations in Zambia: A Review of Zambia's Contemporary CMR history and Challenges of Disarmament, Demobilisation and Reintegration, Institute for Security Studies, Pretoria, 2004, 17–26.

Rustici, Kathleen and Alexandra Sander. "The 2012 Thai Military Reshuffle." Center for Strategic and International Studies, October 12, 2012.

Rustow, Dankwart A. "Transitions to Democracy: Toward a Dynamic Model." *Comparative Politics* 2, no. 3 (April 1970): 337–63.

Sachs, Jeffrey D. *The End of Poverty: Economic Possibilities for Our Time.* New York: Penguin Books, 2005.

—. "It Can be Done." *Economist* 339, no. 7972 (1996): 19–21.

Sachs, Jeffrey D. and Andrew M. Warner. "The Big Push, Natural Resource Booms and Growth." *Journal of Development Economics* 59, no. 1 (June 1999): 43–76.

—. "Sources of Slow Growth in African Economies." *Journal of African Economies* 6, no. 3 (December 1997): 335–76.

Sageman, Marc. *Understanding Terror Networks.* Philadelphia, PA: University of Pennsylvania Press, 2004.

Said, Mohamed El Sayed. "Egypt: The Dialectics of State Security and Social Decay," IPG, 2000, 5–18.

Saideman, Stephen M., David J. Lanoue, Michael Campenni, and Samuel Stanton. "Democratization, Political Institutions, and Ethnic Conflict A Pooled Time-Series Analysis, 1985–1998." *Comparative Political Studies* 35, no. 1 (2002): 103–29.

Saleh, Basel. "Palestinian Suicide Attacks Revisited: A Critique of Current Wisdom," December 2004, 1–16, www.yumpu.com/en/document/view/4474941/suicide-attacks.

Sánchez, Gonzalo. *Guerra y Política en la Sociedad Colombiana.* Bogotá: El Áncora, 1991.

Sandler, Todd. "Collective Action and Transnational Terrorism." *The World Economy* 26, no. 6 (June 2003): 779–802.

Sarre, Rick, Dilip K. Das, and H. J. Albrecht. *Policing Corruption: International Perspectives.* Lanham, MD: Lexington Books, 2005.

Sartori, Giovanni. *Parties and Party Systems: A Framework for Analysis.* Cambridge, UK: Cambridge University Press, 1976.

Savage, Tyrone, "In the Quest of a Sustainable Justice: Transitional Justice and Human Security in the Democratic Republic of the Congo." Paper 130. Institute for Security Studies, 2006.

Schedler, Andreas. *Electoral Authoritarianism: The Dynamics of Unfree Competition.* Boulder, CO: Lynne Rienner, 2006.

—. "The Menu of Manipulation." *Journal of Democracy* 13, no. 2 (2002): 36–50.

—. *The Self-Restraining State: Power and Accountability in New Democracies.* Boulder, CO: Lynne Rienner, 1999.

Schedler, Andreas and Rodolpho Sarsfield. "Democrats with Adjectives: Linking Direct and Indirect Measures of Democratic Support." *European Journal of Political Research* 46, no. 5 (August 2007): 637–49.

Schneckener, Ulrich. "Fragile Statehood, Armed Non-state Actors and Security Governance." *Private Actors and Security Governance, Berlin.* Edited by Alan Bryden and Marina Caparini. Berlin: Lit Verlag, 2006, 23–41.

Schneider, Friedrich and Dominik Enste. "Shadow Economies around the World: Size, Causes and Consequences." *IMF Working Paper*, February 2000.

Schneider, Gerald and Nina Wiesehomeier. "Rules that Matter: Political Institutions and the Diversity-Conflict Nexus." *Journal of Peace Research* 45, no. 2 (2008): 183–203.

Schönteich, Martin and Antoinette Louw. "Crime in South Africa: A Country and Cities Profile." Crime and Justice Programme, Institute for Security Studies Occasional Paper 49 (2001): 1–22.

Scobell, Andrew. "Politics, Professionalism, and Peacekeeping: An Analysis of the 1987 Military Coup in Fiji." *Comparative Politics* (1994): 187–201.

Sebudubudu, David. "The Institutional Framework of the Developmental State in Botswana." In *The Potentiality of 'Developmental States' in Africa: Botswana and Uganda Compared.* Edited by Pamela Mbabazi and Ian Taylor. Dakar: CODESRIA, 2005, 79–89.

Sedra, Mark. "Police Reform in Afghanistan: An Overview." Bonn International Center for Conversion Brief 28 (2003): 32–9.

Sekhri, Neelam and William Savedoff. "Private Health Insurance: Implications for Developing Countries." *Bulletin of the WHO* 83, no. 2 (February 2005): 127–34.

Seligson, M. A. "Populism and the Resurgence of the Left in Latin America." *Journal of Democracy* 18, no. 3 (July 2007): 81–95.

Semerad, Kate and Robert B. Hawkins, Jr. "Conflict Prevention and US Foreign Assistance: A Framework for the 21st Century." The Institute for Contemporary Studies, November 15, 2001, 1–104.

Seznec, Jean-Francois. "Stirrings in Saudi Arabia." *Journal of Democracy* 13, no. 4 (2002): 33–40.

Shafqat, Saeed. "Pakistani Bureaucracy: Crisis of Governance and Prospects of Reform." *The Pakistani Development Review* 38, no. 4, part II (Winter 1999): 995–1017.

Shaw, Matthew. "South Africa: Crime in Transition." Institute for Security Studies Occasional Papers 17 (March 1997): 1–13.

Shambayati, Hootan and Esen Kirdiş. "In Pursuit of 'Contemporary Civilization': Judicial Empowerment in Turkey." *Political Research Quarterly* 62, no. 4 (2009): 767–80.

Shearer, David. *Private Armies and Military Intervention.* Oxford, UK: Oxford University Press, 1998.

Shen, Ce and John B. Williamson. "Corruption, Democracy, Economic Freedom and State Strength: A Cross National Analysis." *International Journal of Comparative Sociology* 46, no. 4 (2005): 327–45.

Shepherd, Geoffrey. "Civil Service Reform in Developing Countries: Why Is It Going Badly?" 11th International Anti-Corruption Conference, Seoul, Korea, May 2003, 1–26.

Sherwood, Robert. "Judicial Systems and National Economic Performance."
Paper delivered at the Inter-American Development Bank's Second Annual
Conference on Justice and Development in Latin American and the Caribbean,
Montevideo, Uruguay, 1995.

Shils, Edward A. and Morris Janowitz. "Cohesion and Disintegration in the
Wehrmacht in World WarII." *Public Opinion Quarterly* 12 (Summer 1948):
280–315.

Shugart, Matthew Soberg and John M. Carey. *Presidents and Assemblies:
Constitutional Design and Electoral Dynamics.* Cambridge, UK: Cambridge
University Press, 1992.

Siddiqa, Ayesha. *"Military Inc.": Inside Pakistan's Military Economy.* London,
UK: Pluto Press, 2007.

Siebold, Guy L. "The Essence of Military Group Cohesion." *Armed Forces &
Society* 33, no. 2 (2007): 286–95.

Siegel, Larry J. *Criminology.* Andover, UK: Cenage Learning Publications,
2008.

Simons, Anna and David Tucker. "The Misleading Problem of Failed States: A
Socio-Geography of Terrorism in the Post 9/11 Era." *Third World Quarterly*
28, no. 2 (2007): 387–401.

Sindzingre, Alice. "Financing the Developmental State: Tax and Revenue Issues."
Development Policy Review 25, no. 5 (2007): 615–32.

—. "The Relevance of the Concepts of Formality and Informality: A Theoretical
Appraisal." In *Linking the Formal and Informal Economy: Concepts and
Policies.* Edited by Basudeb Guha-Khasnobis, Ravi Kanbur, and Elinor
Ostrom. Oxford, UK: Oxford University Press, 2006, 58–74.

Singer, J. David, Stuart Bremer, and John Stuckey. "Capability Distribution,
Uncertainty and Major Power War, 1820–1965." *Peace, War, and Numbers*
(1972): 19–48.

Singh, L. P. "Political Development or Political Decay in India?" *Pacific Affairs*
44, no. 1 (Spring 1971): 65–80

Sloan, Britt and James Cockayne. "Terrorism, Crime, and Conflict: Exploiting
the Differences among Trans-national Threats?" Center on Global Terrorism
Cooperation, Policy Brief, February 2011, 1–11.

"Small Arms and Light Weapons, Africa." Religions for Peace, United Nations,
2008, 1–28.

Smelser, Neil and Faith Mitchell. "Discouraging Terrorism: Some Implications
of 9/11." US National Research Council Panel on Understanding Terrorists in
Order to Deter Terrorism, 2002.

Smith, Benjamin. "Life of the Party: The Origins of Regime Breakdown and
Persistence under Single-Party Rule." *World Politics* 57 (April 2005): 421–51.

—. "Oil Wealth and Regime Survival in the Developing World, 1960–1999."
American Journal of Political Science 48, no. 2 (2004): 232–46.

Snyder, Jack L. *From Voting to Violence: Democratization and Nationalist
Conflict.* New York: Norton, 2000.

—. "Nationalism and the Crisis of the Post-Soviet State." *Survival* 35, no. 1
(1993): 5–26.

Snyder, Richard. "Explaining Transitions from Neo-patrimonial Dictatorships."
Comparative Politics (1992): 379–99.

Snyder, Richard and R. Bhavnani. "Diamonds, Blood, and Taxes: A
Revenue-Centered Framework for Explaining Political Order." *Journal of
Conflict Resolution* 49, no. 4 (2005): 563–97.

Söderbaum, Fredrik. "Modes of Regional Governance in Africa: Neo-liberalism,
Sovereignty Boosting, and Shadow Networks." *Global Governance* 10, no. 4
(October–December 2004): 419–36.

Soderlund, Walter C., "Political Decay and State Collapse: Understanding
Developments in Haiti Surrounding the Overthrow of Jean-Bertrand Aristide."
Paper prepared for presentation at theAnnual Meeting of the Canadian
Political Science Association University of Saskatchewan, May 30–June 1,
2007, 1–19.

Hillel Soifer and Matthias vom Hau. "Unpacking the Strength of the State:
The Utility of State Infrastructural Power." *St. Comparative International
Development* 43 (2008): 219–30.

Sokoloff, Kenneth L. and Stanley L. Engerman. "History Lessons: Institutions,
Factors Endowments, and Paths of Development in the New World." *The
Journal of Economic Perspectives* (2000): 217–32.

Solomon Jr, Peter H. "Assessing the Courts in Russia: Parameters of Progress
under Putin." *Demokratizatsiya* (2008).

Sondhi, Sunil. "Combating Corruption in India: The Role of Civil Society."
Paper prepared for the 18th World Congress of International Political Science
Association, Quebec City, Canada, August 1–5, 2000, 1–30.

Sørensen, Georg. "After the Security Dilemma: The Challenges of Insecurity in
Weak States and the Dilemma of Liberal Values." *Security Dialogue* 38, no. 3
(2007): 357–78.

—. "A State Is Not a State: Types of Statehood and Patterns of Conflict after the
Cold War." In *International Security Management and the United Nations.*
Edited by Muthiah Alagappa and Takashi Inoguchi. New York, NY: United
Nations University Press, 1999a.

—. "Sovereignty: Change and Continuity in a Fundamental Institution." *Political
Studies* 67 (1999b): 590–604.

Southall, Aidan. "General Amin and the Coup: Great Man or Historical
Inevitability?" *The Journal of Modern African Studies* 13, no. 1 (March
1975): 85–105.

Soyinka, Wole. The *Open Sore of a Continent: A Personal Narrative of the
Nigerian Crisis.* New York, NY: Oxford University Press, 1996.

Staats, Joseph L., Shaun Bowler, and Jonathan T. Hiskey. "Measuring Judicial
Performance in Latin America." *Latin American Politics and Society* 47, no. 4
(2005): 77–106.

Starr, S. Frederick. "Clans, Authoritarian Rulers, and Parliaments in Central
Asia." *Central Asia-Caucasus Institute Silk Road Studies Program Paper*
(June 2006): 1–26.

Starr, Joyce R. "Lebanon's Economy: The Costs of Protracted Violence." In
The Emergence of a New Lebanon. Edited by Edward A. Azar. New York:
Praeger, 1984.

Stedman, Stephen. "Conflict and Conciliation in sub-Saharan Africa." In *The
International Dimensions of Internal Conflict.* Edited Michael E. Brown.
Cambridge, UK: MIT Press, 1996.

Stepan, Alfred C. *Rethinking Military Politics: Brazil and the Southern Cone.* Princeton, NJ: Princeton University Press, 1988.

Stepputat, F. and Engberg-Pedersen, L. "Fragile States: Definitions, Measurements and Processes." In Fragile Situations: Background Papers, Danish Institute for International Studies, DIIS, Copenhagen, 2008.

Stern, Vivian. "Problems in Prisons Worldwide, with a Particular Focus on Russia." *Annals New York Academy of Sciences* 953b, no. 1 (February 10, 2006): 113–19.

Stewart, Francis and Graham Brown. "Fragile States: CRISE Overview 3." Oxford University Centre for Research on Inequality, Human Security and Ethnicity (CRISE), 2010, 1–42.

Stohl, Rachel. "Reality Check: The Danger of Small Arms Proliferation." *Conflict and Security* (Summer/Fall 2005): 71–9, 73.

"Suharto Tops Corruption List." BBC News, 25 (March 2004), http://news.bbc.co.uk/2/hi/business/3567745.stm.

Suchlicki, Jaime, ed. *The Cuban Military Under Castro.* Transaction Publishers, 1989.

Suhrke, Astri. "Reconstruction as Modernisation: The 'Post-Conflict' Project in Afghanistan." *Third World Quarterly* 28, no. 7 (2007): 1291–308.

Takeyh, Ray and Nikolas Gvosdev. "Do Terrorist Networks Need a Home?" *The Washington Quarterly* 25, no. 3 (2002): 97–108.

Talbot, Ian. "The Punjabization of Pakistan: Myth or Reality?" In *Pakistan: Nationalism without a Nation.* Edited by Christophe Jaffrelot. New York: Zed Books, 2002, 51–62.

Tambunan, Tulus. "Entrepreneurship Development: SMES in Indonesia." *Journal of Developmental Entrepreneurship* 12, no. 01 (2007): 95–118.

Tan, Netin. "Institutionalized Leadership: Resilient Hegemonic Party Autocracy in Singapore." Paper prepared for presentation at CPSA Conference, Ottawa, Ontario, May 28, 2009, 1–32.

Tangri, Roger and Andrew M. Mwenda. "Military Corruption & Ugandan Politics since the late 1990s." *Review of African Political Economy* 30, no. 98 (2003): 539–52.

—. "Politics, Donors and the Ineffectiveness of Anti-corruption Institutions in Uganda." *Journal of Modern African Studies* 44, no. 1 (2006): 101–24.

Tanzi, Vito and Hamid Davoodi. "Corruption, Public Investment, and Growth." *IMF Working Paper* 139 (1997): 1–23.

Tate, C. Neal. "Courts and Crisis Regimes: A Theory Sketch with Asian Case Studies." *Political Research Quarterly* 46, no. 2 (June 1993): 311–38.

Tate, C. Neal and Stacia L. Haynie. "Authoritarianism and the Functions of Courts: A Time Series Analysis of the Philippine Supreme Court, 1961–1987." *Law and Society Review* (1993): 707–40.

Tedesco, Laura and Jonathan R. Barton. *The State Of Democracy in Latin America: Post-transitional Conflicts in Argentina and Chile.* London, UK: Routledge, 2004.

Tezcür, Murat. "Constitutionalism, Judiciary, and Democracy in Islamic Societies." *Polity* 39, no. 4 (2007): 479–501.

Thachuk, Kimberley. "Transnational Threats: Falling through the Cracks?" *Low Intensity Conflict and Law Enforcement* 10, no. 1 (2001): 47–67.

Thampi, G. K. *Corruption in South Asia: Insights and Benchmarks from Citizen Feedback Surveys in Five Countries.* Berlin, Germany: Transparency International, 2002.

Thies, Cameron G. "War, Rivalry, and State Building in Latin America." *American Journal of Political Science* 49, no. 3 (July 2005): 451–65.

Thomas, Troy S. and Stephen D. Kiser. *Lords of the Silk Route: Violent Non-state Actors in Central Asia.* Boulder, CO: Diane Publishing, 2002.

Thompson, Dennis F. "Mediated Corruption: The Case of the Keating Five." *The American Political Science Review* 87, no. 2 (June 1993): 369–81.

Thompson, Elizabeth. *Colonial Citizens: Republican Rights, Paternal Privilege and Gender in French Syria and Lebanon.* New York, NY: Columbia University Press, 2000.

Thompson, Mark R. *The Marcos Regime in the Philippines.* Baltimore, MD: Johns Hopkins University Press, 1998.

Thorp, Rosemary. *Progress, Poverty and Exclusion: An Economic History of Latin America.* New York, NY: Inter-American Development Bank, 1998.

Tirado, Alvaro. "Violence and the State in Colombia." In *Colombia: The Politics of Reforming the State.* Edited by Eduardo Posada-Carbó. New York, NY: St. Martin's Press, 1998

Tilly, Charles. *Coercion, Capital, and European States.* Oxford, UK: Blackwell Publishers, 1990.

—. "Terror, Terrorism, Terrorists." *Sociological Theory* 22, no. 1 (March 2004): 5–13.

—. "War-Making and State-Making as Organized Crime." In *Bringing the State Back In.* Edited by Peter Evans, Dieter Rueschemeyer, and Theda Skocpol. Cambridge, UK: Cambridge University Press, 1985, 169–91.

Titley, Brian. *Dark Age: The Political Odyssey of Emperor Bokassa.* Montreal, Canada: McGill-Queen's Press, 2002.

Tornell, Aaron and Philip Lane. "Are Windfalls a Curse?: A Non-representative Agent Model of the Current Account." *Journal of International Economics* 44, no. 1 (February 1998): 83–112.

Torres, Magüi Moreno and Michael Anderson. "Fragile States: Defining Difficult Environments for Poverty Reduction." *PRDE Working Paper 1* (August 2004): 1–34.

Trinkunas, Harold A. "The Crisis in Venezuelan Civil-Military Relations: From Punto Fijo to the Fifth Republic." *Latin American Research Review* (2002): 41–76.

Tripplet, Ruth, Randy Gainey, and Ivan Sun. "Institutional Strength, Social Control and Neighborhood Crime Rates." *Theoretical Criminology* 7, no. 4 (2003): 439–67.

Tsuboi, Yoshiharu. "Corruption in Vietnam." Waseda University (2005): 1–8.

Tullock, Gordon. *Autocracy.* Netherlands: Springer, 1987.

Turits, Richard Lee. *Foundations of Despotism: Peasants, the Trujillo Regime, and Modernity in Dominican History.* Stanford, CA: Stanford University Press, 2003.

Turner, Thomas and Crawford Young. *The Rise and Decline of the Zairian State.* Madison, WI: University of Wisconsin Press, 1985.

Ukrist, Pathmanand. "A Different Coup d'Etat?" *Journal of Contemporary Asia* 38, no. 1 (2008).

Ulklah, Akm Ahsan. "Poverty Reduction in Bangladesh: Does Good Governance Matter?" *NAPSIPAG* (2004): 423–42.

Ulloa, Alfie, Felipe Katz, and Nicole Kekeh. "Democratic Republic of Congo: A Study of Binding Constraints." Harvard University (December 28, 2009): 1–246.

Ungar, Mark. "Prisons and Politics in Contemporary Latin America." *Human Rights Quarterly* 25 (2003): 909–34.

United Nations Institute for Disarmament. "Scoping Study on Mine Action and Small Arms Control within the Framework of Armed Violence and Poverty Reduction," September 2006, 1–30.

United Nations Office for Drug Control and Crime Prevention. "Integrated versus Quantitative Methods: Lessons Learned," May 2000, 1–43.

United Nations and the Rule of Law. www.un.org/en/ruleoflaw/index.shtml.

USAID. "Fragile States Strategy. US Agency for International Development PD-ACA-999." Washington, DC: USAID, 2005.

US AID. "Measuring Fragility: Indicators and Methods for Rating State Performance," June 2005, 1–43.

US AID. "Reducing Corruption in the Judiciary," June 2009, 1–47.

United States State Department. "Terrorist Safe Havens: Strategies, Tactics, and Tools for Disrupting or Eliminating Safe Havens," July 31, 2012.

Valenzuela, Arturo. "Latin American Presidencies Interrupted." *Journal of Democracy* 15, no. 4 (October 2004): 5–19.

Van de Walle, Nicolas. "The Economic Correlates of State Collapse." Paper presented at a Conference on State Failure, Harvard University, 2001.

—. "The Impact of Multi-Party Politics in Sub-Saharan Africa." Paper prepared for delivery at the Norwegian Association for Development Research Annual Conference "The State under Pressure," October 5–6, 2000, Bergen, Norway.

Van Rijckeghem, Caroline and Beatrice Weder. "Bureaucratic Corruption and the Rate of Temptation: Do Wages in the Civil Service Affect Corruption, and By How Much?" *Journal of Development Economics* 65 (2001): 307–31.

Van Evera, Steven. "Bush Administration, Weak on Terror." *Middle East Policy* 13, no. 4 (Winter 2006): 28–38.

Verma, Arvind. "Cultural Roots of Police Corruption in India." *Policing: An International Journal of Police Strategies & Management* 22, no. 3 (1999): 264–79.

Vinci, Anthony. "Anarchy, Failed States, and Armed Groups: Reconsidering Conventional Analysis." *International Studies Quarterly* 52 (2008): 295–314.

Von Einsiedel, Sebastian. "Policy Responses to State Failure." In *Making States Work: State Failure and the Crisis Of Governance.* Edited by Simon Chesterman, Michael Ignatieff, and Ramesh Chandra Thakur. Tokyo, Japan: United Nations University Press, 2005, 13–35.

Von Hippel, Karin. "The Roots of Terrorism: Probing the Myths." *Political Quarterly* (2002): 25–39.

Vreeland, James Raymond. "The Effect of Political Regime on Civil War Unpacking Anocracy." *Journal of Conflict Resolution* 52, no. 3 (2008): 401–25.

Walker, Samuel. "A Critical History of Police Reform." In *The Emergence of Professionalism*. Lexington, MA: Lexington Books, 1977.

Walls, Michael. "The Emergence of a Somali State: Building Peace from Civil War in Somaliland." *African Affairs* 108, no. 432 (2009): 371–89.

Wang, Te-Yu. "Arms Transfers and Coups d'État: A Study on Sub-Saharan Africa." *Journal of Peace Research* 35, no. 6 (1998): 659–75.

Wang, Vibeke. "The Accountability Function of Parliament in New Democracies: Tanzanian Perspectives." Chr. Michelsen Institute (2005): 1–26.

Webber, David. "Good Budgeting, Better Justice: Modern Budget Practices for the Judicial Sector." Law and Development Working Paper Series 3 (2007): 1–76.

Weber, Max. *Economy and Society*. Vol. 1. Berkeley, CA: University of California Press, 1978.

—. *Politics as a Vocation*. Minneapolis, MN: Fortress Press, 1972.

Wedeman, Andrew. "Looters, Rent-Scrapers, and Dividend-Collectors: Corruption and Growth in Zaire, South Korea, and the Philippines." *The Journal of Developing Areas* 31, no. 4 (Summer 1997): 457–78.

Weinberg, Leonard B. and William L. Eubank. "Terrorism and Democracy: What Recent Events Disclose." *Terrorism and Political Violence* 10, no. 1 (1998): 108–18.

Weizhi, Xie. "The Semi-hierarchical Totalitarian Nature of Chinese Politics." *Comparative Politics* (1993): 313–30.

Welch, Claude E. "Continuity and Discontinuity in African Military Organization." *Journal of Modern African Studies*, 13, no. 2 (June 1975): 229–48.

Wendt Alexander and Michael Barnett. "Dependent State Formation and Third World Militarization." *Review of International Studies* 19 (1993): 321–47.

Wesley, Michael. "The State of the Art on the Art of State Building." *Global Governance: A Review of Multilateralism and International Organizations* 14, no. 3 (2008): 369–85.

Weyland, Kurt. "Clarifying a Contested Concept: Populism in the Study of Latin American Politics." *Comparative Politics* 34, no. 1 (October 2001): 1–22.

White, Brent T. "Rotten to the Core: Project Capture and the Failure of Judicial Reform in Mongolia." *East Asia Law Review* 4 (2009): 209–76.

White, Robert W. "From Peaceful Protest to Guerrilla War: Micro-mobilization of the Provisional Irish Republican." *American Journal of Sociology* 94, no. 6 (May 1989): 1277–302.

Whitmore, Sarah. "State and Institution Building under Kuchma." *Problems of Post-Communism* 52, no. 5 (September/October 2005): 3–11.

Wickham-Crowley, Timothy. "Terror and Guerrilla Warfare in Latin America, 1956–1970." *Comparative Studies in Society and History* 32, no. 2 (1990): 201–37

Wiarda, Howard. *Critical Elections and Critical Coups: State, Society and the Military in the Processes of Latin American Development*. Ohio University Center for International Studies, 1978.

—. *Dictatorship and Development: The Methods of Control in Trujillo's Dominican Republic*. Gainesville, FL: University of Florida Press, 1968.

Widner, Jennifer A. *Building the Rule of Law: Francis Nyalali and the Road to Judicial Independence in Africa*. London, UK: WW Norton, 2001.

Wilder, Andrew. "Pakistan & Afghanistan: Domestic Pressures and Regional Threats: The Politics of Civil Service Reforms in Pakistan." *Journal of International Affairs* 63, no. 1 (Fall/Winter 2009): 19–37.

Willett, Susan. "Defence Expenditures, Arms Procurement and Corruption in Sub-Saharan Africa." *Review of African Political Economy* 36, no. 121 (2009): 335–51.

Williams, Paul. "Fighting for Freetown: British Military Intervention in Sierra Leone." *Contemporary Security Policy* 22, no. 3 (2001): 140–68.

Williams, Paul D. "Review Article: International Peacekeeping: The Challenges of State-Building and Regionalization." *International Affairs* 81, no. 1 (2005): 163–74.

—. "State Failure in Africa: Causes, Consequences and Responses." In *Africa South of the Sahara*. Edited by G. W. Kingsworth. London, UK: Routledge, 2007, 37–42.

Wintrobe, Ronald. *The Political Economy of Dictatorship*. Cambridge, UK: Cambridge University Press, 1998.

Williamson, John. "A Short History on the Washington Consensus." Paper commissioned by Fundación CIDOB for Conference "From the Washington Consensus towards a new Global Governance," Barcelona, September 24–25, 2004, 1–14.

Wintrobe, Ronald. *The Political Economy of Dictatorship*. Cambridge, UK: Cambridge University Press, 1998.

Wiseman, John A. "Leadership and Personal Danger in African Politics." *Journal of Modern African Studies* 31, no. 4 (1993): 667–70.

Woo-Cummings. Meredith. *The Developmental State*. Ithica, NY: Cornell University Press. 1999.

—. "Diverse Paths toward the Right Institutions: Law, the State, and Economic Reform in East Asia." *Asian Development Bank Working Paper* 18 (April 2001): 1–43.

Woods, Kevin, James Lacey, and Williamson Murray. "Saddam's Delusions: The View from the Inside." *Foreign Affairs* (May/June 2006).

Woodward, Susan L. "Fragile States: Exploring the Concept," 2004, 1–9, http://statesandsecurity.org/_pdfs/Fragile%20States_Exploring%20the%20Concept.pdf.

World Bank. "Building Institutions for Markets." World Development Report 2002. Oxford University Press, 2002.

—. "Doing Business in a More Transparent World," 2012, 1–212.

—. "Public Administration Reform Loan 1&2 to the Kingdom of Morocco," June 25, 2009.

—. *The State in a Changing World: World Development Report* 1997, Oxford, UK: Oxford University Press, 1997.

World Bank Group Work in Low Income Countries under Stress: A Task Force Report. September 2002, 1–53.

World Bank Institute. "Parliaments as Peace-Builders." *Development Outreach* (October 1, 2009).

The World Justice Project. "The WJP Rule of Law Index." http://worldjustice-project.org/rule-of-law-index/.

Worthington, Ross. "Between Hermes and Themis: An Empirical Study of the Contemporary Judiciary in Singapore." *Journal of Law and Society* 28, no. 4 (2001): 490–519.

Wright, Joseph. "Aid Effectiveness and the Politics of Personalism." *Comparative Political Studies* 43, no. 6 (2010): 735–62.

—. "Do Authoritarian Institutions Constrain? How Legislatures Affect Economic Growth and Investment." *American Journal of Political Science* 52, no. 2 (2008a): 322–43.

—. "To Invest or Insure? How Authoritarian Time Horizons Impact Foreign Aid Effectiveness." *Comparative Political Studies* 41, no. 7 (2008b): 971–1000.

Wright, Joseph, and Matthew Winters. "The Politics of Effective Foreign Aid." *Annual Review of Political Science* 13 (2010): 61–80.

Wulf, Herbert. "Security Sector Reform in Developing and Transitional Countries." Berghof Research Center for Constructive Conflict Management, July 2004, 1–20.

Wyler, Liana Sun. "Weak and Failing States: Evolving Security Threats and US Policy." *CRS Report for Congress*, August 28, 2008, 1–27.

Yamani, Mai. "The Two Faces of Saudi Arabia." *Survival* 50, no. 1 (2008): 143–56.

Yates, Douglas. *The Rentier State in Africa: Oil Rent Dependency and Neo-colonialism in the Republic of Gabon*. Trenton, NJ: Africa World Press, 1996.

Yesilkaya, Oezlem. "Whither the State: Understanding State Collapse and Its Challenges." *Internationale Beziehungen—studentische Beitraege* 3 (2007): 7–14.

Young, Crawford. "The Heart of the African Conflict Zone: Democratization, Ethnicity, Civil Conflict, and the Great Lakes Crisis." *Annual Review Political Science* 9 (2006): 301–28.

—. "Reflections on State Decline and Societal Change in Zaire." Typescript, January 1997.

—. "Zaire: The Shattered Illusion of the Integral State." *Journal of Modern African Studies* 32 (June 1994), 247–63.

—. "Zaire: The Unending Crisis." *Foreign Affairs* 57, no. 1 (Fall 1978).

Young, Crawford and Thomas Turner. *The Rise and Decline of the Zairian State*. Madison, WI: University of Wisconsin Press, 1985.

Yong, Tan Tai. "Singapore: Civil-Military Fusion." In *Coercion and Governance: The Declining Political Role of the Military in Asia*. Edited by Muthiah Alagappa. Stanford: Stanford University Press, 2001, 276–93.

Yusuf, Hakeem O. "The Judiciary and Political Change in Africa: Developing Transitional Jurisprudence in Nigeria." *International Journal of Constitutional Law* 7, no. 4 (2009): 654–82.

Zartman, William. *Collapsed States: The Disintegration and Restoration of Legitimate Authority*. Boulder, CO: Lynne Rienner, 1995.

Zimbardo, Philip G. "A Situationalist Perspective on the Psychology of Evil: Understanding How Good People Are Transformed into Perpetrators." In *The Social Psychology of Good and Evil*. Edited by Arthur G. Miller. New York, NY: Guilford Press, 2004, 21–50.

Zoellick, Robert. "Fragile States: Securing Development." *Survival: Global Politics and Strategy* 50, no. 6 (2008): 67–84.

INDEX

Entries in **bold** refer to boxes.

Scottish plants, plaids and wildlife Junk journal

HOW TO USE THIS BOOK

Ideal for just appreciating the magnificence of these prints, drawings and illustrations, to work on top of to create a totally new Creative Journal or for crafters to cut and paste into collages, decoupage, art sketchbooks, junk journals, nature journals or even to cut out and place in photo collages or photo frames to create an art wall.

Printed in Great Britain
by Amazon

44236508R00016